Mastering

Implementing Your
Service Driven Operating Model

Wouter Wyns

Colophon

Title	Mastering 4me
Subtitle	Implementing Your Service Driven Operating Model
Author	Wouter Wyns
Reviewers	Bart Van Brabant, Cor Winkler-Prins, Frank de Jong, Jean-Marie Van Cutsem, Klaas Vandeweerdt, Laurens Pit, Mathijs Sterk, Robbert Brak, Sebastian Ziemiński, Tina van Schelt
ISBN Paperback	978 94 649 4930 8
Lay Out	Jana Lulovska
Copy Editor	Anne Marie O'Donnell
Edition	First edition
Copyright	© 2024, 4me, Inc.
Publisher	CapeIT BV

Foreword by Cor Winkler Prins

In your hands you are holding the ultimate guide to the ultimate service management application. It was written by Wouter Wyns. Wouter and I have been working together for roughly 20 years already. Over those years, we have enjoyed bouncing many ideas off of each other for improving service management applications. Organizations regularly confronted us with a complex requirement that could not yet be met in an elegant way by a service management application. That's when we'd think: "Wouldn't this be useful for some of our other customers as well?" Quite often the answer was a resounding "Yes!" In such cases we'd each try to design a feature that would meet the requirement in a way that benefits many organizations. Then we'd compare our designs and come up with an even better one by building on each other's ideas.

Wouter has helped a great number of large multinationals, government agencies, and managed service providers with their service management implementations. His knowledge of the industry, its best practices and its supporting software solutions is enormous. He also has many years of experience as a practitioner. The last 5 years or so, he spent leading the support department within the 4me company. And when Wouter leads, he leads by example. Whenever the workload of the service desk became too high, he'd roll up his sleeves and work with his team to ensure customers would not experience any delays. Wouter was also in charge of the setup of 4me in the company. As the organization grew, the setup had to keep pace. Initially the 4me application was only used to support 4me's customers, but over time the sales and marketing teams, as well as the HR and finance departments started to streamline their processes in 4me as well.

All this is to say that Wouter knows what he is talking about. I must admit that I still do not understand why he wanted to write this book, though. 4me may seem like an elegant, easy-to-use application (which it is), but looks can be deceiving. 4me is enormous. It has so many features that most companies that have adopted 4me are not even aware of. And that is exactly why it is so great that this book exists; it provides a comprehensive overview of 4me's capabilities. Your organization will probably not even need half of them right now, but knowing that they exist can be extremely valuable in certain environments.

If your organization is planning to implement 4me, make sure that you have familiarized yourself with each chapter, so you know where to find the information you need to make the right implementation decisions. This will benefit your organization as 4me gets deployed in more and more departments, suppliers and customers. If your organization has already been using 4me for some time, this book will give you at least 10 great ideas on how to get way more out of 4me by making use of capabilities that your colleagues probably did not even know existed. And if you are a 4me implementation consultant, this will be your bible. Reference it whenever you are asked to help a customer streamline its more complex cross-organizational workflows.

Above all, though, remember that even minor improvements in the set up of 4me can benefit end users and support specialists countless of times over the years that these small perfections typically remain in place. Use this book as your guide as you implement them, one at a time, to continuously improve the professional lives of your colleagues and customers.

Cor, 3 May 2024

Acknowledgements

I am deeply grateful to a host of individuals whose assistance, guidance, and support were invaluable throughout the process of writing this book.

First and foremost, I extend my heartfelt thanks to Kevin McGibben and Martijn Adams for granting me the time to pursue this project.

Special thanks are due to the founders of 4me—Cor, Laurens, and Mathijs—and the incredible development team whose consistent weekly deployments of new features have made this book possible. Their dedication and ingenuity have been nothing short of inspiring.

I owe a profound debt of gratitude to the reviewers of this manuscript, Bart Van Brabant, Cor Winkler-Prins, Frank de Jong, Jean-Marie Van Cutsem, Klaas Vandeweerdt, Laurens Pit, Mathijs Sterk, Robbert Brak, Sebastian Ziemiński and, Tina van Schelt who tackled the challenging task of sifting through earlier drafts and provided invaluable feedback that significantly enhanced the final product.

Additionally, I express my appreciation to Tina, my partner, who endured my grumpiness during those times when progress was slower than expected. Your support has been a cornerstone of this journey.

Lastly, I thank you, the reader, for taking the time to explore this work. I hope it enriches your understanding and provides insights that prove valuable in your own endeavors.

About the Author

Wouter Wyns, the author of Mastering 4me, is a distinguished service management architect with an extensive background in implementing service management platforms for major players such as HP, BMC, CA, and ServiceNow. With years of experience in providing top-notch support within the 4me ecosystem, Wouter has meticulously crafted this book in response to a question he encountered frequently: "Where can we find a comprehensive resource on all things 4me?" Mastering 4me is his expert answer, compiling insights, best practices, and deep dives into the platform's capabilities. This book is a must-read for anyone looking to leverage 4me to its fullest potential, offering a treasure trove of knowledge that Wouter has accumulated over many years of hands-on experience.

Contents

PART V

Chapter 1 - Introduction

It's All About Enterprise Service Management

In the beginning, there was Service Management, a concept that later evolved into the grander scale known as Enterprise Service Management. Service management, initially rooted in IT, found its foundation in the IT Infrastructure Library (ITIL), a framework still pivotal in this domain.

Now, Enterprise Service Management (ESM) represents a more expansive vision, one that encompasses the orchestration and governance of services across an entire organization. The primary objective of ESM is to streamline service delivery while harmonizing it with the overarching goals of the organization. ESM takes an enterprise-wide and strategic approach to service delivery. It entails the integration of service management processes with other critical business functions such as finance, HR, and facilities.

Translating the traditional ITIL framework language into other domains, like Human Resources, Facilities, and Legal, can sometimes feel awkward or challenging to grasp. However, the underlying essence remains unchanged: delivering valuable services and adeptly managing them.

Throughout this guide, we'll consciously employ the term Enterprise Service Management instead of Service Management, as it underscores the holistic essence of this discipline. These processes should effortlessly transcend organizational boundaries, irrespective of whether an organization provides IT services or not. In the upcoming section, we'll dive into the significance of strategic thinking and action within a company, moving beyond siloed perspectives. The term Enterprise Service Management perfectly encapsulates this forward-thinking approach.

Theory and Practice - The 4me Demo Environment

In the pages ahead, we're going to embark on a journey that seamlessly blends theory with real-life application. We'll guide you through practical examples that effectively connect the dots between knowledge and action.

Welcome to the 4me Demo Environment

The 4me Demo Environment is used for demonstration and training purposes. Enter below the name and password of the 4me Instance that you wish to access.

| Instance Name |
| Password |

Sign In

But delving into this adventure, here's a friendly tip: consider joining the free online '**4me Specialist Training**.' It's a brief yet informative experience that will thoroughly acquaint you with the platform. Moreover, it won't consume your entire day – just a few hours of your time.

Are you ready to become a 4me pro? Your training awaits you at the 4me Training Hub: https://learning.4me.com.

Throughout the specialist training and by studying the examples provided in this book, you'll master the intricacies of 4me. Many of the examples can be found in the 4me demo environment. No need for technical wizardry; all you need is a solid grasp of service management.

Now, here's the exciting part. To access your very own 4me demo environment – a space for exploration, experimentation, and learning – simply visit https://www.4me.com/training-instance. Once you enter your email, keep an eye on your inbox. You'll receive an email containing the keys to your individual demo playground: the demo instance name and password.

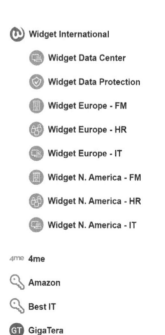

- Widget International
  - Widget Data Center
  - Widget Data Protection
  - Widget Europe - FM
  - Widget Europe - HR
  - Widget Europe - IT
  - Widget N. America - FM
  - Widget N. America - HR
  - Widget N. America - IT
- 4me
- Amazon
- Best IT
- GigaTera

To access your demo realm, simply point your browser to https://4me-demo.com.

Once you've entered into your personal demo instance, your journey begins with an enticing overview of 4me accounts. However, before you rush into your selection, take a moment to peruse the upcoming chapters. These chapters will illuminate the intricate world of 4me accounts, ensuring you're well-prepared for the adventure ahead. Enjoy the ride!

A demo instance automatically expires after 7 days. Should your demo instance expire, don't hesitate to request a new one.

PART I

4me's Service-Driven Architecture

Chapter 2 - The Operating Model

4me is fundamentally designed around the concept of services, embedding this principle into every facet of its functionality. Whether we explore workflows, the 4me shop, time tracking, or the reservations module throughout this book, it's evident that these features are intricately woven into 4me's service-driven architecture. In Chapter 4, we will delve into the nuances of the **Service Chain** and **Service Hierarchy**, which form the backbone of the 4me platform. However, to fully appreciate the service-driven approach 4me champions, we must first anchor our understanding in the broader context of an enterprise's strategic framework.

Enterprise Service Management
is more than Implementing Workflows

What does it truly mean to implement enterprise service management? And where does one begin? All service management frameworks unanimously highlight the importance of managing and enhancing the quality of services, aligning them with the organization's overall objectives. Hence, it's evident that an enterprise service management implementation must commence with a common agreement and a well-defined vision and plan on how service management will be integrated into the organization's operations based on its business strategy. This involves identifying specific service management processes to be employed and understanding how they fit into the broader business strategy.

However, in reality, many enterprise service management initiatives and tool implementations often start from issues or the outdated state of the existing ticketing tool. Occasionally, organizations may conduct a maturity assessment to pinpoint pain points and identify some low-hanging fruit for improvement. Alternatively, it might arise from a simple requirement to replace email-driven processes in HR and Legal departments with a more structured and transparent workflow system. While mandatory alignment checks with the organization's goals and objectives are performed during project budget approval, strategic alignment tends to fade away once the implementation project begins. Consequently, these projects may end up focusing solely on specific business functions by implementing a set of workflows, disregarding the need for strategic alignment.

Why does the apparent necessity for strategic alignment of enterprise service management with business strategy become less apparent when it comes to implementation? The main issue is the gap between strategy and execution. A study [Donald Sull, Stefano Turconi, Charles Sull, James Yoder] revealed that only 28% of executives and middle managers responsible for executing strategy could list three of their company's strategic priorities. According to Andrew Cambell [Andrew Cambell, Mikel Gutierrez and Mark Lancelott], only 5% of employees believe that strategy is their responsibility.
Interestingly, according to Andrew Cambell [Andrew Cambell, Mikel Gutierrez and Mark Lancelott],

operating models engage 95% of employees. The operating model represents what employees know, understand, and feel responsible for within the organization. Furthermore, there exists a direct link between the organization's strategy and its operating model, making the latter a practical and indispensable starting point for every enterprise service management project. Before we delve into how the operating model can form the foundation of each service management project, let's first gain a deeper understanding of its relationship with the business strategy.

From Strategy to Operating Model

The value chain is to business strategy what Newton's law of universal gravitation is to physics—a fundamental concept. Michael Porter introduced the value chain in his book "Competitive Advantage: Creating and Sustaining Superior Performance" in 1985. Unlike merely examining the individual silos that constitute a company, the value chain focuses on systems and cross-boundary processes,

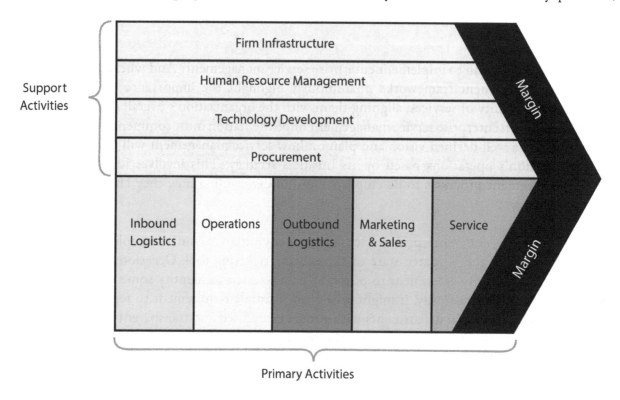

Figure 1: Michael Porter's Value Chain.

understanding how this chain of processes delivers value to consumers through products and services. In essence, the value chain represents the work required to deliver value.

At the corporate level, a distinction is drawn between primary and support activities. In a typical corporate organization, enterprise service management falls under the umbrella of Support Activities. However, for Managed Service Providers (MSPs), enterprise service management constitutes a core part of the primary activities within the value chain, undertaken to deliver value.

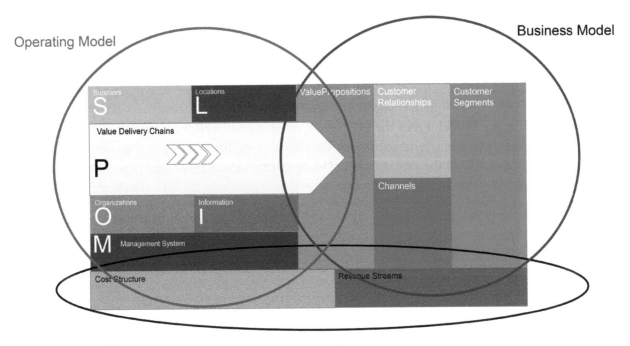

Figure 2: The operating model and business model canvas.

Value chains have gained extensive popularity in strategic management and have been embraced by organizations spanning various industries to enhance their competitiveness and overall performance. While the value chains of companies within the same industry may appear similar at first glance, successful companies in the industry demonstrate distinctive and specific approaches in managing their business. It is precisely these unique approaches that provide them with a competitive advantage and contribute to their success over the competition. This is where the company's strategy comes into play, as it defines the operating model that sets them apart from others. In Chapter 4, we will explore how 4me breathes life into these value chains, transforming them into dynamic service chains and a structured service hierarchy, thereby operationalizing the theoretical framework into tangible, service-driven architecture.

The business model canvas, developed by Alexander Osterwalder, Yves Pigneur, and Gregory Bernarda, and the operating model canvas, introduced by Andrew Cambell, Mikel Gutierrez, and Mark Lancelott, are both great tools for visualizing and comprehending the interconnection between strategy, the value chain, the business model, and the operating model. In this book, we will utilize the operating model canvas to illustrate how an organization's operating model forms the foundation of the service management configuration on the 4me platform. Before delving into the specifics, let's first take a broader look at the overall picture.

Essentially, an organization's strategy consists of three fundamental building blocks:

1. **Value Propositions**: These are located at the center of the overall picture, representing the end of the value delivery chains. They are essential components of both the operating model and the business model. Value propositions define what the organization provides (in the form of services or products) to its customers or beneficiaries.

2. The **Business Model**, on the other hand, identifies the Customer Segments - different groups of people the organization aims to reach and serve, as well as the Channels through which the products and services are distributed to customers or beneficiaries. Additionally, the Business Model outlines the principles of Customer Relationship Management, covering how customers or beneficiaries are acquired, engaged, and retained.

3. The **Operating Model**: From the perspective of enterprise service management, the Operating Model takes center stage. It describes how the activities required to deliver the value are organized and carried out within the organization. The operating model acts as the glue that connects the value proposition (what the organization delivers to its customers) with the necessary actions to make those deliveries.

The Operating Model:
The Blueprint for Enterprise Service Management

There are compelling reasons to consider the operating model of an organization as the primary starting point for an enterprise service management implementation:

- Alignment with Business Strategy: The operating model serves as the execution engine for an organization's business strategy. When properly designed, the operating model is closely aligned with the organization's strategic objectives and actively supports the achievement of its goals.
- Delivery of Products and Services: The operating model encompasses a comprehensive set of processes, structures, capabilities, and resources that an organization utilizes to deliver its products and services. This alignment with the essence of enterprise service management makes it a natural foundation for the implementation.
- Universality Across the Organization: The operating model exists at both the corporate level and within individual business units and domains. As such, it can be applied universally to any part of the organization, providing consistency and coherence in service delivery.
- Employee Engagement: One of the key strengths of operating models is their ability to engage employees. By clearly defining roles, responsibilities, and workflows, the operating model fosters a sense of ownership and collaboration among team members.

By leveraging the operating model as the starting point of an enterprise service management implementation, organizations can create a solid framework that is intrinsically connected to their strategic objectives, optimized for delivering products and services, and universally applicable throughout the organization.

Let's take a closer look at the Operating Model Canvas. At its core are the **Value Delivery Chains**, also referred to as Processes on the canvas. These represent the primary activities that an organization performs to bring its value propositions to life and deliver value to its customers or beneficiaries. These processes are supported by the necessary resources, which are outlined in the canvas.

The **Organizations section** identifies the structure of the organizational units involved in the value

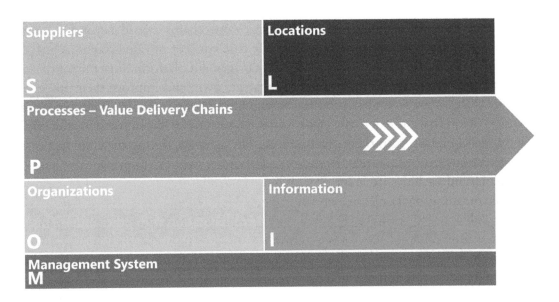

Figure 3: The operating model canvas.

delivery chains. In the context of enterprise service management, these units often correspond to business units or specific service delivery organizations such as EMEA Production, Human Resources, Finance, and others.

The **Suppliers section** defines both the internal and external organizations (partners) that actively participate in the value delivery processes. These suppliers play a crucial role in ensuring the smooth functioning of the organization.

The **Locations section** specifies where the work is carried out and identifies the assets required at these locations to support the execution of the processes.

Information on the canvas highlights the main information systems that are integral to the value delivery chains. These systems facilitate the smooth flow of information and data necessary for efficient operations.

Lastly, the **Management System** section includes the meta processes, which are the processes that managers employ to plan, set targets, make decisions, and measure performance. Additionally, this section should encompass the processes needed to comply with essential frameworks, such as SOC-2, ISO-27001, GDPR, Sarbanes-Oxley Act (SOX), Basel III, and other relevant regulations.

The Operating Model:

Enterprise Service Management Platform Requirements

The interconnection between the operating model and enterprise service management has tangible implications for the capabilities that an enterprise service management platform must possess.

1. The operating model operates without barriers. Value chains extend beyond the confines of individual organizational silos, aligning with the core concept of value chains as introduced by Michael Porter. Similarly, an enterprise service management platform must mirror this principle. It should empower organizational units to organize, own, and improve their processes within the value chains. However, these processes should not be restricted at the boundaries of the unit. Inclusion of internal and external suppliers on the operating model canvas demands efficient and effective collaboration with these organizations. For instance, during the employee onboarding and offboarding process, Human Resources collaborates with IT (to provide or revoke access to IT systems) and Facilities (to grant or withdraw site/building access). The platform must allow dedicated organizational units to own and control process ownership and data within their value chains, while simultaneously facilitating seamless collaboration with other units. This ability to foster cross-functional collaboration is a critical feature that every enterprise service management platform should offer.

2. Adaptability and evolution are vital for business success. As conditions and strategies change, operating models need to evolve accordingly. However, this becomes challenging when an organization's operating model is locked in within an enterprise service management platform due to excessive customization. In such cases, modifying the platform becomes exceedingly difficult, if not impossible. To ensure agility, an enterprise service management platform must be inherently flexible. The operating model should not be embedded through heavy customization. Instead, the platform should incorporate built-in processes that are ready-to-use once the operating model has been defined on the platform.

In the next chapter, we will delve into how this is achieved on the 4me platform. By defining service delivery organizations that own their processes and service chains the support processes come alive and align seamlessly with the operating model. The operating model forms the foundation, and the operating model canvas will serve as a visual aid to illustrate these concepts effectively.

Chapter 3 -
The 4me Account Structure Design

4me Accounts: The Design Pillars

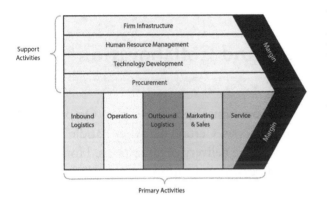

Figure 4: Value chains.

The foundational building block of the 4me platform is the 4me account. To better comprehend the notion of a 4me account, let's revisit Michael Porter's value chains.

Value is generated within an enterprise by various organizational units. Some entities participate directly in the value chains and execute primary activities. Others provide support to these entities. Irrespective of the type of activities they engage in, all these organizational units are potential candidates for getting their own 4me account.

Figure 5: The 4me account structure.

In the business context, units that offer supportive functions like HR, IT, and Facilities Management are commonly termed "Support Functions" or "Support Domains.".

In an enterprise using 4me, it is typical to establish a 4me account for each support function. In the diagram above, these 4me accounts are depicted as circles or bubbles and are referred to as **Support Domain Accounts**. A support domain account encompasses all the data necessary for delivering services.

At the top lies a **Directory Account**. This directory account contains information shared across all support domain accounts. It encompasses the people, organizations, and sites that constitute the enterprise. The directory account also offers self-service portal functionality. This portal serves as a hub where employees can access information and knowledge regarding the support services provided by support functions. Additionally, employees can log requests or report issues to these support functions. The directory account, along with its integrated self-service portal, serves as the gateway and facilitator for the primary activities of an organization to receive support from support functions.

4me Trusts:

Process Autonomy, Data Segregation and Collaboration

The relationship between service delivery organizations can sometimes appear complex. On one hand, each of these entities necessitates autonomy to shape their processes. Certain data they handle might be sensitive and thus unsuitable for direct sharing with other service delivery organizations. However, on the other hand, value chains and support processes shouldn't be confined within the boundaries of these individual organizations; they should extend across other service delivery entities.

Consider the scenario of HR. HR manages sensitive information that should remain isolated from IT, Finance, and Facilities: HR requires **data segregation**. HR also controls processes like onboarding and offboarding. HR has the authority to craft and execute these procedures in alignment with strategic needs and their own expertise. HR also requires **process autonomy**.

A 4me account establishes process autonomy and data segregation. Each service delivery organization can independently oversee processes within their respective support domain account, with their data remaining concealed from other service delivery entities.

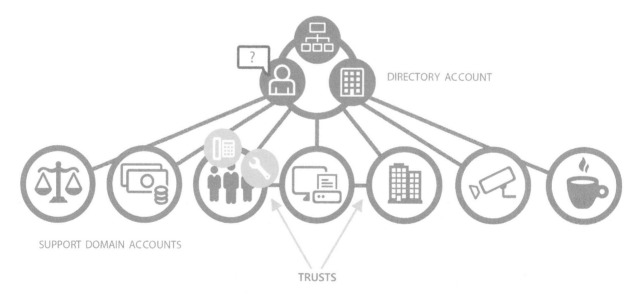

Figure 6: Trusts connecting 4me accounts.

However, certain tasks in the onboarding and offboarding process may involve contributions from other service delivery organizations like IT, Finance, and Facilities. And some level of data sharing becomes necessary for effective collaboration.

To facilitate collaboration and selective data sharing, **Account Trusts** come into play. An Account Trust establishes a connection between two accounts. With a defined trust, a service delivery organization can meticulously determine which data is shared and how they will cooperate. Account Trusts enable collaboration between 4me accounts while upholding process autonomy and data segregation.

Extending Collaboration with External Suppliers

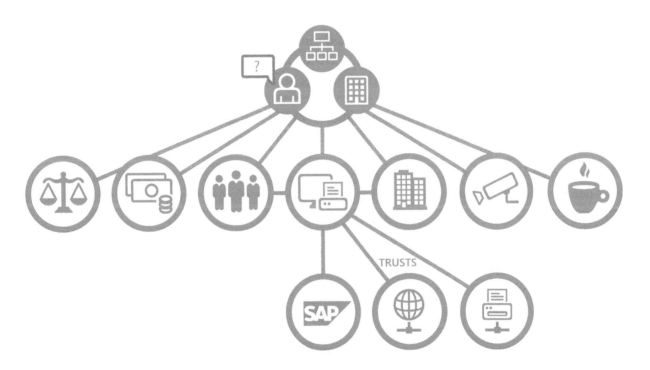

Figure 7: Connecting accounts of suppliers.

In the modern digital enterprise, collaboration transcends the organization's boundaries. Service delivery entities often outsource certain services. But these outsourced services are still integral components of their value chains.

The architecture of 4me enables the extension of value chains beyond the confines of an entity's own account structure. An account trust not only facilitates collaboration between the support domain accounts within an enterprise: an account trust can also be defined between the accounts of two different account structures. The account trusts are what you need to establish customer – supplier relationships.

Standard Accounts

In addition to directory accounts and support domain accounts, there are also **standard accounts**. A standard account is a combination of a directory account and a support domain account. It includes organizational data (like organizations, personnel, and sites) as well as service delivery information. Standard accounts are something from the past. For any new accounts, a directory account is created. Customers can add support domain accounts as needed.

The 4me Account Structure Design for Widget Inc.

When implementing 4me for an enterprise, one of the initial tasks is designing the account structure. This involves determining the necessary 4me accounts and establishing the trusts between them. The account structure serves as the foundational layer of the operating model to be implemented. Typically, this structure is devised during a workshop involving key stakeholders from the customer. The 4me account structure should be envisioned as a long-term plan, even though only a portion may be implemented initially. For larger enterprises, the account structure can facilitate an iterative approach to implementation.

The Operating Model Canvas serves as an excellent foundation for crafting the account structure. Let's delve into the operating model of Widget, Inc., a nice example of a typical enterprise within the demo environment.

Widget, Inc. is a New York-based company in the United States specializing in the production of 'widgets'. The company consists of three primary business units: Widget North America, Inc., Widget Europe, SE, and Widget Data Center, a non-profit IT organization. Within Widget there are six critical support functions: IT, HR, Facilities, Customer Services, Sales & Marketing, and Legal.

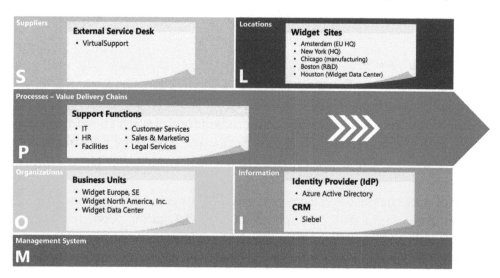

Figure 8: The operating model of the Widget company.

Based on this information, an initial account structure could be envisioned as follows:
- A central directory account, serving as the core entity
- Six support domain accounts aligned with the various support functions

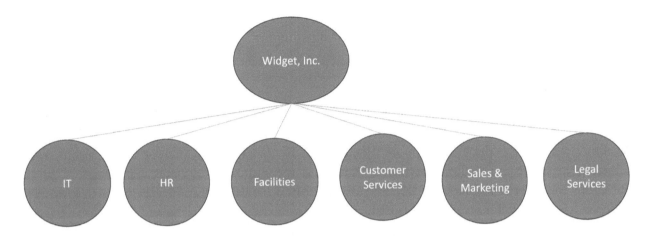

Figure 9: The 4me account structure design for the Widget Company after initial examination.

However, as workshops progress and discussions with stakeholders unfold, new elements will come to light, necessitating adjustments to this initial account structure.

The First Line of an Account - The Service Desk team

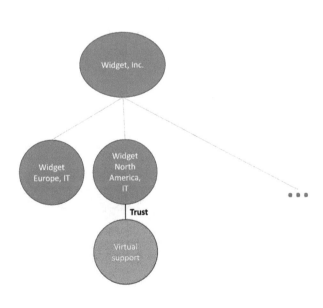

A **Service Desk** team is established within every 4me account to handle tickets that cannot be automatically assigned to a team or to handle incoming chat messages. The service desk team of a 4me account is defined in the **First-Line Support Agreement (FLSA)** record.

Each 4me account can have only one service desk team. In scenarios where an enterprise operates multiple service desks, it becomes necessary to define distinct 4me support domain accounts. Each entity with its dedicated service desk would require a separate 4me account.

This holds true for Widget, Inc. within its IT organization. During the workshop it becomes clear that Widget Europe, Information Technology, maintains its regional service desk

Figure 10: Defining two accounts when two different first line support agreements.

while the IT departments in Widget North America have outsourced their service desk to an external provider called *Virtualsupport*.

Given this information, Widget IT must be split into Widget Europe, IT, and Widget North America, IT. Furthermore, Widget North America, IT needs to establish a trust with the account of VirtualSupport, the external supplier responsible for delivering first-line support.

Process Segregation

Within an enterprise, the same support function can be managed by different organizations, each adhering to specific procedures. A prime example is the Human Resources department. Due to variations in national legislation, HR functions are often handled by local HR units that operate independently in different regions. This setup ensures alignment with local laws and regulations. In such cases, it's advisable to consider dividing the 4me account into multiple accounts. This approach respects process segregation, allowing each service delivery organization to autonomously manage processes and procedures while collaborating with others via account trusts.

Examining Widget, Inc.'s structure unveils the existence of four sites in North America: the corporate headquarters in New York, a manufacturing site in Chicago, a Research and Development center in Boston, and a data center in Houston. Similarly, Widget Europe is headquartered in Amsterdam.

In the case of Widget, Inc., it's apparent that both Human Resources and Facilities are divided into separate European and North American organizations. These units independently manage their processes and procedures, making them suitable candidates for individual 4me support domain accounts.

In the IT domain, there exists a distinct business unit called Widget Data Center, responsible for providing shared IT services to the regional IT departments of Widget Europe, SE, and Widget North America, Inc. This data center unit operates with its own IT processes, procedures, and IT assets, even displaying distinct financial management compared to the regional IT departments. With these unique characteristics, creating a dedicated support domain account for Widget Data Center is prudent. This account should establish trusts with Widget Europe, IT, and Widget North America, IT due to their shared service delivery. Additionally, a trust with the VirtualSupport account is required for the service desk function. This arrangement is depicted in the following illustration:

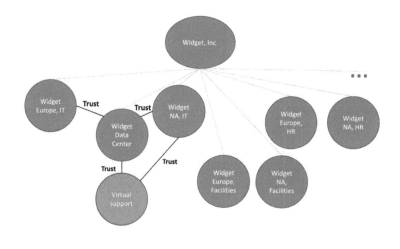

Figure 11: Defining multiple accounts for process segregation.

Data Segregation

Within Widget Data Center, a small team is responsible for IT security and data protection. The team, led by the Chief Information Security Officer (CISO) and including the Data Protection Officer (DPO), typically handles sensitive data that should not be exposed to the specialists from the IT department. As a result, data segregation is required. 4me accounts implement data segregation, ensuring that data in one 4me account cannot be accessed by specialists from other accounts, unless data is exchanged via the trust relationship.

This necessitates adding an extra account to the account structure of Widget Company, namely the Widget Data Protection account. This account will be defined as a Strong Privacy account, which adds an additional layer of security. In the chapter on account settings, we will explain in detail what this entails.

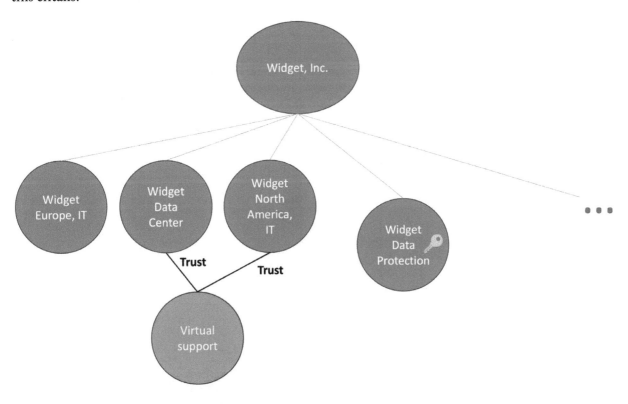

Figure 12: Widget Data Protection needs a separate account for data segregation.

Connecting Suppliers

Let's explore the operating model of Widget Data Center from the perspective of external suppliers. On our operating model canvas, we've incorporated Widget Data Center's 4me-using suppliers: *VirtualSupport* (handling the Service Desk function), *GlobalNet* (providing Network services), *GigaTera* (offering storage services) and 4me (providing 4me support).

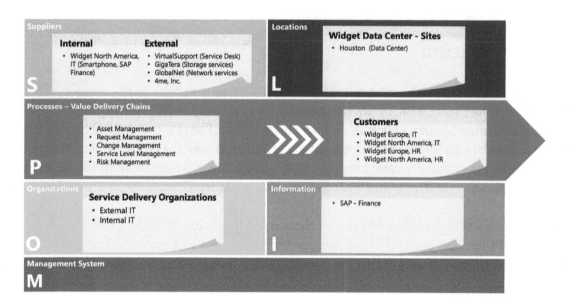

Figure 13: The external suppliers of Widget Data Center working on 4me will have their own 4me account.

These 4me-utilizing suppliers should be integrated into our account structure design, necessitating trusts with their respective 4me accounts.

It's important to note that Widget Data Center has numerous other suppliers beyond the four organizations using 4me. In the subsequent chapter, we will elucidate how all suppliers, regardless of their 4me usage, will be integrated into the Service Hierarchy.

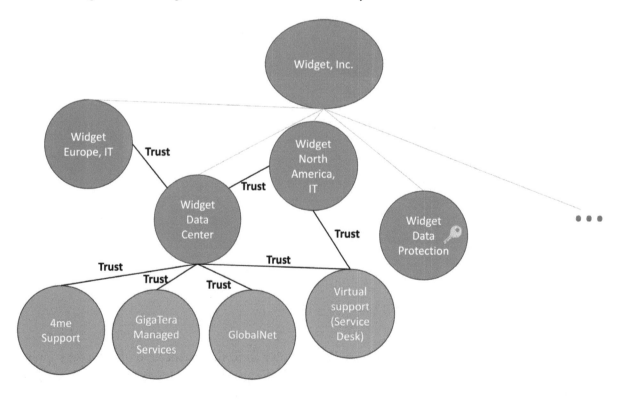

Figure 14: The suppliers of Widget Data Center with a trust to their 4me account.

Internal Customers and Suppliers

During the workshop it becomes clear that Widget Data Center is providing services to other service delivery organizations that have their own 4me account. Notably, Widget Data Center serves as a shared data center to both Widget Europe, IT and Widget North America IT. Additionally, Widget Data Center is involved in tasks assigned by the regional HR departments, particularly in the onboarding and offboarding workflows.

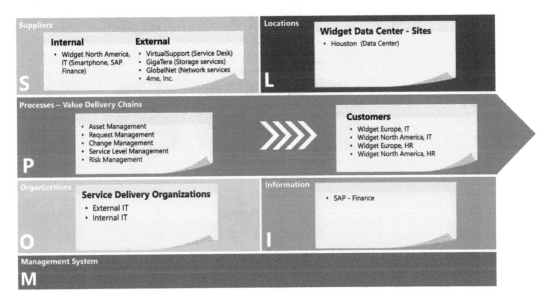

Figure 15: Four internal customers of Widget Data Center have their own 4me account. A trust will need to be established with these accounts.

Consequently, several account trusts must be incorporated into our account structure design:

- A trust between Widget Data Center and Widget Europe, HR.
- A trust between Widget Data Center and Widget North America, HR.
- A trust between Widget Data Center and Widget Europe, IT.
- A trust between Widget Data Center and Widget North America, IT.

It's essential to note that establishing a trust doesn't signify a hierarchy between the two organizations. For most services, Widget Data Center acts as the internal supplier to Widget North America IT. However, for smartphone support and SAP finance support, the roles reverse, with Widget North America IT becoming the supplier to Widget Data Center.

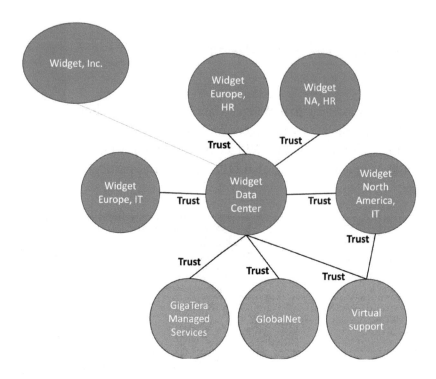

Figure 16: Because Widget Data Center is acting as an internal supplier for other support domain accounts trusts with these accounts must be established.

4me Accounts and Data Protection of Personal Info

Sharing of Personal Information

4me accounts are designed to segregate data, while trusts facilitate collaboration between various organizations. These trusts can be established within a single enterprise or across different enterprises and entities. However, collaboration necessitates the sharing of specific data, which poses a risk of data breaches, especially when exchanging information between entities from separate organizations. This could potentially lead to the disclosure of confidential and sensitive information to external parties. The 4me platform ensures that during collaboration between different organizations, only necessary personal information for the collaboration is exchanged, and nothing more.

Sharing of Ticket Notes

In 4me, comments added to a ticket are referred to as notes. Notes may contain sensitive information that should not be shared outside the organization or with end users. By default, a note in 4me is public and accessible to all users with ticket access. This includes end users, often the ticket requesters and users from other accounts, often the specialists from external suppliers. To restrict access, an internal note can be created, ensuring confidentiality when needed: an internal note is not visible to end users and users from other accounts.

Data Segregation Between Specialists - Strong Privacy Accounts

In certain situations, service delivery organizations dealing with highly sensitive information may require internal data segregation. For instance, within a large HR department, teams dedicated to Employee Benefits and Salary & Compensation services might need to keep their tickets private from other HR teams. This is where the '**Strong Privacy**' account feature is vital. Activating 'Strong Privacy' in account settings ensures that tickets are visible only to assigned teams. Additionally, in these accounts, the default setting for notes is internal, aligning with the focus on processing sensitive information without external sharing.

Data Segregation Between End Users - End user privacy

Effective collaboration and communication within an enterprise are essential. 4me offers built-in features enabling users to mention colleagues and submit requests on behalf of others. However, unrestricted user interaction isn't always desirable. For example, a city or county using the 4me platform to serve its citizens wouldn't want individuals to search for or communicate with all other citizens. 4me offers several options for implementing end-user segregation within an account structure.

- An '**End User Privacy**' **account setting** can prevent such interactions among all (internal and external) end users in the account.
- Alternatively, restrictions can be applied only to external end users in the account by adjusting the '**External end users may mention others**' setting.
- Finally a specific organization can be designated as an **End User Privacy Organization**, limiting communication to its own users.

Account Structure for Business to Consumer (B2C) Support

Let's revisit the initial account structure design, which includes an account dedicated to the business function of 'Customer Services.' This addition is necessary due to Widget, Inc.'s production and sale of 'widgets' to consumers, which requires the provision of customer support services.

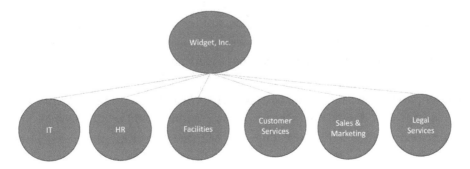

Figure 17: The initial account structure design of the Widget Company.

As previously discussed, internal users, such as Widget employees, access support services through the Self-Service Portal on the directory account. It's important to note that a self-service portal can be configured and customized on each 4me account, spanning directory accounts and support domain accounts. While it's theoretically possible to grant consumer access via self-registration to the Customer Services support domain account or the directory account, the most logical approach is to establish a separate account structure (directory account and one support domain account) for the customer portal.

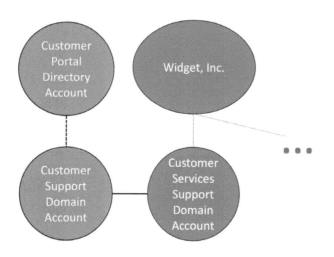

Figure 18: A typical B2C account structure design.

This approach is motivated by communication needs and the imperative of safeguarding personal information. Each account has its distinct set of email designs and templates. Given the likely differences in email designs and templates used for internal and external communication, it's prudent to define (external) customers within a separate account structure. This separation also ensures that the personal information of both Widget employees and external users remains better protected. So we enhance the account structure by introducing the customer portal as a separate account structure. This involves establishing a trust link between the Customer Services account—where customer services are provided—and the Customer Portal support domain account, which serves as the home for consumers and features an appealing self-service design.

Account Structure Design for a Managed Service Provider (MSP)

A Managed Service Provider (MSP) typically performs the same business functions as other enterprises, such as Human Resources, Legal, Financial Services, and Internal IT. However, the core activities of an MSP are carried out by one or more managed service delivery organizations. This central service delivery organization serves as a supplier to external customer organizations.

Let's revisit an example from the 4me demo environment: Gigatera Inc. This company, a managed service provider, offers storage and data center services to its customers. Take a close look at the Operating Model of their service delivery organization 'GigaTera Managed Services' pictured below.

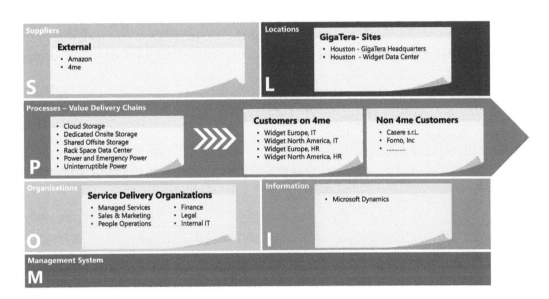

Figure 19: The operating model of GigaTera Managed Services.

External Customer Organizations

On the right-hand side of the value delivery chain in the operating model of GigaTera Managed Services you can find the external customers. In 4me each customer must be defined as an organization. **Internal customer organizations** belong by design to the directory account. The customers of MSPs are external customers and here we have a choice: an **external customer organization** can be defined in the directory account, in the support domain itself or in a trusted account structure.

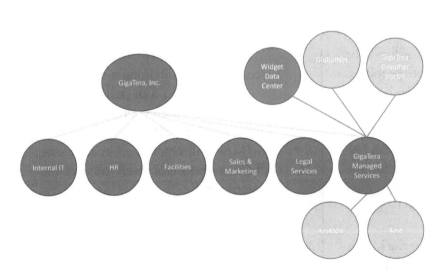

Figure 20: Connecting customers working on 4me.

Now, check the operating model again: a distinction has been made between external customers working on 4me and those without 4me. For those external customers working on 4me the design is straightforward: they have their own 4me account and the MSP will establish a trust with the support domain account of the customer for which they act as the supplier. In the example, Widget Data Center has a supplier contract with GigaTera Managed Services which results in a trust between both accounts.

What about the customers that don't work in 4me? For these external customers, all three possibilities are available. There is not a 'best' solution: all three possibilities have their advantages and disadvantages.

Registering External Customers in a Trusted Account Structure

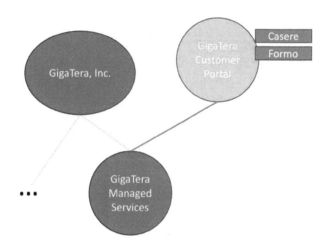

A first approach is to define a separate account structure that will be used as the customer portal. It is even possible to define a dedicated customer portal for only one customer. Due to the overhead this probably only makes sense when such a customer intends to start working on 4me in the future.

Figure 21: MSP with the customers defined in a standard customer portal account.

Pros	Cons
• There is a clear separation between the MSP's organizational structure and the organizational structures of the external customers; the administration of the customer records can only be performed by the MSP's personnel who have the necessary role for this in the stand-alone account. • The specialists of the MSP will not be able to accidentally mention people of customers unless these specialists have the Specialist role of the stand-alone account. • The design of the self-service portal of the stand-alone account can be very different from the design for the self-service portal for the MSP's own employees, which is defined in the MSP's directory account. • The single sign-on option for the MSP's internal employees will not need to become visible to the customer's people when they log into the self-service portal of the stand-alone account.	• The MSP will not be able to link organizations, people or sites of the customers to records that are stored in the MSP's account (think for example of linking users and sites to a configuration item registered in one of the MSP's support domain accounts). • There is additional administrative overhead for maintaining a completely separate account and the trust relations it has with the support domain account(s) of the MSP. • The MSP will be charged at least one billable user (the account owner) for the account.

Registering External Customers in the Support Domain Account

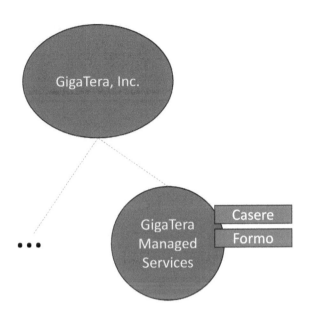

It is possible to define the customer organizations in the support domain account. This reduces administrative overhead and makes it possible to link sites defined in the support domain account to the customers.

Figure 22: Defining the customers in the support domain account.

Pros	Cons
• There is still a clear separation between the MSP's organizational structure (registered in the MSP's directory account) and the organizational structures of the external customers (registered in this special support domain account); the administration of the customer records can only be performed by the MSP's personnel who have the necessary role for this in this support domain account. • Only the employees of the MSP who have the Specialist role of this support domain account in which the customers are registered will be able to mention people from customers. This may avoid, for example, one of the MSP's HR specialists mentioning a customer employee in a request from one of the MSP's employees. • The extra support domain account within the MSP's directory structure is free of charge.	• The people, organizations and sites of the external customers can only be related to the records that are registered in this support domain account of the MSP. If the MSP, for example, wants to use people or site records of customers in requests linked in the Sales & Marketing support domain account or in the Data Protection account of the MSP, then this will not be possible. • If the MSP decides to acquire another MSP that provides very different services, it may be best to provide the acquired organization its own support domain account. It will not be possible for the acquired company to set the coverage in an SLA for a customer that is registered in another support domain account.

Registering External Customers in the Directory Account

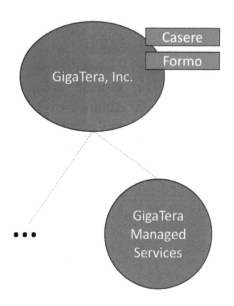

Finally, one can define the external customer organizations in the directory account. Be aware that if single sign-on is enabled for the internal users, the external users must be able to bypass the standard SSO configuration.

Figure 23: Defining the external customers in the directory account.

Pros	Cons
• The people, organizations and sites of the external customers can be related to the records that are registered in any of the MSP's support domain accounts. This provides a lot of flexibility and reduces administrative complexity. • There are no additional costs for registering the customer organizations, their people, and sites in the MSP's directory account.	• When an employee of one of the customers logs into the self-service portal of the MSP, this person will see the single sign-on (SSO) option for the MSP's internal staff. This can be avoided by setting up a separate SSO Configuration for each external customer and providing each customer with their unique SSO login URL. • Any specialist of the MSP (e.g. also HR specialists) can accidentally mention a person from a customer organization in a request from another customer organization or from one of the MSP's employees. When they do, though, they will see the following warning: @ Add Mention ⚠ You mentioned an external person. Are you sure that you want to give access to this request to Abbie Lindt of Microsoft Sales North America? Yes No *Figure 24: Warning when mentioning an external person.*

	• It may not be clear which site records belong to a customer and which belong to the MPS, unless a naming convention is used for sites that includes the customer's name.

Account Structure Design - Best Practices

In theory, it's possible to create a separate 4me account for each team, but this approach is far from ideal. Every additional account introduces more settings to manage and increases administrative overhead. While collaboration can occur between accounts, it's generally smoother within a single account. Therefore, the primary rule when designing an account structure is to minimize the number of accounts.

For instance, let's reconsider the proposed account structure for GigaTera Managed Services. It includes both an Internal IT account and a Managed Services account. If the same individuals provide both internal IT and managed services to customers, consolidating these into a single account can be a wise move.

 **Best Practice**	So, the first and foremost rule is to define as few accounts as possible. However, there are compelling reasons why you might need to segment an account into multiple accounts:

Data Segregation: Sometimes, privacy, data protection, or compliance regulations mandate the separation of data.

Process Segregation: There are scenarios where distinct maturity levels and objectives exist among different organizations, divisions, or locations. Also, when the same service gets different service owners, knowledge managers, or change managers for different organizations or locations a split might be required.

Service Desk Differences: Different organizations, divisions, or locations may have their own unique service desk. Remember, each 4me account can have only one service desk team.

Finally, **different user groups** may necessitate separate 4me accounts under the following circumstances:

- Identity Providers: When these groups have their own Identity Provider for provisioning and Single Sign-On (SSO).
- Self-Service Needs: Groups of users may require their own self-service portal designs or specific communication formats, including unique email designs and templates.

The 4me Environments and 4me Accounts

4me is more than just a cloud platform; it's a gateway to efficient, service driven enterprise service management on a global scale. In an ideal world, a single environment could host all the 4me accounts for every customer across the globe. But, as we know, our world isn't perfect. Various countries and regions have established their own strict data privacy regulations, and personal data must remain within the boundaries of the respective territory.

This is where 4me shines. It's designed to ensure that personal data is securely stored within specific regions. To achieve this, 4me divides its platform into secure segments, aptly named "environments." Currently, 4me offers environments in Australia, the European Union, Switzerland, the United Kingdom, and the USA, with the potential for more to come.

However, the 4me platform doesn't stop there. Companies often require a dedicated quality assurance environment during implementation and continuous improvement of their 4me accounts. For each regional environment, there's both a quality assurance and a production environment.

Within these regional test and production environments, countless 4me accounts can be seamlessly connected through trusts. Each account boasts a **unique account ID**—a string of up to 40 characters. These IDs can include letters (a-z, A-Z), digits (0-9), and hyphens (-), mirroring URL encoding restrictions. And yes, you guessed it, these account IDs are used within the URL to access each 4me account within a specific 4me environment.

The domain of these URLs is governed by the environment. So, here's the URL syntax breakdown:

Region	QA Environment	PROD environment
Australia	*account-id*.au.4me.qa	*account-id*.4me.au.4me.com
Europe	account-id.4me.qa	account-id.4me.com
Switzerland	*account-id*.ch.4me.qa	*account-id*.ch.4me.com
United Kingdom	*account-id*.uk.4me.qa	*account-id*.uk.4me.com
United States	*account-id*.us.4me.qa	*account-id*.us.4me.com

Creating 4me Accounts: Process and Essential Settings

Setting up a new directory account within 4me necessitates a formal process initiated through direct engagement with 4me. Upon the establishment of a valid contractual agreement and the provision of all necessary information, the 4me support team commits to creating a new directory account within one business day. For existing directory account holders, adding a support domain account is a capability reserved for the *directory account owner*. The requisite information for either requesting a new account or creating a support domain account includes:

Name	Description
Account ID	The unique identifier of the 4me account. Ensure it includes a reference to the name of your organization!
Account name	This is a crucial identifier, as it will be displayed prominently across the 4me platform, including the browser title bar and the account sign-in page.
Support URL	The 4me platform is where users can get support. But what if the user cannot access 4me? How do they find support when they cannot access the main support platform in the first place? To resolve this issue, you should define the Support URL in the account settings: enter a website URL, email address, or telephone number. If **john.doe@widget.com** is found in our records, you will receive an email from us with instructions for setting a new password. If you do not receive this email, please check your junk mail folder. Or contact us at **001-253.36.67.67** for further assistance. **Back to the sign in page** *Figure 25: The telephone number defined in the Support URL is given when the user tries to reset the 4me password*
Currency	
Language	The 4me platform supports multiple languages, enabling the translation of custom fields and knowledge articles. Initially, you must select a default language—preferably one universally understood by your specialists. It's advisable to finalize this choice before go-live, as changes post-launch can lead to translation discrepancies.
Time zone	While individual users can personalize their time zone settings, the account-wide default time zone is established here, offering a baseline for all new users.

Time format	Choose between the 24-hour and 12-hour clock formats. This selection sets the default time format for new users, though it remains customizable on an individual basis.
Start of the week	Important for time tracking: The start of the week is used as the first day of the week when determining whether someone's weekly time registration goal has been exceeded.
Account owner	Although an account may have several administrators, there is only one *account owner*. This individual possesses exclusive rights to alter security settings and add new support domain accounts. It's recommended to appoint at least one additional account administrator who, in the owner's absence, can adjust the account owner's email address in the system to assume control if necessary.

The Organization of a 4me Account

In 4me, each support domain account is designed to represent a specific service delivery organization. Directory accounts symbolize the overarching organization itself. Upon the creation of any 4me account, it is inherently associated with an organization. This initial linkage is crucial, as the account cannot be re-associated with a different organization after its creation, though the organization's name within 4me can be modified if necessary.

Directory Account Creation:

- With the inception of a directory account, an organization corresponding to the account name provided during setup is automatically generated. This primary organization holds a unique status within 4me, serving as the root for internal organizational structure.
- Any child organization added under this primary organization is recognized as **an internal organization**, indicative of internal departments or divisions such as HR or IT Services.
- Conversely, any organization not directly descending from this primary organization is deemed **external**, typically representing suppliers or external customers.

Support Domain Account Addition:

- The *account owner* of a directory account possesses the authority to introduce additional support domain accounts. This process is facilitated through the "Support Domain Accounts" section within the directory account's settings console.
- A crucial aspect of setting up a support domain account is its affiliation with an internal organization. This entity is the service provider within the 4me architecture, for example, an HR department or a Shared Service Center.

- During the creation of a support domain account, the administrator is presented with a choice: select an existing internal organization (which has not been previously linked to a support domain account) or opt to leave the organization field empty. In the latter case, a new internal organization bearing the same name as the account will be automatically generated.

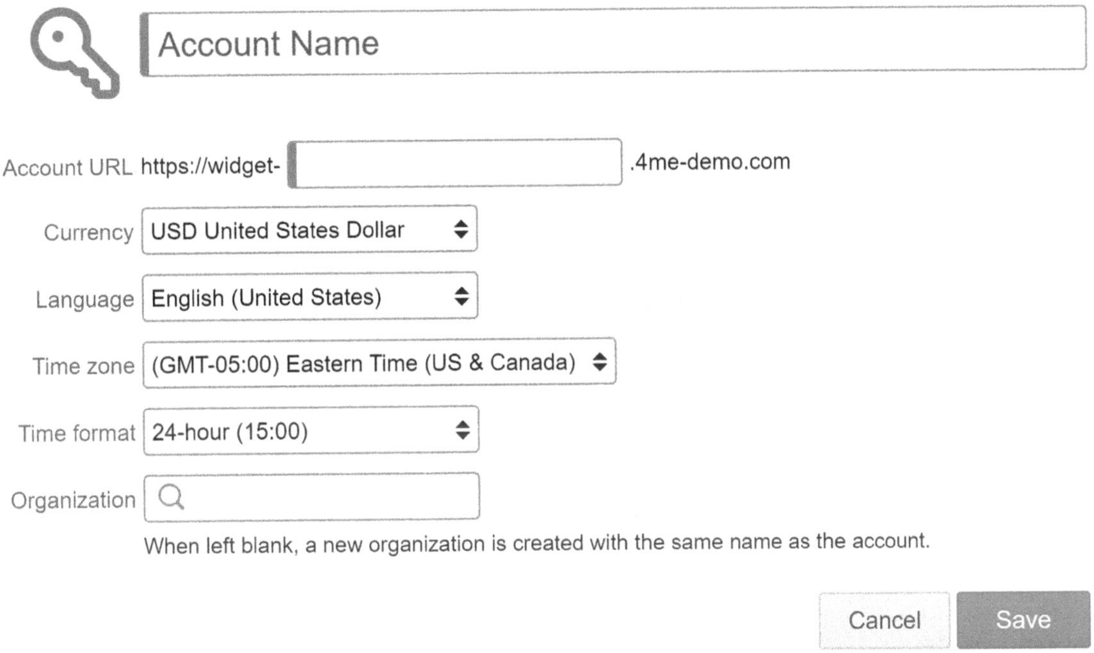

Figure 26: Support Domain Account creation by the account owner.

Account Security Settings

To adjust security settings, you must hold the *account owner* role. These settings are typically established once during the initial configuration and seldom modified thereafter. You may need to reach out to your security officer and check the security policy of the organization to ensure compliance with these settings.

Account Settings:

- **Strong Privacy**: Enforces rigorous data segregation within the account, allowing teams to view only the tickets for which they are responsible.
- **End User Privacy**: Restricts end users from viewing or mentioning each other and from registering requests on behalf of one another.
- **Internal Notes and Internal UI Extension Fields Visible in Other Support Domains**: Implements strict data segregation within a directory account structure; internal notes and custom fields are not accessible to specialists from other accounts.

- **External End Users May Mention Others**: Typically, external users should only mention individuals from their own organization. However, in cases where external personnel (like contractors) are integrated into operations, enabling them to mention others within the organization can be beneficial.
- **Default Organization**: Specifies the default organization for automatically created person records through inbound email or self-registration, ensuring each record is associated with an organization.

Security:

- **Idle Session Timeout**: Determines the duration of inactivity before a user must re-authenticate. Defaulted to 4 hours for user convenience but can be adjusted to meet stricter security policies. Note: Administrative control sessions have a fixed idle timeout of 15 minutes.
- **Two-Factor Authentication Required**: Although SSO implementations usually handle two-factor authentication, administrators can always circumvent SSO. Thus, enforcing two-factor authentication within 4me is recommended for enhanced security.
- **Allowed Extensions**: 4me predefines a list of safe file extensions. This list can be customized to reflect your organization's security policy, noting that 4me includes built-in antivirus and malware protections.
- **Maximum File Size**: The default file upload limit is 2GB. For additional security, this limit can be reduced.

Password Policy:

- **Maximum Password Length**: Align with your organization's security policy.
- **Password Expires In**: Adjust according to your security policy.
- **Enforce Password History**: Ensure compliance with your security policy by preventing the reuse of recent passwords.

Creating Trusts between Accounts

In 4me, the mechanism to facilitate collaboration across different service delivery organizations is through the creation of trusts between accounts. *Account owners* and *administrators* have the capability to initiate the trust-creating process by extending an invitation to the administrators of another account. This initiation of trust is a proposal that requires acceptance; a trust relationship is established only after the invitation is accepted by the receiving account's administrators.

Key Aspects of Creating Trusts:

- **Initiation of Trust**: The process begins with an *account owner* or *administrator* proposing a trust by sending an invitation. This step signifies the intent to collaborate but does not automatically establish a working relationship.
- **Acceptance Required**: The establishment of a trust is contingent upon the acceptance of the

invitation by one of the administrators of the invited account. This mutual agreement ensures that both parties are willing and ready to engage in collaboration.

- **Defining the Scope of Collaboration**: The mere creation of a trust does not dictate the terms or extent of collaboration between the accounts. Detailed collaboration parameters need to be defined either through account trust settings or by establishing Service Level Agreements (SLAs). The specifics of how trusted accounts will interact and collaborate are crucial and will be elaborated upon in subsequent chapters.

Invite 4me Account

Enter the account ID of the 4me account with which you want to set up a trust relation:

> gigatera-managed-services

Enter a message for the account administrator(s) of the other account. Include an email address and/or phone number if you want to enable them to contact you for questions:

> As discussed, GigaTera will become our new partner for storage services

When inviting an existing 4me account to set up a trust relation, an email message is sent to the owner of the specified account. The recipient must click the link in the email and accept the invitation to complete the process.

> Cancel   Invite

Figure 27: Creating an account trust invitation.

Trusts with Directory Accounts

Trusts between a directory account and its associated support domain accounts are implicit, given their inherent connection within the 4me architecture. That's why it is impossible to establish a trust relationship between a directory account and its support domain accounts.

However, a directory account may establish a trust with a support domain account belonging to a different directory account. This arrangement can be particularly beneficial for organizations looking to outsource administrative responsibilities of their directory account to a 4me partner. Once a trust is established, administrative roles, such as the directory account administrator role, can be delegated to the trusted account, facilitating a collaborative management approach.

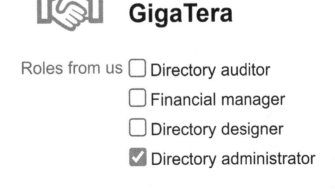

Figure 28: Providing the Directory Administrator role to a trusted account.

Examples in the demo environment

 **Demo** | **Accounts and Trusts in the Demo Environment**

(ti) **Widget International**

    🖥 **Widget Data Center**

    🛡 **Widget Data Protection**

    🏢 **Widget Europe - FM**

    👥 **Widget Europe - HR**

    🖥 **Widget Europe - IT**

    🏢 **Widget N. America - FM**

    👥 **Widget N. America - HR**

    🖥 **Widget N. America - IT**

4me **4me**

🔑 **Amazon**

🔑 **Best IT**

GT **GigaTera**

    GT **GigaTera Managed Services**

Alright, let's dive into the 4me demo world! Picture this: you log into the demo and boom – a whole universe of predefined accounts is at your fingertips, like a buffet of digital delights. Our previous pages were just a teaser, featuring organizations you'll find right here in the demo.

Top of the list? Widget International, the directory account of the Widget Organization. Want a backstage pass? Peek at Annex B for a list of demo users. For your first act, let's roll with Widget International. Log in as randy.barton@widget.com (psst, the password is '4me'). Who's Randy? Just your average Joe in the Widget Europe Finance department. But when he logs in, he's like a VIP entering the Self-Service Portal. Try to register a request and check the support domain accounts made available for Randy.

Done playing Randy? Time to logout. Hint: Randy's pic in the top right is your ticket out.

Next mission: switch to the Widget Data Center account. Enter stage left: howard.tanner@widget.com. Who's Howard? The account owner of the Widget Data Center support domain account.

 As Howard, hit the Settings console (left toolbar, can't miss it), then Account Trusts. You will find 10 account trusts, a few more than what we designed in the previous paragraph. Try to define another trust with yet another account. Use Annex B as a guide.

Chapter 4 –
The Service Hierarchy and Service Catalog

Unveiling the Service Hierarchy:
Driving the Operating Model Forward

In the previous chapter, we explored how service delivery organizations are defined as accounts within 4me. These 4me accounts serve as the interconnected gears that drive the entire organizational operating model, extending to interactions with both customer and supplier organizations.

However, what's still missing are the engines that propel these gears forward. Let's revisit the diagram that encompasses the operating model, business model, and financial model of an organization.

At the core of both the operating model and business model lie the value propositions. Value propositions define what an organization offers in the form of services or products to its customers. An enterprise has its own unique value propositions, as do all the service delivery organizations that constitute the enterprise. In terms of enterprise service management, a value proposition comprises services. Even when products are delivered, it's imperative to view them within the context of a specific service.

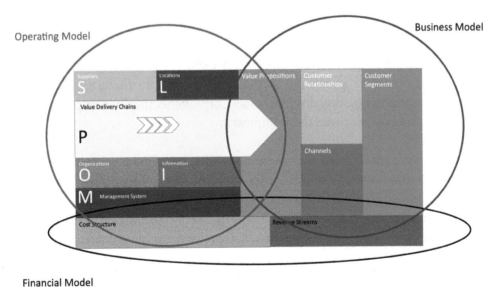

Figure 29: The operating model, the business model and the financial model.

Therefore, the driving force behind these 4me accounts, these interlocking gears, is none other than services. In enterprise service management, these services are not endpoints; delivering a service to a customer can be a complex process that involves multiple skills and resources. This implies that delivering a service to a customer may necessitate the involvement of multiple supporting services.

This interconnected chain of services that ultimately delivers a value proposition is referred to as a **Service Hierarchy**.

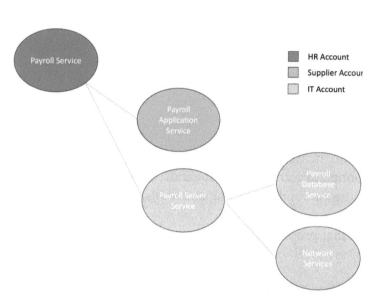

Let's elucidate this concept with an example. Imagine a scenario within a Human Resources account where the Payroll Service has been meticulously defined. Any questions or issues pertaining to this service are efficiently managed by a dedicated Human Resources team known as the *Payroll Management* team. In this scenario, the configuration of the Payroll Application has been entrusted to an external supplier. If the Payroll Team encounters a query or issue that falls outside their domain of expertise, they will initiate collaboration with the external supplier. Meanwhile, the infrastructure housing the payroll application is provided by an internal IT department.

Figure 30: The service hierarchy of a payroll service.

Therefore, should any technical issue arise, the HR team will promptly involve the IT team responsible for maintaining the servers hosting the payroll application. On occasion, the root cause of a technical glitch may not originate within the servers but could be linked to the database system or network. In such instances, the server team will coordinate with the database management team or the network team. This example underscores the inherent complexity and logical structure that characterizes a service delivery organization. Often, the provision of end-to-end support for a service necessitates the involvement of numerous teams boasting diverse skill sets. Simultaneously, it exemplifies how the service-driven approach in 4me adeptly addresses this complexity.

The Service Hierarchy is the lynchpin of the operating model. It defines a coherent support flow. This flow materializes when a support team responsible for a specific service engages with the support team of a supporting service. In essence, the service hierarchy or service chain is the embodiment of the operating model in action, defining the pathways within a service delivery organization. Moreover, it seamlessly connects these pathways with both internal and external service delivery organizations.

In 4me the service catalog and the related service hierarchy consist of the following 4 record types:

1. Services
2. Service Instances
3. Service Offerings
4. Service Level Agreements

In the upcoming sections, we will delve into each of these crucial record types.

Defining the Service Catalog and Service Hierarchy in 4me

The Service: Defining the Value in 4me

When setting up 4me, defining your services is non-negotiable. In 4me, the Service record is a first-class citizen, and Services take center stage. Yet, the journey to establishing a service catalog is a road less traveled by many service delivery organizations. The hesitation often stems from the nebulous concept of what exactly constitutes a 'service,' exacerbated by the theoretical definitions found in leading frameworks.

The ISO20000 framework encapsulates a service as *'a means of delivering value to customers by facilitating outcomes they desire, without burdening them with ownership costs and risks.'* Similarly, ITIL V4 expands on this by introducing value co-creation, suggesting that *'a service enables value co-creation by facilitating outcomes customers want to achieve, without forcing them to bear specific costs and risks.'*

Though these definitions offer a high-level understanding, they fall short of providing the concrete guidance organizations seek when attempting to pinpoint and delineate their own services. This gap between theory and application contributes to the reluctance of many organizations to embark on defining their service catalog. Often, 'lack of maturity' is cited as the main reason for not defining the organization's **Service Catalog** (= collection of the services delivered).

This is incorrect. Any service delivery organization, regardless of their 'maturity,' can identify the services they are providing. Most importantly, identifying services is not as complex as it may seem and can be accomplished through a few workshops. Experienced individuals in a service delivery organization do understand the operating model of their organization. By defining the service catalog, existing knowledge is uncovered and made explicit.

The key success factor for a service definition workshop is to start from best practices service catalogs. Even if the operating model of similar service delivery organizations differs depending on the company or organization's strategy they belong to, some of the services they deliver will be the same. An HR organization will most likely be responsible for a Payroll service, and most Facilities Management organizations will provide 'Building Maintenance' and 'Building Access and Security.' 4me has published best practices catalogs, see also Annex C. Use these service catalogs as the starting point to identify your services. Once the audience is acquainted with these well-known services, they can add the services that are specific to their organization.

 | Use the 4me best practices service catalog as the starting point for your service catalog.

When identifying services, always think in terms of **Utility**; this is about 'What the service does.' A good service is 'fit for purpose,' providing the utility and functionality the business and its users need. It should be possible to describe 'What the service does' in a Service Description, a few lines that explain to the users what it is all about. The service record helps the business understand what is delivered. For example, the Payroll Service could be described as:

> *'The Payroll service ensures the timely payment of salaries and bonuses, as well as the withholding of taxes.'*

Here is a list of common misunderstandings often encountered during service definition workshops:

- Problem management, incident management, or knowledge management are not services. They don't bring value to the customer on their own. The Payroll service brings value to the customer. Providing knowledge articles related to the Payroll service does provide value, but knowledge management is just an activity or practice that is part of service delivery and should not be defined as a separate service.
- *'Restoring a file from a backup'* is not a service. It is a standard request that belongs to the IT service: 'File Services.'
- 'HR Services' and 'Business Applications' are too high-level to be considered services. HR Services need to be further broken down into more specific services.

Defining the Service Record

In addition to its name and description, the service record must specify the **Service Provider**—the organization responsible for delivering the service. This is particularly crucial when billing or charging is involved, as this organization will issue invoices to customers.

Aligned with 4me's service-oriented approach, the service record also delineates responsibilities for key process roles, such as the Change Manager, Knowledge Manager, and Problem Manager. Of particular importance is the Service Owner, who is responsible for ensuring that the service level targets outlined in the Service Level Agreements (SLAs) for the service are consistently met.

Figure 31: Defining a service. The service provider is the organization that provides the service. When billing or charging is involved, this organization will send the invoices to the customers.

Bringing Services to Life: The Role of Service Instances

The second record type is the **Service Instance**. The service instance brings the service to life; it is the 'instantiation' of the service in a service delivery chain. This means that the service instance identifies the team accountable for the delivery of the service or part of the service. We will refer to this team as the **Support Team**.

Payroll Service

Figure 32: The Payroll Service consists of two service instances each with its own support team.

In a complex environment, it may be necessary to define multiple service instances for one service. For example, consider the Payroll Service offered to all employees in a multinational enterprise. The operating model may require the definition of a local Payroll Management team per country due to country-specific payroll legislation. This can be achieved by defining a service instance for each country. In our example, if there's a 4me account named 'Human Resources Europe,' representing the service delivery organization for all human resources' services in the European region, two service instances, 'Payroll Services Germany' and 'Payroll Services UK,' would be created for the Payroll Services. Each of these service instances will have its own support team.

In Facilities, Retail, and IT environments, it is often necessary to divide a service into multiple service instances based on the location where the service is delivered. Each location may have a dedicated team responsible for service delivery.

Network Connectivity Service

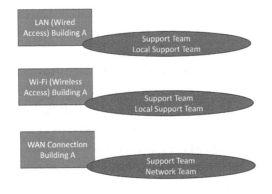

Figure 33: A service instance per location.

Another reason to divide a service into service instances by location is availability management. For instance, in retail, the HVAC (Heating, Ventilation, and Air Conditioning) service is available in each shop. It makes sense to visualize the unavailability of the HVAC service and measure its availability per shop. If this is required, the HVAC service should be divided into service instances per shop. In Facilities Management, creating a service instance per building for the Building Maintenance service is advantageous. In IT, it is a best practice to split the Network Connectivity service into LAN (wired connectivity), Wi-Fi (wireless connectivity), and WAN (connection to the network backbone) service instances per site.

Apart from enabling more accurate availability monitoring, it also facilitates better asset and configuration management. For example, in the case of the Wi-Fi service, having a service instance per site allows for linking Wi-Fi routers to the corresponding site-specific service instances. In IT, this implies that a service instance can define a service infrastructure comprising all the hardware and software components it encompasses.

Another scenario where splitting a service into multiple service instances is warranted is when specific customer organizations receive their own service offerings and service level agreements. For instance, HR might provide a specialized Payroll service for managers, enriched with additional knowledge articles and faster response times. In this case, the Payroll service can be split into two service instances: the *Standard Payroll Service* (Instance) and the *Payroll for Managers Service* (Instance).

Network Connectivity Service

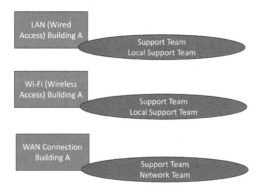

Figure 34: A service instance per environment (Test and Production).

MSP SAP SuccesFactors Service

Figure 35: A service instance per customer.

Another example is the differentiation between production and test systems in IT. Apart from having separate service infrastructures for each environment, they cater to distinct customer audiences. The Service Level Agreements (SLAs) for test environments are typically less stringent than those for production environments. These factors justify defining separate service instances for production and test environments.

Managed Service Providers (MSPs) typically deliver just a few services to multiple customers. For example, an MSP that offers a managed service for the SAP SuccessFactors platform to various customers will define one service called 'SAP SuccessFactors' and create a service instance for each customer, often named 'SAP SuccessFactors for Customer X.'

Lastly, a crucial recommendation, especially in IT environments, is to avoid overengineering the configuration. A complex IT environment can consist of thousands of service infrastructures. From a service management perspective, it does not always make sense to define a separate service instance for each of them. For example, in a building, each floor might have its own Wi-Fi and LAN routers. In theory, network connectivity could be unavailable on one floor while available on others, leading to consideration of defining a service instance for each floor. However, unless certain floors are involved in critical activities, it is often more practical to create a single service instance for LAN and Wi-Fi covering the entire building. Furthermore, splitting a service into multiple service instances, if necessary, is not overly complex and can be done at a later stage.

When to split a service in multiple service instances?	
	1. When different support teams are accountable for different parts of the service. 2. When there is a need to visualize and monitor the availability of different parts of the service. 3. When the service is composed of multiple service infrastructures. 4. When different parts of the service require specific service level agreements. And always avoid overengineering!

As a general rule, service delivery organizations providing HR services, legal, and financial services typically maintain just one service instance for each service, bearing the same name as the service they represent.

Service Instances and the First-Line Team

In the chapter on Account Structure Design, the concept of the first-line team was introduced: In every 4me account, a **first-line** or **service desk team** is established to handle tickets that cannot be automatically assigned. It is also possible to define a first-line team for a service instance. The first-line team is not accountable for the service instance but is responsible for the initial processing of requests routed to the service instance. When the first-line team of a service instance is not able to resolve the request, they can easily forward it to the support team of the service instance. In many cases, the service desk team of the account will also act as the first-line team of all the service instances provided to the customers.

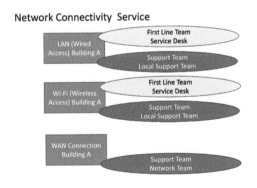

Figure 36: Defining first line teams when relevant.

For example, in the case of the Network Connectivity service, the first-line team of the LAN and Wi-Fi service instances will probably be defined and set to the service desk of the IT account. When a user registers an incident, the service desk will perform initial analysis and only forward the request to the support team when they are unable to resolve the issue. In this example, for the WAN service instance, which defines the connection between the local network and the network backbone, no first-line team is defined. That's because end users will not register issues directly with this service instance; instead, they will register incidents against the LAN or WiFi service instances. The service desk and eventually the local support team will analyze the incident. When they find out that the network connectivity issue occurs due to an issue with the WAN connection between the local network and the network backbone, the incident will be linked to the WAN service instance and assigned to the network team. In such a setup, the WAN service instance is not customer-facing, and the service desk will not be involved. In the paragraph on SLAs, we will describe how this support flow can be defined in 4me.

Defining the Service Instance Record

The service instance record requires a name and must be linked to a specific service. Selecting a service automatically copies the first-line and support team details from the service record to the service instance record, although these can be modified if necessary.

A key attribute of the service instance record is the maintenance window, which consists of a designated 4me calendar and a corresponding time zone. This window specifies the recurring periods during which preventive maintenance likely to disrupt the service can be carried out. This information is critical in change management processes. If a task related to a service instance is scheduled outside of its maintenance window, a warning will alert users that the planned implementations may need to be rescheduled.

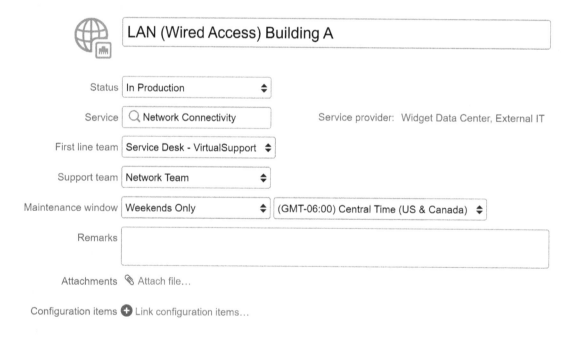

Figure 37: Defining a service instance. 4me will automatically assign requests to the right team based on the first line and support team definitions.

Service Offerings: The Promise of Service Excellence

The third component of the Service Hierarchy is the **Service Offering**. The service offering defines the service's fitness for use or **warranty**, outlining the promises made to the customer regarding what they can expect from the service. This includes the following elements:

- **Response and Resolution Times**: Specifies how quickly new requests will be responded to and resolved. The 4me platform utilizes these definitions to calculate target response and resolution times. These targets are communicated to requesters, team members, management, and customer representatives, providing clarity on when to expect a response and resolution. These metrics can be customized for various request types (cases, incidents, requests for information, requests for change, and standard requests). For incidents, targets can even be set for different impact levels. Targets are calculated within specified **Support Hours**, which are calendar-based, allowing exclusion of weekends and holidays. Different support hours can be defined as needed.
- **Service Availability**: Specifies when the service is available **(Service Hours)** and the guaranteed **Availability** of the service during these hours (measured as a % on a monthly basis). Additionally, you can define **Reliability** (indicating how many times the service can become unavailable during service hours) and the expected technical **Performance** (e.g., maximum technical response time for platform access).
- **Continuity Targets**: Concerning service infrastructures, Continuity targets can be set, such as the Recovery Time Objective (RTO) and Recovery Point Objective (RPO).
- **Contractual Agreements**: Covers various contractual agreements, including performance expectations, termination conditions, penalties, reporting frequencies, limitations, and more.
- **Billing Information**: Especially crucial for Managed Service Providers, the service offering includes a section specifying how activities performed when delivering the service will be charged to the customer. This information enables the 4me platform to provide all necessary details for generating invoices to external customers or charging services provided to other internal organizations.

When is it appropriate to distinguish between service hours and support hours?	
	Service hours become relevant when a service infrastructure is provided, such as the Shop Access service in Retail or the Email service in IT. Consider the example of the Shop Access service: Facilities management teams handle requests to grant access to a shop for a new employee during regular business hours, typically from 9:00 AM to 5:00 PM. These are the support hours. However, let's suppose the shop's opening hours extend from 9:00 AM to 8:00 PM on weekdays, including Saturdays. These are the service hours and they must align with this extended calendar. This also carries operational implications: it implies that shop employees should have the means to contact Facilities Management outside of regular business hours when a serious issue with the shop access occurs. Often, a dedicated phone number is shared with the business for use during interventions outside of regular support hours.

While it is necessary to define at least one service offering for each service, it is not advisable to delve into the specifics of service offerings on a per-service basis initially. Instead, a more effective approach is to standardize service offerings and establish some standard levels of service offerings. This exercise involves assessing the services being offered and categorizing them based on their business criticality. It is a good practice to define 2 to 4 levels of business criticality.

For example, in HR, the Payroll service might be categorized as 'Critical,' necessitating faster response times, while the Retirement Planning service, which requires less stringent response times, might be categorized as 'Normal.'

For Managed Service Providers (MSPs), service offerings often depend on customer contracts. However, implementing 4me presents an opportunity to standardize in what can be a chaotic landscape. This standardization effort will require the involvement of the presales and sales teams. Generally, they will appreciate a standardized service offerings portfolio, which can enhance their efficiency.

	Standardize the service levels for different services to include 2 to 4 levels. It's recommended to define at least 2 levels to allow the 4me platform to generate more precise targets for critical requests. Use clear and easily recognizable labels for the service levels.

After completing the exercise to identify the different service levels (e.g., Gold, Silver, Normal), proceed to define the specifics of the service offerings, including response and resolution targets, and, if applicable, service hours and availability. Once these definitions are in place, it becomes relatively straightforward to create one service offering for each service level and replicate this service offering across all services.

Defining the Service Offering Record

The service offering record is the most detailed among the four record types that make up the service hierarchy in 4me. However, once the initial service offerings are established, they can be easily replicated using the 'Duplicate Service Offering' action.

After duplication, it is essential to at least update the name, the service, and the summary to reflect the specifics of the new offering. In a standardized environment, other fields may not require adjustments.

Before creating your first service offering, it's important to establish 4me calendars for Service hours and Support hours. For precise target calculations, ensure these calendars include recognized bank holidays.

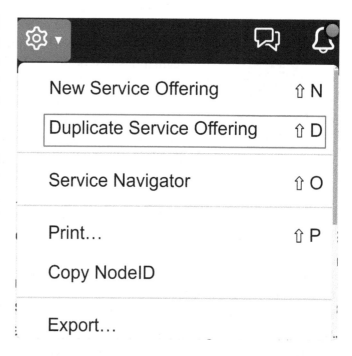

Figure 38: Duplicate a service offering.

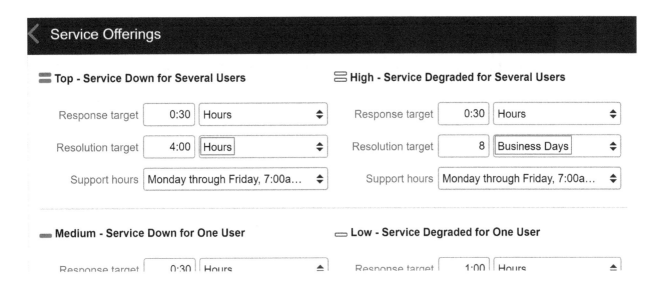

Figure 39: Defining the response and resolution targets on a service offering. For incidents these targets can be defined for each impact level. Targets can be defined in hours or business days and the target calculation will be based on the selected calendar (Support hours).

Service Level Agreements: Sealing the Service Commitment

The fourth record type, the **Service Level Agreement** (SLA), connects the service instance and service offering and links the service instances to the service hierarchy. By defining the service level agreements, the interconnected chain of service instances representing the service hierarchy is established. The service instances serve as nodes in the service hierarchy with links to support teams, assets, configuration items, and knowledge articles.

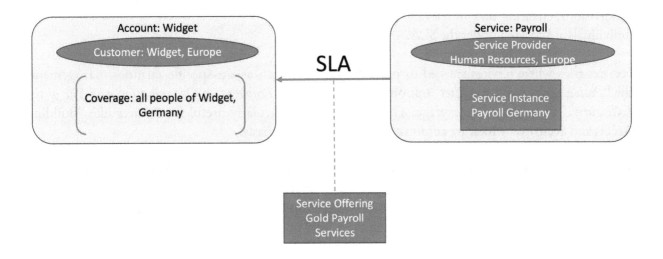

Figure 40: An SLA is linked to a service offering. It connects the service provider and the service instance (the starting point at the right side) to the customer (the end point at the left side).

In essence, an SLA is a relationship with an initiator (starting point) and a recipient (end point). The initiator is the **Service Provider**, representing the '***Who***' and the **Service Instance** defining the '***What***' is being provided.

The endpoint determines the **Customer**, which is the organization billed for the service delivered. Another key element is the **Coverage**, specifying the individuals who are provided the service instance. If a person is covered, the service instance becomes visible to them in the self-service portal. It's important to distinguish between customer and coverage. For example, while both the SLAs for the service instances *'Payroll UK'* and *'Payroll Germany'* list Widget Europe as their customer, their coverages differ: *'Payroll UK'* covers employees of Widget UK, whereas *'Payroll Germany'* is specific to Widget Germany employees.

The SLA is associated with a **Service Offering**. As mentioned earlier, the service offering outlines the commitments made by the service provider to the customer.

The SLA Coverage Options

The 4me platform offers an extensive array of coverage options for service level agreements (SLAs), catering to various organizational needs. Among these options, *"People of the Following Organizations and Descendants"* is most commonly utilized. This selection is ideal when services are intended for the entire organization or specific subdivisions, ensuring that all relevant individuals are covered under the SLA.

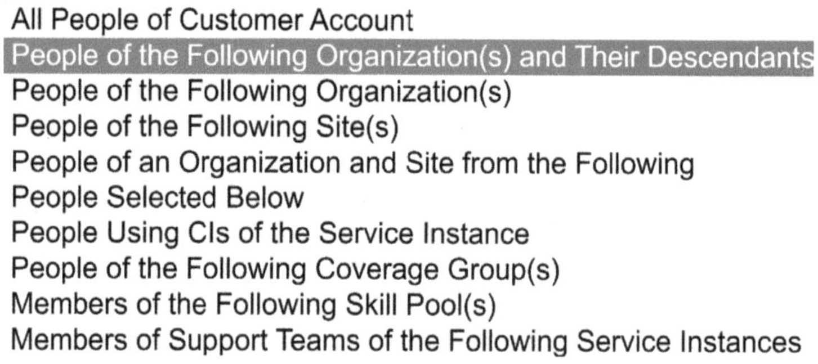

All People of Customer Account
People of the Following Organization(s) and Their Descendants
People of the Following Organization(s)
People of the Following Site(s)
People of an Organization and Site from the Following
People Selected Below
People Using CIs of the Service Instance
People of the Following Coverage Group(s)
Members of the Following Skill Pool(s)
Members of Support Teams of the Following Service Instances

Figure 41: The SLA coverage options.

For scenarios where services are tied to physical locations, such as site-specific facilities management, the *"People of the Following Sites"* option or the combined *"People of an Organization and Site of the Following..."* ensure precise coverage. This approach is particularly useful for services like "Building Access and Security," which are administered on a site-by-site basis.

Services that cater to users of specific company assets, such as smartphones or vehicles, can benefit from a more targeted approach. By cataloging each company smartphone and car as a Configuration Item (CI) and associating these CIs with their users, the *"People Using CIs of the Service Instance"* coverage option dynamically encompasses only those utilizing these assets.

Furthermore, the platform supports the creation of skill pools—groups of individuals sharing the same skill set, such as financial controllers or software architects. These pools facilitate the provision of specialized services to members through the *"Members of the Following Skill Pool(s)"* coverage option.

While the platform offers several other coverage choices, the "People of the Following Coverage Groups" option stands out for its unparalleled flexibility. Custom **SLA Coverage Groups** can be crafted within the Settings console, employing filters and, if needed, a search phrase to delineate specific groups, such as VIPs. This feature allows for a tailored coverage definition.

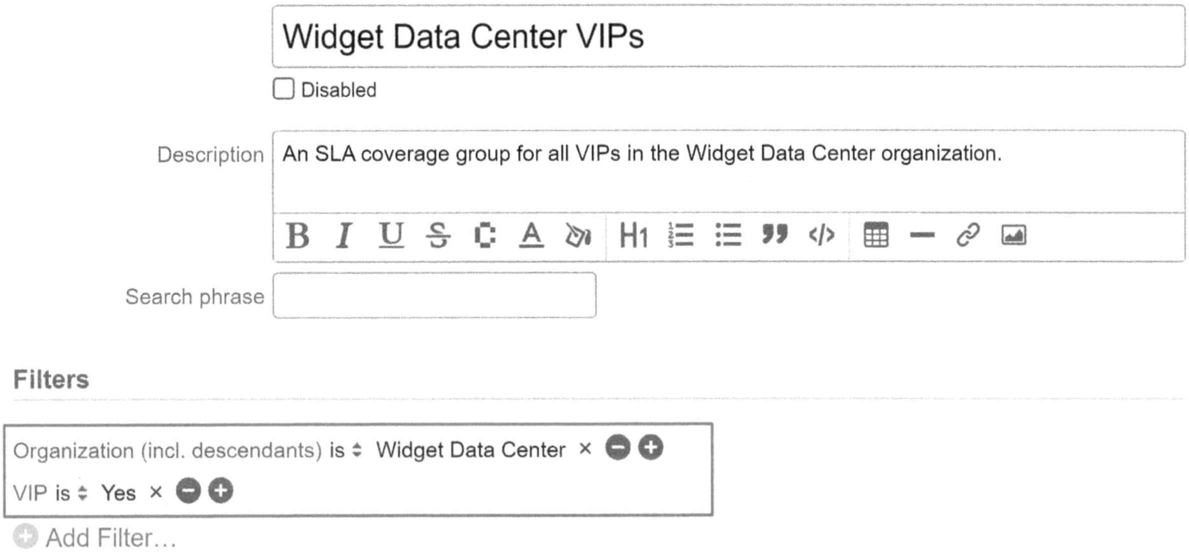

Widget Data Center VIPs

☐ Disabled

Description | An SLA coverage group for all VIPs in the Widget Data Center organization.

B *I* U̲ S̶ C A ✎ H1 ≣ ≔ 𝟗𝟗 </> ⊞ — 𝒫 🖼

Search phrase |

Filters

Organization (incl. descendants) is ⇕ Widget Data Center × ⊖ ⊕
VIP is ⇕ Yes × ⊖ ⊕
⊕ Add Filter…

Figure 42: An SLA coverage group for VIPs.

Providing a Supporting Service - Defining a Child Service Instance

We observed that defining both a first-line team and a support team on a service instance allows for easy escalation of requests from the first-line team to the support team. In complex environments, it is often necessary to involve additional teams to resolve an issue, particularly when the issue is related to a supporting service. For example, in the case of the Network Connectivity service, an issue with the WAN Connection service instance exemplifies this scenario. Initially, a network connectivity issue may be reported by an end-user on the LAN or Wi-Fi service instances. However, once it becomes evident that the network connectivity problem stems from an issue with the WAN connection (the network connection between the local network and the organization's network backbone), the ticket should be linked to the WAN Connection service instance. Subsequently, the 4me platform will automatically assign the ticket to the Network team for resolution.

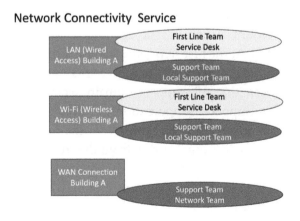

Figure 43: The network connectivity service.

In this scenario, an SLA needs to be created with the '*WAN Connection*' service instance as the starting point. The WAN Connection will become a **child service instance**. The LAN and Wi-Fi service instances will become the endpoints of the SLA. They are the **parent service instances**. This configuration can be defined with the coverage option '*Members of the support teams of the following service instances*' and by selecting the LAN and Wi-Fi service instances as the (parent) service instances.

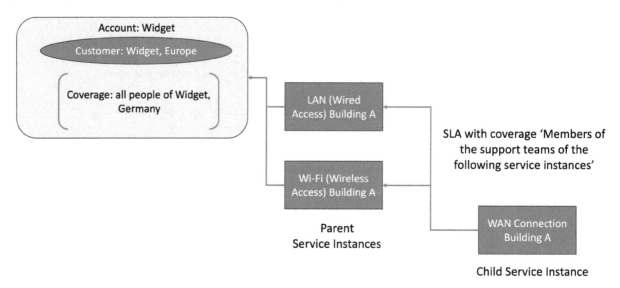

Figure 44: The service hierarchy of network connectivity. The SLA for the service instance 'WAN Connection Building A' has the coverage set to "Members of the support teams of the following service instances". The selected service instances are 'LAN (Wired Access) Building A' and 'Wi-fi (Wireless Access) Building A'. These are the parent service instances.

Providing a Supporting Service to Another 4me Account

The unique account structure of 4me facilitates collaboration across different service delivery organizations. Consider the earlier example of the Payroll service, where the configuration of the Payroll Application is managed by an external supplier.

In the account structure, the supplier has its own account structure. For defining a cross-account SLA, the first step is to establish a trust relationship between the two accounts, such as between the HR support domain account and the Supplier support domain account. Subsequently, the supplier can create the SLA and designate the organization from the trusted account as the customer. Next, the service level manager in the customer account should define the coverage of the SLA.

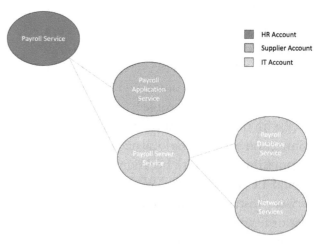

Figure 45: The cross-account payroll service hierarchy.

Defining the SLA Record

To define or modify a Service Level Agreement (SLA), the service level manager role is required. Initially, an SLA record is created in the account of the service provider. It requires a name, a customer, a service level manager, a service offering, a service instance, and a start date. Optionally, you can also define a notice date and an expiry date, and the service level manager will receive notifications as these dates approach.

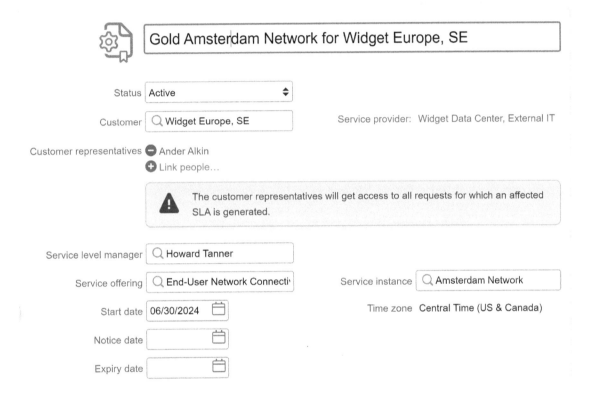

Figure 46: Defining an SLA. A name, a customer, a service level manager, a service offering, a service instance, and a start date are required.

Implement a Clear Naming Convention for SLAs	
	To enhance clarity and facilitate easier SLA reporting, adopt a consistent naming convention. A recommended format includes the service offering level, the service instance name, and the customer. For example: *Gold Payroll Services for Widget Europe*

The process for defining an SLA differs when setting up *cross-account SLAs*, where a service provider offers a service instance to another service delivery organization (account). For cross-account SLAs, the endpoint of the SLA is defined in the target account, and customer representatives and coverage must be defined by someone with the service level manager role in the customer account.

The definition of the Customer organization on the SLA record determines whether an SLA is cross-account:

- If the Customer is an organization within the same account structure and not linked to a support domain account, it is not a cross-account SLA. In this scenario, a service level manager in the service provider account is responsible for defining the customer representatives and coverage.
- If the Customer belongs to a trusted account from a different account structure, it qualifies as a cross-account SLA. Here, a service level manager in the trusted account must set the customer representatives and coverage. Additionally, the service level manager in the customer account can modify the customer organization to any organization within their account.

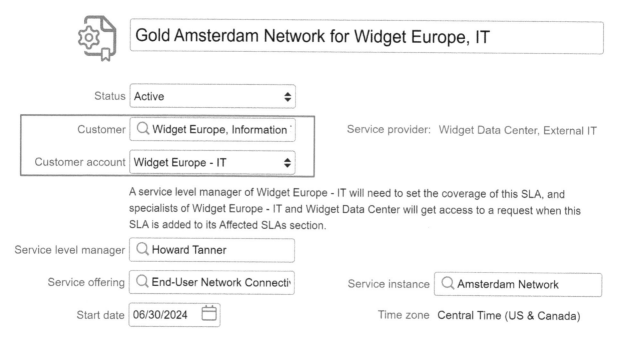

Figure 47: When the customer organization is linked to another support domain account in the same account structure a new field becomes available: the 'Customer account'. By setting the Customer account to the account of the customer, the SLA turns into a cross-account SLA. The service level manager in the customer account will need to define the coverage of the SLA.

- When the Customer is an organization within the same account structure and linked to a support domain account, things are more complex. An extra field will appear on the SLA record: the **Customer account** field.
  - If the account linked to the customer organization is not involved in the service delivery and the customer organization only acts as the paying entity, the Customer account field should be set to the service provider account. A service level manager in the service provider account will then define the customer representatives and coverage.
  - If the account linked to the customer organization is involved in the service delivery, the Customer account field should be set to the customer account. A service level manager in the customer account is then required to define the customer representatives and coverage. The service level manager in the customer account can define the service instance of the SLA as a child service instance of its own service instances.

Service Integration and Management (SIAM)

4me's architecture is exceptionally well-suited for supporting Service Integration and Management (SIAM). This management approach is tailored for organizations that utilize multiple service providers. Below, we explore how the service hierarchy within 4me facilitates the integration of services from various providers through a customer account.

Outsourcing Business Services Through Cross-Account SLAs

Cross-account SLAs enable service delivery organizations to outsource business services seamlessly to other accounts. This process is completely transparent to end users.

For instance, in the demo environment, the Email service is provided by Widget Data Center to Widget Europe, IT, another support domain account within the Widget account structure. In Widget Europe, IT, coverage is set for all users from Widget Europe, SE, and its descendant organizations.

To end users, it appears as though the email service is internally provided by Widget Europe, IT. However, the 4me platform automatically routes tickets related to the email service to the support team at Widget Data Center. While specialists in Widget Europe, IT are not directly involved in handling these tickets, the setup grants them full visibility.

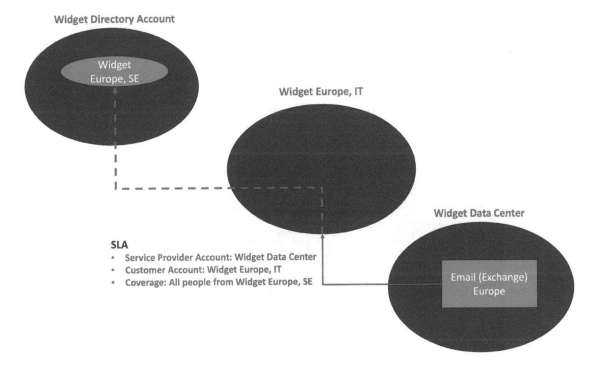

Figure 48: Widget Europe, IT has outsourced the Email service to Widget Data Center.

Defining and Managing Suppliers

4me offers three approaches for defining and managing services provided by external suppliers:

1. **Direct Integration with a 4me Customer**: If the external supplier is also a 4me customer, the setup is straightforward. A trust relationship must be established between the customer account and the supplier account. The supplier defines the SLA, and in the customer account, coverage is set. Coverage can be directed to end-users for business services or can define the supplier service as a child service of a business service.

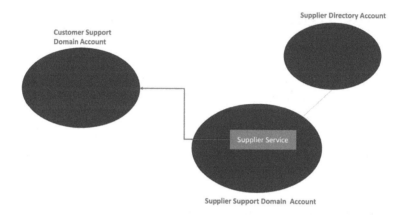

Figure 49: Integration with a supplier working in 4me.

2. **Integration with the service management system of the supplier**. A 4me account structure should be created for the supplier, with the supplier's service catalog defined within this account.
   a. **Simple Email Integration**: Suitable for non-business-critical, low-volume integrations involving non-sensitive data.
   b. **API-Based Integration**: For business-critical, high-volume integrations or when ticket data is sensitive, a full integration between the 4me platform and the supplier's service management system is recommended. This can be achieved via 4me's Open API or through standard integrations offered by 4me's technology partners.

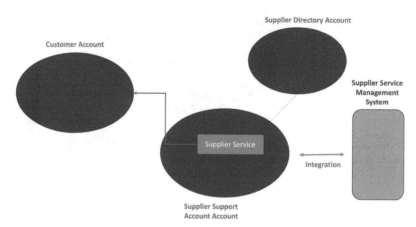

Figure 50: Integration with the service management system of the supplier.

3. **Managing Non-Integrated Suppliers**: For suppliers who are neither integrated within 4me nor provide integration capabilities, the customer's IT support team must manually manage interactions. Such suppliers should be defined as external organizations within the customer's 4me account. Subsequently, services provided by these suppliers can be specified, designating the supplier organization as the service provider. The support team responsible for these supplier service instances should be the team that will manually handle the supplier ticket registration. Finally, the service offering and the corresponding SLA with the supplier are established.

In this configuration, when a ticket requiring supplier intervention is assigned to the internal support team, a special field, called the supplier request ID, is made available in the 4me ticket to track the supplier's ticket reference.

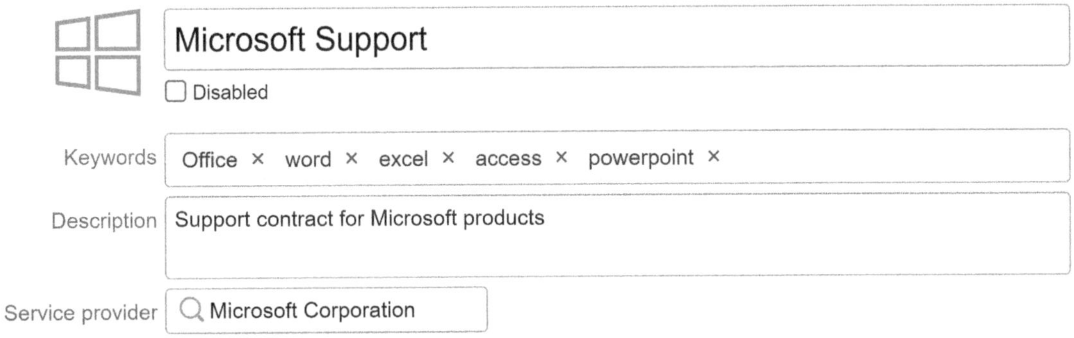

Figure 51: Defining a service for a supplier who is neither integrated within 4me nor provides integration capabilities. The supplier should be defined as an (external) organization in the 4me account of the customer. Next the service provided by the supplier can be specified, designating the supplier organization as the service provider.

The Provider Reports: The SIAM Control Center

Once all supplier services and SLAs are defined and incorporated into the customer's operating model through the service hierarchy, the customer gains comprehensive visibility into supplier activities and performance. Regardless of the operational setup—whether suppliers operate within their own 4me accounts, use their own service management systems with an integration to 4me, or simply have their services and SLAs outlined in 4me with manual ticket handling by the customer's support team—all KPIs defined in the service offerings are tracked and measured.

Visibility into all supplier activities is consolidated within the **Provider Reports** section of the **Analytics console**. These provider reports offer customers complete insights into the performance and activities of all their suppliers.

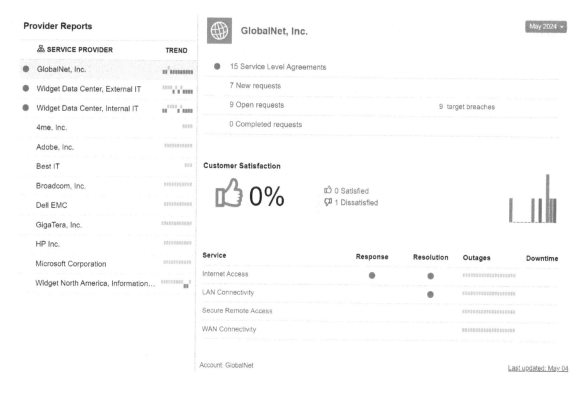

Figure 52: All the suppliers are added to the Provider Reports in the Analytics console.

Demo

The Service Catalog and Service Hierarchy
The service hierarchy of the Personal Computing Service

Let's embark on an exciting journey through the demo environment to witness the 4me platform in action, starring Randy, an accountant at Widget Europe's Finance Department, who's on the verge of a caffeine overload due to his sluggish PC.

Picture Randy, coffee cup in hand, glaring at his PC that's still booting up after what feels like an eternity. Frustrated, he decides it's time for action. In this demo, we'll follow Randy as he navigates the self-service portal to get some much-needed IT intervention.

First stop: Randy logs in as randy.barton@widget.com at Widget International.

He clicks on 'New Request' - because it's time to get some work done between coffees.

Browsing through the list, Randy selects 'Information Technology' under support domain accounts, aiming straight for 'Personal Computing'.

Choosing 'None of the Above', he fills in the details about his snail-paced login times and submits his plea for help.

Voilà! Without Randy selecting specifically, his ticket finds its home with the '*Personal Computing for Finance*' service instance, thanks to the smart SLA covering him.

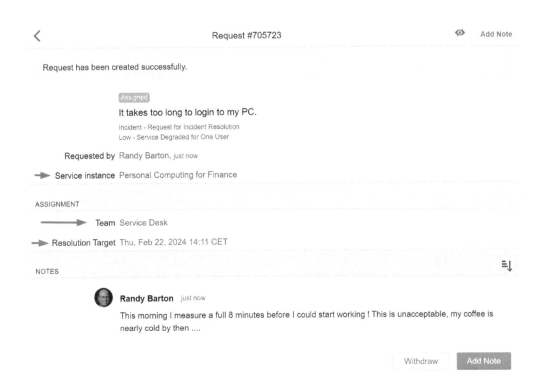

Figure 53: The ticket registered on the self-service portal. Note how 4me detects the correct service instance and assigns to the correct team with the right resolution target.

Enter Joseph Baker, a member of the service desk team at Widget Europe, IT, who suspects a mischievous Group Policy Object (GPO) behind Randy's issues. He knows that GPOs are part of the directory services. Joseph's steps:

Joseph logs in as **joseph.baker@widget.com** at **Widget Europe -IT**.
After logging in, he finds Randy's ticket awaiting attention in his inbox.

Using 4me magic, Joseph edits the ticket, causing the **Service Hierarchy Browser** to appear, revealing all the supporting services as **child service instances** under Personal Computing.
With a flick (or a drag and drop) of Directory Services onto Randy's ticket.
He adds an internal note about his suspicions regarding the GPO and passes the baton, all set for the next step.

Figure 54: Check the Service Hierarchy Browser on the right side: it displays all the supporting services as child service instances. And so much more, all within the service-driven context provided by 4me.

Ellen logs in as **ellen.brown@widget.com** at **Widget Data Center**.
After logging in, she finds Randy's ticket in her inbox.

What you've just witnessed is the 4me platform, flexing its service-driven muscles, effortlessly navigating through organizational silos and geographical boundaries to bring Randy's coffee and PC woes to the attention of the right IT heroes. This, folks, is the Widget IT operating model in full swing, powered by 4me.

The First Line Support Agreement of an Account

For every support domain account, defining a **First Line Support Agreement (FLSA)** is essential. A First-Line Support Agreement outlines the primary support framework for the account: The FLSA defines a "fallback" team for the 4me platform when the service catalog and service hierarchy do not specify a team assignment for a ticket. This scenario typically arises when an account receives a simple, unstructured email: the 4me platform cannot determine which service should be linked to the ticket generated from the inbound email. In such instances, the FLSA provides a necessary resolution mechanism.

The designated first line of an account, commonly the **Service Desk team**, does not necessarily need to be a part of the account itself. When a trust relationship exists between two accounts, one can establish a First-Line Support Agreement with the trusted account. The cross-account FLSA designates a specific team to function as the outsourced service desk. For example, in the demo environment, the VirtualSupport account performs the service desk role for both Widget Data Center and Widget North-America IT.

In the framework of service desk outsourcing contracts, it is common to define service desk KPIs (Key Performance Indicators). These KPIs should be incorporated into the First-Line Support Agreement. Once these targets have been defined both the customer and the provider of the service desk services can monitor these KPIs through the out-of-the-box FLSA reports that can be found in the Analytics console.

Figure 55: A first-line support agreement from VirtualSupport to Widget Data Center. It includes typical service desk KPIs like pickup targets and first call resolutions.

FLSA0001029 First line support agreement for Widget Data Center

June 2024 ▾

KPI	Target	Actual	Past 12 Months
Pickups within target ⓘ	>= 85%	100.00%	
First call resolutions ⓘ	>= 40%	100.00%	
Service desk only resolutions ⓘ	>= 50%	100.00%	
Service desk resolutions ⓘ	>= 60%	100.00%	
Rejected solutions ⓘ	< 10%	0.00%	

Service Desk Customer Satisfaction

👍 0 Satisfied
👎 0 Dissatisfied

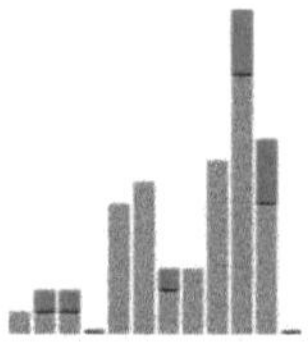

Service Desk Activity ⓘ	Count
Registration of new requests completed on first call	0
Registration of new requests not completed on first call	0
Updates of existing requests	0
Completion of existing requests	0
Totals	**0**

Figure 56: The FLSA reports measuring the service desk performance.

PART II

The Core of 4me

A Foundation for Service Excellence

Introduction

In the previous chapters, we've witnessed how 4me empowers organizations to define their operating models around services. By establishing the account structure and service hierarchy, the foundation is set. Once your organization's service-driven operating model is framed within the 4me platform, you're ready to take off.

This strategy offers significant advantages. It ensures a quick implementation process while maintaining a top-tier, mature, and service-centric approach. Moreover, it promotes agility. If your organization needs to adjust its operating model, rest assured you're not locked in; adapting within 4me is seamless.

This flexibility stems from the standardization of core functionalities. For example, predefined status values for all ticket types are in place. This not only saves you from designing these essential features but also enables you to start operating as soon as the platform is configured. Additionally, it fosters collaboration among various internal and external entities, all seamlessly working on the same tickets.

In this part, we delve into the heart of 4me's functionality and core processes. It's important to note that beyond this core and standard functionality, 4me offers customization for procedures, workflows, and data records to suit your organization's unique needs. This adaptability will be explored in Part III. Also, please be aware that neither this chapter nor this book serves as a user manual. For detailed instructions, refer to the free online training provided by 4me. In this part, we will explore core functionality from the perspective of the service management architect, the designer, and the administrator of a 4me configuration.

Chapter 5 - Foundational 4me Records

People, Organizations and Sites

Enterprise Service Management revolves around people. These individuals are part of organizations and often work at specific locations within company sites. This trio of elements—people, organizations, and sites—is foundational to any enterprise service management system and extends its importance beyond. As we explored at the beginning of this book, an organization's operating model encapsulates all this information, shaping the design of the 4me account structure. Moreover, this information is intricately woven into the service-driven ethos of the 4me platform. It influences which services a user sees on the self-service portal, dictates procedures by dynamically sending approvals to an individual's managers, determines the delivery locations for goods ordered via the 4me shop, and decides which organization pays for the time spent on services, among other things.

Note that a directory account is not designed for direct service delivery activities; it doesn't host a service catalog or manage tickets. Its primary purpose is to centralize and manage foundational elements such as people, organizations, and sites. The diagram below provides an overview of the internal organizations, sites, and person records within the Widget directory account and illustrates how these elements are interconnected.

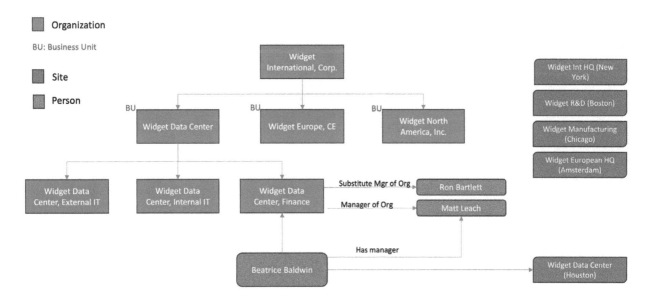

Figure 57: People, organizations, and sites in the Widget company.

Internal, External and Trusted Organizations

Every 4me account is inherently linked to a specific organization record. For directory accounts this linkage is to the primary internal organization, which acts as the central node or root from which all other **internal**

organizations branch out. This primary internal organization represents the core entity or the main corporate structure for which the entire 4me account structure is configured. It forms the basis for categorizing all affiliated departments, divisions, or related entities under its umbrella as internal organizations. Some of these internal organizations represent service delivery organizations and are linked to a support domain account.

Conversely, any organization not directly descending from the primary organization of the directory account is categorized as an **external organization**. This differentiation is critical for enforcing data protection protocols within 4me, ensuring that individuals associated with external organizations have limited access to sensitive information, in alignment with privacy and security standards.

Moreover, within the context of a support domain account, there emerges a third categorization: **trusted organizations**. Unlike internal or external organizations, trusted organizations are those external entities with which there exists a formal trust relationship *and* a service level agreement (SLA). Trusted organizations could be customers or service providers engaged through SLAs.

Please note, the role of *account administrator*, *service level manager* or *configuration manager* is necessary to add or modify an organization record.

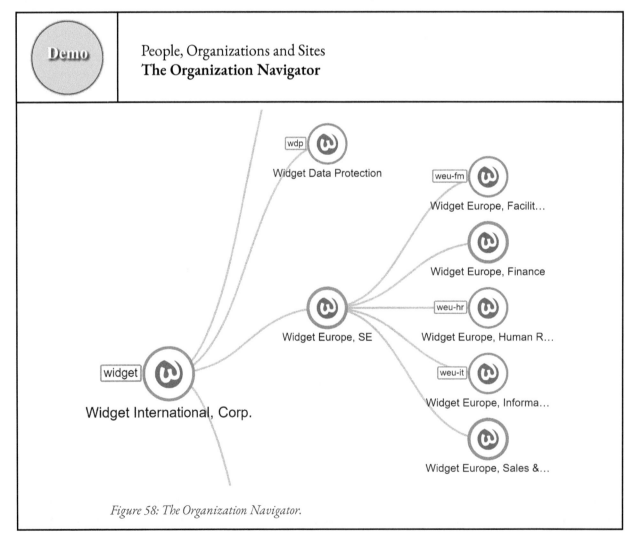

Figure 58: The Organization Navigator.

4me has a cool feature to visualize the organizational structure: the Organization Navigator that can be found in the Analytics console.

- Log in as howard.tanner@widget.com to Widget International.

  - Go to the Analytics Console.
  - Select the Organization Navigator

Can you see which of these organizations are linked to a 4me account?
- Next, go to the record console and check all the Organizations defined in the directory account. Which organizations are not displayed in the Organization Navigator?

The Business Unit and Region Fields for Internal Organizations

Internal organizational structures can be quite intricate, often comprising multiple levels. In 4me, it's not only possible but advisable to outline a company's comprehensive organizational layout. The more precise the organization's information, the more tailored and efficient the support can be. However, this level of detail can pose challenges for management reporting. To facilitate higher-level consolidation of reports, internal organizations can be designated as a **Business Unit**. This classification enables the aggregation of information from all descendant entities up to the business unit level for reporting purposes.

Similarly, the **Region** field serves a parallel function. It facilitates the consolidation of reporting across a specified group of organizations, allowing for regional analysis and insights.

The Region Field and Financial ID for Trusted Organizations

Trusted organizations typically represent external service providers or customer organizations. The records for these organizations are not created within your account but within the accounts that you have established a trust with. However, your account can still contain specific information about these trusted organizations. For example, an account administrator has the capability to assign a trusted organization to a region. This feature is particularly beneficial for managing external customer organizations. It allows a Managed Service Provider (MSP) to generate consolidated reports by region, offering insights into customer distribution and service coverage across different areas.

Equally significant is the Financial ID field for trusted organizations. This ID serves as the unique identifier for the external customer organization within the MSP's financial systems. It is an essential piece of information for integrating service management activities with billing procedures.

The Contact Info for Organizations

Within the 4me platform, an *account administrator* has the ability to enrich organization records with comprehensive contact details. This information can include telephone numbers, email addresses, and physical addresses. Importantly, this contact information is also accessible in the records of trusted organizations.

In scenarios where swift action is crucial, such as emergency situations or incidents concerning cybersecurity, having direct access to the appropriate contact information is invaluable. Regulations like NIS2 or CMMC further underscore the importance of this, mandating service management organizations to have their emergency contact details readily available. In 4me, this can be achieved with the **'Emergency'** contact type for telephone numbers and email addresses of organizations.

4me Sites and Locations

A site within 4me serves as a geographical marker, offering precise answers to questions regarding the location of specific entities such as personnel and configuration items. This geographical linkage not only identifies a user's workplace but also pinpoints the location of assets.

The level of detail or granularity for defining a site in 4me can vary, tailored to the specific needs of each setup. This flexibility is crucial, given the diverse ways sites are utilized within the platform. Here are a few examples of how sites might be leveraged:

- **SLA Coverage Definitions**: Ensuring service coverage accurately corresponds to where individuals are based.
- **Configuration and Asset Management**: Identifying precise storage or installation locations for assets, ranging from stock rooms to computer rooms.
- **4me Shop Deliveries**: Determining the delivery addresses for ordered items.
- **Custom Procedures**: Allowing for the automation of actions based on site-specific processes.

 Widget Manufacturing Center

Street address **5225 South Harper Avenue**
Chicago, IL 60615
United States ⊙ ⟵———

Time zone **Central Time (US & Canada)**

Figure 59: A 4me site record. Note the 'Show on map' marker that will open Google Maps.

Creating a site record in 4me is straightforward, focusing on providing an address and selecting a time zone. Due to the relative permanence of sites, adding or removing them is an action reserved for users with the Account Administrator role. This ensures stability in the organizational structure.

Locations, on the other hand, offer a more granular and dynamic approach. Configuration managers have the flexibility to specify locations on the fly when associating an asset with a site. This could be as specific as indicating the exact room where an asset is located. Newly created locations are automatically linked to their respective site. When a site is specified for a person or asset, existing locations within that site are suggested.

Figure 60: A 4me location is dynamically linked to the selected site.

People

People and Organizations

In 4me, the concept of people is tightly intertwined with organizations. Every individual, represented within 4me by a person record, must be associated with exactly one organization. This stringent requirement is not arbitrary but a necessary measure for both security and data protection. By knowing the organizational affiliation of each user, 4me can apply the appropriate data protection rules, distinguishing between internal and external organizational membership.

4me Specialists and End Users

In 4me, every individual with access to the platform is initially considered an **end user**. This broad categorization includes anyone who logs into a 4me account where they are recognized, thereby gaining access to the **self-service portal** associated with that account. Typically, an end user utilizes the self-service portal for informational purposes or to submit requests. It's important to note that, within the 4me ecosystem, end users do not require a dedicated license to access the self-service portal, which means their access does not incur any service credit costs.

However, when an individual's role within their organization involves the processing and management of tickets, they are designated as a **specialist**. Upon logging into a 4me account where they hold this designation, specialists are directed to a different interface, called the **Specialist Interface**. Beyond the basic specialist designation, individuals can be granted additional roles based on their specific duties within the service delivery process. These roles range from '*Service Desk Analyst*' and '*Service Desk Manager*' to '*Workflow Manager*,' among others. Each role confers distinct permissions and capabilities within the 4me platform.

Note that beyond the specialist role, there are distinct roles including *Account Owners, Account Administrators, Auditors, Account Designers* and *Financial Managers*, all of which are licensed users.

4me Roles: Simplifying Security

Embracing simplicity and security, the 4me platform adheres to a clear philosophy. Unlike some service management platforms that rely on Access Control Lists (ACLs) to create custom roles, 4me has chosen a different path. Access Control Lists (ACLs) offer flexibility but at the cost of added complexity and heightened risk of data breaches. 4me believes that the complex challenge of maintaining and monitoring role access is a responsibility best left to the platform's developers.

To this end, 4me has implemented a straightforward and sturdy security model. It utilizes a limited number of predefined roles, with access permissions for these roles explicitly defined and integrated into the platform. This approach ensures a balance between flexibility and simplicity, leveraging the design of 4me accounts and privacy settings to accommodate diverse needs without compromising on security.

Access within these roles is rigorously monitored. Each weekly release is accompanied by an extensive suite of automated testing scripts designed to verify that new functionalities have not violated any security protocols, maintaining the integrity of the platform's role-based access control.

The list below provides highlights of the various roles within 4me, not an exhaustive description of each role's access rights. Detailed access rights will be explored throughout this book as we discuss different features and records.

- **Account Owner**: Each 4me account has a single Account Owner. In order for someone to become the owner of an account, this person must already have the Account Administrator role. Once someone has been designated as the owner of an account, this person will get the exclusive rights to alter fundamental account settings and to access and modify security-related configurations.
- **Account Administrator**: An Account Administrator plays a pivotal role in the day-to-day maintenance and operational integrity of a 4me account. While multiple individuals can be appointed as Account Administrators, a best practice is to appoint at least one in addition to the Account Owner, limiting the total number to two or three. Responsibilities include assigning roles within the account, managing trust relationships with other 4me accounts, and overseeing the creation and modification of key account records such as Organizations, Teams, People, Sites, Calendars and Holidays. Furthermore, Account Administrators have the authority to enable integrations, access and review all non-financial information, audit trails and logs, create and share analytics dashboards. Importantly, in accounts where privacy settings are configured for heightened data protection, Account Administrators retain visibility across all records.
- **Account Designer**: The Account Designer role is specifically tailored for configuring and customizing of the 4me environment. Key responsibilities include adjusting the account and self-service portal aesthetics, customizing PDF and email designs, and configuring request and workflow templates as well as automation rules. It's important to note that, despite their extensive configuration capabilities, Account Designers do *not* have visibility into tickets.
- **Auditor**: The Auditor role is designed to grant comprehensive oversight without the ability to alter data. Individuals with this role have the capability to view all record fields across the account, including detailed audit trails. However, to maintain data integrity and security,

Auditors are expressly restricted from adding, modifying, or deleting any records. This role is crucial for conducting thorough reviews and ensuring compliance with internal policies and external regulations.

- **Financial Manager**: Specializing in the management of sensitive financial data, the Financial Manager plays a pivotal role in overseeing financial aspects such as invoices and contracts. This role is uniquely authorized to access and manipulate financial fields across various records. The safeguarding of financial details, including the 'Cost per hour' on person records, is exclusive to Financial Managers.
- **Specialist**: A Specialist is the backbone of service delivery, engaging directly in ticket resolution across one or more teams. In environments without strong privacy settings, Specialists have visibility into all tickets. They are also empowered to contribute knowledge articles and log risks, when the risk management features are active. The Specialist role serves as a foundation for the following, specialized roles within 4me.
    - **Service Desk Analyst**: While all specialists have access to the service desk console, only Service Desk Analysts can select all users within their account and its related directory account. A service desk analyst can add new person records, facilitating immediate support for new users.
    - **Service Desk Manager**: Building on the Analyst role, the Service Desk Manager has additional authorities, such as deleting notes within a 14-day window, initiating broadcasts, and revising request templates. This role is also responsible for managing user feedback and ensuring support quality.
    - **Problem Manager**: Dedicated to the identification of root causes of reported or anticipated incidents and the proposal of permanent fixes, a Problem Manager is integral to continuously improving service stability. Aligned with 4me's service-driven approach, it is possible to define a problem manager for each service.
    - **Workflow Manager**: Tasked with the creation and management of workflows, a Workflow Manager ensures the efficient progression of tasks according to the predefined process flows. Aligned with 4me's service-driven approach, it is recommended to assign a Workflow Manager to each service. This role, particularly in the context of ITIL and service management principles, is called the **Change Manager** of the service, signifying a dedicated point of responsibility for overseeing all changes throughout the service's lifecycle.
    - **Release Manager**: Responsible for planning, scheduling, controlling, and implementing releases, this role ensures that all aspects of a release are conducted smoothly and efficiently. In line with 4me's service-driven framework, it is beneficial to assign a Release Manager to each IT service.
    - **Project Manager**: Responsible for overseeing projects from initiation to completion, Project Managers ensure that objectives are met, stakeholders are engaged, and resources are efficiently utilized.
    - **Service Level Manager**: This role is pivotal in shaping the service catalog and structuring the service hierarchy within 4me. It involves the detailed tasks of creating, modifying, and overseeing services, service instances, service offerings, and service level agreements (SLAs). Additionally, the Service Level Manager is entrusted with the creation and modification of first line support agreements for the account.
    - **Configuration Manager**: Charged with managing the configuration and asset landscape, Configuration Managers ensure that assets are accurately tracked, utilized, and maintained.

Elevated End User Roles: Key Contacts and Customer Representatives

End users primarily interact with the platform through the self-service portal to submit and track their requests. End users can also handle approval tasks assigned to them by workflow managers and project managers. However, certain end users require broader visibility into requests beyond their own. This is where the roles of **Customer Representative** and **Key Contact** come into play, both of which enhance an end user's capabilities without necessitating a billable license.

Customer Representatives are defined on SLAs as liaisons between the service provider and the customer organization. To effectively fulfill their role, they need insight into all requests from people who are covered by the SLAs they oversee, alongside dashboards to track the performance of the providers of these SLAs.

The *Key Contact* role represents another elevated End-User role, granting visibility into all requests registered for individuals within their organization or its subsidiaries. Same as for customer representatives, this access is facilitated through the "All Requests" and "Dashboards" options in the self-service portal. Typically, MSPs designate key contacts within their client organizations to manage and follow up on requests on behalf of their colleagues.

It's important to note that the key contact role is irrelevant within directory accounts, as these accounts do not handle requests directly. Instead, key contacts are assigned within support domain accounts. An end user can be a key contact for his organization for the requests in one support domain account and be an end user without this elevated access in another support domain account.

Elevated End Users: Key Contacts and Customer Representatives
Dashboard Sharing with a Key Contact

Time for a little exploration in the world of Widget accounts with David Whitney, our finance expert at Widget Europe. Not only does he crunch numbers like a pro, but he's also the key contact for the European Finance department in both the IT and Facilities Management support domain accounts. Picture this: David's about to receive a shiny new toy—a KPI dashboard for all requests registered by someone from the finance department. The account owner of the directory account will define this dashboard.

- Log in as account.owner@widget.com to Widget International.
    - Navigate to the Analytics Console.
    - Edit the dashboard Request Management KPIs.
    - Click on "Shared with key contacts."
    - Select the organization Widget Europe, Finance.
    - Access the people records.
    - Select David's person record and ensure he has the key contact role in the IT and FM accounts.
- Log in as david.whitney@widget.com to Widget International.
    - Choose Dashboards from the menu.
    - Check the Request Management KPIs dashboard.

Figure 61: David Whitney, a key contact, gets access to a shared dashboard on the self-service portal.

User Provisioning

While it's crucial for 4me to maintain up-to-date information about the company's personnel, organizations, and site details, managing this data directly within 4me might not be ideal. Typically, such information is best maintained outside of 4me, ensuring that the platform isn't the primary source of truth.

In most enterprise settings, this critical information resides within the **Identity Provider (IdP)** service. The IdP, integral for facilitating single sign-on (SSO) across various business applications including 4me, should ideally handle the real-time provisioning of user details, along with their associated organizational and site information, directly into 4me.

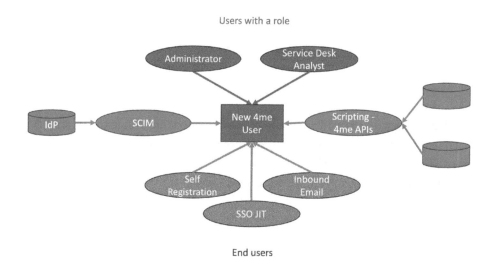

Figure 62: User provisioning - multiple options.

Beyond IdP integration, user provisioning can also occur through manual entry by *account administrators* or *service desk analysts*, end-user actions like *self-registration*, inbound email or Single Sign-On Just-In-Time provisioning (SSO JIT), or custom scripts leveraging 4me's open APIs.

Exploring Person Record Fields

Understanding the fields within a person record is crucial, regardless of the provisioning method – whether it's through 4me's APIs, custom scripts, or SCIM (System for Cross-domain Identity Management - the standard for user provisioning to cloud applications).

- **Primary Email Address**: Within a directory account structure, the primary email uniquely identifies a person.
- **Authentication ID**: Identity Providers (IdPs), such as Active Directory, Google, Octa, and OneLogin, provide unique identifiers for Single Sign-On (SSO) authentication. These should be

stored in the Authentication ID field. The Authentication ID must be a unique value within a directory account structure.

- **Support ID**: A number or code that service desk analysts can request for identification during support calls. This might be a security badge number, IT login ID, or customer number. The support ID can be used in the service desk console to quickly find a person. MSPs often validate a caller by asking for their organization's customer number.
- **Employee ID**: Assigned by HR, this unique identifier can be used to quickly locate a user within the service desk console or as a unique identifier for integration with the HR system.

Personal and Contact Information

Providing additional details like job title, VIP status, and the user's site and location can enhance the support experience. Users may also have secondary email addresses, phone numbers, and messaging IDs (e.g. for Microsoft Teams, Slack or WhatsApp) linked to their profiles.

Personal Preferences

To accommodate global users across different time zones and languages, 4me allows users to set their time zone, preferred time format, and language. These can be adjusted by the users themselves through the *Personal Preferences* menu.

Manager Assignment

Automated manager approval assignments in request fulfillment frequently make use of the link between users and their managers within 4me. It's important to note that a manager can be linked to individual person records, and a manager and a substitute manager can be designated at the organizational level. For approvals you have the option to use either the direct manager specified in the user's person record or the manager and their substitute defined at the organizational level. When time tracking is enabled, managers at the organizational level are granted access to view the time entries submitted by individuals within their organization.

Resource and Cost Management

Work hours and cost per hour are crucial for resource scheduling and cost management. Work hours determine a person's availability for ticket assignments and resource planning, while the cost per hour is vital for tracking and managing service costs. Access to cost information is restricted to users with the *financial manager* role.

Manual User Provisioning

Account administrators and *service desk analysts* are empowered to manually create and update person records within 4me. Often, organizations employ a hybrid approach to onboarding new users: automated processes are utilized for initial user record creation, while manual intervention is applied for assigning specific roles, and if necessary, associating the user with the appropriate organization.

 **Tip**

When a service desk analyst initiates the creation of a new user, that person's record is generated within the 4me support domain account where the analyst operates. However, the ideal scenario is for these user records to reside within the directory account. 4me elegantly addresses this: if a person record with an identical primary email address is subsequently created in the directory account, either through automated provisioning or manual input by an administrator, and a matching record is found in a support domain account, 4me automatically migrates this record to the directory account.

Enabling Self-Registration for Streamlined User Onboarding

In certain scenarios, allowing users to register themselves is not only the best approach but sometimes the only viable one. This method proves particularly beneficial for Managed Service Providers (MSPs) operating a customer portal, where the key contacts within an external organization might change without prior notice to the MSP. It's also invaluable for retailers and government agencies aiming to offer consumers and citizens an easy way to register and track their requests. Through self-registration, the burden of creating individual person records for each end user is eliminated.

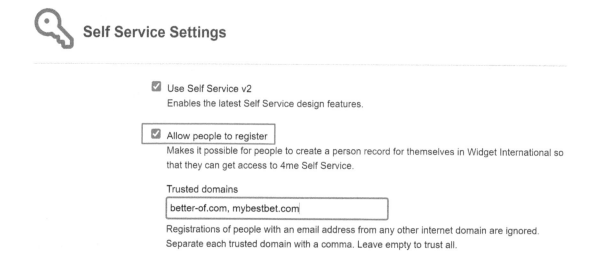

Figure 63: Allow people to register in the Self-Service Settings.

Activating self-registration is straightforward: simply enable the '**Allow people to register**' option within the Self-Service Settings of your 4me account. To maintain control over who can self-register, you can restrict this ability to specific internet domains by entering them into the **Trusted Domain** field. This ensures that only email addresses from approved domains can create user accounts.

A crucial aspect of self-registration is the automatic linkage of new users to an organization. By default, self-registered users are associated with the **Default organization** specified in the Account Settings. For security purposes, this default organization should be external, with end-user privacy settings activated, ensuring that new users cannot view or interact with internal or other external users. For MSPs, an additional step may be required to associate these new users with the appropriate customer organization.

Upon enabling the self-registration feature, a 'Register as New User' button will appear on the account's login screen.

Guest or Anonymous Login - Whistleblowing Accounts

In response to the EU Whistleblower Directive enacted at the end of 2021, organizations are now required to establish internal reporting mechanisms that allow for anonymous submissions. These channels must safeguard the whistleblower's identity, restrict access to unauthorized personnel, and ensure a thorough review of reports by a designated individual or department.

4me offers the necessary features to serve as a comprehensive whistleblowing platform, enabling individuals to report misconduct or ethical violations anonymously. This capability allows guests to self-register as anonymous users and submit requests without revealing their identity. Upon selecting the '**Continue as a Guest**' option on the login page, guests are directed to the self-service portal, where they can anonymously file a request.

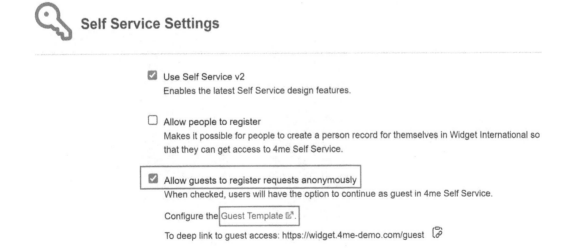

Figure 64: Self-Service Settings for enabling anonymous (guest) login.

To activate anonymous guest reporting, enable the '**Allow guests to register anonymously**' option in the 'Self Service Settings' of the settings console. Within this section, you can also configure the **'Guest' person record**, which serves as a template for each anonymous session. This template allows for the customization of guest preferences and the assignment of a generic identifier, which will be prefixed to a unique number (e.g., 'Guest 1', 'Guest 2'). The guest account is associated with an organization that enforces end-user privacy settings.

Best Practices for Whistleblower Accounts	
	1. Establish a **dedicated whistleblower account** with tightly controlled specialist access. 2. Set up a **specific service** and a straightforward request template that is exclusively available to the whistleblower account. 3. Publish a **public knowledge article** within the whistleblower account detailing the organization's whistleblowing policy and procedures to guide potential reporters.

User Provisioning via SCIM

SCIM, or System for Cross-domain Identity Management, addresses the demand for a standardized protocol in cloud software platforms for managing identities. Defined by the Internet Engineering Task Force (IETF) in September 2015, SCIM 2.0 quickly became the go-to standard for software vendors, cloud services, and enterprises, including major identity providers (IdPs), SaaS applications, and cloud platforms like 4me.

At its core, SCIM facilitates a one-way push of user and group data from the IdP to the cloud application. It necessitates a neutral data model, requiring mapping at both ends: the IdP maps its fields to SCIM, and the application maps SCIM fields to its own data fields.

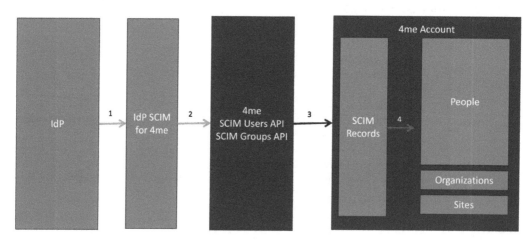

Figure 65: 4me's integration with SCIM.

The integration process with SCIM in 4me involves four main steps:

- **Mapping at the IdP**: Configure the IdP to map its data fields to the SCIM specifications.
- **Provisioning to 4me**: The IdP SCIM app sends user and group data to 4me's SCIM API.
- **Creation of SCIM Records**: 4me's SCIM API processes this data, creating corresponding SCIM records within the 4me account, typically a directory account.
- **Mapping to 4me Records**: Automation rules within 4me then map the SCIM data to person records and, if applicable, associate these records with the correct organization and site.

Implementing SCIM essentially involves straightforward configuration steps, making it accessible even for those new to the concept. The setup process requires collaboration between the 4me account administrator and the IdP administrator - for instance, the administrator managing Microsoft Active Directory. The primary task for the IdP administrator is to install and configure the IdP's 4me SCIM app, such as the Okta SCIM app or the Microsoft Azure app.

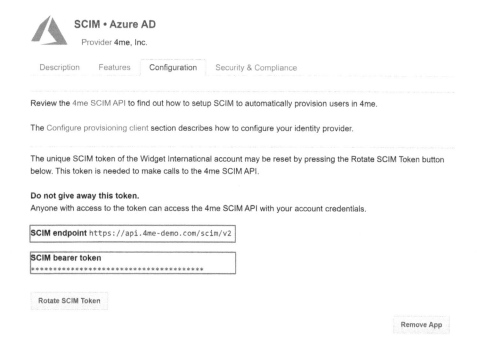

Figure 66: Setting up SCIM with Azure Active Directory in 4me.

From the 4me side, the account administrator adds the 4me SCIM app available in the 4me App Store, located within the Settings console. This action generates the necessary SCIM endpoint and SCIM bearer token, which the IdP administrator will need to finalize the connection between the IdP and 4me.

Customizing SCIM Provisioning

Despite involving two distinct administrative roles, setting up SCIM is designed to be uncomplicated. The heavy lifting is done by the SCIM application and 4me's built-in automation rules, which automatically map the incoming SCIM data to the corresponding person and organization records in 4me. The out-of-the box configuration can be customized as needed. Collaboration between the Identity Provider's (IdP) SCIM app and 4me allows for precise mapping, ensuring that specific fields from the IdP can be directly aligned with 4me's fields. For instance, with the Microsoft Azure 4me SCIM app, it's possible to tailor the provisioning process, mapping specific Azure Active Directory attributes to 4me's SCIM custom fields. This level of customization is detailed in both Microsoft's documentation and 4me's developer guide (available at https://developer.4me.com/v1/scim/users/#fields), offering a comprehensive list of fields for mapping. Furthermore, 4me enables adjustments to SCIM automation rules to fit the unique mapping needs between SCIM and 4me's person records, a topic we'll explore further in the chapter dedicated to Automation Rules.

Other User Provisioning Methods

Not every Identity Provider (IdP) supports SCIM provisioning for 4me, and sometimes, essential details like person, organization, or site attributes reside outside the IdP's database. In such cases, you're not left in the lurch! You can still ensure seamless user provisioning through custom automation scripts that tap into the rich capabilities of the open 4me API. For everything from syntax to functions, dive into the wealth of resources available on the 4me Developer Site (https://developer.4me.com). Here, you'll find the tools and guidance needed to tailor user provisioning to your organization's unique landscape.

4me and Single Sign-On Integration

Incorporating 4me as your new enterprise service management solution shouldn't mean adding another password to your users' collection. Ideally, users should seamlessly authenticate using your organization's Identity Provider (IdP) services, such as Okta, OneLogin, or Microsoft Azure Active Directory (Azure AD). 4me smoothly integrates with these services through the most widely adopted single sign-on (SSO) protocols:

- **SAML 2.0**: A staple for web-based applications, known for its security and wide adoption.
- **OpenID Connect (OIDC)**: A newer, JSON-based protocol that builds on OAuth 2.0, offering a streamlined and modern approach.

Both SSO protocols are secure, robust, and supported by major IdPs, making them excellent choices for integrating 4me with your existing authentication systems. The choice between SAML and OIDC often comes down to the specifics of your IT architecture and preferences. Consulting with your IdP administrator on which protocol best suits your needs is a good step.

Setting up SSO in 4me is straightforward and quick, typically taking less than an hour. It involves a simple exchange of technical information between your IdP and 4me's SSO service. You can find the Single Sign-On Configurations option in the 4me Settings Console, where you can easily add and manage your SSO setups.

	Provide to the IdP admin	**To obtain from the IdP admin**
SAML V2.0	• Assertion Consumer Service (ACS) URL: https://url-account/access/saml/consume	• Logout URL • SAML SSO URL • Certificate fingerprint
OpenID Connect (OIDC)	• Redirection URI: https://url-account/access/oidc	• Logout URL • Client Identifier • Client Secret • Issuer identifier

SSO Setup Insights

- **Role Requirements**: Only users with the account administrator role can set up SSO configurations.
- **Support Domain Account Configuration**: A support domain account can leverage the SSO setup from the directory account, simplifying management across your organization.
- Multiple SSO Configurations: It's possible to have several SSO configurations within a single account. The first configuration listed is the default and is automatically used with the standard account URL. Each configuration receives a unique identifier that can be appended to the account URL, creating specialized URLs for users depending on specific SSO configurations.
- **Notifications and SSO**: 4me sends notifications with links to tickets or records. To ensure users are directed to the appropriate SSO configuration from these links, SSO configurations can be associated with specific organizations. Thus, links in notifications to users within these organizations will automatically include the correct SSO identifier.
- **IP Range-Based SSO Selection**: You can configure SSO selection based on IP ranges, accommodating different SSO configurations for users accessing from inside versus outside the organization's network. When a user accesses the 4me account from inside or outside the IP range, the SSO configuration will be displayed as a selectable login option.
- **Displaying All SSO Options at Login**: To show all SSO options on the login screen, define an IP range of 0.0.0.0 and select 'Outside these IP ranges.' This setting ensures all SSO configurations are visible since the condition is always met.
- **Bypassing SSO for Administrators**: Administrators can bypass SSO by navigating to a special URL (https://your-account-url/access/normal). This is crucial for ensuring access in case of SSO issues. While this bypass option can be made available to all users, it's generally recommended to restrict it to maintain the integrity of your SSO policy.
- **Bypassing 4me's Two-Factor Authentication (2FA) with SSO**: It's typically recommended to activate the 'Two-factor authentication is required' security setting in your account to enhance security. However, when users are authenticating through SSO, it might not be necessary or desirable to prompt them for an additional 4me two-factor authentication code. To ensure a

streamlined login process via SSO without compromising security, ensure you select the option '*Do not ask a user authenticating via this Single Sign-On to enter a 4me two-factor authentication code*'. This setting effectively bypasses the 4me's built-in 2FA for users logging in through SSO.

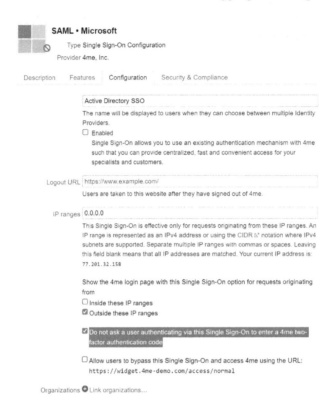

Figure 67: Setting up SCIM with Azure Active Directory in 4me.

- **SAML – Selecting the Identifier**: In 4me, a person's primary email address serves as their unique identifier. However, names and consequently email addresses can change over time, for example when someone gets married. To ensure seamless authentication with the Identity Provider (IdP) during SAML authentication that isn't reliant on an email address, 4me allows the use of the authentication ID present in the person record. When used, it's critical that the user provisioning proces includes mapping the IdP's unique identifier to the **Authentication ID** field in 4me person records.

When SCIM is used for user provisioning the IdP's unique identifier should be mapped to the **ExternalID** SCIM field in the IdP SCIM configuration. Next, in 4me in the SCIM User automation rule, the **ExternalID** should be mapped to the **Authentication ID** field of the 4me person record.

Embracing Simplicity with 4me's Single Sign-On Just in Time Provisioning

4me isn't solely about streamlining the service management process; it's about simplifying every aspect of the user experience, beginning with how new users enter the platform. With Single Sign-On Just in Time (SSO JIT) provisioning, the moment a user steps through the digital door of 4me via their Identity

Provider (IdP) for the first time, they're not just greeted with the message 'User record unknown'. Instead, 4me automatically adds a new person record for them. And it doesn't stop there—each subsequent login refreshes their record, ensuring their details are always up to date.

However, simplicity doesn't equate to overlooking details. While SSO JIT might initially capture just the essentials like a user's name and email, it's designed to work hand-in-hand with SCIM provisioning. This dynamic duo ensures that while the welcome mat is rolled out with JIT, the finer details and fuller profile are provided courtesy of SCIM's comprehensive data mapping.

	Speaking of names, 4me keeps it straightforward. Forget juggling titles, first names, middle names, surnames and suffixes across multiple fields—4me consolidates them into a single field: the **Name**. But, heed the wisdom of company policies on name ordering; a mismatch between SCIM and SSO JIT configurations could turn names into a game of flip-flop. Consistency in field mapping is key to placing all parts of the full name in their proper place and keeping them there.

The Four 4me Ticket Types

A ticket created by an end user in 4me is referred to as a **Request**, pure and simple. Whether an end user submits a ticket asking about remaining holiday entitlements, requests an additional holiday for the birth of a child, or reports an issue with accessing the payroll system, all such submissions are treated as requests within 4me.

Each request is categorized for efficient handling. Possible categories include:

- **Incident**: For reporting issues.
- **RFI (Request for Information)**: For all inquiries.
- **RFC (Request for Change)**: To request something.
- **Complaint**: For expressing dissatisfaction.
- **Compliment**: For positive feedback.
- **Other**: When the request does not fit any other category or is out of scope.
- **Order or Fulfillment**: Specifically used within the context of the 4me shop.
- **Reservation**: Specifically used within the context of the 4me Reservations feature.

A unique category, **Case**, is distinct from the first six mentioned categories. When a service delivery organization prefers not to differentiate among these categories, it can enable **'Case management'** in the account settings. This approach simplifies the process for the support organization: whether a submission is an Incident, RFI, RFC, Complaint, Compliment or something else, it is categorized as a Case.

While end users primarily interact with requests, support teams deal with various record types, including:

- **Tasks**: The basic units of workflows that outline the procedures of the service delivery organization.
- **Project Tasks**: Fundamental elements of a project.
- **Problem**: A service management concept where recurring or anticipated issues are analyzed deeply to identify and address the root cause. A problem is distinct from an incident. An incident can be completed when a temporary fix or workaround is offered to help users get back to work as soon as possible.

4me Ticket Targets

Tickets represent various types of work, each requiring prioritization. This is the reason every 4me ticket can be assigned specific targets: pickup, response, resolution, and analysis.

Pickup targets are designated for the frontline team, typically the service desk team of an account. The pickup target only exists for requests and is not dependent on the SLA or its service offering. It measures how fast the first line picks up new requests from the customers. The target can be defined in the account's **First Line Support Agreement**.

The **response target** specifies the timeframe within which a team member should begin addressing the ticket. A response target can only be defined for requests. It's important to note that 4me places significant emphasis on response time; merely accepting a ticket or assigning it to a team member is not sufficient. A response in 4me signifies that active work on the ticket has commenced, which is when it reaches the 'In Progress' status.

Please note, that 4me also recognizes that a response has been provided when a request is assigned to a child service instance or when a request's status is set to 'Workflow Pending.' This status indicates that a workflow associated with the request has been initiated. This is seen as the start of active work on the ticket.

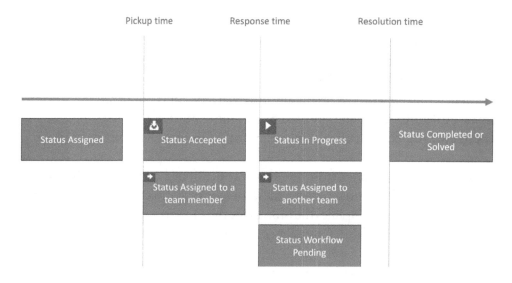

Figure 68: Tickets, statuses, and targets.

Resolution targets can be tailored to requests, workflow tasks and project tasks. The resolution target is a predetermined timeframe at which a ticket should be fully resolved. This target is crucial as it sets clear expectations for the duration of the work to be accomplished. It is the benchmark against which the timely and satisfactory resolution of tickets is measured.

4me implements a consistent approach across all four ticket types, standardizing status fields and actions in the top bar. They all have the statuses Assigned, Accepted and In Progress. And the same icons are available in the top header bar of the ticket to move through these statuses.

However, there are nuances in how targets are set, varying by ticket type. While these differences may not need to be understood by the members of support teams handling the tickets, it is crucial for service management architects and team managers to grasp them.

Primarily, SLAs and their service offerings apply only to requests, the only type of ticket an end user can submit. The agreement between the end user and the service delivery organization is encapsulated within the SLA and its service offering, where response and resolution targets are established in accordance with a support calendar. For instance, a critical incident may receive 24/7 support, whereas the resolution timeframe for a standard request is based on business hours only.

Workflow tasks and project tasks do not have a response target. Their resolution target is calculated automatically based on task duration, assignment time, and the work hours of the assigned team.

Problem tickets are treated distinctly. Setting a resolution target for a problem is impractical due to the complexity and unpredictability of resolving such issues. The focus in problem management is on analyzing recurring and anticipated issues to identify their root cause and, for recurring issues, to devise a workaround. This is why an **'Analysis target'** can be set for problem tickets.

Adjusting Expectations:

Setting a Desired Completion Date Beyond the SLA Resolution Target

In an imperfect world, the resolution targets defined in SLAs and their accompanying service offerings may occasionally be unattainable due to circumstances beyond the support organization's control. Consider a scenario where a user poses a complex RFI (Request for Information) to HR regarding payroll, necessitating input from an expert currently on vacation. Or perhaps a user requests a new laptop battery but is away for the next two weeks, preventing the support team from installing the new battery. In such instances, the original resolution target is likely to be exceeded.

Thankfully, 4me provides a mechanism for support team members to specify a "Desired Completion" date for the request. Upon setting this new target, the requester is notified, effectively managing their expectations without misusing the feature. Importantly, if the manually set Desired Completion date extends beyond the initially calculated resolution target, it is this new date that is considered for SLA reporting purposes. Consequently, requests with adjusted completion dates are not marked as SLA breaches.

Figure 69: Setting the desired completion.

Utilizing Desired Completion for Requester-Specified Deadlines

The "Desired Completion" feature is not solely for adjusting expectations when delays are anticipated; it can also serve to inquire about the requester's timeline for when certain tasks or deliveries are required. In the forthcoming chapter on Customizing 4me, we will explore how such deadlines can be gathered through a custom field and then automatically transferred to the Desired Completion field of a request via an automation rule. This flexibility allows the Desired Completion field to serve as a dynamic tool for specifying an on-demand and ad-hoc resolution target.

Urgency or Adding Emotional Intelligence on Top of Targets

While many service management systems determine priorities and SLA targets based on the widely recognized **impact x urgency** formula, 4me adopts a distinct approach that aligns with its overarching design philosophy: being service driven and simplifying the workload for support teams.

Specifically, 4me employs an **impact x service criticality** algorithm for incidents. This method simplifies the process for support teams by requiring them to only assess the impact, choosing from four clear-cut options. The dimension of service criticality is inherently factored into the service offering, automatically applied when a service or service instance is selected.

This algorithm operationalizes your SLAs and agreements with the business. For instance, it might dictate that individual access issues to the SAP service (with a 'medium' impact level) are resolved within eight hours—a timeline generally acceptable to most users. However, for a financial controller facing month-end reporting deadlines, an eight-hour wait could be critically detrimental. This is where the concept of urgency comes into play.

In 4me, urgency is represented as a binary flag that can be applied to any ticket, giving it a special designation and ensuring it appears prominently at the top of the inbox. This feature is designed to capture the support organization's immediate attention. While the established ticket targets remain unchanged, support teams are exceptionally encouraged to prioritize and give additional attention to tickets marked as 'Urgent.' This practice exemplifies the application of emotional intelligence in service management, recognizing the human element behind the ticket handling.

Request Tags: Enhancing Ticket Categorization

4me keeps ticket forms streamlined with a limited number of fields to minimize administrative overhead and maintain lean processes. However, the Tags feature offers specialists a flexible, lightweight method to add supplemental information to a request. Tags not only enable powerful and straightforward filtering but also allow users to view all related records by simply clicking on a tag in the 'All Requests' view.

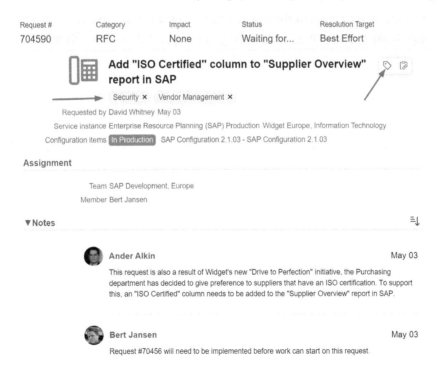

Figure 70: Adding a tag to a request.

NAME	REQUEST COUNT	CREATED
Policy issue	1	04:18am
vendor Management	1	just now

Figure 71: Account administrators can manage available tags through the Tag section in the Settings console.

Demo

Navigating 4me Ticket Targets
A Peek into Howard Tanner's Inbox

Dive into the dynamic world of ticket management with Howard Tanner at Widget Data Center, as he skillfully prioritizes his workload using 4me's ticket targets and the urgency flag. This practical example showcases the seamless integration of customer expectations into daily operations.

- Log in as howard.tanner@widget.com to Widget Data Center.
  - Right at the top of his inbox sits an urgent request. Despite being tagged with a 'Best effort' target—indicating the absence of a contractually fixed resolution time—it screams for immediate attention, thanks to its urgency flag.
  - Howard notices the rest of his tickets are neatly arranged according to their target dates, ensuring a structured approach to his workflow.
  - Curious about the impact of the urgency flag, Howard selects the urgent ticket. He navigates to the Actions menu, symbolized by the gear icon, and chooses to 'Remove Urgent Flag'.
  - With a quick refresh of his inbox, Howard witnesses the once top-priority request gracefully descend nearly to the bottom of his list. The urgency flag's removal repositions the ticket, ensuring that it gets prioritized with the other 'Best effort' tickets based on the moment they were registered (the oldest gets listed on top).

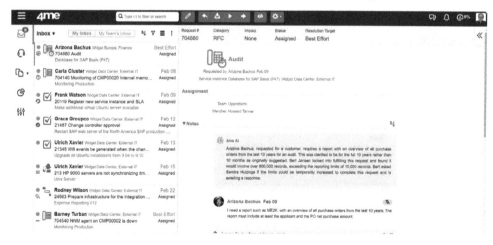

Figure 72: An urgent ticket in Howard's Inbox.

Notes: Streamlining Communication in 4me

4me is committed to simplifying work; hence, it eschews the proliferation of fields like long descriptions, extra comments, solution fields, and others that some service management platforms favor. Such fields often disperse crucial information across numerous locations, complicating the user experience. Instead, 4me utilizes notes, appended to tickets in chronological order, with user preference dictating their sorting from oldest to newest or vice versa.

A ticket can accommodate a virtually unlimited number of notes—technically up to 2,500, a limit unlikely to be reached unless a ticket transforms into an entire book. Each note can be extensive, supporting up to 64 KB of text, images, and embedded videos. Every note features a unique identifier, which can be copied for easy reference in future communications or when linking to notes in other tickets. Furthermore, **referencing** other tickets is streamlined with the use of the **hashtag (#)**, facilitating the search for tickets by ID or subject.

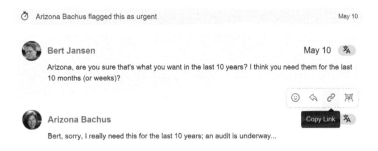

Figure 73: Copying the link to a note.

Notes extend beyond the confines of 4me ticket types and are accessible on all records where communication is essential, including releases, workflows, projects, and risks. The ability to reference a request within a note on a risk record, for example, proves invaluable as it facilitates direct linkage to actions undertaken to mitigate the risk.

Diverse Media Types in Notes

Notes can originate from various sources: directly from users, through the API, from incoming emails, emails sent from within a ticket, system-generated alerts (e.g. SLA clock stoppages), or via automation rules. The **medium** of a note, while automatically determined by 4me, is of little concern to users but can offer valuable insights in automation contexts.

Distinguishing Between Internal and Public Notes

Effective communication also involves discerning what information should remain concealed. For this purpose, 4me differentiates between **internal** and **public** notes within requests. Public notes are accessible to anyone with ticket access, while internal notes are confined to users with specialist or administrator roles within the account where the note was created. **Internal notes** are not visible to the end users or to the specialists of other accounts. This distinction ensures that sensitive information is shielded from unauthorized viewers.

Specialists who hold roles across multiple 4me accounts may encounter situations where they need to add an internal note to a request. In such cases, they must choose the account in which the note will become visible. This selection is facilitated by the **internal note account switche**r feature, allowing for precise control over the internal note's allocation.

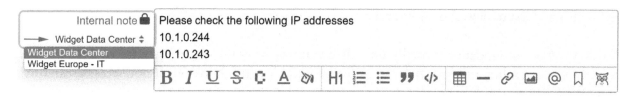

Figure 74: An Internal Note with the note account Switcher.

Deleting Notes and Understanding Note Ownership

Mistakes happen, and occasionally sensitive information that shouldn't be shared with a broader audience is mistakenly included in a note. Such notes require deletion, but this must be balanced with the need for auditability and the integrity of the process. To safeguard against the inappropriate removal of information that could influence decision-making, 4me enforces strict guidelines for note deletion:

- Deletion is restricted to account administrators and service desk managers within 14 days of the note's creation. Notes older than this period can only be deleted by the account owner.

- A system note stating "Redacted by [Administrator's Name]" replaces the deleted note, keeping the audience informed of the deletion. This action is also recorded in the audit trail of the record for transparency.

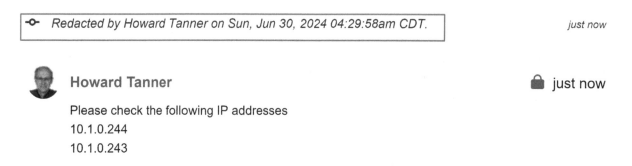

Figure 75: A deleted note is replaced by a system message.

Understanding note ownership is crucial in this context. Internal notes belong to the account where they were created, while public notes are considered "owned" by the 4me account associated with the creator's organization. This delineation has significant implications:

- An administrator and a service desk manager can only delete notes created by individuals within their directory account structure. For example, notes added by specialists from a supplier on a customer-assigned request can only be deleted by administrators within the supplier's account, not the customer's.
- This ownership rule also affects data handling; exporting public notes from requests must be performed at the directory account level and will only include public notes made by members of your organization.

	When it comes to sharing sensitive information such as passwords and security tokens, caution and best practices must be strictly observed. These types of information should never be included in notes within the 4me platform. Instead, 4me offers a **secure chat functionality** specifically designed for the safe transmission of sensitive data.

Chapter 6 - Request Templates: Making the Service Catalog Actionable

We have seen that the service hierarchy is the backbone of 4me's service-driven structure. It is a connected chain of services essential for operationalizing a 4me account. Once established, users can begin submitting requests. By default, these requests are categorized as 'Incident' (or 'case' in a Case Management account). Specialists on the support team, typically service desk analysts, should reassess and accurately categorize each new request assigned to them. This step, however, introduces unnecessary overhead. Why not enable end users to specify their needs directly from the outset?

This is where request templates come into play. By preparing request templates for services, users are empowered to select a specific action. For instance, adding templates like '*I have a question concerning a pay slip*' and '*Request a copy of a pay slip*' transforms the service catalog into a dynamic tool for user engagement.

Managing Request Templates

Users with the *account designer* or *service desk manager* role can create or modify request templates. Empowering *service desk managers* with this capability facilitates an agile approach to continuous improvement, allowing for the creation of new templates in response to recurring requests.

The Request Template Subject

Creating a request template necessitates only one mandatory field: the Subject. This field is pivotal as it guides end users in finding the template on the self-service portal, assists service desk analysts in locating it within the service desk console, and helps support team members identify it in the Service Hierarchy Bar (SHB).

The '**Copy subject to requests**' option might seem minor but significantly affects usability. For example, if a template titled '*I have a question related to the payroll service*' is used, enabling this option means the subject auto-populates in the self-service portal. This could lead to a cluttered inbox for the team, with multiple requests bearing the same generic subject. Disabling this feature encourages end users to craft more descriptive subjects, enhancing clarity in the team's inbox.

The Request Template Service

Given the platform's service-driven nature every record in 4me typically links to a service. However, the requirement to link a template to a service does vary by request category. Four request categories do not necessitate a service definition:

- **Complaints** and **Compliments**, which relate to the service delivery organization as a whole.
- The **'Other'** category, for requests that fall outside the scope of provided services.
- The **'Order'** category, which is handled differently, as detailed in the chapter dedicated to the 4me Shop.

That said, typically, 99% of request templates fall under 'Incident,' 'Request for Information,' or 'Request for Change' categories. For these, defining both a subject and a service is necessary. In a Case Management account, the category will always be 'Case' (except for reservations or order/fulfillment request templates used in the 4me Shop). For a case, the selection of a service is not mandatory, though highly recommended.

Managing Request Template Visibility

Certain request templates, like *'Termination for cause'* or *'Replace a desktop,'* should not be visible to end users, as these decisions are typically made by HR or IT team members. This is where visibility options come into play. Disabling the **'End users' visibility** option keeps the template off the self-service portal and out of sight from end users.

In some cases, templates might be made visible to end users but hidden from team members and or vice versa, to accommodate two different scenarios of request submission: via the self-service portal or via the service desk console. Additionally, a template can be made invisible to both groups for integration purposes, allowing external systems to utilize these 'invisible' templates when generating new requests in the 4me account.

Figure 76: Request template subject, service, and visibility.

Keywords, Registration Hints, Instructions, and Notes

Keywords play a crucial role in making request templates easier to find.

Registration hints provide valuable guidance to both end users and service desk analysts upon selecting or applying a request template. Well-crafted instructions can boost efficiency by eliminating the need for follow-up queries due to missing or incorrect information.

Instructions are intended for the support staff and are not visible to end users. Detailed and clear instructions can dramatically improve both the efficiency and the quality of the support provided. Investing time and effort into developing these instructions pays dividends in streamlined operations.

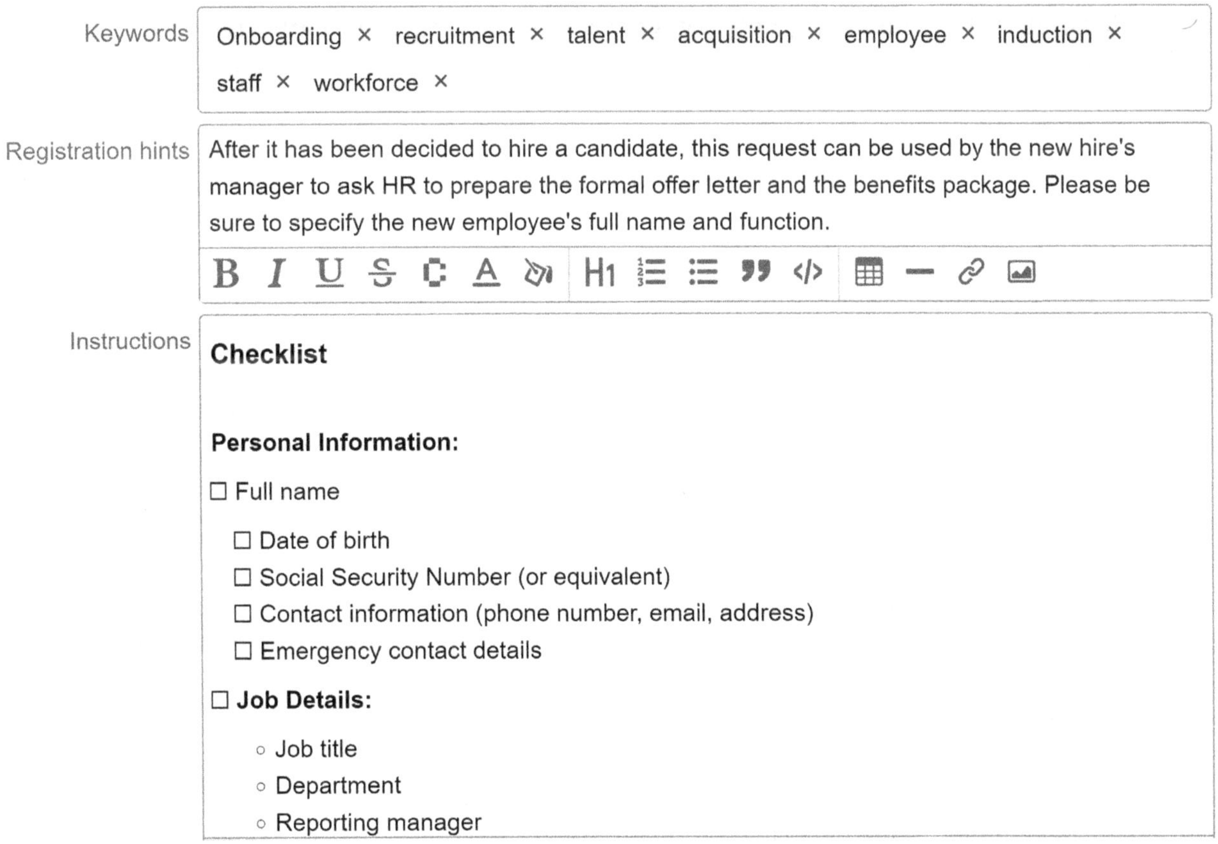

Keywords	Onboarding × recruitment × talent × acquisition × employee × induction × staff × workforce ×
Registration hints	After it has been decided to hire a candidate, this request can be used by the new hire's manager to ask HR to prepare the formal offer letter and the benefits package. Please be sure to specify the new employee's full name and function.

B *I* U S̲ C A ✒ H1 ☰ ☰ ❞ </> ▦ ─ 𝒫 🖼

Instructions

Checklist

Personal Information:

☐ Full name

   ☐ Date of birth
   ☐ Social Security Number (or equivalent)
   ☐ Contact information (phone number, email, address)
   ☐ Emergency contact details

☐ **Job Details:**

   ○ Job title
   ○ Department
   ○ Reporting manager

Figure 77: Request template keywords, registration hints and instructions. The instructions field in this example includes a checklist.

- If a lengthy manual or instructions document is necessary, include a **hyperlink** within the document to the instructions.
- Utilize the **rich text formatting** options to enhance the readability of the instructions. Keep in mind that you can incorporate images and embed videos into the instructions.
- Take advantage of the **checklist** functionality. Once the request is registered and assigned, the assignee can then mark or unmark the items on the list, even with the request in View mode. All changes made to these checklist items are remembered and audited.

The information entered in the Note field of a template is automatically transferred to the Note field of the corresponding request when the template is applied. This functionality proves beneficial for integrations: instead of embedding note content within the integration script, it's more efficient to include it directly in the request template.

Streamlining Request Assignments with 4me Templates

Defining the Assignment section within a request template is optional, thanks to the 4me platform's reliance on the service hierarchy for precise assignment. When a request is initiated via a template - either by an end user through the self-service portal or by a service desk analyst in the Service Desk Console - a service instance is always selected. Each service instance is linked to a designated support team and, optionally, a first-line team. This organizational structure facilitates the automatic routing of requests to the appropriate team, even when no specific assignment team is selected in the template.

However, it's often advisable to explicitly assign a team within the template when the service (or service instances) associated has both a first-line team and a support team defined. Determining whether the first-line team or the support team should handle these is a decision to be made jointly by the managers of these teams and reflected in the template.

In some cases, it may be decided to allocate a particular request template to a specific team for operational efficiency. For example, facilities management might oversee Access Control & Key Management across multiple sites, each with its service instance and local support team. Yet, a central team might be more suited to handle requests like '*Request access to a building.*' Such teams are referred to as **template teams**, and they, along with the first line and support teams, are listed on top in the team selection field within the Specialist Interface.

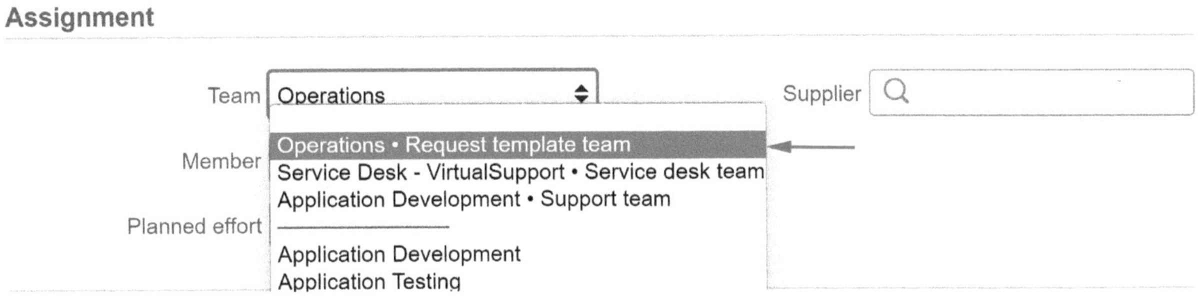

Assignment

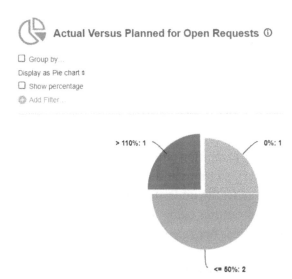

Figure 78: The team field on a request sets the first line team, the support team and the template teams on top.

Noteworthy Fields in the Assignment Section: Supplier and Planned Effort

Supplier Field: If a request necessitates action from an external service provider not working in 4me, this entity must be listed as an external organization within the account or its directory account. Specifying a supplier in the template auto-populates this field when the request is generated, introducing a **Supplier request ID** field for tracking purposes. The assigned team member will then liaise with the supplier, referencing the supplier's ticket ID in the Supplier request ID field.

Planned Effort: This field estimates the effort needed to resolve a request. While predicting the necessary effort for incidents and RFIs is challenging, future advancements, possibly through AI, could enable 4me to make accurate effort estimations and automatically provide a value for this field. For RFCs and certain cases, where the effort can be accurately estimated based on predefined instructions, defining the planned effort is crucial for garnering insightful data.

The planned effort is utilized in an insightful 4me report: the *Actual Versus Planned Effort* report. This report becomes significantly more valuable when filtered by Template, as it meticulously examines deviations and outliers, shedding light on the precision of initial effort estimates. Outliers, in particular, often highlight instances where processes may have diverged from expectations.

Figure 79: Actual versus planned effort.

Defining Standard Service Requests

Services often require specific request templates to be accessible to certain end users while remaining hidden from others. For instance, the HR service "Payroll" might receive requests from financial controllers for an overview of employee pay slips. To facilitate these requests, a template titled "*Request for the Monthly Pay Slip Report*" can be made available. However, this template should not be visible to all end users.

This selective visibility is achievable by creating a dedicated service offering named "*Payroll Services for Financial Controllers.*" By linking the "*Request for the Monthly Pay Slip Report*" template to this specific service offering, the request template becomes a **standard service request**. A standard service request is only visible to the users that are covered by an SLA that is linked to the service offering that includes the standard service request.

In the example above, an SLA 'Payroll Services for Financial Controllers' will be defined. This SLA will be linked to the service offering 'Payroll Services for Financial Controllers,' and the SLA should only cover the financial controllers.

In summary, all request templates not tied to a service offering will be accessible to all users that are covered for the service of the request template. However, linking a request template to a service offering changes this dynamic. Now, the template becomes available only when a service instance with an SLA and service offering connected to the template is selected, and when the requester is covered by the SLA.

Managing Targets

Standard Requests and Keeping Promises

Setting resolution targets for standard requests is more than just a good practice; it's essential for managing user expectations and preventing unnecessary follow-up inquiries for status updates. While requesters may generally understand and accept missed targets for incidents and complex RFIs—especially when they see notes being added that describe the efforts being made to resolve their issues—this leniency often does not extend to standard requests or straightforward RFIs.

For these types of requests, meeting the set resolution target is critical. Users view these targets as promises, and failing to fulfill them can lead to significant dissatisfaction and erode trust in the service delivery organization. This underscores the importance of not just setting realistic resolution targets but also ensuring that your service delivery team has the resources and processes in place to meet these targets consistently. When defining resolution targets for standard requests, it's crucial to do so with a commitment to keeping those promises, thereby maintaining a high level of customer satisfaction and trust.

Defining Resolution and Response Targets

The concept of standard service requests extends beyond merely specifying which users have access to specific request templates. By associating request templates with service offerings, it becomes possible to define detailed response and resolution targets, as well as pertinent billing information. This feature is particularly valuable for Managed Service Providers (MSPs), who commonly categorize their service offerings based on quality levels, such as " Bronze," "Silver," and "Gold." Within these differentiated service offerings, MSPs have the flexibility to include all or selected request templates as part of their standard service requests, assigning unique response and resolution targets to each template.

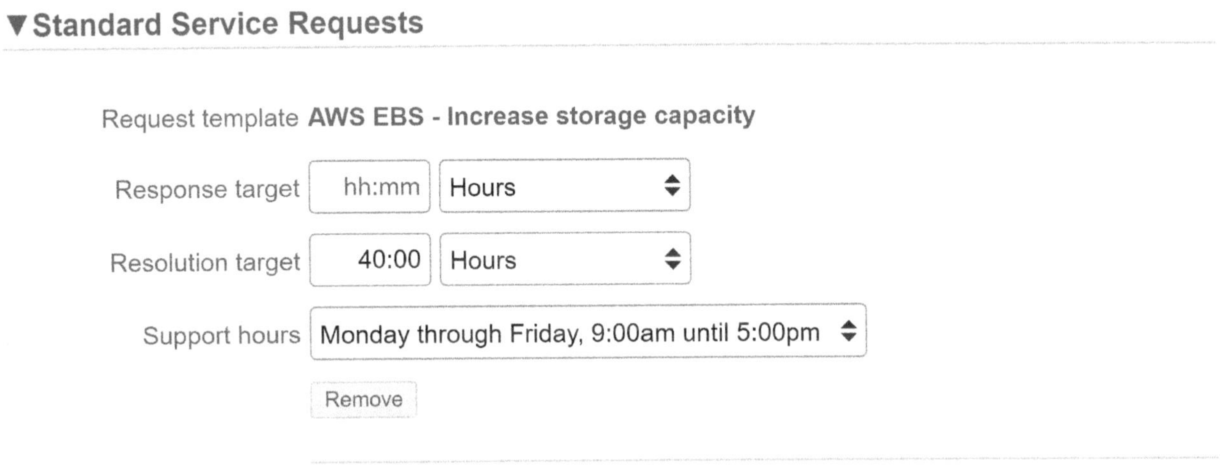

▼ **Standard Service Requests**

Request template **AWS EBS - Increase storage capacity**

Response target   [hh:mm] [Hours ⬍]

Resolution target   [40:00] [Hours ⬍]

Support hours [Monday through Friday, 9:00am until 5:00pm ⬍]

[Remove]

Figure 80: A request template linked to a service offering becomes a standard service request.

The Simplified Approach to Resolution Targets with Desired Completion Time

Linking request templates to service offerings allows for setting specific response and resolution targets. However, this method introduces an additional layer of administration. For services targeting a singular group, underpinned by a unified SLA and service offering - and when response targets are not necessary - there exists a simple alternative: setting the desired completion time directly within the request template.

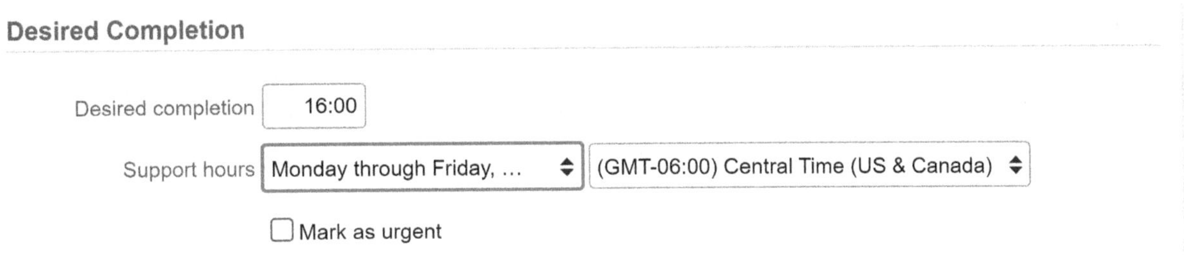

Desired Completion

Desired completion [16:00]

Support hours [Monday through Friday, ... ⬍] [(GMT-06:00) Central Time (US & Canada) ⬍]

☐ Mark as urgent

Figure 81: The desired completion time and urgency flag on a request template.

Previously, we explored how specialists can adjust the desired completion time on individual requests, signifying a concord between the requester and the support team. This level of mutual understanding can also be pre-established at the request template level, embedding a pre-agreed resolution timeframe directly into the template itself.

Incorporating Urgency Right from the Start

Within the Desired Completion section of the request template, there's an option to designate the requests generated from this template as 'Urgent' from the outset. This feature is particularly useful for instances requiring prompt attention, such as when a user reports a data breach.

The Actionable Servivce Catalog
Data Protection Request Templates

In this demonstration, we'll explore how a meticulously crafted service catalog can enhance security and data protection measures at the Widget company. Recognizing the importance of security, Widget has invested significantly in raising awareness among its employees about potential threats. A critical component of this initiative is the establishment of a support domain account specifically for the data protection team, responsible for overseeing the organization's digital security.

Randy Barton, a financial controller at Widget, encounters what he suspects to be a phishing attempt: an email, seemingly from the CEO, sent to his private address, requesting a confidential financial report. Recognizing the potential threat, Randy decides to report it:

Randy logs in as **randy.barton@widget.com** at **Widget International**.
- He clicks on 'New Request'.
- From the list, Randy selects Data Protection.
- Next he selects 'Data Breaches and Security Incidents (SIR).
- Now Randy reviews the list of standard requests.

This scenario underscores the value of having of having well-defined request templates. Such precision not only empowers users to report security incidents accurately but also equips the security team with detailed analytics on the types of incidents occurring, enabling them to respond more effectively and enhance the organization's overall security posture.

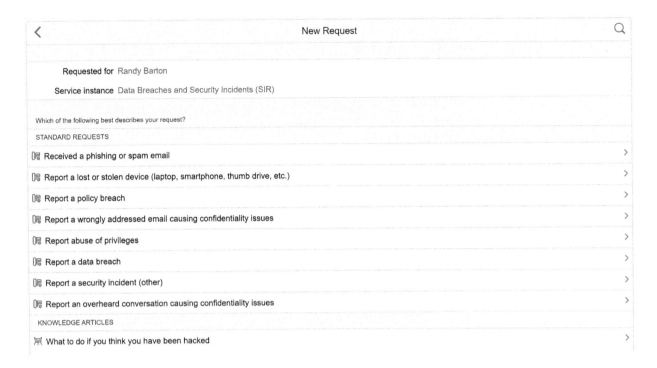

Figure 82: The actionable service catalog for a security service.

Chapter 7 - Workflows - Unleashing the Power of 4me

Congratulations! By now, you've laid the foundations for your 4me environment, weaving together the account structure, populating it with people, organizations, and sites, and crafting a meticulously designed service catalog and hierarchy. This groundwork ensures that users can effortlessly submit requests, which are then smartly routed to the appropriate teams for resolution. Even at this stage, 4me stands head and shoulders above what you'd typically expect from a service management platform.

"Enterprise Service Management is more than implementing workflows!". That was our rallying cry in the opening chapters, a declaration aimed at broadening your horizon beyond the nuts and bolts of workflow diagrams. Yet, here we stand—quite a few pages later—poised to dive headfirst into the very subject we've been circling around. Why, you ask? Because, as much as we've championed the idea that enterprise service management transcends the realm of workflows, the truth is, there's no escaping their gravitational pull. They are the silent gears and invisible threads weaving through the tapestry of any robust service driven operating model. Workflows are the baton-wielding maestros ensuring every section of our service delivery orchestra plays in harmony. Here's why embarking on this workflow odyssey is not just important but downright essential:

- **The Symphony of Standardization**: Workflows bring a crucial level of standardization to the handling of service requests, especially vital in environments involving multiple teams or various service delivery organizations (across different 4me accounts). This standardization guarantees that each request is processed with a consistent approach.
- **A Transparent Concerto**: The clarity and traceability offered by workflow functionality illuminate every step of the service delivery process. By making the progression of the workflow visible to requesters, it enhances their understanding of the process, which helps to set realistic expectations. For service owners and team members, this transparency is instrumental in tracking task progress in real time, pinpointing delays or inefficiencies, and facilitating strategic improvements in service operations.
- **The Rhythm of Compliance**: Embedding compliance controls within workflows is a strategic move to ensure successful adherence to regulatory frameworks. Workflows aid in the detailed recording of actions and decisions, providing the necessary documentation for compliance and audit trails. This level of detail not only meets regulatory demands but also bolsters accountability, making it clear who was responsible for what actions and when.
- **Automating the Choreography**: By automating the execution of repetitive and routine tasks, workflow functionality significantly reduces the dependency on manual input. This acceleration of the service delivery process not only enhances efficiency but also decreases the likelihood of human error, contributing to more reliable and consistent service outcomes.

Let the symphony begin!

Introducing Key Roles:
Workflow Manager and Account Designer

In the realm of service delivery, *specialists* primarily focus on execution, adhering to established procedures and workflows without altering their structure. The foundational procedures of a service delivery organization are encapsulated within workflow templates. To amend these workflow templates, one requires the roles of an **Account Administrator** or an **Account Designer**.

Subsequently, workflows are generated from these templates, under the oversight of a designated **Workflow Manager**. The *workflow manager* oversees the orchestration and management of workflows.

Workflows: The Fundamental Framework

Recall that in 4me, end users are primarily acquainted with requests. However, a request can initiate a workflow. As mentioned earlier, these requests are often generated from a request template. Furthermore, a request template can be associated with a **workflow template**, which in turn is linked to **task templates**.

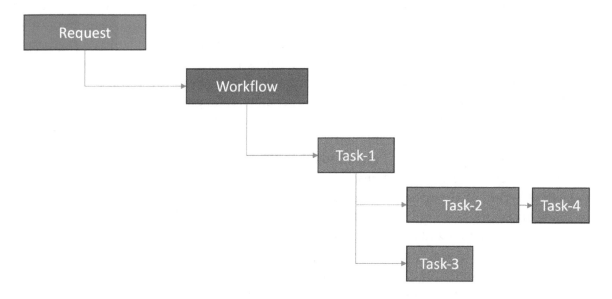

Figure 83: A request is linked to a workflow with workflow tasks.

In certain instances, a single workflow may serve multiple requests. This is particularly common in IT, where several requesters might seek the same enhancement. In such cases, all related requests can be consolidated under a single workflow.

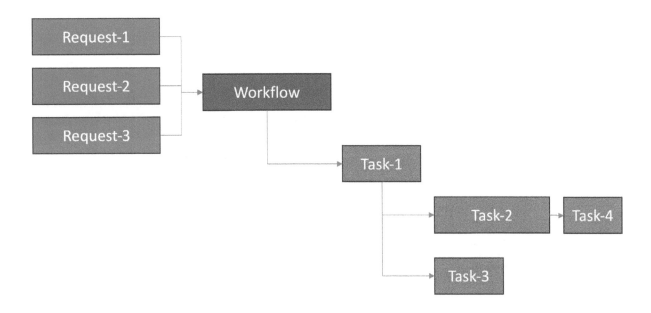

Figure 84: Multiple requests related to a workflow.

Moreover, in the IT domain, a workflow may be connected to a problem record. This approach is utilized to investigate the underlying cause of recurring incidents. Once identified, a solution to eliminate the root cause is proposed, often necessitating a change coordinated via a specific workflow. Notably, the workflow, through its associated problem record, communicates back to all users impacted by the issue.

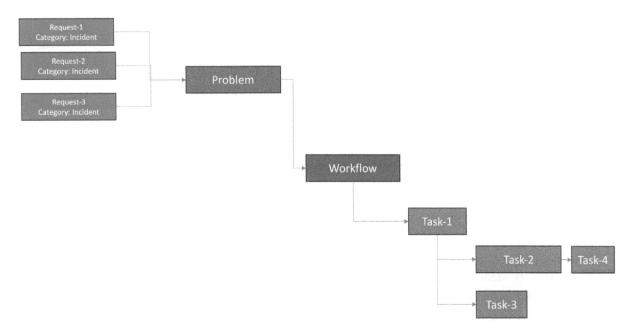

Figure 85: From a request over a problem to a workflow.

Workflows can also be aggregated into a release, especially within IT practices like "Change Enablement," which rely extensively on workflows. This aspect will receive further attention in the chapter dedicated to the 4me best practice process models.

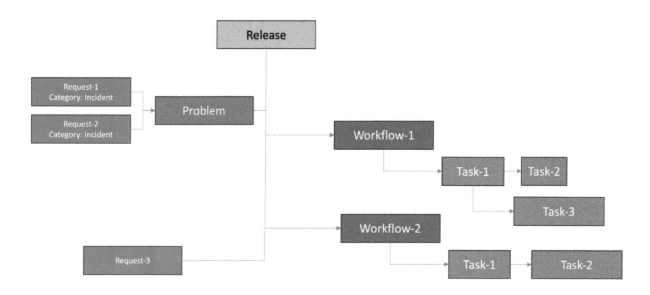

Figure 86: A release bundling multiple workflows (changes).

While workflows are typically auto-generated by linking a request template to a workflow template, they can also be manually initiated. This manual creation, however, requires the Workflow Manager role. Workflow Managers have the capability to link requests and problems to new workflows using the action "**Relate to New Workflow ...**". Workflow managers can even initiate workflows independently of any other record. Nevertheless, initiating a workflow invariably begins with the selection of a workflow template.

It's advisable to discourage the practice of starting workflows without a clear underlying reason. Workflow Managers should be encouraged to **always begin with a request**, as it clarifies the origin, purpose, and rationale behind the workflow's initiation.

Task Templates: The Building Blocks

The foundation of standardizing procedures within workflows is the creation of **workflow templates**. Workflow templates are fundamentally composed of **task templates**, each serving as a blueprint for tasks and falling into one of four categories:

- **Risk & Impact**: Commonly utilized in IT change management and applicable across various domains, these tasks involve the identification and evaluation of the potential risks that could cause the implementation of the change to fail. These tasks are also used to identify ways to minimize the impact of the implementation on the users that will be affected by the change. Completed risk & impact tasks typically influence the subsequent steps in the workflow.

- **Approval**: Unique in that they can be assigned to any user, including those without a license, approval tasks allow for broader organizational engagement.
- **Implementation**: Often considered the most critical, implementation tasks focus on executing the work required to fulfill the objectives of the workflow.
- **Automation**: Future discussions will cover automation rules in depth, including how they can streamline workflow steps. Automation tasks, distinguished by their simplicity, do not require many of the fields and options necessary for other tasks. For instance, specifying a team is unnecessary because an automation task activates automation rules or integrations directly, bypassing the need for manual team involvement.
- **Order**: Specific to transactions within the 4me Shop, details on order tasks will be elaborated in a dedicated chapter.

Instructions and Notes in Task Templates

Just as detailed **Instructions** in a request template significantly enhance support efficiency and quality, the same applies to task templates. Precise and comprehensive instructions in a task template can markedly boost the effectiveness and consistency of support delivered.

Similarly, the **Note** field in a task template is mirrored in the Note field of the created task. This feature proves valuable when tasks are generated through an integration, shifting the maintenance of task-related notes to the maintenance of the task template instead of the maintenance in the integration layer.

Task Note Behavior: Copy Notes to the Workflow

When team members add notes to tasks, they have the option, via a checkbox beneath the note field, to duplicate these notes to the associated workflow record. Generally, adding notes directly to the workflow record is unnecessary, as workflows primarily serve as a placeholder for tasks. However, in scenarios where workflows are actively managed by a workflow manager—who may schedule, cancel, or append tasks—such as in sales and marketing processes for handling RFPs (Requests for Proposals) or creating marketing collateral, it's beneficial to copy task notes to the workflow record. This consolidation causes the workflow manager to be notified without the need to review each task individually.

Figure 87: The task template. Modifying the category will hide or show other fields.

To circumvent the common oversight of failing to select the 'Copy notes to workflow' option, it's prudent to enable '**Copy notes to workflow by default**' in the task template settings.

Note Behavior for Implementation and Risk & Impact Tasks

The behavior of the note field upon task completion - whether making a note mandatory or optional - is configurable, ensuring flexibility. As a general guideline, avoid mandating notes for straightforward task completions where a simple acknowledgment of completion suffices, as this adds no value.

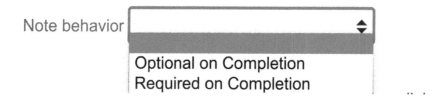

Figure 88: Define the notes behavior on task completion.

Note Behavior for Approval Tasks

The inclusion of comments by approvers during the approval process poses a question: should comments be allowed, optional, or required? While rejection of a task necessitates an explanatory note, approvals offer flexibility in note policy. Allowing notes during approval introduces the possibility of conditional approvals, which, if not meticulously managed, can lead to oversight of the approver's conditions, potentially impacting subsequent actions.

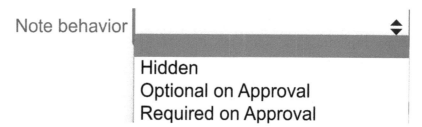

Figure 89: Note behavior for approval tasks.

Three strategies to manage approval notes include:

- **Unconditional Approvals Only**: Set the Note behavior to 'Hidden'. Concealing the note field to prevent the addition of conditions, requiring approvers to reject tasks to stipulate any conditions. When it happens on a regular basis that approvers only want to approve under certain conditions this approach will create overhead.
- **Mandatory Notes with Default Copying**: Set the Note behavior to 'Required on Approval'.

Make sure to automatically copy the note to the workflow. In this approach, specialists working on the workflow should always review the workflow record for any approver comments.

- **Optional Notes with Automation**: Set the Note behavior to 'Optional on Approval'. Offering the least administrative burden, this option allows notes to be added at the approver's discretion. But this approach requires implementing automation rules to ensure that any conditions noted are communicated effectively to relevant parties.

Choosing the right strategy depends on balancing the need for detailed communication against the administrative overhead for workflow managers and stakeholders.

Pausing SLA Timers: When Accountability Lies Elsewhere

A common hurdle in meeting the resolution target of standard request involves waiting for approvals from organizational managers, whether they're business managers, financial controllers, or direct supervisors of the requester. Previously, we touched upon the importance of a service delivery organization's commitment to "Keeping Promises" in handling standard requests. However, if managerial approval consistently delays resolutions, it's unfair to hold the service delivery organization responsible. To address this, the **"Provider not accountable"** flag can be activated in tasks. This pauses the SLA clocks for requests that are linked to the workflow when the provider organization is waiting for the task to be completed by the customer.

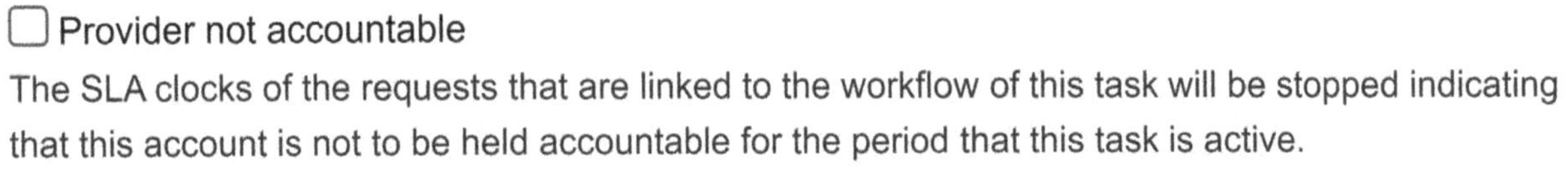

☐ Provider not accountable
The SLA clocks of the requests that are linked to the workflow of this task will be stopped indicating that this account is not to be held accountable for the period that this task is active.

Figure 90: The "Provider not accountable" flag on task templates. The SLA clock for requests linked to the workflow will be stopped.

Risk & Impact and Implementation Task Assignments

Risk & Impact and Implementation tasks must be assigned to a team. Similarly to request templates, if the task requires an action from an external service provider not integrated into 4me, the **Supplier** organization can be defined in the task template. This action automatically populates the **Supplier ID** field when the task is assigned, enabling tracking. The assigned team member will then liaise with the supplier, referencing the supplier's ticket ID in the Supplier ID field.

In addition to a team, tasks can be assigned to the *workflow manager* and or the *service owner*. These individuals are defined within the service record, and because a workflow is always associated with a service, the assignee will be dynamically selected from the service record. This is particularly useful in these workflows where active management by the workflow manager is anticipated.

Assignment

Team	[▲▼]	Supplier	[🔍]
Member	[🔍]		

☐ Workflow manager
☐ Service owner

Planned duration [hh:mm]
Planned effort [hh:mm]

☐ Work hours are 24x7
☐ Mark as urgent

Figure 91: Assignment of implementation and Risk & Impact task templates.

Assignments for Approval Tasks

Approval tasks are assigned to individuals rather than teams, often requiring dynamic role-based assignments to ensure flexibility and continuity. Typical roles in the approval process include the *workflow manager*, *service owner*, the original requester, or the requester's managerial chain. While any known person record within the account or directory can technically be selected, relying solely on individual assignments poses risks should that individual exit the organization, necessitating updates to task templates.

To mitigate this, approvals are sometimes defined by role (e.g., financial controllers approving purchases or software architects reviewing designs), incorporating these individuals into a **skill pool**. Assigning the approval task to this pool broadens the approver base, maintaining process integrity regardless of personnel changes. It's important to specify the **minimum number of approvals** needed for proceeding, noting that once this threshold is met, the task is canceled for the remaining approvers, preventing them from approving or rejecting the task.

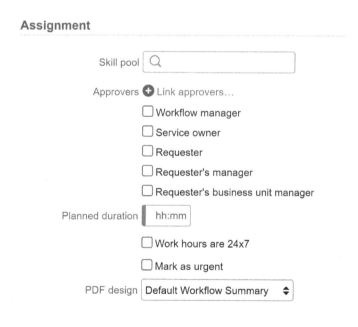

Figure 92: Assignment for an approval task template.

Approval Delegation: Ensuring Continuity in Service Management

Effective service management heavily relies on efficient resource management, which must account for periods when individuals are unavailable due to holidays, sick leave, or training sessions. To address this, 4me allows users to set an **out-of-office period** during which they can nominate an *approval delegate*. This feature ensures that any approval tasks assigned to the person during their absence are automatically redirected to their designated delegate.

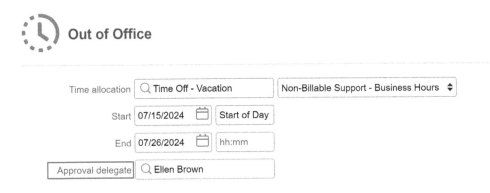

Figure 93: Every user can define an out-of-office period with a delegate for approvals.

Should the delegate act on an approval task, the corresponding task assigned to the original approver is instantly canceled to prevent duplicate actions. Conversely, if the original approver decides to approve a task—perhaps while relaxing on a beach in southern France, using the 4me Mobile App—the delegate's approval task is likewise canceled.

This mechanism is crucial in scenarios requiring approval from distinct roles. For example, when an approval task is assigned to the service owner and the financial manager, and requires at least two approvals, the required number of approvals would have be reached if the service owner and the service owner's delegate would both approve it. By ensuring that, as soon as the service owner has approved the task, the service owner's delegate can no longer approver it, the financial manager's approval is still required in order for the workflow to proceed.

Planned Duration and Planned Effort

Remember, ticket targets are crucial for support teams, enabling them to prioritize their workload effectively and manage requester expectations efficiently. The **Planned duration** specified in a task template directly influences the resolution target for that task. Visibility of a task in the inbox is triggered once its status changes to 'Assigned,' indicating that all preceding tasks have been completed successfully. Initially, the resolution target for a task is determined based on an anticipated assignment time, factoring in the actual or expected resolution times of all preceding tasks. Upon task assignment, the resolution target is recalculated based on the moment the task was assigned and the planned duration.

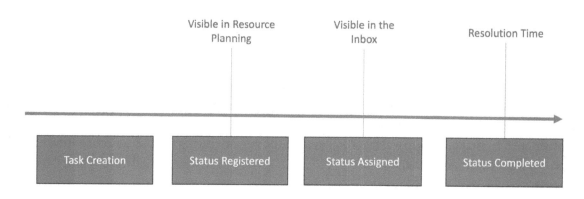

Figure 94: The lifecycle of a task.

Resolution target calculations take into account the **Work hours** defined for the assignee's team, which may exclude weekends and bank holidays. This can be overridden by checking the box **'Work hours are 24 x 7.'** This feature is particularly useful for implementation tasks within IT changes, which frequently occur outside of normal business hours.

When enabling time tracking (which we strongly recommend) you should define the **Planned effort** for the task. This will enable better resource planning and quality control.

It's important to note that end users do not have visibility into tasks and their respective resolution targets. Instead, their expectations are set based on the resolution target of the request tied to the workflow. To ensure seamless service delivery, the anticipated target for the workflow's final task should be set to complete before the request's resolution target. Incorporating a buffer time into the resolution target of the request (or template) compared to the cumulative resolution target of the workflow template is considered a best practice. Make sure to enable the 'Provider not accountable' flag on tasks for which your organization cannot be held responsible.

Approval Tasks: Ensuring Clarity and Compliance through PDF Designs

Workflows within 4me are instrumental in upholding organizational policies and procedures, laying a foundation for compliance adherence and fostering good governance. The approval process, in particular, requires robustness and auditability. It is crucial that the information forming the basis of an approval is precise and remains unchanged post-approval to maintain the integrity of the decision-making process. This is where PDF designs come into play.

PDF designs allow for the precise definition of information necessary for approvers to make informed decisions. When a task is assigned to an approver, a PDF file is generated based on the designated template and attached to the approval task, ensuring that approvers have all the relevant details at their disposal.

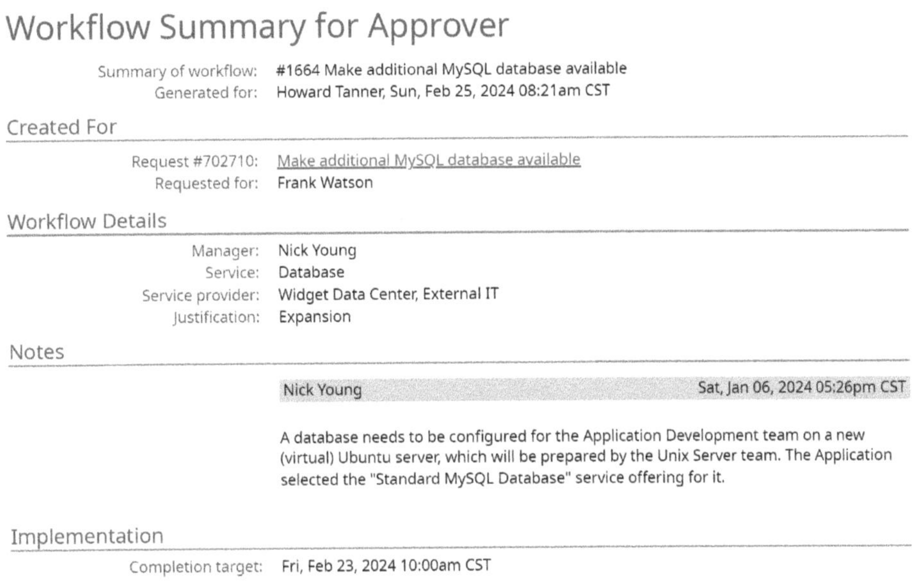

Workflow Summary for Approver

Summary of workflow:	#1664 Make additional MySQL database available
Generated for:	Howard Tanner, Sun, Feb 25, 2024 08:21am CST

Created For

Request #702710:	Make additional MySQL database available
Requested for:	Frank Watson

Workflow Details

Manager:	Nick Young
Service:	Database
Service provider:	Widget Data Center, External IT
Justification:	Expansion

Notes

Nick Young	Sat, Jan 06, 2024 05:26pm CST

A database needs to be configured for the Application Development team on a new (virtual) Ubuntu server, which will be prepared by the Unix Server team. The Application selected the "Standard MySQL Database" service offering for it.

Implementation

Completion target:	Fri, Feb 23, 2024 10:00am CST

Figure 95: The default PDF design for approvals.

Every new 4me account comes equipped with a Default Workflow Summary PDF design. This standard design offers a comprehensive overview of the workflow, including implementation tasks and associated requests, which may be overly detailed for certain approval scenarios. Additionally, there may be a desire to incorporate company branding, such as adding a logo. You can customize the default PDF design and create custom PDF designs tailored to meet specific requirements. Guidance on PDF Design customization will be provided in an upcoming chapter.

Implementation Tasks: Assessing Impact on Services and Configuration Items

In many instances, workflows are designed to manage maintenance or changes affecting service infrastructure or physical devices. For example, in facilities management, servicing HVAC (heating, ventilation, and air conditioning) systems may result in temporary outages. Similarly, in IT, upgrading a server might lead to brief periods where an application is not accessible.

To address this, implementation tasks include an '**Impact**' field, allowing for the classification of the task's potential effects—using 'TOP' and 'HIGH' impact codes—to signify that the implementation may cause unavailability or degradation of services (such as reduced air conditioning efficiency) for multiple users.

When specifying an impact level, it's considered best practice to also identify which service instance(s) or configuration item(s) will be affected by the task. This not only clarifies the scope of impact but also aids in planning and communication with stakeholders. The upcoming chapter on 4me's best practice processes will offer further insight into leveraging this information within the framework of Change Enablement practices.

Figure 96: The impact of a change on the related service instance and configuration items.

Workflow Templates:

Crafting the Foundation of Efficient Workflows

Workflow templates serve as the architectural blueprint from which workflows are generated. After defining the task templates that will create the tasks—the fundamental components of any workflow—these elements are assembled within a workflow template to produce an operational workflow. Before delving into the nuances of constructing a workflow schedule by linking task templates into a predefined sequence, it's beneficial to explore some of the key attributes found in the workflow template record.

Workflow Categories: Balancing Standardization and Flexibility

The drive to standardize procedures is pivotal for organizations aiming to scale operations efficiently and boost predictability and customer satisfaction. Consequently, the primary emphasis in developing workflows through workflow templates is placed on the **'Standard'** category.

However, the dynamic nature of service delivery in a rapidly evolving landscape introduces unpredictability. There are scenarios where an organization may embark on unfamiliar ventures, accompanied by both known and unknown risks. For significant initiatives demanding extensive resources and substantial budgets, formal **project management** or **agile methodologies** are typically employed. Yet, for smaller endeavors—those estimated at less than 10 days of effort and involving only a single team—a **'Non-**

Standard' workflow may be more appropriate. In such workflows, the workflow manager plays an active role, adjusting tasks and scheduling as necessary. Organizations should establish clear policies for managing non-standard changes, including risk assessments and requisite approvals. The non-standard change process within IT Change Enablement offers a valuable model.

Urgent circumstances also necessitate deviations from standard procedures. Whether it's addressing immediate dismissals, accommodating tight proposal deadlines in presales, or deploying hotfixes for IT outages, **'Emergency'** workflow templates provide a framework for swift action. Policies outlining emergency protocols typically allow for expedited approvals by designated line managers, with post-factum registrations ensuring compliance with all relevant rules and regulations. The emergency change process within IT Change Enablement offers a valuable model.

Additionally, there exists a fourth category: the **'Order'** workflow template. These templates are specifically designed for use within the 4me Shop and will be further explored in the chapter dedicated to the 4me Shop.

Workflow Justification and Types: Guiding Strategic Investments

Understanding the allocation of resources is crucial for the management of any service delivery organization. It's essential to discern whether spending is directed towards expansion, improvement, maintenance, or compliance. To facilitate this understanding, the **'Justification'** field is incorporated both in the workflow template and the workflows generated from it.

For instances where an additional layer of classification is required beyond category and justification, the account administrator has the capability to define **'Workflow Types'** within the Settings console. This feature allows for further segmentation and reporting on workflow initiatives. For example, within the IT domain, distinguishing between changes made to infrastructure versus applications can offer valuable insights.

The Service Association of Workflow Templates

Designating a service to a workflow template is not a requisite. This flexibility might raise eyebrows, considering the workflows generated are typically associated with a service. Opting not to link a workflow template to any service renders it 'free-floating,' making it versatile enough to be utilized for various requests or problems.

This characteristic is particularly beneficial for managing 'non-standard' and 'emergency' workflows, which embody the overarching policies of a service delivery organization rather than being tied to a singular service. These types of workflows are often initiated manually in connection with a specific request, at which point the service association is derived automatically from the related request.

For standard workflow templates, however, specifying a service is advisable. Be aware that when linking a request template to a workflow template, only those workflow templates associated with the same service as the request template are selectable.

Breaking through the Organizational Silo's

Workflow Collaboration Between Different 4me Accounts

A major obstacle to efficient procedure execution is the difficulty of navigating through organizational silos. These barriers frequently result in procedural delays, miscommunication, and errors, ultimately undermining the quality of end-to-end processes.

A key strength of the 4me platform is its capability to break down these barriers. Within 4me, service delivery organizations are configured as accounts. Establishing a trust relationship between accounts allows these accounts to collaborate effectively. As detailed in the previous chapter, service hierarchies and their associated SLAs can span multiple accounts, providing a channel for requests to flow seamlessly from one account to another.

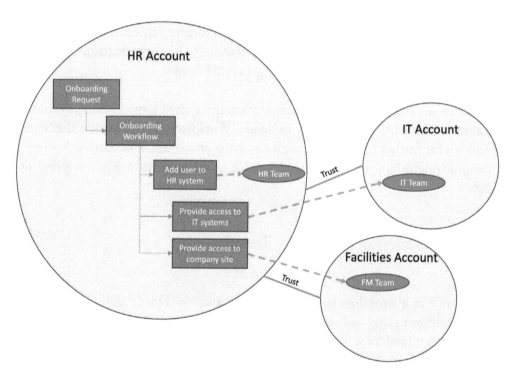

Figure 97: Assigning tasks to teams in trusted accounts.

Embracing a similar ethos, workflows can extend across different accounts. Through account trust settings, an account administrator can specify that their account is open to receiving tasks from another account.

However, allowing a trusted account to assign tasks within your account raises data protection concerns, especially when the trusted organization is entirely separate. There may be reservations about permitting specialists in the trusted account to access all personnel and teams within your organization.

To facilitate workflow collaboration between two trusted accounts while safeguarding personal data, the following trust settings are available for the account administrators:

- ***Trusted Account* can assign workflow approval tasks to anyone in our account**: When enabled, workflow managers in the trusted account can view and assign any individual in your account as approvers for approval tasks. This setting grants comprehensive access to all personnel in your account for the purpose of approval task assignment.
- ***Trusted Account* can assign workflow tasks to our key contacts and specialists**: Selecting this option restricts the visibility of the trusted account to key contacts and specialists when assigning approval tasks.

For Risk & Impact and Implementation tasks, which are typically assigned to a team, enabling this setting allows specialists in the trusted account to view all your teams when assigning tasks. However, further refinement is possible; by selecting specific teams, you limit the trusted account's visibility exclusively to those teams.

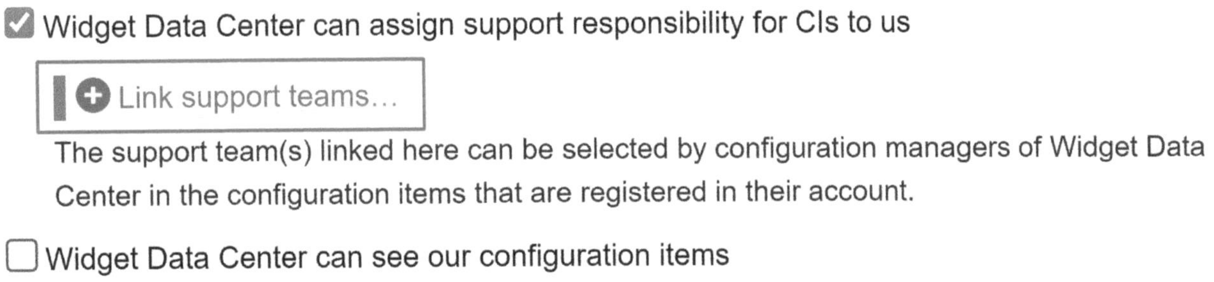

☑ Widget Data Center can assign support responsibility for CIs to us

The support team(s) linked here can be selected by configuration managers of Widget Data Center in the configuration items that are registered in their account.

☐ Widget Data Center can see our configuration items

Figure 98: Allowing task assignment from a trusted account with the possibility to limit the assignment to certain teams.

Orchestration at Work:

Using Request Generation to Streamline Multiple Workflows

Procedures often encompass nested, more detailed procedures. An illustrative case is the HR onboarding workflow, which, at a glance, may seem straightforward with steps like:

1. Defining the user in HR systems.
2. Granting the user access to IT systems.
3. Providing the user access to company sites and buildings.

Yet, within IT, granting system access is far from a singular task; it unfolds as a comprehensive workflow comprising multiple tasks. IT departments, seeking autonomy over their processes, prefer not to have HR embed these tasks within the HR workflow.

Instead, IT adds an '*IT Access*' service to their catalog, which includes everything needed, such as a service instance, a service offering, and a '*Give the user access to IT systems*' request template. They also set up an SLA (Service Level Agreement) for this service, considering HR as the customer.

HR defines who gets this service by setting the SLA coverage for their team. In the HR onboarding workflow template the task template, '*Give the user access to IT systems*' is assigned to the HR team.

Here's what happens when the HR onboarding workflow is started:

- The '*Give the user access to IT systems*' task is assigned to the HR team.
- An HR team member registers a new request using the 'IT Access' service and chooses the 'Give the user access to IT systems' template. The status of the HR task is set to 'Waiting for ….'.
- Over in IT, this kicks off the request with a workflow to set up the access.
- Once IT finishes the setup, the workflow and request are completed.
- The HR team member receives a notification.
- The HR team member then completes the task in the HR Onboarding workflow.

While manageable, this manual process does impose a burden on HR.

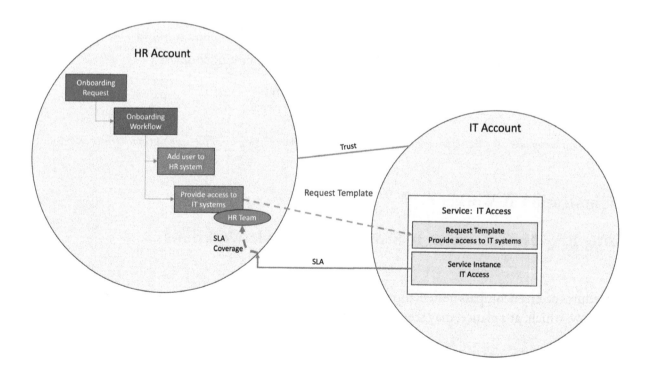

Figure 99: The manual procedure. An HR team member will register a request to IT for the IT access.

Indeed, 4me offers the capability to automate these manual steps through simple configuration. Within both task templates and tasks, a '*Request Template*' field facilitates end-to-end automation. By selecting the IT account's request template within an HR task template, a request is automatically generated in the IT account upon assignment, logically linking the HR task and IT request. Subsequently, the HR task status shifts to '*Request Pending*', removing it from any inbox as the action moves to the IT request. Upon completion of the associated IT workflow, the HR task is updated to 'Completed', all without requiring manual intervention.

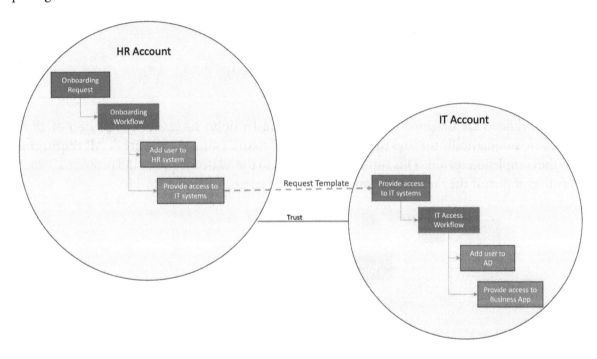

Figure 100: Request generation allowing fully automated linking of two workflows in two different accounts.

Don't Forget about the Service Instance

When linking a request template to a task template the option to select a service instance becomes available. It's crucial to remember that requests, of the category incident, RFI or RFC, must always be connected to a specific service instance. The best practice is to explicitly specify the service instance in the task template. This will avoid issues when multiple service instances are available and the 4me platform is not able to determine the appropriate service instance to select.

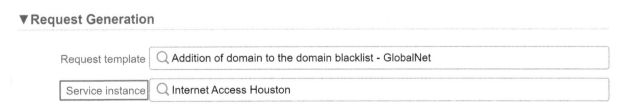

Figure 101: Request generation in a task template. It is a good practice to select the service instance.

Orchestrating Between Request and Related Workflow

The seamless integration of a request template with a workflow template automates the creation of a workflow upon request initiation. 4me ensures synchronization between the workflow, its tasks, and any related requests, establishing a harmonious operation. This section delves into the key principles of this orchestration.

Workflow Escalation on Failure: Managing Disruptions

Standard workflows are designed to operate autonomously; upon successful completion of all tasks, the workflow automatically updates to the '**Completed**' status, citing '**Complete – All requirements met**' as the completion reason. This automation extends to the related requests and problems, which are set to auto-complete if they're in the 'Workflow Pending' status.

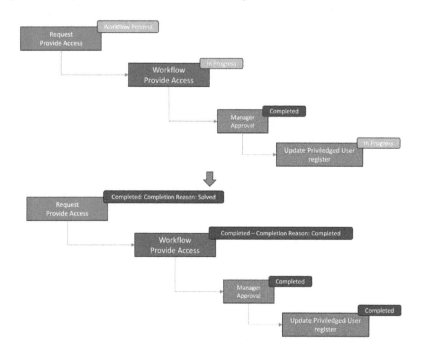

Figure 102: On workflow completion, the related request is autocompleted.

However, the path of standard workflows is not always smooth. Consider a scenario where an end user submits a request for a high-specification PC using a standard request template. This request, due to its cost or specific requirements, may face rejection from a business unit manager via an assigned approval task, causing the workflow to enter the '**Progress Halted**' status. The workflow manager is then alerted to intervene and determine the next steps. Similarly, if the business unit manager approves the request but the requested PC model is out of stock, the tasked IT specialist might mark the task as '**Failed**', again halting the workflow's progress and prompting an action from the *workflow manager*.

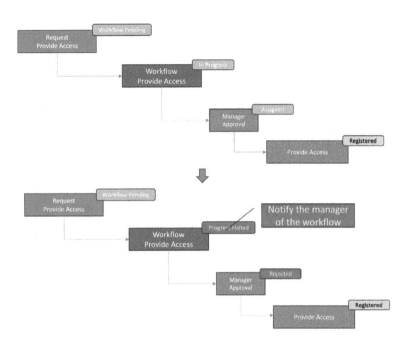

Figure 103: When the workflow fails, the workflow gets the status 'Progress Halted' and the workflow manager is involved. A workflow fails when someone rejects an approval task or when a specialist sets the status of a task to 'Failed'.

The critical decision for the *workflow manager* in such situations is whether to conclude the workflow with a 'Rejected' or 'Failed' reason. Directly auto-completing the associated request or problem might bypass the opportunity to communicate effectively with the requester about the failure and discuss possible alternatives. Hence, a related request or problem is only automatically marked as completed if its status is 'Workflow Pending' and the workflow concludes successfully.

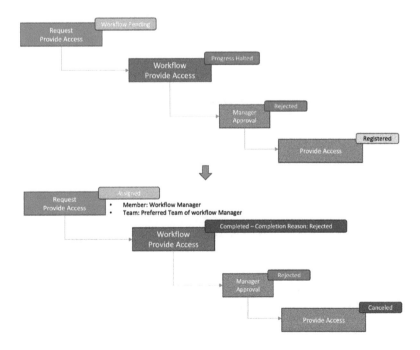

Figure 104: When the workflow is unsuccessfully completed, the related request is assigned to the workflow manager.

Assigning the requests or problems related to a failed workflow necessitates thoughtful consideration. By default, this responsibility falls to the *workflow manager*, presumed to be well-versed in the workflow's intricacies. When the workflow manager sets a workflow to 'Completed' and indicates in the Completion reason field that the execution was not entirely successful, the related requests and problems that are in the status 'Workflow Pending' are automatically updated to the status 'Assigned'. This normally ensures that these requests and problems are assigned to the *workflow manager* so that this person can inform the requesters and problem managers about the situation.

Yet, in specific circumstances, such as the procurement of new PC equipment, it might be more apt to assigning the request to a dedicated support team, like Personal Computing. This adjustment can be configured in the workflow template with the checkbox '**Assign related requests and problems to workflow manager**'. When unchecked and when a workflow is related to a request or problem, the actual assignment of the request or problem upon the unsuccessful completion of the workflow will not be modified.

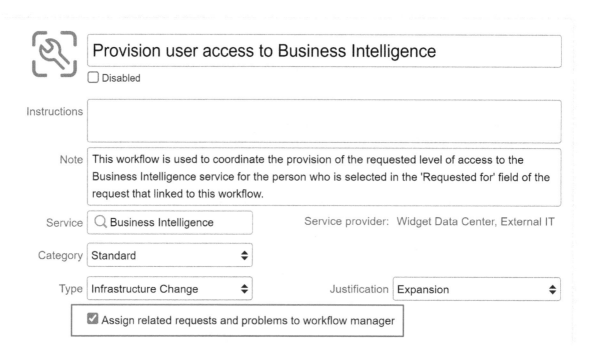

Figure 105: Defining the assignment of the related requests and workflow on a workflow template.template, the workflow manager can be set.

Identifying the Manager of the Workflow

Determining the manager of a workflow is straightforward when the workflow is manually initiated, typically being the individual who creates it. When a workflow is automatically generated through the linkage of a workflow template there are two possibilities:

- The workflow manager can be selected on the request template while linking a workflow template.

Figure 106: When linking a workflow template to a request template, the workflow manager can be set.

- A recommended strategy is to leverage the service-oriented architecture of 4me, which facilitates the designation of a *change manager* for each service. This *change manager* is tasked with overseeing service modifications, including the management of the workflows related to the service. If the *workflow manager* is not specified in the request template, the *change manager* of the service will become the workflow manager.

Seamless Continuation Beyond Workflow Completion

In certain cases, it may be advantageous to continue working on a request even after the associated workflow has been completed.

A common example includes standard requests that only require approval. For these instances, a straightforward workflow consisting solely of a manager's approval task suffices. To facilitate continued action on the request post-workflow completion, the **'Assign after workflow completion'** option can be enabled within the request template. This approach ensures that after the approval has been provided, the request is set to 'Assigned' so that a specialist will start to work on it.

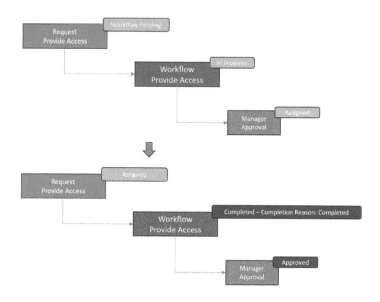

Figure 107: Continue working on the request on completion of the workflow.

Concurrent Visibility and Management of Requests and Workflows

When setting request to the 'Assigned' status while its workflow is still progressing, the request will become visible in team inboxes. This enables a specialist to concurrently address the request while others work on the tasks of the workflow.

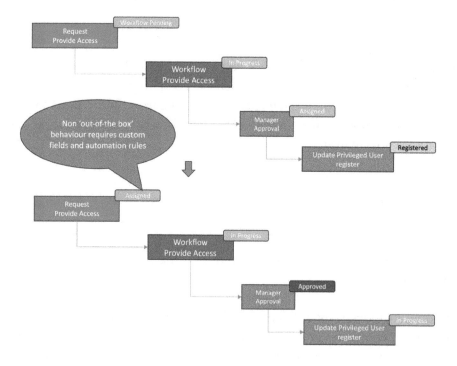

Figure 108: In this scenario it is more efficient to assign the request to the support team once the manager has approved the task. The last task in the workflow can be processed in parallel with the task.

This approach proves beneficial under specific conditions. For example, consider a scenario involving a request and workflow template designed to grant IT system access. This process includes an approval task followed by request assignment to the service's support team for access provision. However, when administrator access is given, an extra task must be performed to register the user on a Privileged User register. In this scenario, it's impractical to delay request assignment until this last task is finalized. By setting the request to 'Assigned', work progresses independently on both the request and the workflow without waiting for the workflow task's completion.

It's important to highlight that effectively managing this scenario involves leveraging automation rules to overwrite the out-of-the box 'Workflow Pending' status based on a certain event. Further details on customizing workflows with automation rules will be covered in a forthcoming chapter.

Crafting the Workflow Schedule

After finalizing the task templates and the overarching workflow template, the next step involves establishing the workflow schedule. This schedule outlines a sequential or parallel flow of tasks required for execution.

Grouping the task templates into phases will later help communicate workflow progress to requesters. While it's not necessary to disclose every detail of the workflow to requesters, providing them with updates on major milestones helps in managing their expectations and reducing inquiries to the service delivery organization.

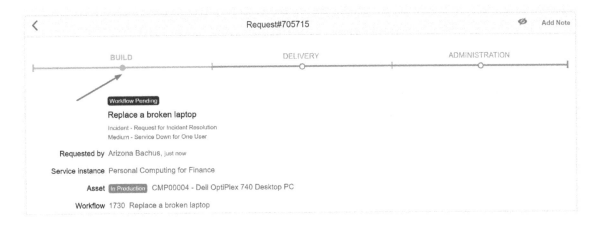

Figure 109: The workflow phases are exposed to the requester in the self-service portal.

Connections are then established between predecessor and successor tasks through a straightforward drag-and-drop interface: by clicking the green dot behind the predecessor task and dragging it to the successor task.

We've previously discussed how workflow failures, such as the rejection of an approval task or the failure of a task, result in the workflow's status updating to 'Progress Halted' and the subsequent notification of the workflow manager. However, not all deviations necessitate halting progress. For scenarios where a standard fallback plan exists for rejections or task failures, an exception or rework flow can be defined.

Workflow Control: Exception Flows

To navigate alternative paths in the event of rejections or failures, exception flows can be delineated within the workflow's Gantt chart. This involves creating two distinct pathways from a predecessor task to its successor: one for success and another for failure. To define the failure path, instead of simply clicking the green dot behind the task and dragging it to the successor task, the shift or control key must be pressed and held while dragging. This action transforms the green dot into a red dot, and dragging it to the desired successor task creates a red, dashed line.

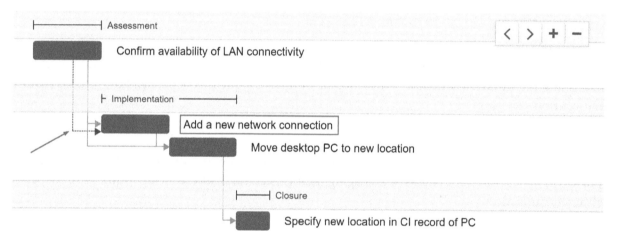

Figure 110: Defining an exception flow

Consider a workflow for installing a network printer. The process starts with an assessment to verify network connectivity at the intended location. Depending on the outcome, the workflow diverges:

Successful Assessment:

- The task to "Install network printer" is set to "Assigned".
- The task to "Add network connection" is marked as "Canceled".

Failed Assessment:

- The task to "Install network printer" remains "Registered".
- The task to "Add network connection" is set to "Assigned".
- After completing the "Add network connection" task, the workflow resumes with the "Install network printer" task being assigned.

Exception Flows

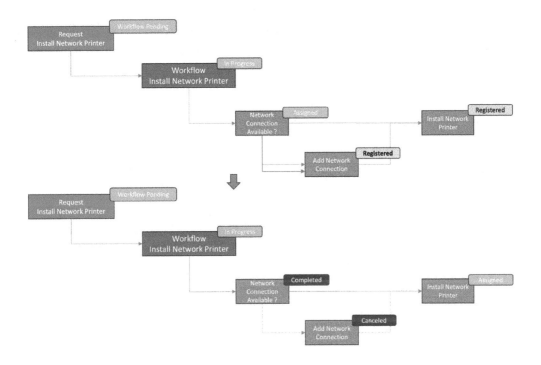

Figure 111: Check the good-day scenario in an exception flow.

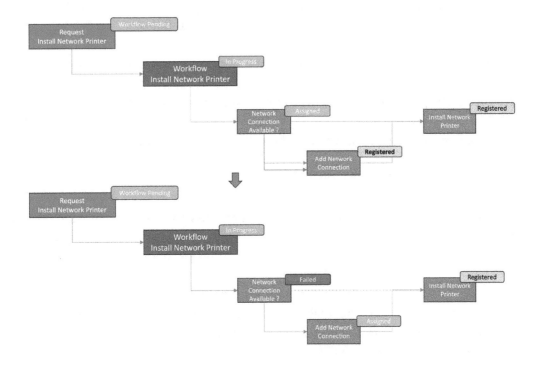

Figure 111: Check the bad-day scenario in an exception flow.

Workflow Control: Rework Loops for Process Iteration

In various operational scenarios, a rejection or task failure requires revisiting previous steps in the workflow rather than halting progress or diverting to an alternative path. This iterative process is facilitated through the creation of rework loops, enabling workflows to dynamically adapt to feedback and corrections.

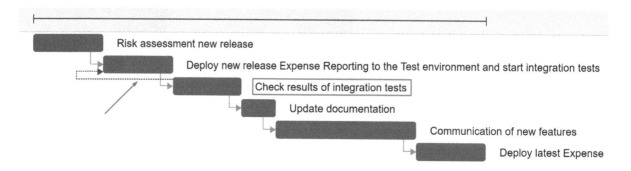

Figure 112: Example of a rework loop.

Rework loops are established similarly to exception flows within the Gantt Chart of a workflow template. However, rather than progressing to a subsequent task of an alternative branch, the workflow is designed to loop back to a preceding task for revaluation or correction. This is achieved by linking a task back to a previous task with the aid of the shift or control key, signifying the loop back for rework.

An illustrative example of rework loops in action involves a Managed Service Provider (MSP) handling a customer's request for a minor enhancement. The process unfolds as follows:

Initial Analysis: The MSP evaluates the enhancement request and formulates a proposal.

Approval Request: The proposal is submitted to the customer for approval.

Upon receiving the customer's response, the workflow diverges based on the decision:

Approval Granted:

- The task to implement the enhancement is activated ('Assigned' status), moving the workflow forward towards completion.

Rejection:

- The workflow loops back to the analysis phase allowing for adjustments or clarifications to the proposal. The analysis task gets the status 'Assigned' and the tasks 'Create a proposal and 'Customer approval of the proposal' tasks are returned to the status 'Registered'.
- The implementation task remains in 'Registered' status, on standby until the revised proposal gains approval.

Rework Flows

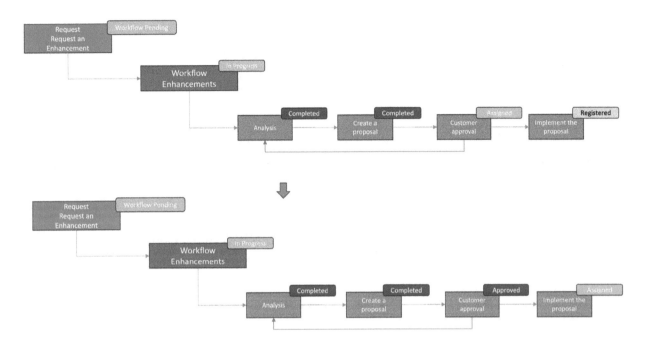

Figure 113: Check the good-day scenario in a rework loop.

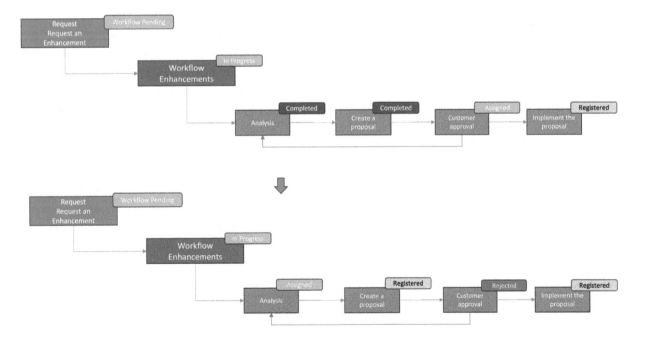

Figure 113: Check the bad-day scenario in a rework loop.

Note the potential for a workflow to become indefinitely entangled within a rework loop if continual rejections occur. To prevent such scenarios, the 4me platform monitors the number of rejections for each approval task. If an approval task is rejected **10 times**, the system intervenes by halting the rework loop, and the workflow status automatically updates to 'Progress Halted.'

Workflow Control: Mastering Recurring Workflows

Recurring workflows are essential for tasks that necessitate regular execution, whether for compliance, HR evaluations, or maintenance purposes. These workflows ensure tasks are consistently performed and documented, fulfilling both operational and audit requirements.

Examples of Recurring Tasks

- **Compliance Controls**: Certain frameworks mandate annual verification of privileged access registers.
- **HR and People Operations**: Team leads are often required to conduct annual performance reviews with their members.
- **Facilities and IT Maintenance**: Routine tasks must be scheduled daily, weekly, monthly, or yearly to maintain operational integrity.

Key Considerations for Recurring Workflows

- **Consistency**: : By scheduling recurring tasks they will not be accidentally forgotten.
- **Auditability**: Documentation of task completion is automatically captured as proof for audits.

Recurring workflows, facilitated by the Recurrence section in a workflow template, are straightforward to set up and manage. Note that at least one task template must be incorporated into the workflow for actionable execution.

A potential hiccup in scheduling is the occurrence of tasks on bank holidays. To mitigate this, workflows can be linked to a calendar excluding such days, ensuring tasks are triggered on the next available workday.

Figure 114: A recurring workflow template. By specifying a calendar the workflow will only be scheduled during normal support hours excluding bank holidays.

Managing Recurring Workflows

Each recurring workflow necessitates a *workflow manager* to oversee operations in case of any issues. Recurring workflows allow the selection of a *Manager* directly within the Recurrence section. Alternatively, leaving this field blank defaults the responsibility to the *change manager* of the associated service.

Workflows and Workflow Templates
Data Protection Request Templates

In this demonstration, we'll observe the process of managing a request involving a single approval task is managed from initiation to completion. Randy Barton, the financial controller at Widget, needs to register a new product in SAP in preparation of its upcoming product launch. This task requires approval from Randy's manager, Jim Lithgow. Once Jim has approved the request, Bert Jansen, the SAP expert at Widget, will proceed and register the product.

Randy logs in as **randy.barton@widget.com** at **Widget International**:

- He navigates to 'New Request'.
- Randy selects the Information Technology support domain.
- From the list, he chooses Enterprise Resource Planning (SAP).
- Next, he selects the request template 'Register new Widget product in SAP'.
- Finally he fills out the form and submits the request.

Jim, Randy's manager, logs in as **jim.lithgow@widget.com** at **Widget International**:

- He checks the Inbox.
- He selects the task that is waiting for his approval.
- He checks the workflow summary PDF.
- He approves the task.

Bert, the SAP specialist, logs in as **bert.jansen@widget.com** at **Widget Europe, Information Technology**.

- He checks the Inbox.
- He selects the request from Randy.
- He notes that the related workflow is completed.
- Opening the workflow, he sees that it was Jim Lithgow who provided his approval.
- Backing out of the workflow, Bert follows the instructions and completes the request.

Chapter 8 -
Navigating the 4me User Interfaces

Exploring User Experience in 4me: When Simplicity Meets Speed

As we delve deeper into the world of 4me, having unraveled its architectural essence and foundational elements, we pivot towards a crucial aspect that ultimately defines its success: the user experience. This chapter is dedicated to understanding how both end users and specialists engage with the 4me platform, experiencing firsthand the benefits of its service-driven design.

At the heart of 4me's user experience lies its hallmark simplicity. Users interact with a system that, despite its complex orchestration and robust architecture, presents a straightforward and intuitive interface. End users seek quick resolutions to their inquiries and issues, largely indifferent to the sophisticated mechanics operating behind the scenes. Similarly, specialists aim to perform their duties efficiently, relying on the platform to streamline their workload and minimize administrative effort. The service-driven backbone of 4me is instrumental in delivering this seamless experience, ensuring that both user groups can focus on their immediate needs without unnecessary complexity.

Moreover, 4me stands out as the fastest enterprise service management system available, boasting average transaction times of less than 0.5 seconds. This exceptional performance is akin to navigating the digital equivalent of a luxury sports car: users enjoy the ride, oblivious to the powerful engine and innovative technology under the hood. They simply benefit from the speed, reliability, and comfort, confident in their swift and safe arrival at their desired outcomes.

This chapter invites you to buckle up and explore the interfaces that make 4me a leader in user satisfaction and operational efficiency, underscoring why it's heralded as the fastest enterprise service management system on the planet.

The End User Perspective

In the world of 4me, users are provided with a variety of access channels, ensuring they can reach out for support or information through the means most convenient for them. Here are the five primary ways users can connect with 4me:

1. **The Self-Service Portal**: This is the central hub for all users, designed as a one-stop shop for accessing services, information, and support. It's where users can submit and track requests, find answers in knowledge articles, and much more.
2. **The 4me Mobile App**: For those on the move, the 4me app brings the power of the self-service portal to iOS and Android devices. It offers a streamlined interface tailored for mobile use, ensuring

users can request help, update tickets, and access services anytime, anywhere.

3. **Phone Support**: Users can reach out to the service desk via telephone. This traditional method is enhanced by 4me's Computer Telephony Integration (CTI), allowing service desk analysts to efficiently log and manage requests during the call.

4. **Inbound Email**: Submitting requests or reporting issues can be as simple as sending an email. 4me seamlessly integrates email-based communications into its service management process, ensuring these interactions are tracked and managed just like any other request.

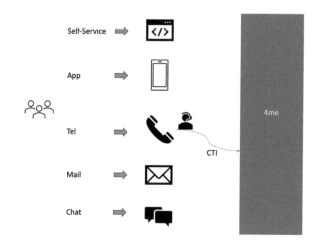

Figure 115: The available channels for a user to connect with the 4me platform.

5. **Chat and Virtual Agent**: Users can contact the Service Desk via support chat or even via the Virtual Agent, advanced chatbot technology integrated in 4me.

The Self-Service Portal

In the corporate landscape, employees typically access services through the directory account's self-service portal. External customers, on the other hand, connect via a customer-specific account. A Managed Service Provider (MSP) can set up (external) customer organizations in various ways, as discussed: within their own directory account, a support domain account, or through a trusted account structure. Regardless of the setup, each 4me account features a distinct self-service portal, customizable to reflect the account's unique branding and design. Users can access their account's self-service portal via a URL structured as follows:

https://account-id.account-domain/**self-service**

For instance, accessing the demo environment's Widget International directory account would be through https://widget.4me-demo.com/self-service. End users need not append /self-service to the URL; they're automatically redirected to the self-service portal upon login.

Best Practice

A user can function as a specialist in one support domain account and as an end user in another support domain account. That's why specialists will occasionally log in to the self-service portal of the directory account. To streamline access for specialists who primarily log into support domain accounts, it's beneficial to set up a **Custom Link** directly to the self-service portal. An account administrator can add custom links via the option with the same name in the Settings console. Custom links are URLs that are conveniently shared within the Actions menu (the gear button in the toolbar).

The Self-Service Design

The self-service portal serves as the primary interface between your organization and those seeking support, whether they are employees within the company or external customers. As a digital embodiment of your service delivery organization, the self-service portal not only facilitates access to support and services but also significantly influences the perception of service excellence. For many users, it represents the initial point of interaction with your organization.

Recognizing this critical role, 4me has dedicated substantial effort to ensuring that its self-service design technology adheres to the latest standards, culminating in the release of **Self Service v2**. This updated version offers an intuitive, user-friendly interface, and activating it within the Self Service Settings of the Settings console is highly recommended. There's no advantage to clinging to outdated versions when such an advanced option is available.

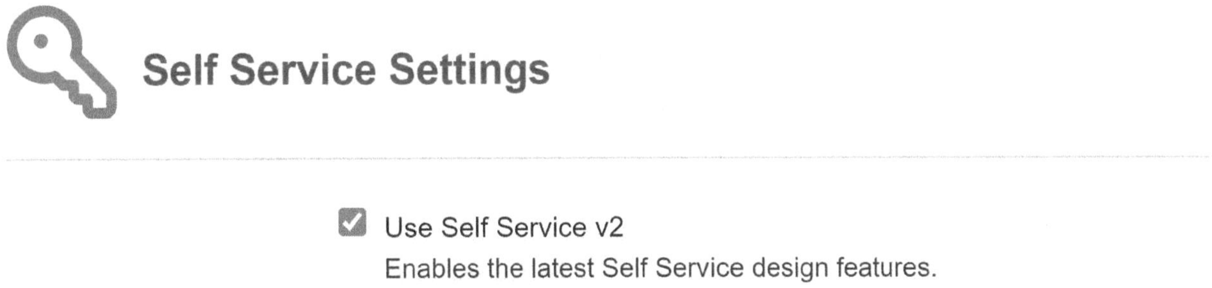

 **Self Service Settings**

☑ Use Self Service v2
Enables the latest Self Service design features.

Figure 116: Use Self Service v2.

To aid in the design of a compelling and effective self-service portal, 4me offers eight exemplary designs, ready for use and exploration in the demo environment. These designs, named after the demo accounts in which they have been set up, showcase a variety of aesthetics and functionalities to cater to diverse organizational needs: GlobalNet, Ultra Max Super Stores, GigaTera, Retter, Inc., Widget International, Widget Data Protection, Widget North America - Human Resources and VirtualSupport.

Within the Self-Service Design section, you have the ability to:

- Explore these pre-configured designs,
- Select and apply any design to your portal,
- Customize the selected design,
- Preview how the design appears on a mobile, tablet, and desktop devices,
- Toggle between light and dark modes to ensure accessibility.

The self-service design functionality provides the flexibility to customize elements such as HTML, CSS, and the background image, allowing for the creation of a portal that aligns perfectly with your organization's corporate identity and user experience goals. While a comprehensive guide on customizing the self-service design will be covered later, initially, leveraging one of the available designs and simply updating the logo is a straightforward process for those with basic web design skills.

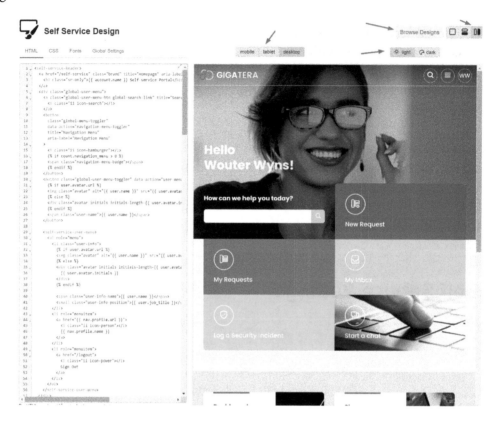

Figure 117: Browse through Self Service designs.

Optimizing the Multi-Language Experience on Your Self Service Portal

In today's global business environment, catering to the diverse linguistic needs to users is crucial for an enterprise service management platform. The 4me platform acknowledges this necessity by offering a self-service portal that supports multiple languages, making it a truly user-friendly solution for a global audience. This one-stop-shop enables users to obtain information or support in their native language.

4me's out-of-the-box self-service portal designs come with design elements that are pre-translated into more than 30 languages. This feature ensures that users are immediately greeted with a familiar linguistic environment. Additionally, when organizations incorporate custom phrases into their self-service design, these phrases are integrated into 4me's translation module. This allows administrators to add translations, further personalizing the experience for users.

While there are approximately 7,000 languages spoken worldwide, it is impractical for any organization, including 4me, to support every single one. Users have the option to select from 60 languages in their profile settings, with the potential for additional languages to be included in the future. However, it is important to manage expectations regarding language support. If a service portal offers a language option but does not provide complete translation for all content, users might encounter a mix of translated and untranslated text, leading to confusion and a disjointed experience. To prevent this, organizations have the flexibility to limit the number of languages they support on their portal, ensuring that each supported language offers a fully translated and coherent user interface.

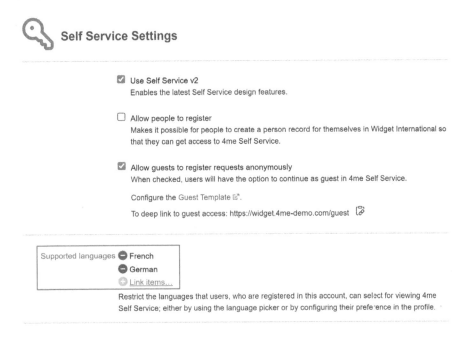

Figure 118: Limit the supported languages in the Self Service Settings.

Refining Support Domain Self Service Settings

The architecture of the Self-Service Portal in a multi-domain support environment is designed to ensure efficient access to necessary support services that can be spread over multiple support domains, such as HR, Finance and IT. The portal allows the users to navigate through the service catalog of each of these support domain accounts.

It's essential to understand the distinction between the design and functionality layers within this structure. While the design elements like colors and fonts for these pages are determined by the self-service design of the directory account, the actual behavior and content displayed are governed by the settings within each support domain account.

Now, let's delve into the specific Self Service Settings managed by each support domain account:

- **Allow requests to be submitted on behalf of someone else**: This setting enables users to submit requests on behalf of colleagues. In support domains focused on sensitive data like HR or security and data protection, this option is often disabled.
- **Allow shop articles to be ordered on behalf of someone else**: Similar to the above, this facilitates the ordering of shop articles on behalf of others.

- **Require the selection of a service**: This setting aims to refine the request submission process by ensuring users categorize their requests under specific services.
- **Require the selection of a request template**: By enforcing the use of predefined request templates, this setting helps standardize requests, facilitating more accurate team assignment, quicker resolution and consistency in service provision.
- **Allow knowledge article feedback**: Enabling this feature allows users to provide feedback on knowledge articles. In most support domains, it is recommended to enable this option.
- **Allow key contacts to see the assignee of requests**: This setting enhances transparency by allowing designated key contacts to view the assignee of requests.

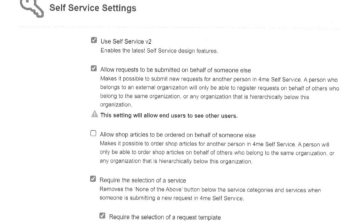

Figure 119: Self Service Settings in a support domain account.

Best Practice

A Managed Service Provider (MSP) should activate the '**Require the selection of a service**' and '**Require the selection of a request template**' options. This requires the MSP to precisely define the services and standard requests available to their customers, but it ensures that requests will be routed to the correct team with the information that team needs to work on it. Typically, this means that for each service, at least one request template should be established for incidents, information requests, and non-standard change requests.

The 4me Mobile App: Accessibility on the Go

The 4me platform extends its functionality beyond the desktop, offering a seamless mobile experience through its self-service portal. This feature is not limited to end users; it also caters to specialists, especially those in field service roles, with access to the My Inbox and the My Team's Inbox views. The mobile interface, designed with simplicity in mind, is fully responsive, ensuring optimal usability on both tablets and smartphones. The 4me app, compatible with iOS and Android devices, can be easily downloaded from the Apple App Store or Google Play Store. Upon installation, users are prompted to enter the account ID associated with their self-service portal, which is typically the ID of the directory account.

The Managed Configuration of Mobile Devices

In today's digital age, securing mobile access is paramount for enterprises. To enhance both security and user experience, many organizations implement a managed configuration for employee mobile devices, typically through Mobile Device Management (MDM) or Unified Endpoint Management (UEM) systems. The 4me app supports mobile device management by allowing the configuration of essential settings such as the *account URL* and *Single Sign-On (SSO)* references directly within an MDM or UEM system.

Figure 120: The 4me app using the responsive self-service design.

Phone Support and Computer Telephony Integration (CTI)

Despite the rapid advancement of digital communication channels, many support organizations continue to offer phone support to their customers. While it's perceived that this mode of support may diminish over time, it remains a vital channel for many users today. Traditional phone support can introduce inefficiencies, such as wait times for callers and the need for service desk analysts to manually verify the caller's identity.

To streamline this process, the 4me platform integrates with Computer Telephony Integration (CTI) technology. This integration enables automatic identification of the caller through their phone number or a provided support ID. Consequently, the service desk analyst's console can automatically display the relevant user as soon as the call is connected. Furthermore, if the caller mentions a specific ticket ID during the call, the corresponding request can be instantly accessed, significantly reducing the duration of calls and improving the customer experience.

For organizations looking to enhance their phone support capabilities, implementing CTI with the 4me platform is straightforward. Detailed specifications and setup instructions are available on the 4me Developer site: https://developer.4me.com/v1/cti.

Inbound Email

Inbound Email Addresses and Processing in 4me Accounts

Every 4me account is assigned a unique inbound email address that adheres to a standardized format. This email address structure allows for the direct submission of emails into the 4me system, facilitating the creation of requests, notes and even person records from those emails. The format for these inbound email addresses is as follows:

- For general emails: account-id@mail.environment
- For team-specific emails: team-email-identity.account-id@mail.environment

The table below outlines the specific domains used for inbound email addresses across different 4me environments, segmented by region:

Region	QA Environment	PROD environment
Australia	*account-id*@mail.au.4me.qa	*account-id*@mail.au.4me.com
Europe	*account-id*@mail.4me.qa	*account-id*@mail.4me.com
Switzerland	*account-id*@mail.ch.4me.qa	*account-id*@mail.ch.4me.com
United Kingdom	*account-id*@mail.uk.4me.qa	*account-id*@mail.uk.4me.com
United States	*account-id*@mail.us.4me.qa	*account-id*@mail.us.4me.com

Upon receiving an email, it is first placed into the Inbound Email queue, accessible by the account administrators. This queue acts as a preliminary holding area where emails undergo initial scrutiny—a "sanity check" aimed at filtering out spam and potentially harmful content. Only emails that pass this initial security assessment are processed further.

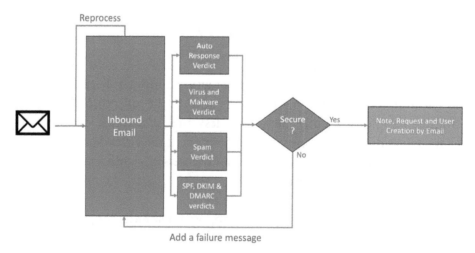

Figure 121: Step 1 in the inbound email process: the sanity checks.

The subsequent processing of an inbound email is governed by the Email Policy settings specific to the account.

Bidirectional Communication through Email Replies in 4me

Enabling seamless communication between service delivery organizations and their clients or external partners is crucial for efficient service management. This is particularly relevant when email notifications are sent out requiring input from a customer—such as through the "Waiting for Customer" status—or when reaching out to a key contact of a supplier not integrated within the 4me platform via email from a note. The expectation is for these parties to respond promptly, with their replies being automatically added to the relevant 4me record as notes.

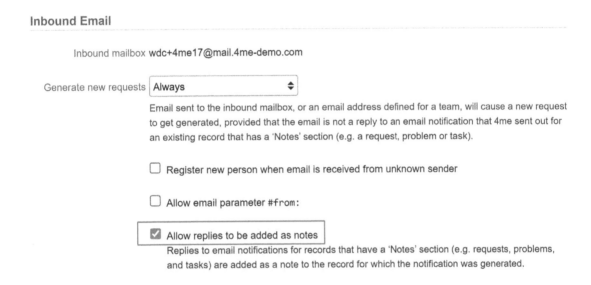

Figure 122: Inbound email policy: allow replies to be added as notes.

To facilitate this process, the "**Allow replies to be added as notes**" option must be activated within the Inbound Email section of the email policy settings. With this feature enabled, 4me employs email threading to associate incoming emails with their original threads initiated by 4me. This capability is based on the analysis of Message-IDs, which are unique identifiers stored in the hidden headers of email messages. Email clients use these IDs to ascertain whether an incoming email is part of an ongoing conversation. Leveraging this functionality, 4me can append incoming emails as notes to the corresponding 4me record, thereby enhancing collaboration with external entities.

Consider a scenario where an email is dispatched from a 4me note to an external supplier's contact who is not predefined in 4me. If the contact replies and includes a colleague in the Cc field, and the colleague subsequently joins the email thread while keeping the original 4me-generated email in Cc, the 4me system will recognize the incoming message as part of the conversation. Consequently, it will add the email as a note to the relevant 4me record, even if the new participant wasn't initially defined within the 4me environment.

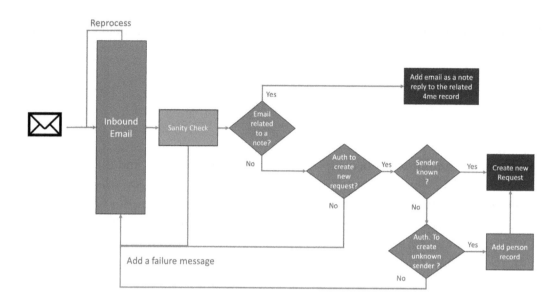

Figure 123: Step 2 of the inbound email process.

In situations where incoming emails lack associated message-IDs, 4me attempts to match the conversation to existing records by scanning the email's subject and body for numerical strings that could correspond to a ticket ID within the recipient's account. Successfully identifying a match ensures that the reply is appropriately appended as a note to the corresponding ticket.

Generating New Requests via Inbound Email in 4me

Creating new requests through inbound email is a feature available in 4me, contingent upon the **'Generate new requests'** setting's activation. While this capability can streamline request submissions, it's crucial for service delivery organizations to carefully consider its implications. Email submissions often omit critical details required for comprehensive request processing. For instance, a Human Resources department requiring specific information for job openings might use a form with mandatory fields to ensure all necessary data is captured. Relying on email for such requests could result in missing information and additional overhead for HR staff to transfer data from emails to the structured form and having to contact the sender for any missing information.

However, for Managed Service Providers (MSPs) or customer support operations in a B2C (Business to Consumer) environment, email might be the most practical or even the only viable channel. In these cases, a notable challenge is the automatic association of the email sender with the requester role in the new request. Particularly for MSPs or customer support, the email sender might not be previously registered in the 4me account. Enabling the **"Register new person when email is received from unknown sender"** option within the inbound email policy allows the auto-creation of a person record for the sender. The person record will be associated with the default organization specified in the account settings. This default organization typically ensures end-user privacy, restricting visibility and interaction with other users, which is ideally suited for B2C contexts.

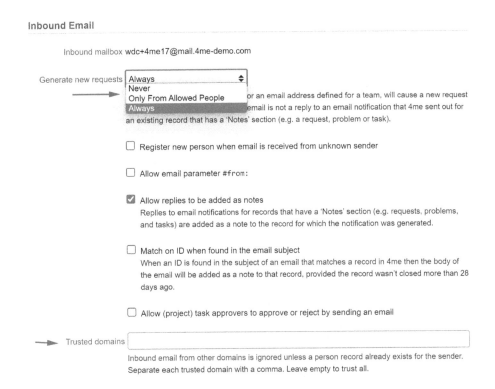

Figure 124: The Inbound Email section in the Email Policy of a 4me account to specify whether new requests can be generated.

In an MSP scenario, further steps might be necessary to associate the new user with the correct customer organization and potentially assign a key contact role, either as part of manual request processing or through automation.

For MSPs concerned about security and misuse, a recommended practice is to accept emails exclusively from customer domains. This can be achieved by specifying '**Trusted domains**' within the inbound email policy settings, enhancing control over who can generate requests via email.

Note that the 4me platform cannot link a simple, unstructured email to a specific service. Instead, such emails will be categorized under 'Other'. The resulting request will be assigned to the account's first-line team, as specified in the **First Line Support Agreement**.

Inbound Email Policy Integration Parameters

4me's inbound email functionality can also serve as a straightforward method for establishing integrations, particularly with monitoring systems. The inbound email API includes parameters for automatically categorizing requests, associating them with specific configuration items, and linking them to the appropriate service instance. Additional parameters relevant to integrations include:

- *Generate new requests from allowed people*: allowing creation of new requests from specified sources, typically to accommodate alerts from monitoring applications.

- *Allow email parameter #from*: to facilitate submissions from web forms or support portals directly into 4me. The use of the #from parameter allows the correct requester to be linked to each new request.
- *Skip auto response check*: disabling auto-response checks to prevent the system from rejecting emails containing auto-response headers, ensuring seamless integration feedback.

These integration capabilities will be detailed further in the subsequent chapter on Integrating with 4me.

Approval by Email

Email serves as a user-friendly medium for managing approvals, even when compared to interacting with a self-service portal. Many managers who frequently receive approval requests prefer this approval option. They often find it more convenient to respond with a straightforward yes or no via email, possibly from their smartphone, rather than first navigating to the self-service portal.

However, approving via email, while convenient, raises security concerns. Since this process doesn't require logging into 4me, it's imperative to ensure the organization's email system is securely configured to authenticate the identity of the person responding to the approval request. Please consult with your organization's security office to determine if email-based approvals are permissible within your organization.

To activate approvals by emails, 4me includes a specific setting within the 'Email Policy' section titled **'Allow (project) task approvers to approve or reject by sending an email.'** This setting, when enabled, allows the 4me platform to determine the nature of the reply—approval or rejection—by scanning for a predefined token. The standard tokens for approval and rejection are set to ✔ and ✖, respectively, though they can be customized in the email policy settings.

☑ Allow (project) task approvers to approve or reject by sending an email

⚠ Approving by email is less secure than approving via the user interface.

Approval token

| ✔ |

This token will be placed in the subject of (project) task-approval emails and recognized by 4me as an approval of the related (project) task.

Rejection token

| ✖ |

This token will be placed in the subject of (project) task-rejection emails and recognized by 4me as a rejection of the related (project) task.

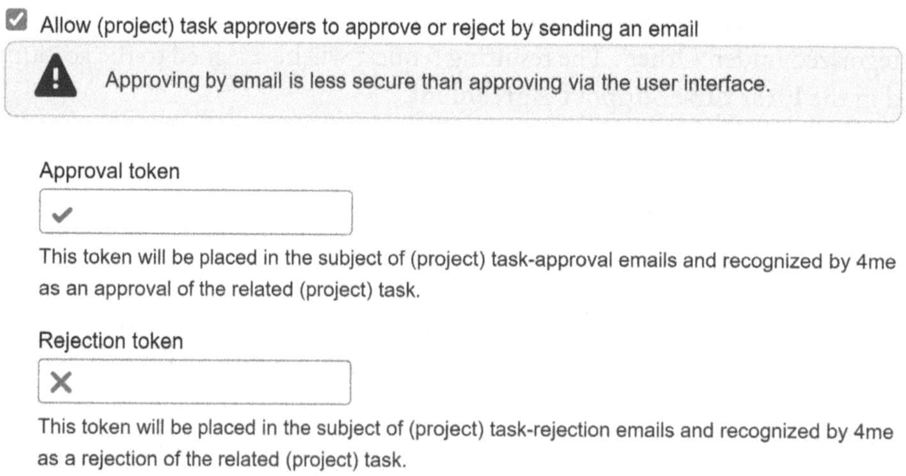

Figure 125: Allow approvals by email in the Email Policy settings.

For the email-based approval mechanism to function, modifications to the task approval email templates are necessary. Typically, such an email template would include links directing the approver to the self-service portal for approving or rejecting tasks. These can be substituted with specific email template fields designed for workflow task and project task approvals, namely '*Task Assigned to Approver*' and '*Project Task Approver Assignment*', incorporating {{approve_task_by_email_link}} and {{reject_task_by_email_link}} fields.

When an approver clicks on these links within an approval email, a preformatted reply is generated, containing the appropriate token and task ID. Whether a note is required in the body of the approval email depends on the configuration within the 'Note behavior' field of the task template. For rejections, providing a reason within the email body is always mandatory. Responses to approvals and rejections conducted via email are recorded as notes within the associated task.

Support Chat and the Virtual Agent

In the evolving landscape of customer support, there is a noticeable shift from traditional telephony to digital methods such as chat for instant communication between end users and support organizations. Within the 4me platform, this modern approach is facilitated through the **Support Chat** feature and the integration of a chatbot, known as the **Virtual Agent**. Users have the convenience of contacting the service desk either via support chat or through the advanced capabilities of the virtual agent, or both.

Setting up the support chat feature in 4me is straightforward and user-friendly. To enable this feature, the '**Allow support chats**' option must be selected in the Self-Service Settings of the support domain account.

Each support account independently determines whether to make Support Chat available to their users. In the Self-Service Design ensure the 'Show Support Chat' option is checked under Global Settings. This step adds the support chat button to the self-service portal.

Figure 126: Support chat on the self-service portal.

Once these steps are completed and assuming a user is covered by an SLA for at least one service within an account that provides support chat, the Support Chat feature will appear in the bottom-right corner of the self-service portal. For end users eligible for services across multiple support domains with Support Chat enabled, they must first select the appropriate support domain.

☑ Allow support chats

Allow covered users in 4me Self Service to start chats with your service desk team. In accounts where Self Service V2 is not enabled, the {{support_chat}} widget must be added in the Self Service Design.

Figure 127: In the Self-Service Settings of a support domain account support chat can be enabled.

Furthermore, each support domain account requires a designated 'contact center' to handle incoming chat messages. Typically, this role is filled by the service desk team, as defined in the First Line Support Agreement. The availability of Support Chat within any given support domain is determined by the support hours outlined in the First Line Support Agreement (FLSA). Users will receive a notification if they attempt to initiate a support chat outside of designated support hours.

Implementing support chat can introduce additional demands on the service desk team, which is where the **Virtual Agent**, an integrated chatbot within 4me, becomes valuable. Available 24/7 and powered by artificial intelligence, the Virtual Agent comprehends the full context of services provided by the support domain accounts. It can assist users effectively, providing accurate answers from knowledge articles or guiding them to the most appropriate service and request template. Should the issue remain unresolved, the Virtual Agent can seamlessly transfer the chat to a service desk representative.

It is worth noting that when support chat is enabled, a specific first-line KPI, the **Support Chat pickup target** can be incorporated into the First Line Support Agreement, recognizing that the pickup target for chats should likely be far more stringent than the pickup target for requests.

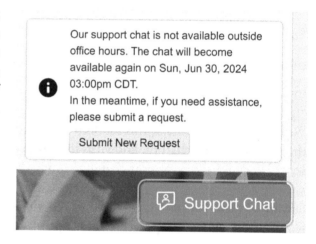

Our support chat is not available outside office hours. The chat will become available again on Sun, Jun 30, 2024 03:00pm CDT.
In the meantime, if you need assistance, please submit a request.

Submit New Request

🗨 Support Chat

Figure 128: Support Chat unavailable message.

▼ Targets

Support chat pickup target	0:01
Pickup target	0:15

The Specialist Perspective - The Specialist Interface

The Inbox: Streamlining Ticket Assignments in 4me

Simplifying the way work flows, the 4me Inbox streamlines the workday of specialists by gathering every ticket in one central hub. Say goodbye to the hassle of sifting through various modules and endless queues. Everything a specialist needs to do is prioritized in their inbox, making their work life smoother and more efficient.

The Inbox console is equipped with comprehensive functionality, including keyword filtering (simply type a phrase into the search bar), the ability to switch between multiline and grid views, column customization (exclusive to grid view), column sorting, and the addition of filters. Specialists can personalize their view by saving these settings, even setting a preferred layout as the default. By default, tickets are organized by target date, a practice designed to prioritize tickets with the most urgent targets at the top, ensuring high-priority tasks are addressed first.

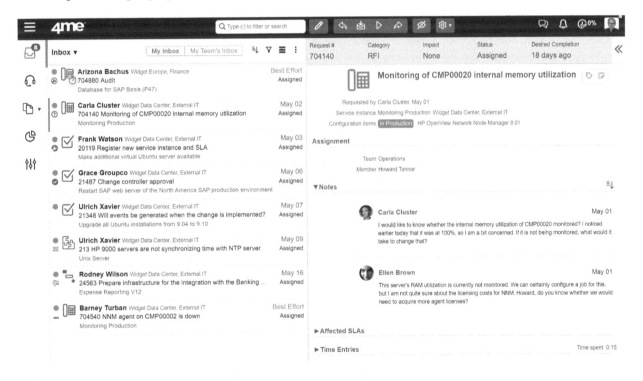

Figure 129: The 4me Inbox.

The number 4 holds significance in 4me, as it represents the **four main ticket types**: requests, problems, tasks (belonging to workflows), and project tasks. The ticket types serve as the foundation for all work conducted in 4me. Additionally, 4me encompasses a vast array of records such as workflows, projects, configuration items, products, agile boards, product backlogs, contracts, risks, and more. In the specialist interface, these records are accessible via the **Records Console**. However, they do not appear in the inbox, even when they are associated with a user. For instance, agile boards, product backlogs, projects, workflows, and risks each have a manager. When an action is required from the manager, it should be initiated through one of the four ticket types. To manage a project, a project task is added and assigned to the project manager; similarly, to address a risk, a request is created and referenced in a note of the risk.

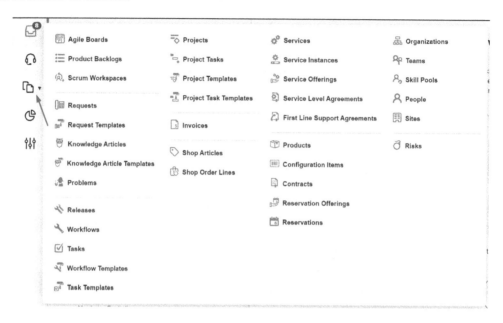

Figure 130: All 4me records in the Records Console.

For a ticket to be visible in a specialist's inbox, it must first be assigned to a team that the specialist is a part of. Incorrect ticket assignments can lead to chaos and increased overhead within a service delivery organization, particularly those that are complex and comprise many teams. 4me addresses this challenge through its service hierarchy: when a request is associated with a service, the service hierarchy automatically directs the request to the appropriate team. Similarly, problems require linkage to a service upon creation, which then automatically assigns the problem to the service's support team. The process for assigning workflow tasks and project tasks differs slightly, with workflow managers determining team assignments either through template definitions or manual assignment.

After a ticket has been allocated to a team, it still requires assignment to an individual member. In this context, the Inbox offers two primary views: **My Inbox** and **My Team's Inbox**. My Team's Inbox provides a comprehensive overview of tickets assigned to any of the user's teams, while My Inbox displays the tickets that require the specialist's direct attention. Understanding the nuances of a Team record in 4me is crucial for fully appreciating the My Inbox view, as these details significantly impact how assignments are managed.

Figure 131: The My Inbox and My Team's Inbox views.

4me Teams and Member Assignments

A pivotal attribute of a team is the **team coordinator**. Any team member can assume this role, or it can be left unfilled. The coordinator role, along with the Auto-assign feature, dictates the method of assignment management within the team. There are three approaches to handling member assignments:

1. **Dispatching**: The team coordinator oversees the queue and distributes tickets to team members using the **Forward** button in the toolbar. This method suits larger teams or those at an earlier stage of development.
2. **Pulling**: With no designated coordinator, unassigned tickets will appear in all team members' My Inbox view. Team members are encouraged to regularly check their inbox and claim tickets by clicking the **Accept** or **Start** button. This approach is ideal for smaller teams or larger teams with a high level of maturity.

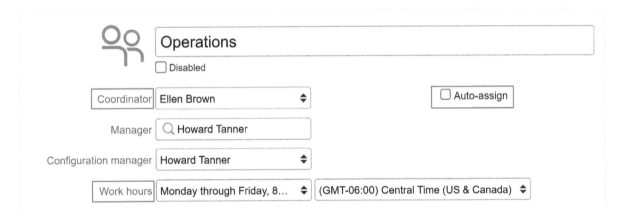

Figure 132: The team fields affecting member assignments.

3. **Auto-assign**: When activated, this feature allows the 4me platform to automatically distribute tickets among team members. If auto-assignment is unsuccessful, the ticket remains unassigned until one of the manual methods is employed to assign it. This method is ideal for large teams where each member has similar responsibilities and capabilities.

Sophisticated Auto-Assignment in Teams

The auto-assignment feature in 4me goes beyond a basic round-robin algorithm. It begins by evaluating the next target for the ticket assigned to the team, focusing on the "Assignment Timeframe", which is the period between the current moment and the ticket's next target.

Auto-assignment then identifies which team members are eligible to receive the ticket. Eligibility is determined by several factors:

- **Availability Status**: Team members can mark themselves as temporarily unavailable using the 'Set Yourself as Away' option. Naturally, those indicating their unavailability will not be considered for ticket assignments.
- **Out-of-Office Periods**: Team members can specify their out-of-office periods. Anyone whose out-of-office period coincides with the ticket's assignment timeframe will be excluded from auto-assignment.
- **Work Hours**: Each team member's work hours are defined by linking their person record to a calendar. If a specialist's work hours have not be defined, the team's work hours are applied. Only those team members whose work hours overlap with the assignment timeframe are considered eligible.

Once the pool of eligible team members is established, the system counts the number of tickets already assigned to each member that are in the status of Assigned, Accepted, or In Progress, and also have the next target within the assignment timeframe. The member with the fewest such tickets becomes the 'winner' and is assigned the new ticket.

Project Tasks and Approval Tasks

Approval tasks or project tasks that are directly assigned to a specialist appear in the My Inbox view of the specialist but not in the My Team's Inbox.

Integration of Support Chat into the Inbox

When support chat is enabled, service desk team members receive an audible notification alerting them to incoming chats, emphasizing the need for a quick response. The new support chat messages appear directly in the team's inbox, and the 4me platform automatically generates a corresponding request. The dialogue with the user is recorded in a 'Conversation' linked to this request.

A service desk analyst can 'Accept' the chat, which then removes it from the collective team inbox. This allows the analyst to engage directly with the user. Having accepted the chat, the analyst has the flexibility to conclude the chat when needed and focus on resolving the associated request. If necessary, the chat can be returned to the team queue for further assistance by another team member.

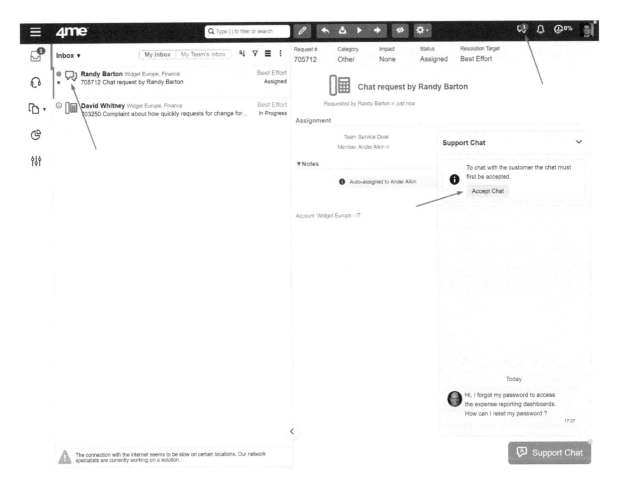

Figure 133: A support chat in the Inbox.

The Service Desk Console: A Hub for Service Excellence

The service desk console serves as the central hub for *service desk analysts*. It features a single search field that enables analysts to locate users quickly. Adhering to the strict data segregation enforced by the 4me account framework, analysts can access and interact with both internal and external users listed within the accounts in which they have the service desk analyst role and within the corresponding directory account.

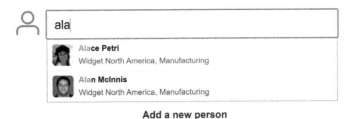

Figure 134: Selecting a requester in the Service Desk Console.

When an account delegates its service desk function to a trusted account, the administrator of the account should grant the trusted account the *service desk analyst* role via the trust. Next, the administrator of the trusted account should establish a First Line Support Agreement for the customer's account. Finally, he should provide the *service desk analyst* role of the customer account to the service desk team members. With this setup the service desk analysts in the trusted account will be able to select all people from the customer account in the service desk console.

Suppliers who only provide support services, rather than full-service desk functions, to a customer account do not need access to all of the customer's end users. In such cases, the supplier's service desk analysts won't be able to select customer users directly from their service desk console. However, it may still be beneficial for the customer's specialists to contact the supplier's service desk by phone. To facilitate this, the customer's administrator can enable the setting **"Trusted Account service desk analysts can submit requests for our specialists"** within their account trusts. This setting allows a supplier's service desk analyst to select a specialist from the customer directly in their service desk console.

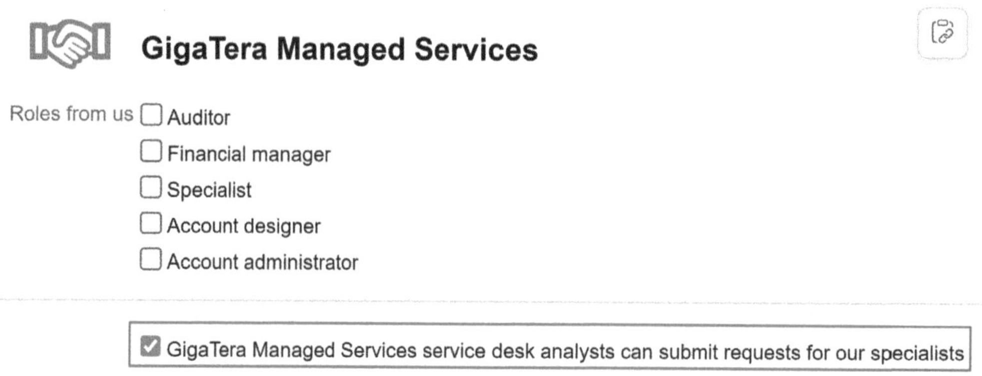

Figure 135: The account trust setting to allow the service desk analysts in a trusted account to register requests for the own specialists.

Once a user is selected in the 4me service desk console, a service desk analyst unlocks vital support information! Picture having the user's contact details at your fingertips, a crystal-clear timeline of their journey through both open and resolved requests, and direct insights into how satisfied they've been with the support they received.

But that's not all—also visualize having an in-depth view of the services the user is entitled to, and a list of the user's assets. It's all there, providing everything one needs to deliver outstanding, informed support with a personal touch!

Importantly, within the structure of a directory account, a service desk analyst has the capability to view all users who are registered in the directory account, even if their support domain account does not directly offer services to these individuals. This feature enables support domain accounts to provide 'best effort' support under exceptional circumstances. For example, if a user visits a regional office and requires assistance from the local service desk, the analysts of the local service desk can register a new request for the user, even though this user is not covered for support from this service desk.

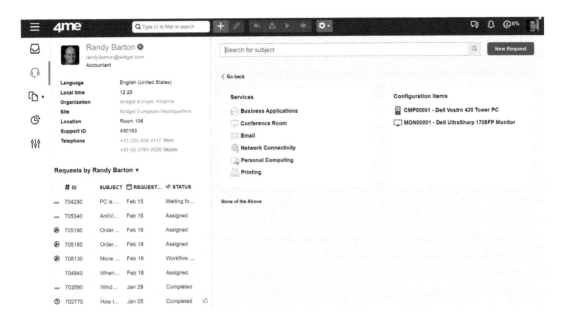

Figure 136: The 4me Service Desk console supporting service excellence.

Unlocking Insights Reports and Dashboards in 4me

Reports Unveiled: Navigating 4me's Analytics for Informed Service Management

Within the 4me Analytics console lies a treasure trove of over 400 reports, each equipped with a multitude of filters—potentially offering over 8,000 unique perspectives on your enterprise service management data. While this might seem daunting, it's designed with a purpose: to underpin the drive for service excellence with comprehensive, real-time data insights. This wealth of information serves as the foundation for informed decision making and continuous improvement.

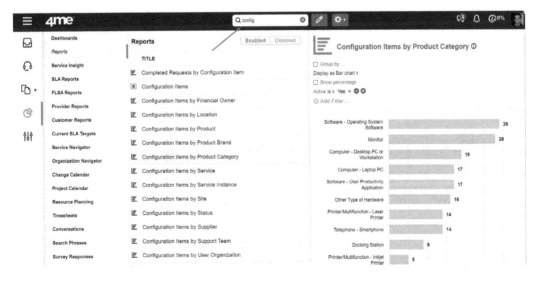

Figure 137: Enter a keyword in the search bar to find a set of reports.

4me champions the principle of transparency within service management. True service excellence is achieved when every member of the service delivery team engages in identifying and contributing to improvement initiatives. By democratizing access to these extensive reports, 4me ensures that insights into service performance are available to all specialists, adhering to the privacy and data segregation policies of each account.

However, it's essential to note that by default, reports focusing on individual performance are not activated. This acknowledges the sensitivity of such data and the necessity for clear communication regarding their usage within organizational and legal frameworks before they are made available.

Dashboards

Transitioning from the individual reports, the real game-changer comes in the form of dashboards. More than just a library, dashboards in 4me allow for the integration and interactive exploration of multiple reports, enhanced by both report-specific and dashboard-wide filters. Every new 4me account is equipped with standard KPI dashboards that spotlight key processes, which account administrators can tailor or expand upon.

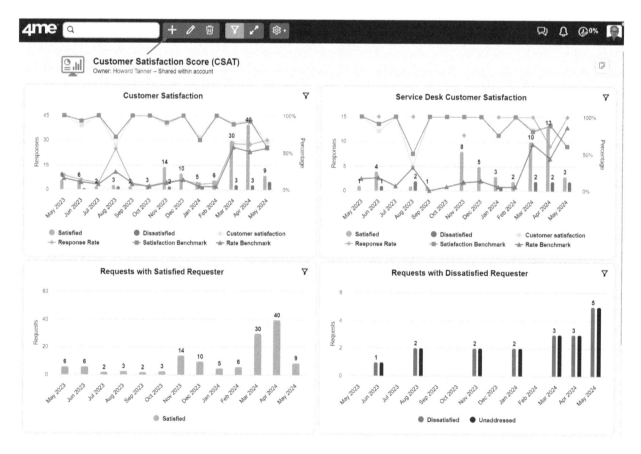

Figure 138: Add a new dashboard to the out-of-the-box KPI dashboards in a 4me account.

Furthermore, each specialist has the autonomy to create personalized dashboards, choosing to keep them private or share them across teams, skill pools, or with all specialists in the account.

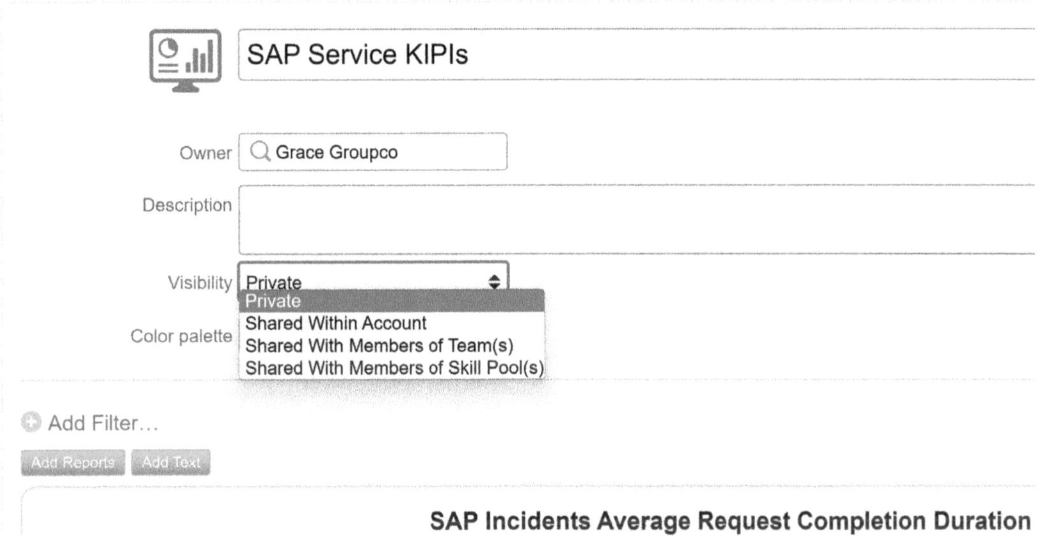

Figure 139: All specialists can define and share dashboards.

The dashboard functionality extends into the directory account, offering a panoramic lens through which to view enterprise service management processes across various support domain accounts. Within this higher-level perspective, the directory account administrator has the capability to construct consolidated dashboards. These dashboards provide insights across different domains facilitating comparison of KPIs among various support domains.

Moreover, the *account administrator* is empowered to design and share dashboards tailored for key contacts and customer representatives. For instance, dashboards can be shared with key contacts, granting them visibility into requests associated with their organization and its branches. Additionally, customer representatives can access dashboards focused on the services they oversee, ensuring they have a clear picture of the service performance and user satisfaction. Note that not only an *account administrator*, but also a *service level manager* is able to share dashboards with customer representatives.

Enhancing Dashboard Clarity and Appeal

A dashboard's value is significantly amplified when its data is clear and comprehensible to its viewers. To facilitate this, 4me provides areas for detailed descriptions both for the dashboards, as well as each individual report they contain. Whenever a description is populated, an informational icon materializes next to the dashboard and report titles. Hovering over this icon reveals the descriptive text.

Moreover, 4me allows the integration of rich text fields directly into the dashboard layout. This feature enables the addition of comprehensive, readily visible instructions or explanations, clarifying the data presented. Beyond textual information, this rich text field can also accommodate logos and other images.

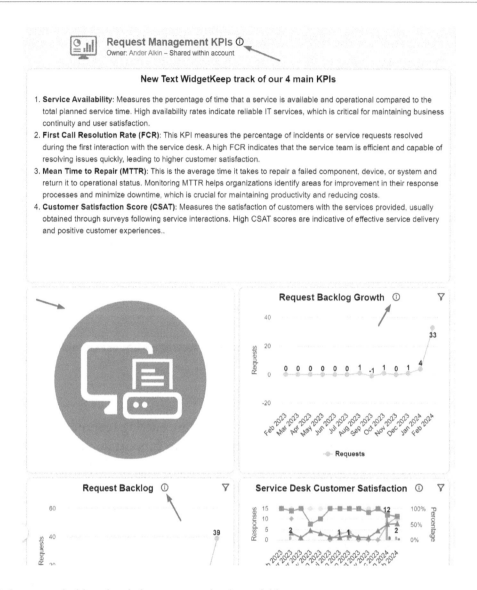

Request Management KPIs ⓘ
Owner: Ander Alkin – Shared within account

New Text WidgetKeep track of our 4 main KPIs

1. **Service Availability**: Measures the percentage of time that a service is available and operational compared to the total planned service time. High availability rates indicate reliable IT services, which is critical for maintaining business continuity and user satisfaction.
2. **First Call Resolution Rate (FCR)**: This KPI measures the percentage of incidents or service requests resolved during the first interaction with the service desk. A high FCR indicates that the service team is efficient and capable of resolving issues quickly, leading to higher customer satisfaction.
3. **Mean Time to Repair (MTTR)**: This is the average time it takes to repair a failed component, device, or system and return it to operational status. Monitoring MTTR helps organizations identify areas for improvement in their response processes and minimize downtime, which is crucial for maintaining productivity and reducing costs.
4. **Customer Satisfaction Score (CSAT)**: Measures the satisfaction of customers with the services provided, usually obtained through surveys following service interactions. High CSAT scores are indicative of effective service delivery and positive customer experiences..

Figure 140: Enhancing a dashboard with descriptions and rich text fields.

Default and Inbox Dashboards: Setting the Stage for Daily Insights

The first dashboard a user encounters upon entering the Analytics console is the **Default Dashboard**. It should present information that resonates with every specialist, offering a snapshot of relevant metrics and updates. *Account administrators* have the authority to designate a dashboard as the account's 'default'.

Specialists typically start their daily routine in the Inbox console. To enhance this experience, why not offer specialists a brief yet comprehensive overview of the current state of affairs within their support domain account as they enjoy their morning coffee? The *account administrator* possesses the capability to assign a dashboard as the **Inbox Dashboard**. By doing this, instead of the standard 4me Welcome page, specialists are greeted with this custom dashboard right alongside their Inbox.

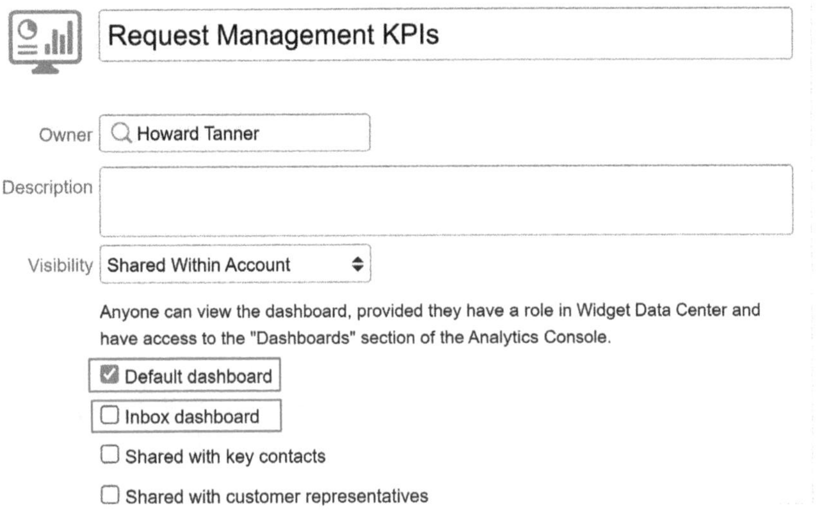

Request Management KPIs

Owner   Howard Tanner

Description

Visibility   Shared Within Account

Anyone can view the dashboard, provided they have a role in Widget Data Center and
have access to the "Dashboards" section of the Analytics Console.

☑ Default dashboard
☐ Inbox dashboard
☐ Shared with key contacts
☐ Shared with customer representatives

Figure 141: Defining the Default and Inbox dashboards.

Extending Dashboard Visibility: Secure Sharing and Public Display

For organizations leveraging large screens to provide real-time updates, 4me dashboards are an invaluable tool. These displays offer continuous insight into metrics and updates crucial for communicating team performance and broader employee engagement. The **'Enter Full Screen'** option, accessible from the dashboard's toolbar, optimizes these dashboards for larger displays, ensuring they're easily readable even from afar. Additionally, dashboards set to full-screen mode refresh every five minutes.

To securely display 4me dashboards on these public screens without requiring individual logins, it is recommended to use the **Shareable Dashboard URL** feature. Generating a shareable URL for a dashboard is straightforward: select *'New Shareable URL...'* from the dashboard's Actions menu to produce a unique URL and associated access token.

https://io.4me-demo.com/dHFMAE

Created by Howard Tanner
Created Sun, Jun 30, 2024 07:27am CDT
Dashboard Request Management KPIs

This URL is protected with the access token below. When you share this URL with someone, also give them the access token, preferably via a separate and secure communication channel.

Access token   e6gPApuoA743T0SKC91gGh7uxoUjJABVoNtEP56YRMsAfldNAeA

Account: Widget Data Center   Last updated: just now

Figure 142: Generating a Shareable Dashboard URL with a QR code and a token.

When a dashboard is accessed via a shareable link, it reflects the access permissions of the user who generated the link within 4me, while disabling the ability to drill down into detailed records. This ensures data security, particularly when displayed in common areas, and allows for the safe sharing of dashboard information with external stakeholders, without granting them access to sensitive information in individual records.

Printing and Scheduling Dashboards

While hard copy documents are becoming less common, 4me recognizes the necessity for adaptability and documentation in various formats. The platform utilizes its PDF design capabilities not just for workflow summaries, but also for generating professionally formatted PDF files of dashboards. Although printing dashboards on paper is generally discouraged to promote sustainability, this PDF feature is invaluable when it comes to scheduling and distributing dashboards via email. Within the Actions menu of a dashboard, users can find the 'Schedule...' option. This allows all specialists to select a preferred PDF design, set a recurrence schedule, identify recipients, and customize the email body content.

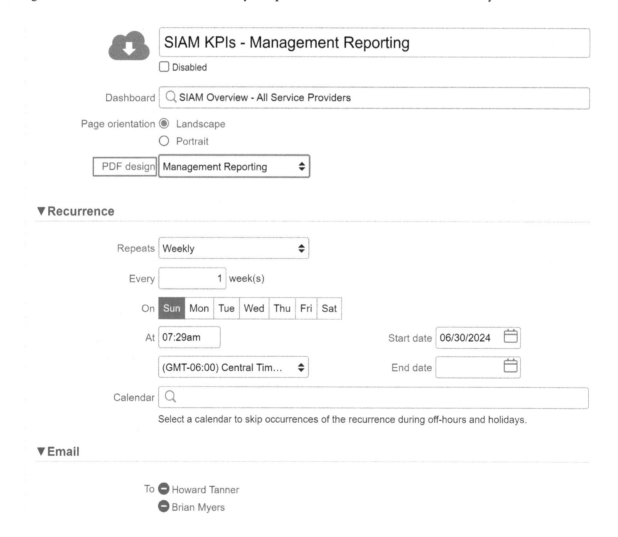

Figure 143: Scheduling and emailing a dashboard, available for all specialists in the dashboard's Actions menu.

4me's Commitment to Accessibility

4me is dedicated to ensuring that its platform is accessible and inclusive for all users, including those with visual impairments and other disabilities. This commitment is evidenced by continuous efforts to align with the **Web Content Accessibility Guidelines (WCAG)** as established by the World Wide Web Consortium (W3C). These guidelines are essential for making web content more accessible, encompassing a range of recommendations such as providing text alternatives for non-text content, ensuring content is easily navigable and adaptable, and enhancing the readability of web pages and presenting them in a predictable order.

In adherence to this commitment, regular and automated tests are conducted to evaluate the accessibility compliance of the 4me service. These assessments are systematically aligned with the development cycle, occurring weekly to coincide with the introduction of new features and updates.

First Time User Click-Through Agreement

Organizations using 4me can present their terms and conditions to users, requiring acceptance upon their first login. This functionality is enabled through a setting called 'Your Privacy & Terms' located in the 'Legal & Compliance' section of the Settings console. When the Click-through agreement field is populated with rich text, all first-time users—or users upon any subsequent edits to the agreement—must accept these terms before they can log in. Users can review the privacy statement and the date of their last agreement acceptance in the 'My Profile' section.

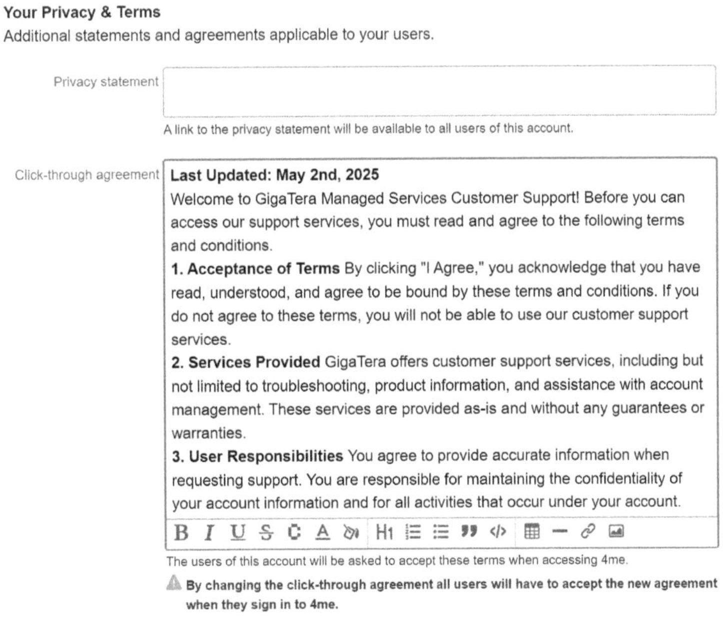

Figure 144: Example of a click-through agreement that each user must accept upon first accessing the customer portal.

Chapter 9 - Communication and Swarming

Enterprise service management is fundamentally about people. While the design of the account structure might perfectly mirror the operating model, and the service hierarchy along with the service catalog may be meticulously crafted, with underlying procedures that are both efficient and robust, the ultimate success of these practices hinges significantly on the competencies of the individuals involved and the effectiveness of communication among them. Although the 4me platform doesn't influence the competencies of its users, it is designed to facilitate communication, making it as seamless and efficient as possible.

Centralizing Communication with 4me's Notification Center

 At the core of all communications within 4me lies the Notification Center, accessible both through the specialist interface and the self-service portal for end users. As processes and procedures unfold, various events—both those integrated into the design and ad-hoc occurrences triggered by stakeholders— may notify the current stakeholders and even bring new ones into the loop.

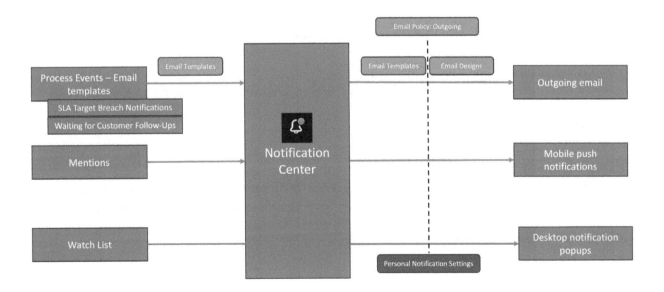

Figure 145: The Notification Center.

Fine-tuning Notification Settings for Effective Communication

Achieving effective communication is not just about receiving alerts for pertinent events; it's equally about filtering out unnecessary notifications to avoid information overload. In today's environment, where many are overwhelmed by excessive emails and messages across platforms, the risk of overlooking critical notifications is real. 4me addresses this by empowering both specialists and end users to customize their notification preferences.

Opting out of Team Assignment Notifications

Specialists, for example, can opt out of team assignment notifications, which is particularly beneficial for members of coordinator-less teams who would otherwise be notified of every team assignment.

Suppressing Email Notifications

All users have the option to suppress all email notifications or configure settings to receive email alerts only when offline.

Identifying Offline Status in 4me:

A user is considered offline under the following circumstances:

- After 10 minutes or more of inactivity.
- When utilizing the '**Set Yourself as Away**' action, accessible via the user's profile picture or initials on the toolbar.
- Throughout any defined out-of-office periods.

The **presence indicator**—a green dot next to a user's name—helps colleagues ascertain whether a user is online.

Leveraging Built-In Notification Systems on Windows and iOS (Mac) Devices

The 4me platform integrates with the built-in notification systems on Windows and iOS (Mac) devices. 4me users can choose their preference for receiving notification pop-ups—whether to always receive them, never, or only for important messages. A message is considered important if it directly involves the user, such as when a ticket is assigned to them, they are mentioned, or a new note is added to a ticket in their personal inbox.

Triggering Notifications

Activating Notifications by Enabling Email Templates

Within 4me, the Email Templates feature, accessible via the Settings console, serves a dual purpose: defining *when* and *to whom* notifications are to be sent out, and *what* information to include in the notification if it is sent out by email.

Every 4me account comes with many standard email templates already prepared for notifications. Each of these standard email templates serves a specific purpose. When an email template is activated, it tells 4me that a notification needs to be sent out when its conditions are met. For instance, the New Request email template notifies the person who submits a new request, except when its status is updated to "Waiting for Customer" or "Completed".

If the preferences of the recipient specify that this person does not want to receive the notification as an email, 4me will still send out a notification if this person's preferences allow this. Initially, all email templates in a new 4me account are disabled (with the exception of crucial user access notifications) to prevent premature alerts when the account is still being configured.

 Best Practice	• Enabling notifications for an account should be done just prior to go-live. The easiest way to do this is through a straightforward export/import that removes the Disabled flag from the email templates. • Activation must extend to the directory account and any support domain accounts prepared for go-live • Don't activate the **'Timesheet – Past Week Incomplete'** template unless universally applicable based on an organizational policy that everyone should fill out the timesheets of the past week to total 100% of their organization's workweek.

Utilizing Mentions for Effective Notifications

The use of mentions in 4me is a dynamic method to ensure individuals are notified promptly, enhancing collaboration and communication. By incorporating the @ symbol in a note within any ticket, users with appropriate access can directly mention and notify other users. This functionality becomes especially crucial in scenarios involving critical incidents or urgent matters, where it enables specialists to rapidly convene a multidisciplinary team of experts from various domains. This collaborative approach, often referred to as '**swarming**,' proves invaluable for swiftly addressing high-impact issues by pooling collective expertise.

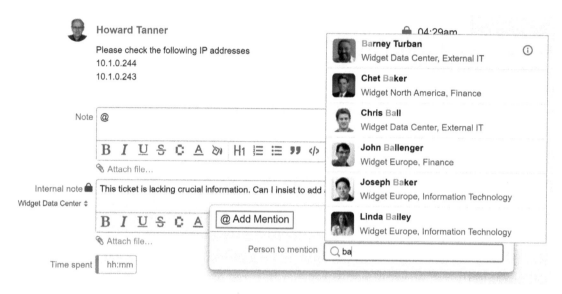

Figure 146: Mentioning a User.

In practice, it is advisable within 4me to maintain the request under the original support team's purview until an in-depth incident analysis reveals the root cause. Subsequently, the request can be accurately reassigned by applying the affected underpinning service instance, leveraging the service hierarchy browser for precision.

Users should also note the **presence indicator** and the **information icon** next to mentioned users. The information icon offers quick access to contact details and to the '**Start chat**' feature.

The Mention functionality in 4me is designed with strict adherence to data protection principles. For instance, specialists are prohibited from mentioning end users in internal notes or accessing the contact information of users outside their directory account structure unless they hold roles across these structures.

Enhancing Visibility with Watchlists

In the dynamic flow of service management, requests might initially come to you or your team, and as they navigate through the service hierarchy, they might be directed to a supplier in a different 4me account. Although the request may no longer appear in your inbox, staying informed about its resolution could still be crucial to you. Similarly, if you're addressing a problem that might interest others within your organization, ensuring they're notified of progress and resolution is essential. This is where the **watchlist** feature becomes invaluable.

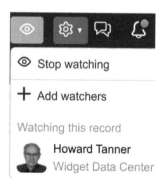

The watchlist allows you or any other user with the appropriate access rights to the ticket to keep an eye on it. Adding a ticket to your watchlist means you, along with anyone else listed, will receive notifications whenever a note is added to the ticket. These notifications are powered by the '*Watchlist Item Updated*' email template.

To view the tickets you're watching, simply switch your inbox view to the **Watchlist** view.

Customizing Process Events

Managing Customer Engagement: Waiting for Customer Follow-Ups

When managing requests or workflow tasks, there are instances where the resolution hinges on customer input, such as requiring additional information or an action on their part. To address this, specialists can leverage the '*Waiting for Customer*' status, effectively pausing the associated SLA clock to await the customer's response. This pause is crucial for maintaining SLA accuracy but presents a challenge in keeping the service delivery process moving. Accumulating a backlog of requests pending customer action is far from ideal for any service delivery organization, which emphasizes the need for a proactive approach to re-engage customers.

To automate customer reminders, follow-up records can be established and associated with service offerings. This linkage allows for precise adherence to follow-up protocols, tailored to the context of each service. Organizations might adopt a universal policy for 'Waiting for Customer' follow-ups, applying it across all service offerings and request types, or they may choose to implement these reminders solely for services deemed business-critical.

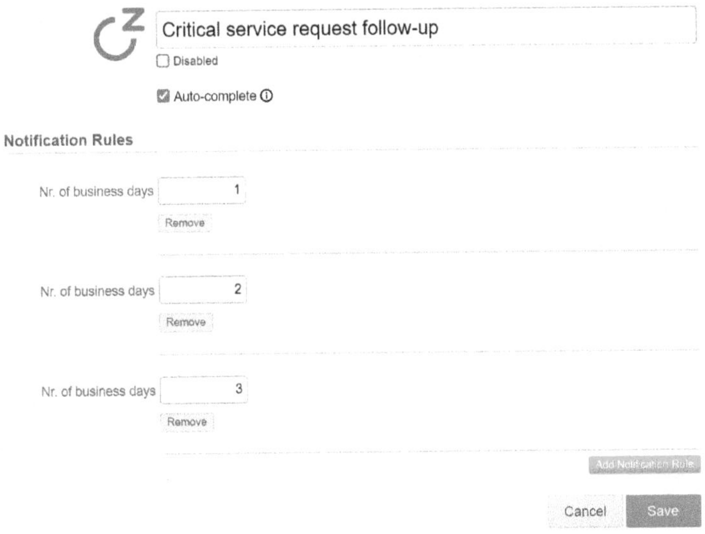

Figure 147: Defining a Waiting for Customer Follow-up.

A follow-up record can encompass up to five notification rules, delineating the number of business days after which a reminder should be dispatched to the customer. These notifications are crafted based on the '*Waiting for Customer Follow-up*' email template. For situations where customer responsiveness remains absent, enabling the **Auto-complete** option within follow-up records ensures requests do not linger indefinitely. The final notification, aligned with the last follow-up rule, triggers this auto-completion using the '*Waiting for Customer Auto Completio*n' template, thereby minimizing the backlog of inactive requests.

Standard Enterprise Resource Planning (SAP)

Status **Available**

Service Enterprise Resource Planning (SAP) Widget Europe, Information Technology

Service hours 24x6 (Monday through Saturday) Amsterdam

Responses within target >= **80%**

Resolutions within target >= **80%**

Availability >= **99.8%**

Reliability <= **2** outages / month

Follow-up Critical service request follow-up

Performance **The transaction of a user logging on to the service (the reference transaction) is not to take longer than 60 seconds.**

Figure 148: Linking a follow-up to a service offering.

Proactive SLA Management with Breach Notifications

For Managed Service Providers (MSPs), adherence to service level agreements (SLAs) is not just about meeting performance benchmarks; it often has financial implications, including penalties for SLA breaches. Given the high stakes, merely tracking SLA compliance through dashboards may not suffice. Dashboards, while informative, might not offer the proactive control needed to avert SLA breaches, leaving MSPs reactive rather than preventive in their approach.

Recognizing this critical need for a more forward-looking strategy, the 4me platform equips service delivery organizations with an advanced SLA notification system. This system is designed to alert key stakeholders about potential SLA breaches well before they occur, enabling timely interventions to maintain SLA compliance. Setting up SLA Notification Schemes is a task reserved for users with the *service level manager* or *account administrator* role.

An **SLA Notification Scheme** is specifically tailored to each request type within a service offering, allowing for granular control over SLA monitoring. For instance, a distinct notification scheme might be established for top-impact incidents associated with business-critical services, while a different scheme could be applied to standard requests like 'Replace a Broken PC'. These schemes utilize the **'Upcoming Resolution Target for Affected SLA of Request'** email template.

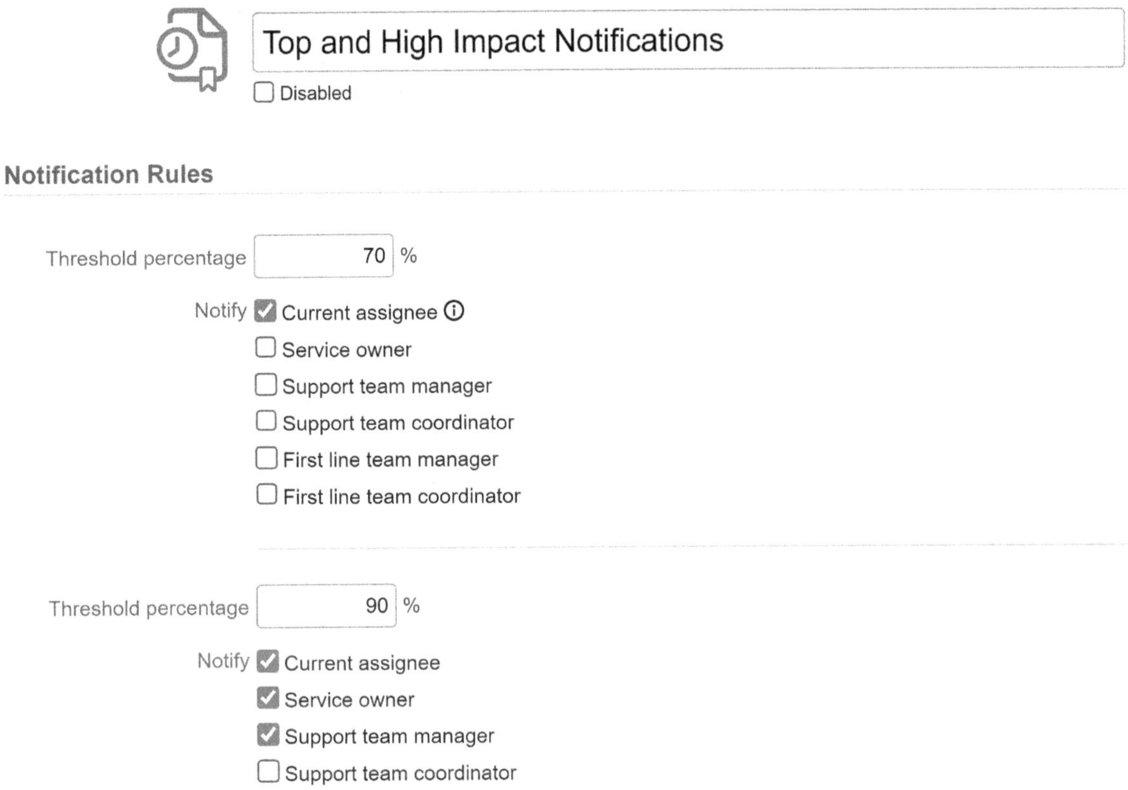

⏰ **Top and High Impact Notifications**

☐ Disabled

Notification Rules

Threshold percentage [70] %

Notify ☑ Current assignee ⓘ
☐ Service owner
☐ Support team manager
☐ Support team coordinator
☐ First line team manager
☐ First line team coordinator

Threshold percentage [90] %

Notify ☑ Current assignee
☑ Service owner
☑ Support team manager
☐ Support team coordinator

Figure 149: Defining an SLA Notification Scheme.

Each SLA Notification Scheme can include up to three notification rules, with each rule defined by a threshold percentage. This percentage dictates the timing for dispatching notifications relative to the resolution target, factoring in the support hours outlined in the service offering.

For example, consider a high-impact incident with an 8-hour resolution target and a notification rule set at a 25% threshold. If the incident is logged on Friday at 4:00 PM, with support hours from Monday to Friday, 9:00 AM to 5:00 PM, the notification would be scheduled to go out 2 hours post-incident logging. However, due to support hours, this would effectively be sent at 10:00 AM on Monday, providing a timely reminder to address the incident before breaching the SLA target.

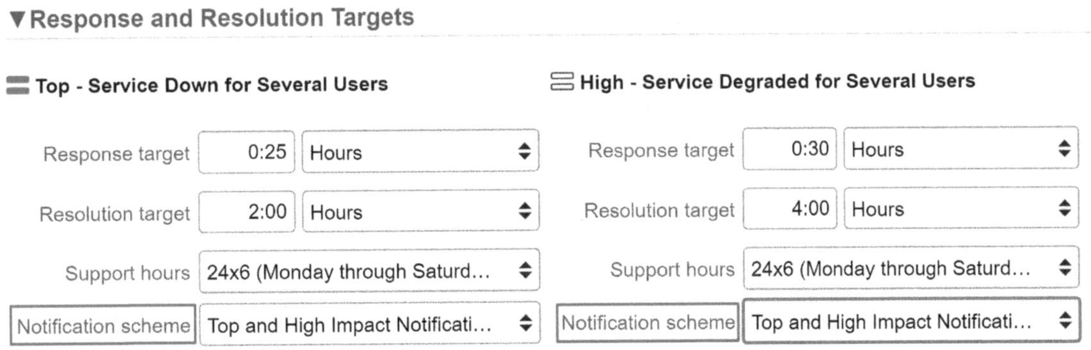

▼ **Response and Resolution Targets**

▬ Top - Service Down for Several Users   **☰ High - Service Degraded for Several Users**

Response target	0:25	Hours ⬍	Response target	0:30	Hours ⬍
Resolution target	2:00	Hours ⬍	Resolution target	4:00	Hours ⬍
Support hours	24x6 (Monday through Saturd... ⬍	Support hours	24x6 (Monday through Saturd... ⬍
Notification scheme	Top and High Impact Notificati... ⬍	Notification scheme	Top and High Impact Notificati... ⬍

Figure 150: Linking an SLA Notification Scheme to a Service Offering.

When establishing a notification rule, it's essential to specify the key stakeholders who will receive notifications. This list encompasses the service owner, the request's assignee, as well as the manager and coordinator of both the first line team and the support team associated with the relevant service instance.

Outgoing Email

Determining the Source Account for Email Notifications in 4me

Notifications within 4me can trigger email communications, which are influenced by various settings within the 4me accounts, dictating both the behavior and format of outgoing emails. It's essential to recognize that a request or task can be visible across multiple 4me accounts, allowing specialists from these accounts to mention stakeholders from across the service delivery chain. This inter-account communication raises the question: which account's settings are applied when an email notification is dispatched?

In 4me, the account responsible for sending out an email is referred to as the "**Notification Account**." Crucially, the determination of the Notification Account is made from the perspective of the notification recipient, not from the service delivery organization initiating the communication. For instance, if an end user from a customer account encounters an issue that the internal support team escalates to an external supplier, the specialists from the supplier's account can mention the customer's requester in their communications. Despite this cross-account interaction, any email sent to the customer's requester will utilize the email templates and settings of the customer's support organization.

This approach ensures that emails received by users are consistent with the branding and communication policies of their primary service provider, maintaining a seamless and coherent user experience even when multiple service providers are involved in resolving a request or task.

Customizing Email Content and Translations

Email templates dictate the subject and body of messages for various events, featuring placeholders (e.g., {{request_id}}, {{recipient_name}}) that dynamically populate with relevant information. These templates are customizable and translatable to match the recipient's language.

Please note that the 'Translations' option is accessible under the 'Actions' menu. This option directs you to the translation module for the chosen email template. Simply select your desired language, and 4me will automatically generate a translation suggestion for you.

Email Designs for a Professional Touch

To complement the email content, 4me allows for the customization of email designs, incorporating elements like company logos, contact information, and disclaimers in the headers and footers. Multiple email designs can be created and associated with different templates.

Enhancing Email Deliverability with 4me's Outgoing Email Policy

The 4me platform's outgoing email policy focuses on ensuring emails are not marked as spam upon receipt and clearly indicate the sender's identity to recipients. A critical aspect of this policy is the customization of the "From" email address, which includes both a display name and an email address. Customizing this field to feature an email address from your organization, such as 'hr-servicedesk@ mycompany.com', requires verification that 4me is authorized to send emails from your domain. This is where SPF, DKIM, and DMARC technologies play a pivotal role in authenticating email messages, enhancing security, and mitigating spam, phishing, and spoofing.

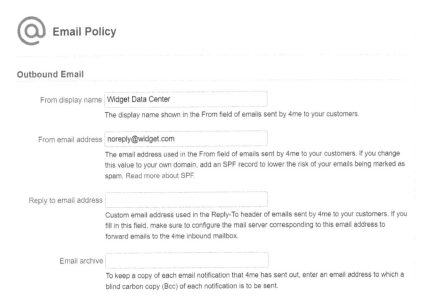

SPF (Sender Policy Framework)

What It Is: SPF is a system that allows an email domain owner to specify which mail servers are permitted to send email on behalf of their domain.

How It Works: When an email is sent, the receiving mail server checks the SPF record in the domain's DNS settings to verify that the email came from an authorized server. If the email is from an unauthorized server, it can be flagged as spam or rejected.

What to Do: Your DNS administrator must update the DNS records to include an SPF record for 4me, for instance, include:_spf.4me.com for the EU production environment or include:_spf.us.4me.qa for the US QA environment.

DKIM (DomainKeys Identified Mail)

What It Is: DKIM provides a way for an email to include a digital signature, which verifies that an email was indeed sent from the domain it claims to be from and that its content has not been altered in transit.

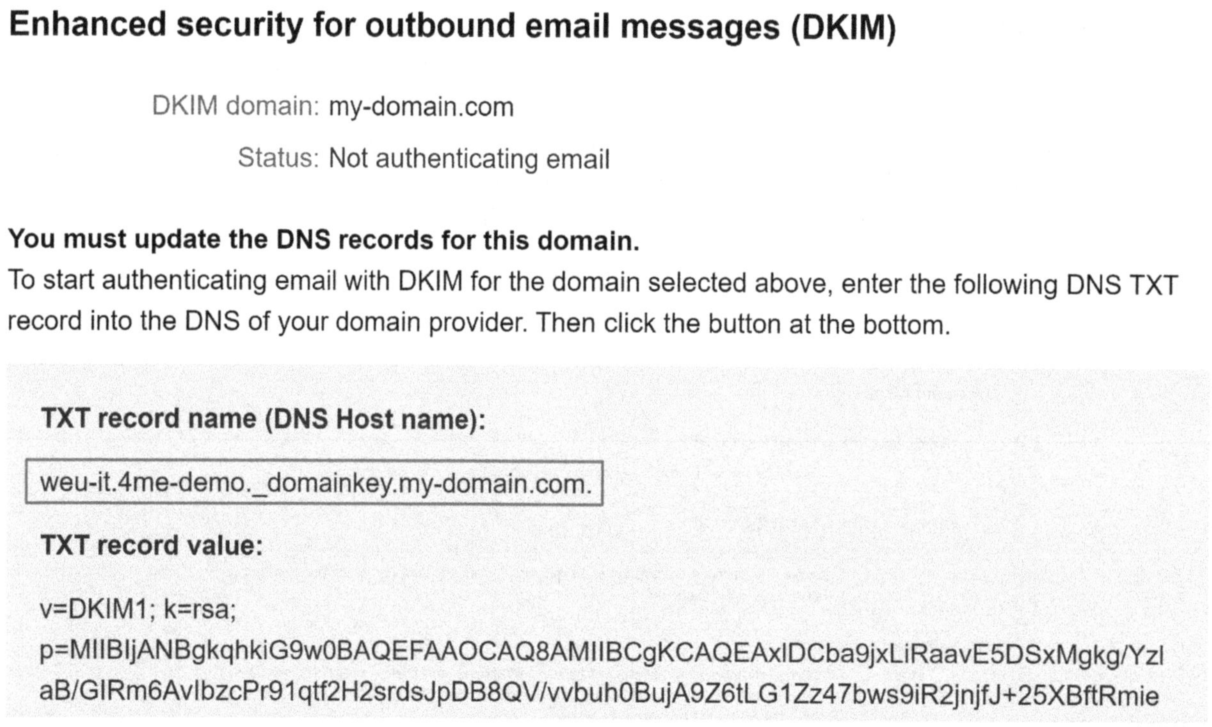

Enhanced security for outbound email messages (DKIM)

DKIM domain: my-domain.com

Status: Not authenticating email

You must update the DNS records for this domain.
To start authenticating email with DKIM for the domain selected above, enter the following DNS TXT record into the DNS of your domain provider. Then click the button at the bottom.

TXT record name (DNS Host name):

weu-it.4me-demo._domainkey.my-domain.com.

TXT record value:

v=DKIM1; k=rsa;
p=MIIBIjANBgkqhkiG9w0BAQEFAAOCAQ8AMIIBCgKCAQEAxlDCba9jxLiRaavE5DSxMgkg/Yzl
aB/GIRm6AvIbzcPr91qtf2H2srdsJpDB8QV/vvbuh0BujA9Z6tLG1Zz47bws9iR2jnjfJ+25XBftRmie

Figure 151: Setup DKIM in the Email Policy.

How It Works: The sending server attaches a unique DKIM signature to the header of each email. The receiving server then looks up the sender's DKIM public key published in their DNS records to check the signature's validity. If the signature matches, it confirms the email hasn't been tampered with and is genuinely from the stated domain.

What to Do: Add a DNS TXT record with the public key, obtained by activating the DKIM setup in 4me's Email Policy settings. Please note that the DKIM configuration needs to be set up only once in the 4me directory account. For support domain accounts, you have the option to specify the use of DKIM keys from the directory account.

DMARC (Domain-based Message Authentication, Reporting, and Conformance)

What It Is: DMARC builds on SPF and DKIM by allowing domain owners to specify how an email that fails SPF or DKIM checks should be handled.

How It Works: DMARC policies are published in the domain's DNS records. These policies tell receiving mail servers what to do with emails that fail SPF or DKIM checks (e.g., reject the email, quarantine it, or let it pass but report the failure to the sender). DMARC also provides a way for email receivers to report back to the sender about emails that pass or fail these checks.

What to Do: Define a DMARC policy in your DNS. Setting up a reporting channel back to 4me for failed emails can aid in monitoring and enhancing email security practices.

Collaborating with your DNS and email administrators to implement these measures is essential for the successful delivery of email notifications sent out by 4me.

Setting Up an Email Archive in 4me

4me allows for the creation of an Email Archive, which is essentially an email address designated to receive copies of all outgoing emails from a 4me account. This feature is particularly useful for troubleshooting instances where users claim not to have received an email. By verifying the presence of the email in the archive, administrators can ascertain whether an email was indeed dispatched. Should the email be located in the archive on a different email server than the organization's primary server, it indicates that the email intended for the user is being held up within the organization's email system, thereby isolating the issue to the internal email infrastructure.

 Limit access to the 4me Email Archive as much as possible so that it is used only for troubleshooting email delivery issues. Ensure that the establishment of an email archive complies with your organization's data protection policies to avoid any potential privacy concerns.

Sending Emails Directly from Notes in 4me

4me's mention function facilitates easy involvement of organization members in ticket resolution and collaboration with individuals in other 4me accounts. However, the reality for some service delivery organizations is that not all potential stakeholders can be predefined in 4me. For instance, a healthcare organization might need to communicate with various government entities on an ad-hoc basis, or a retail company may need to contact a supplier or their logistics partners unexpectedly.

To accommodate such needs, 4me permits sending emails from any record type capable of containing notes, including assignments (i.e. requests, problems, workflow tasks, and project tasks), as well as releases, workflows, and projects. Activating this functionality requires the creation of an additional email template for each relevant record type. Furthermore, you can define a specific Email Design with its own disclaimer for external communications. For example, a healthcare organization could develop a library of preformatted email templates for frequent inquiries to government bodies.

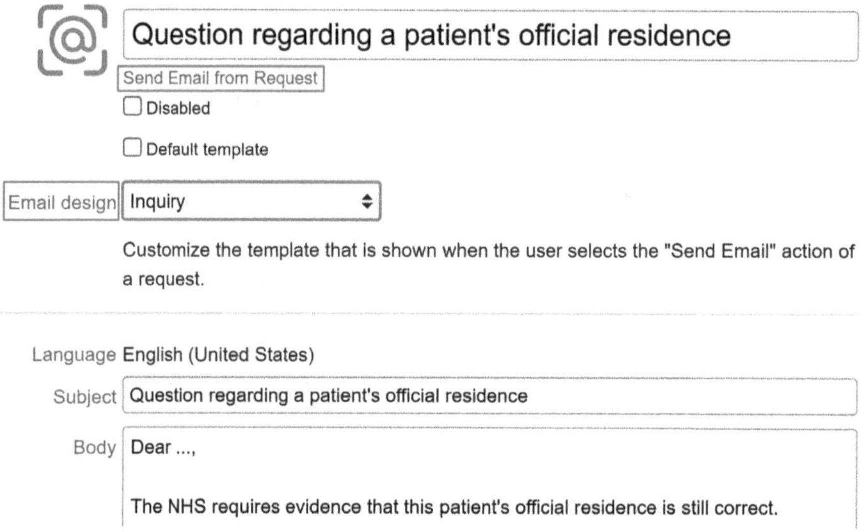

Figure 152: Defining a New Email Template.

A simple selector next to the note's field label transforms the Note field into an Email form, which, besides the usual content, includes fields for selecting an email template and specifying To and Cc addresses. Filling out this form is as intuitive as using any standard email client, with the Subject and Body pre-populated based on the chosen email template.

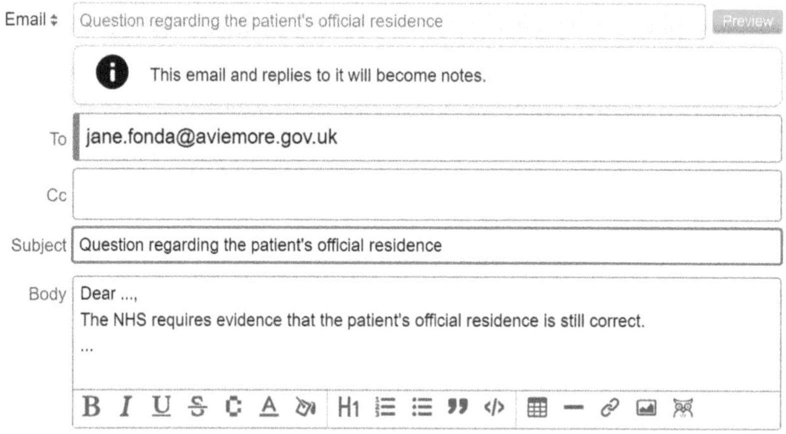

Figure 153: Sending an email from a note.

A Preview button lets users see how the email will appear with the selected design before sending.

When an email is dispatched from within 4me, the content of that email is automatically added as a note to the record from which the mail was sent. It's important to recognize that for requests, if the email was created from the Internal note field, the note that gets added once the email is sent will be internal. This ensures that the content of the email remains confidential, inaccessible to end users or specialists associated with trusted accounts. What's more, any replies to the email will also be added as internal notes to the record.

Sending an email through 4me to individuals not yet registered in the account effectively opens up global collaboration possibilities, leveraging email as a universal communication medium. However, it's worth noting the inherent security limitations of email, despite advancements such as SPF, DKIM, DMARC, and encryption technologies. While email remains ubiquitous in business, its security is not infallible, and perceptions of email as an outdated medium among younger generations suggest that future communication preferences may evolve towards platforms like WhatsApp or Slack. The flexible architecture of 4me ensures readiness for such shifts, potentially extending note-based communication to whichever platform becomes the business standard.

Beyond Notifications

Broadcasts: Enhancing Service Delivery Through Proactive Communication

A pivotal strategy in elevating the efficiency of a service delivery organization is to proactively inform customers to preclude the need for request submissions, thereby conserving organizational resources. This preemptive approach can be effectively achieved through the dissemination of knowledge articles or timely communications about specific events. For instance, notifying customers about current or impending service unavailability due to maintenance is a proactive communication strategy. 4me broadcasts serve this very purpose, designed to inform users via the self-service portal, the specialist interface or the 4me app. To add a broadcast the *service desk manager* or the *administrator* role is required.

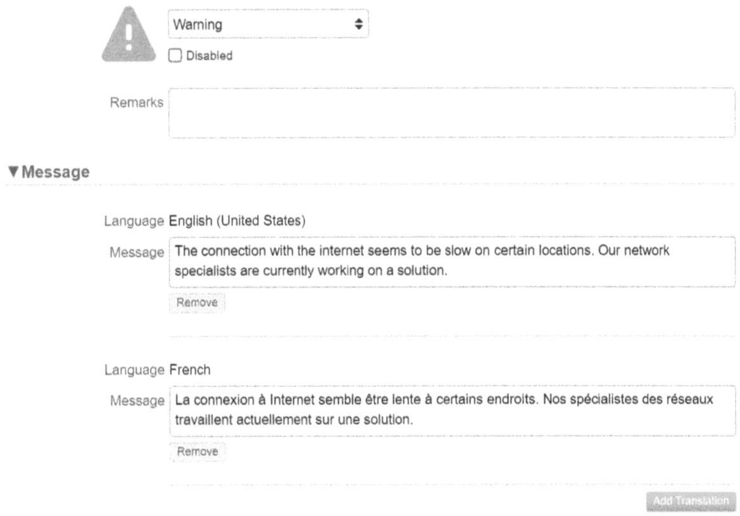

Figure 154: 4me broadcasts are multilingual.

Fully Integrated Broadcasts in 4me's Service-Driven Architecture

Broadcasts in 4me are not just ancillary messages but are fully embedded within its service-driven framework, embracing the platform's multilingual capabilities. This allows broadcasts to be targeted at specific audiences, such as the users of a service instance that is about to undergo maintenance. This makes broadcasts more relevant, which, in turn, makes broadcasts an effective means of communication. The visibility settings of a broadcast offer comprehensive options to fine-tune the audience, ensuring the message reaches only those it is intended for.

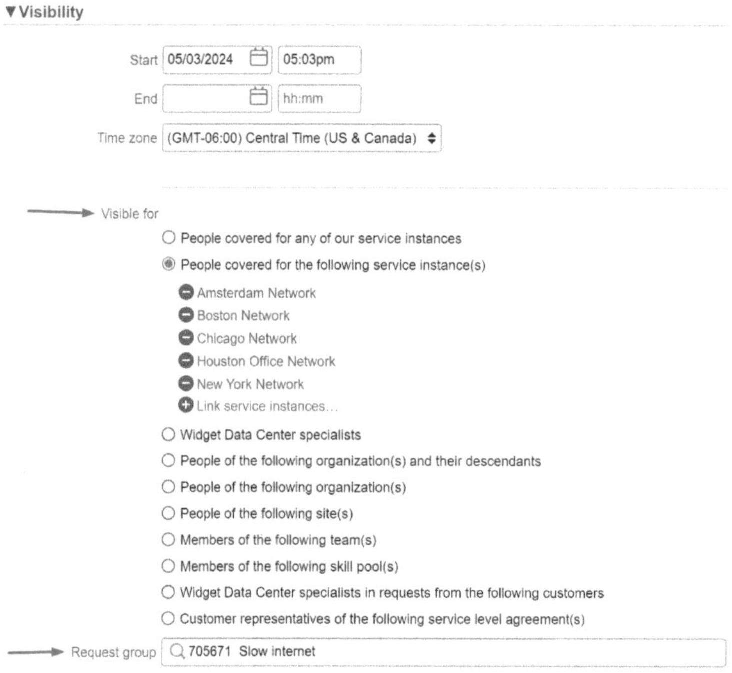

Figure 155: The Visibility options for broadcasts.

Major Incident Communication Through Request Groups

In the event of a major incident, it's common practice to consolidate multiple related requests into a request group. Broadcasting about the major incident informs users about the ongoing issue. Linking a broadcast to the request group makes the **I'm Also Affected** button available in the broadcast. When a user clicks on this button, a new request is generated for the users and automatically added to the group. This ensures that, when the issue has been resolved and the group is completed, all of the requests of the group are also automatically completed and all users who indicated that they were affected are immediately notified so they know they can get back to work.

Broadcasts Targeted at Specialists for Specific Customers

For Managed Service Providers (MSPs), broadcasting to specialists about issues related to specific customers can be crucial. For example, if a customer is significantly behind on payments, specialists might be advised to consult with the account manager before proceeding with support tickets. With the broadcast visibility option '***Specialists in requests from the following customers***' broadcasts can be tailored for visibility to specialists when they open requests from specific customers.

Email Broadcasts: Extending Reach Beyond 4me

While broadcasts within 4me require users to access the platform to view messages, there are scenarios where a direct push of information is more effective. By creating an email template for broadcasts, organizations can extend their communication reach by, for example, sending emails to customer representatives of a particular service. This feature is especially beneficial for customers without direct access to 4me, offering a bridge for important communications. As 4me continues to evolve, it is anticipated that more options will be introduced to also allow broadcasts to be sent out as text messages using different instant message services.

4me Connect: Integrating Communication Tools for Enhanced Collaboration

4me Connect merges essential communication functionalities such as chat, video, and screen sharing into a unified feature set, designed to facilitate instant and efficient collaboration within organizations. Accessible through the chat avatar found on both the toolbar and individual person records within the same directory account structure, 4me Connect empowers specialists to initiate conversations as needed. The presence indicator on a person's record provides immediate visibility into their availability for a video conference.

Integration with Microsoft Teams for a Unified Communication Experience

Recognizing the widespread adoption of Microsoft Teams as a primary communication platform in many organizations, 4me offers seamless integration with Teams through an app available in the 4me App Store. This integration ensures that specialists initiating chat sessions within 4me can leverage the full capabilities of Teams (rather than 4me Connect) for both chat and video conferencing, providing a consistent and familiar user experience.

The setup process for the Teams integration within 4mc is designed for simplicity and ease of use. Upon adding the Teams app from the 4me App Store, organizations are presented with just one straightforward configuration option: whether or not to use the 4me primary email address as the identifier for Teams when no specific User Principal Name (UPN) is associated with a person record. The UPN serves as a unique identifier in Teams, ensuring that users are correctly matched between the two platforms.

Chapter 10 - 4me Core Processes

4me Best Practices Process Models

At the heart of 4me's robust service-driven architecture lie several core built-in processes. These are both a necessity and a significant advantage. As a multi-tenant system, 4me seamlessly integrates service delivery organizations within a single company and across different companies, making these core processes indispensable.

The inclusion of core out-of-the-box processes offers a tremendous advantage by enabling quick starts and lean implementation cycles. The need for lengthy process design workshops, along with the subsequent build, test, and maintenance phases, is greatly reduced. The quality of these processes is exceptional, benefiting from the open-source principle: thousands of users provide continuous feedback, leading to refined and optimized process flows. This collaborative improvement process ensures that the built-in processes in 4me are of unparalleled quality, something that individual organizations would find challenging to replicate independently.

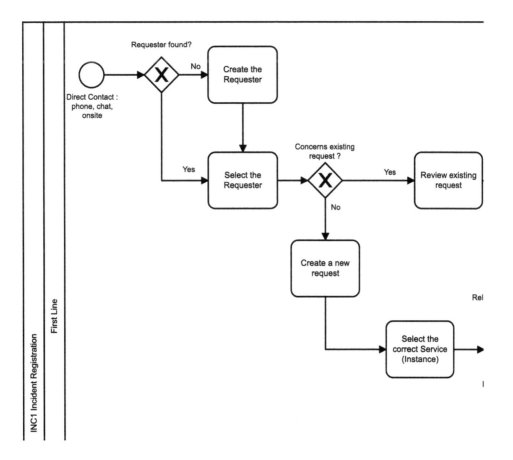

Figure 156: Incident registration - an example of a BPMN diagram in the 4me process documents that 4me shares with its customers.

Despite the strength of these core processes, 4me recognizes that organizations may have unique process requirements. This is where customization comes into play. In Part III of this book, we'll explore how 4me's processes can be tailored to meet specific organizational needs. Understanding the foundational, unchangeable core is essential before embarking on customization. To aid in this, 4me provides detailed process documentation, including process diagrams adhering to the open BPMN (Business Process Model and Notation) standard. These resources are shared with customers, allowing them to modify and adapt the processes according to their needs and to meet various compliance requirements. Contact your 4me partner or 4me support for access to these process documents. In this chapter, we will focus on some essential principles embedded in the 4me core processes.

Deciding on Process Implementation

Within the 4me platform, the Account Settings section of the Settings console allows administrators to enable or disable specific process functionalities. In 4me, access to process functionalities such as Agile, Problem Management, Release Management, Configuration Management, and Risk Management is not governed by licensing fees; all features are available at no extra cost. However, activating these processes should be a well-considered decision. It's not advisable to enable functionalities solely because they are available without additional charge. An organization should ensure that there is sufficient awareness, training, and policy in place before enabling these functionalities.

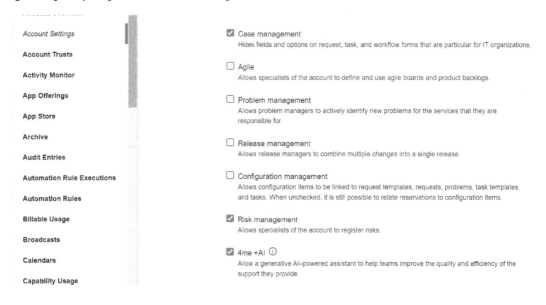

Figure 157: Process implementation options in the Account Settings.

Streamlining with Case Management: Beyond ITIL Terms

The ITIL framework, established in the late 1980s, has significantly influenced the terminologies and practices in enterprise service management. While terms such as 'incident' or 'request for change' (RFC) are standard within ITIL, they may not always resonate outside the IT department, especially in areas like Human Resources, Legal, Finance, or Sales & Marketing. In these departments, the concept of handling each ticket as a **'Case'** is often more relatable and less complicated.

In 4me, all user-related tickets are treated as requests, ensuring interoperability between departments like HR, IT, and Sales & Marketing. However, for simplicity and clarity in non-IT domains, organizations can choose to implement **case management**. In a case management-enabled account, every request is classified as a case, eliminating the need to select an impact level and avoiding ITIL-specific terminology such as incident and RFC.

Opting for case management does not limit cross-departmental collaboration. Cases from a case management account can still be seamlessly transferred to traditional IT service management accounts and vice versa. For instance, when IT assigns a request initially categorized as an 'incident' to Sales & Marketing, it simply gets adapted to the case format. Conversely, when HR needs IT assistance, they adapt by selecting an appropriate ITIL-defined category and impact, maintaining the required structure for IT services.

Orchestration of Requests on a Multi-Account Environment

The Request Life Cycle

Every ticket registered by a user is considered a **request**. In a case management account these requests will be referred to as "cases." In a typical IT account, the requests will receive different categories based on their nature, such as incident, RFI (Request for Information) or RFC (Requests for Change). However, regardless of the category or the type of account, a request always follows the same status options and lifecycle. This enables seamless collaboration between case management accounts and IT-oriented accounts: in both environments, the same statuses, actions, and logic apply.

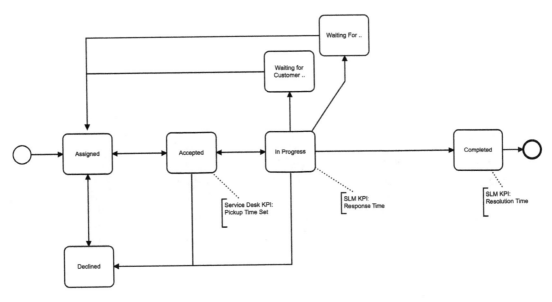

Figure 158: The life cycle of a request.

Account of Request and Request Accounts

Within the service hierarchy, a request may traverse and appear in multiple 4me accounts with different statuses. This situation arises when, for example, after a supplier resolved or declined a request and set its status to *Completed*, causing the same request to appear with the status *Assigned* in the customer's account. How is this managed given that a request typically has only one status field? The answer lies in the creation of a **Request Account** record each time a request appears in a new 4me account. A Request Account record hosts a limited set of fields, including the status field for that account, allowing the same request to exhibit different statuses across various accounts. For specialists working within these accounts, the underlying mechanics of Request Account records remain transparent; they continue to interact with what they perceive as "the" request, viewed from their account's perspective.

The Request Account record also plays a crucial role in analytics and continuous improvement efforts. It includes "hidden" fields such as **Assignment Count** and **Reopen Count**, which are essential for detailed reporting. These metrics are account-specific and are maintained within the Request Account record.

18

Figure 159: Report on how many requests for VIPs required at least two reassignments in an account.

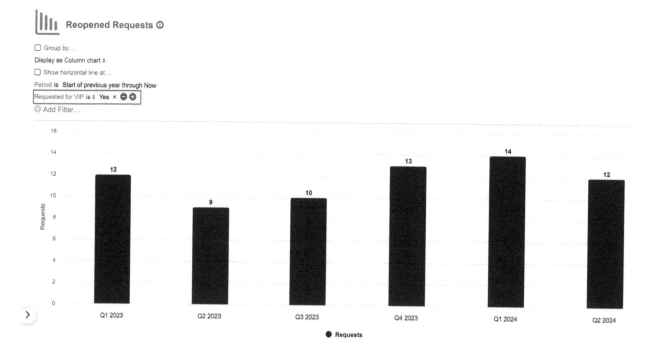

Figure 160: Report on how many requests for VIPs have been reopened in the account.

While a request may have multiple Request Account records, the request itself also belongs to a specific account. This is the account of the organization that is responsible for providing first line support to the requester of the request. For example, if an IT request is submitted, it is owned by the IT support domain account of the customer, regardless of subsequent assignments to teams in other accounts. This entity 'owns' the request. Consequently, the 'Account' filter found in various request-related reports corresponds to the account in which the request is registered. It's particularly useful for generating accurate request reports within a directory account, ensuring that requests are correctly categorized by their origin, even when they have been worked on by multiple support domain accounts.

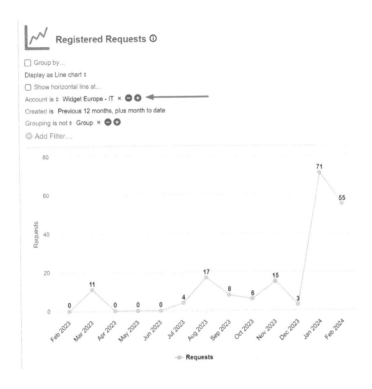

Figure 161: Selecting the account of requests in a report in the directory account.

Transferring a Request

Occasionally, a requester may mistakenly select the incorrect support domain account when submitting a request. For example, they might choose the IT support domain account for an issue that actually pertains to the Payroll application, which should have been directed to the HR support domain account.

In such instances, the support team in the IT department has the option to use the **Forward** button in the toolbar above the Inbox, not to reassign the ticket within IT, but to transfer the request entirely to a different support domain account, such as HR in this example. When transferring a request, there is no need to select a specific HR team; 4me automatically assigns the request to the HR service desk team as designated in the HR account's first line support agreement. Additionally, the Transfer action triggers the removal of the Request Account record from the IT account, rendering the request invisible to IT specialists. This is particularly beneficial as the request, which may evolve into an HR 'case,' could contain sensitive information not meant to be accessible by IT personnel.

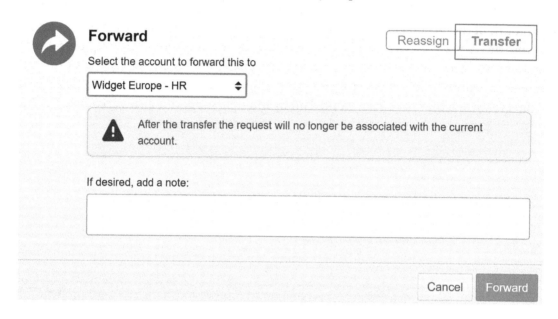

Figure 162: Using the forward button to transfer a request to another support domain account.

Declining Requests and Tracking the Assignment Trail

The first action available in the toolbar of the Inbox is 'Decline.' Utilizing the 'Decline' action returns the request to its previous assignment state. If a request is assigned to a team member by the team coordinator, declining it will move the request back to the team's queue. Team members might decline a request for various reasons, such as:

Figure 163: The Decline action.

- Insufficient time to meet the response and resolution targets due to other commitments (e.g. holiday leave, project work).
- Lack of necessary knowledge or access rights to address the request.

Similarly, when a team coordinator declines a request, it is reassigned to the previous team. The reasons for this could include:

- Missing information that should have been provided by the previous team.
- Incorrect assignment as the current team is not responsible for addressing the issue.

4me keeps track of all assignments through an '**Assignment Trail**,' a breadcrumb-like path that tracks the journey of each request across different teams and accounts. This trail ensures that when a request is declined, it can be sent back correctly, even if that means moving it to a team in a different account. However, it's important to note that a specialist cannot decline a request back to the end user. Once the request reaches the initial team in the assignment trail, it can still be declined to the service desk team of the account of the request, but the service desk cannot decline it further.

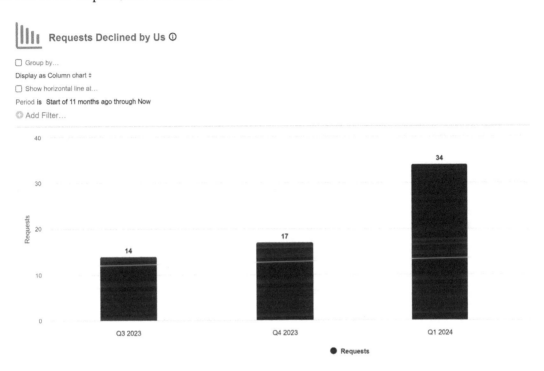

Figure 164: Service Excellence and measuring the number of declines.

A high number of declined requests can signal underlying issues; perhaps there's a problem with the service hierarchy. It could also indicate a gap in knowledge or training. To maintain and enhance service excellence, 4me provides reports designed to track the frequency of declines within an account.

Managing Customer Interaction Across Multiple Accounts

In environments with multiple account structures, where requests may pass from a customer account to a supplier's account and subsequently to a supplier of that supplier, complex customer-service provider relationships are formed.

When a secondary supplier marks a request as completed, it is the first supplier's responsibility to verify the resolution. Similarly, when a secondary supplier changes the status of a request to 'Waiting for Customer', the supplier is waiting for its customer (the first supplier); not the original requester.

The first supplier must address the inquiry or, lacking the necessary information, also change the status to 'Waiting for Customer' to engage the internal service provider. The query reaches the end user only after the internal service provider deems it necessary and also sets the status to 'Waiting for

Customer'. This ensures that validations are made at each level of service hierarchy before reaching the requester.

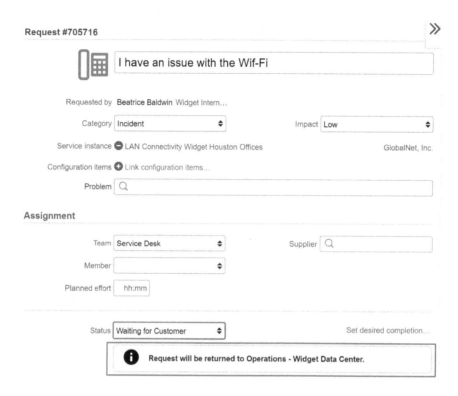

Figure 165: 4me displays a message when the status 'Waiting for Customer' is selected, clarifying to which team the request will be assigned.

In this multi-tiered process, when the 'Waiting for Customer' or 'Completed' status is selected, it assigns the request back to the *'Team of the Customer'* from the previous account in the service chain. This mechanism ensures that each layer in the service hierarchy is accountable and responsive to the preceding layer.

Incident Management

Navigating Major Incidents with Precision

Murphy's Law, familiar to many, ominously predicts, "Anything that can go wrong, will go wrong." This principle underscores the critical need for a robust major incident management procedure to address severe disruptions effectively.

Understanding Major Incidents

In service management, an incident refers to any event disrupting normal service operations. A situation escalates to a major Incident when it severely impacts a business service, leading to a significant operational productivity reduction. These are typically easy to identify due to an influx of related service desk calls and tickets, escalating managerial concern and stress within the organization. The onset of a major Incident often triggers a blend of stress, frustration, and urgency, making a calm and coordinated response mechanisms crucial.

Crafting a Major Incident Management Procedure

The **Major Incident Management procedure** outlines specific, actionable steps for responding to major Incidents, aiming to streamline the resolution process in high-pressure circumstances. The *incident manager* plays a pivotal role, assembling a dedicated team of multidisciplinary engineers to diagnose and address the issue. By extracting these experts from their routine duties and facilitating a focused communication channel, the incident manager ensures that all efforts are directed towards a swift resolution.

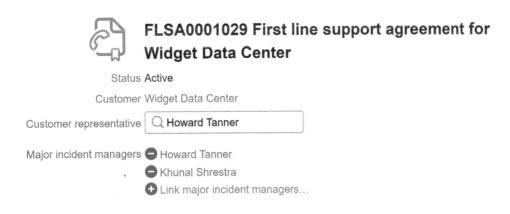

Figure 166: Defining incident managers will enable the major incident management functionality.

Equally important is the management of external communications, informing stakeholders and end users about ongoing resolution efforts to alleviate service desk pressure and maintain organizational transparency. Regular updates are vital until service restoration. Once the major incident has been resolved a thorough post-incident review is required to identify improvement opportunities and implement the necessary changes to prevent recurrence.

Each organization's major incident management process is specific, necessitating detailed instructions on who to inform, by which means, and at what frequency. This is something that you will always need to add to the 4me core incident management process description of your organization.

Leveraging the 4me Platform for Major Incident Management

4me offers the necessary features for the declaring and managing of major Incidents. The platform enables specialists to mark potential major incidents for management review. By tagging a service disruption as a

'Proposed' Major Incident, the relevant incident managers arc alerted to assess and either accept or reject the proposal.

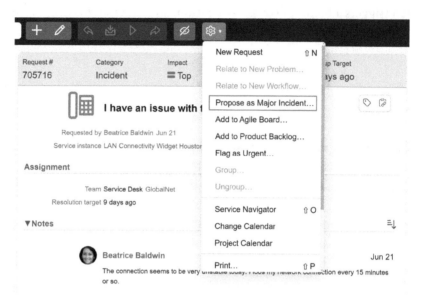

Figure 167: A specialist can propose a TOP impact incident as a candidate for the major incident management process. The incident managers will be notified.

To enable Major Incident Management within a 4me account, define the organization's *incident managers* within your first line support agreement. Specialists can then propose incidents as 'major' directly from their interface. The system's design ensures all designated *incident managers* receive immediate notifications.

Availability Management and Incident Management

An incident with the impact 'Top' means that the related service instance is down, causing an outage of the service for the users of that instance. This information is immediately reflected on the self-service portal for the end users, as well as in the Service Navigator for specialists.

When a specialist completes a top-impact request, he will need to define the start and end time of the outage. Remember that it was possible to define the service hours and an availability target on a service offering. Using these data points, the 4me platform is able to provide accurate availability figures for the services. These figures can be found in all the SLA reports of the Analytics console.

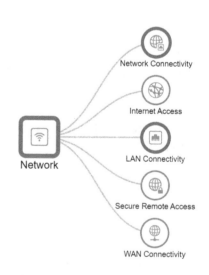

Figure 168: Outages are visualized in the Service Navigator section in the Analytics console.

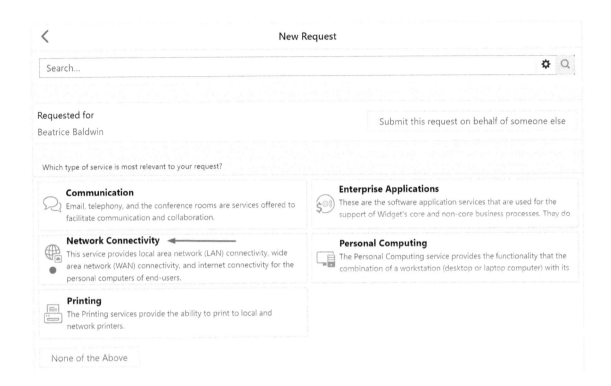

Figure 169: Outages become visible on the Self Service Portal.

Figure 170: Outages and availability tracking on the SLA Reports, a section of the Analytics Console.

Problem Management

Problem management is a fundamental service management practice. The undeniable value of problem management - reducing the number and impact of incidents - underscores its importance. Yet, the problem management process is characterized by its simplicity. According to ITIL 4, the process encompasses three main phases: problem identification, problem control, and error control. While the process is simple, identifying the root cause of an incident can be challenging and time-consuming.

Overcoming Common Challenges

However, the real challenge lies not in the complexity of identifying the root cause but in initiating the process itself. Many organizations falter in maintaining an active problem management practice due to the difficulty in identifying recurring incidents among potentially tens of thousands of tickets. This is where the concept of 'service-driven' problem management becomes crucial. By categorizing incidents under specific services and assigning a dedicated problem manager—regarded as a 'service matter expert'—to each service, organizations can streamline the identification process, making the 'haystack' more manageable.

Leveraging 4me for Efficient Problem Management

In 4me, problem managers are provided with a specialized view in the Records console, named '**Requests for Problem Identification**'. This view lists all completed requests associated with their service domain, highlighting those that may warrant further investigation because they are like to recur or because represent a service outage. Here's how 4me facilitates problem management:

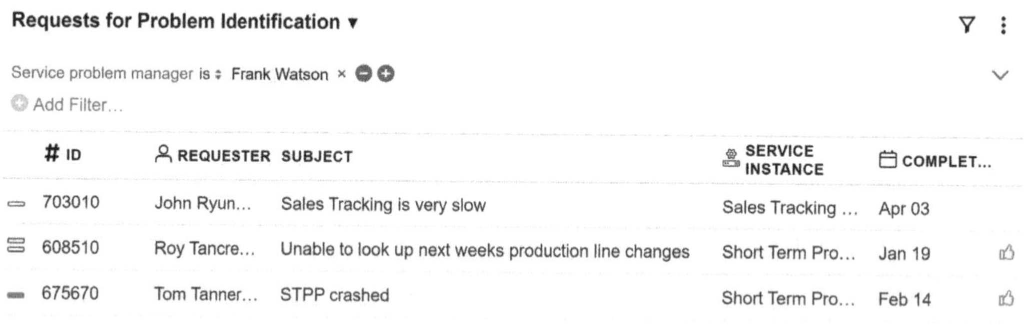
Requests for Problem Identification ▾
Service problem manager is ⬍ Frank Watson ×
Add Filter...
ID
REQUESTER
SUBJECT
SERVICE INSTANCE
COMPLET...
703010
John Ryun...
Sales Tracking is very slow
Sales Tracking ...
Apr 03
608510
Roy Tancre...
Unable to look up next weeks production line changes
Short Term Pro...
Jan 19
675670
Tom Tanner...
STPP crashed
Short Term Pro...
Feb 14

Figure 171: The Requests for Problem Identification view.

- **Request Review**: Problem managers can quickly review completed requests. If an incident's root cause has been addressed, marking it as 'Reviewed' removes it from the problem identification view.

- **Problem Creation**: Should further action be deemed necessary to avert future occurrences, problem managers can easily 'Relate to New Problem...' directly from the Actions menu, creating a new problem record and automatically relating it to the request.

Figure 172: Relate to a New Problem or set as Reviewed.

IT Change Management - Change Enablement

When ITIL v4 was unveiled, it brought with it a refreshing transformation from the traditional "Change Management" to "Change Enablement". This shift signifies far more than mere wordplay; it heralds a new era that aligns more closely with today's dynamic, agile-driven environments and DevOps cultures. Gone are the days when change management was synonymous with slow, bureaucratic processes that could stall the momentum of improvement initiatives and company growth. The conventional model, often anchored by the weekly meetings of the change advisory board (CAB) and orchestrated by a solitary change manager, was increasingly viewed as a bottleneck rather than a facilitator of value.

Even before the advent of ITIL v4, 4me was pioneering a more streamlined, efficient approach to managing changes.

The Service Driven Change Manager

One of the fundamental shifts in this new approach is moving away from the traditional centralized change manager role. Instead, 4me champions the concept of assigning a change manager for each individual service. This adjustment aligns perfectly with the essence of change management as a practice of risk management, where the primary goal is to assess and mitigate potential risks associated with implementing changes. This is especially crucial when considering:

- **Impact on Business Services**: Assessing whether the implementation of a change might degrade or interrupt services. It involves considering if monitoring solutions will be impacted, necessitating coordination with those responsible for oversight.
- **Capacity Impact**: Evaluating whether the change will require additional resources such as CPU or memory, thus affecting the service's capacity.
- **Post-Implementation Impact**: Determining the potential instability or functionality changes that a change might introduce to business services. This also involves considering whether additional training or communication is necessary.
- **Resource Requirements**: Identifying the necessary resources for implementing the change and their availability, including evaluating the complexity of the change to decide if it should be managed as a project.

✈ Expense Reporting

Category	Enterprise Applications
Description	The Expense Reporting service provides the ability to submit, review, approve, track and pay expenses incurred for Widget-related business. The service offers the functionality needed to support all Widget employees regardless of where they are based geographically.
	The Expense Reporting service relies on cost center and reimbursement status information from the Finance (SAP) service.
Service provider	Widget Data Center, External IT
Survey	General Service Rating Survey

▼ Responsibilities

Support team	Application Development
Service owner	Frank Watson
Release manager	Frank Watson
Change manager	Grace Weller
Knowledge manager	Thomas Wicker

Figure 173: *The Change Manager on a Service record.*

In this refined approach, there is a clear differentiation between service matter experts and the change manager. These experts are instrumental in answering the critical questions regarding business impact, capacity, post-implementation effects, and resource requirements associated with any change. On the other hand, the change managers collect assessments and insights from various service matter experts, synthesizing this information to make informed decisions regarding the risk associated with the change. Furthermore, the change managers are responsible for the overall planning and coordination of the changes for their service.

The Virtual Change Advisory Board

The virtual change advisory board introduces a more fluid and responsive approach to change approvals. With 4me, there is no longer a need to wait for a weekly CAB meeting. The platform's approval tasks enable the organization of a virtual CAB as soon as the service's change manager completes the risk assessment. This transforms change management from a weekly batch process into a continuous process.

For routine changes with minimal risk, the service's change manager may have the autonomy to proceed with planning and implementation without further approvals. For changes that could result in service downtime during operational hours, it may require the involvement of customer representatives and the service owners of the impacted services. High-risk changes might warrant the attention of the operations manager or even the CIO.

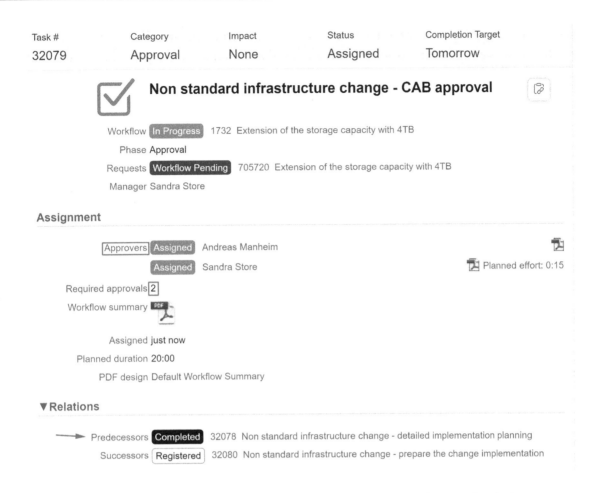

Figure 174: A virtual CAB with the implementation planning task as a predecessor. In this example only the service owner and change manager of the service need to give an approval.

An organization may choose to retain the weekly CAB meetings to review only these high-risk changes, ensuring that this meeting remains focused and efficient. Following agile principles, significant responsibility is delegated to the service support team and its change manager, empowering them to determine whether escalation to higher management is necessary.

Establishing a Unified Change Policy

Central to an agile and coherent change management framework is the role of the change process owner. This key figure is tasked with crafting, overseeing, and refining the agile change enablement process throughout the organization. Although the decentralized approach empowers the individual change managers for the different services, their activities should still fall within a universal framework.

The change process owner sets up this framework by establishing a comprehensive change policy. This policy outlines uniform risk assessment criteria and standardized escalation procedures to be followed by all change managers. By ensuring that all changes, regardless of their origin within the organization, adhere to this overarching policy, the change process owner ensures consistency, mitigates risk, and maintains alignment with organizational objectives and compliance requirements. This structured approach ensures that, while agility and speed are prioritized, they do not come at the expense of control or quality.

Facilitating Change Enablement with the 4me Platform

4me equips your organization with the necessary tools for efficient change management through its request and workflow templates. These templates are pivotal, especially when dealing with Non-Standard changes, also recognized as 'Normal' changes in ITIL terminology.

Adopting best practices, it's recommended to craft distinct request templates for each service concerning non-standard change requests. This ensures that every change has a clear rationale, answering the essential 'why' behind each modification. This clarity is crucial; without understanding the underlying need, proceeding with a change can be counterproductive. The initial request serves as a foundation, helping to discern whether a situation calls for a change or needs escalation to a project. Subsequently, a workflow manager can link the request to an appropriate workflow, selecting from predefined workflow templates aligned with organizational policies.

Active Workflow Management: The Role of the Change Manager

In the realm of change enablement, the service-specific *change manager* assumes the critical role of *workflow manager* for the change process. Unlike standard changes, where the workflow manager's intervention is minimal, the non-standard change workflow demands proactive oversight. The *change manager* is tasked with engaging service experts, conducting thorough risk assessments, orchestrating the approval process, and meticulously planning the implementation phase. This may involve coordinating multiple tasks and ensuring all stakeholders are aligned and informed.

Therefore, it is imperative that the *change manager* is well-versed with the 4me platform's functionalities regarding task assignments, risk assessments, and scheduling. Effective training in the *change manager* role is essential to grasp the nuances of active workflow management, ensuring the change process is handled with expertise and precision.

Planning Non-Standard Change Implementation Tasks in 4me

Effective planning of non-standard change implementation tasks is crucial for smooth execution. In the 4me platform, detailed *implementation* task definition ensures clear communication and coordination across the support organization. Be sure to specify the correct information in each implementation tasks, specifically:

- **Team** and **Member** to which the task will be assigned for execution.

- **Start no earlier than**: The date and time at which work on the task may begin, provided that its predecessors have been completed successfully.
- **Planned duration**: The time that is expected to elapse from the moment the task is assigned until the task is completed.
- **Planned effort**: The estimated effort required to complete the task.
- **Work hours are 24x7**: If left unchecked, the task completion target will be calculated using team's work hours.
- **Relations – Service instances**: Identify the service instances that will be impacted by the execution of the task to ensure visibility.

The Change Calendar in 4me

The Change Calendar is an essential tool for overseeing planned changes across the different services and change managers:

- **Accessing the Change Calendar**: You can find the Change Calendar in the Analytics console of the 4me platform. This feature provides a visual overview of scheduled changes.
- **Visibility of Changes by their Implementation Tasks**: An implementation task appears on the Change Calendar once it has been linked to one or more service instances.
- **Proactive Conflict Identification**:
    - **Resource Conflicts**: The Change Calendar alerts when a specialist is scheduled to work on multiple tasks as the same time.
    - **Service Infrastructure Conflicts**: The Change Calendar identifies tasks which execution is scheduled to overlap with other tasks that will affect the same service instance or service instances higher in the service hierarchy.

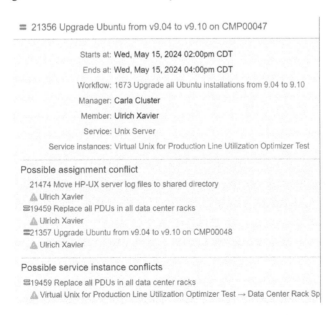

Figure 175: The 4me Change Calendar identifying resource and infrastructure conflicts.

Identifying Recent Changes in 4me

Post-implementation of non-standard changes carries the inherent risk of introducing new issues. For any support organization, it's crucial to stay informed about recent changes as they can often lead to the root cause of newly reported incidents

In 4me, the **Recent Changes** are prominently displayed in the Service Hierarchy Browser (SHB). This ensures that support teams can quickly identify the changes made to the service instance that appears to be affected by a new issue.

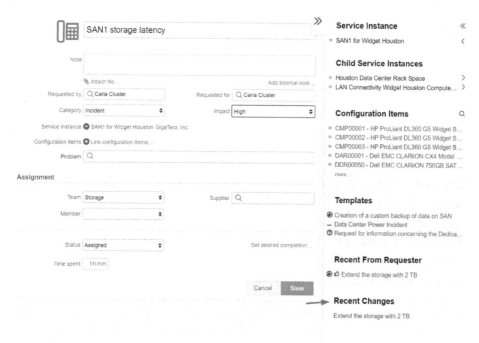

Figure 176: Recent Changes in the SHB.

Enhancing Efficiency: Beyond Basic Change Enablement in 4me

The 4me platform provides robust out-of-the-box functionality for change enablement, such as the intuitive 'Recent Changes' feature on the Service Hierarchy Browser (SHB) and the dynamic conflict detection in the Change Calendar. These features significantly streamline the change management process, making it more efficient and effective for organizations. However, to truly optimize change enablement, we recommend taking advantage of 4me's customization and automation capabilities. This involves:

- **Custom Assessment Forms**: Enhance the change request process by creating custom forms that cater specifically to your organization's needs. Tailored assessment questions can lead to more informed decision-making and a smoother change process.

- **Automated Risk Assessment and Approval**: Utilize UI Extensions to perform risk assessments based on predefined criteria and automation rules to automatically route change requests to the appropriate approvers. This reduces manual effort and speeds up the approval process.
- **Streamlined Implementation Scheduling**: Automate the scheduling of implementation tasks based on the information provided during the change assessment and planning phase.
- **Instructions and Checklists**: Include detailed instructions in the task templates for the people who will be asked to execute tasks that are based on these templates. In many cases, a checklist can make it easier for the assignee to keep track on the steps that need to be taken to complete the task.

By customizing workflow templates and employing automation rules, your organization can further reduce manual tasks, minimize errors, and ensure that changes are implemented swiftly and effectively. In Part III, we will explore how to apply custom fields and automation rules within the 4me platform to elevate your change enablement process to the next level.

Stay tuned for the next demo scenario, where we will demonstrate how these advanced customizations and automations can be implemented in 4me.

Demo

Change Enablement
Demo of GigTera's Non-standard Change Process

Imagine a critical moment at Widget Data Center: Carla Cluster, a dedicated member of the Unix server team, detects a looming issue. The onsite storage, SAN1, crucial for their UNIX servers, is alarmingly close to full capacity, sitting at less than 10% available space. This storage is crucial to several business services that Widget International depends on. The provider responsible for the SAN1 service instance is GigaTera Managed Services, known for their robust and secure data solutions.

Faced with this challenge, Carla doesn't hesitate. She springs into action and logs a detailed request to GigaTera Managed Services to extend SAN1's storage capacity with an additional 2 TB - a significant upgrade to ensure smooth operations.

Enter Sandra Store, the astute change manager specializing in SAN storage. She understands the critical nature of this request. Recognizing the urgency, Sandra quickly takes charge of Carla's request, linking it to a non-standard change template specially designed for such significant modifications.

Join us as we step into their shoes: Watch how this scenario unfolds, illustrating the seamless integration of request management and change enablement in 4me.

- Log in as carla.cluster@widget.com to Widget Europe, IT.

- Go to the Service Desk Console.
- Select Dedicated Onsite Storage.
- Select None of the Above.
- Set the subject to "Extend the SAN1 storage with 2 TB".
- Add a note: "The SAN1 storage is for 90% in use. Please extend it with 2 TB."
- Set the category to RFC and add two minutes for time spent.
- Save.

- Login as sandra.store@gigatera.com to GigaTera Managed Services.
  - In the Inbox, select the request from Carla Cluster.
  - In the Actions menu (gear button), select "Relate to a New Workflow…".
  - Select the workflow template "Non-standard infrastructure change' and click on New….
  - Select the Justification: "Expansion".
  - Save.
  - Go to the Inbox.
  - Select and edit the Risk & Impact task.
  - Set the status to Completed.
  - Set the Short description to "Extend the storage".
  - Set the Implementation Plan to "See document".
  - Set service impact to Unavailable.
  - Set the proposed time to Saturday evening at 18:00.
  - Set the Duration to 30 minutes.
  - Set Risk - Likelihood to Highly Unlikely.
  - Set Risk – Impact of failure to Low.
  - Add note: "This must be planned during the weekend".
  - Save.

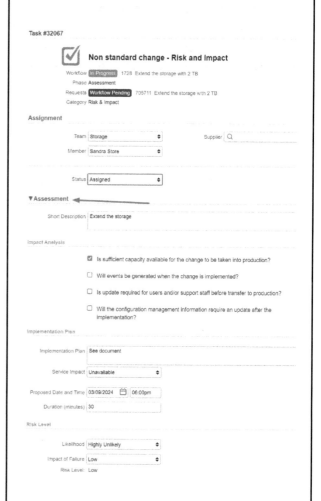

Figure 177: A customized change enablement assessment form in GigaTera Managed Services.

Configuration and Asset Management

Simplifying Configuration Items and Assets

In service management frameworks like ITIL, there's a clear distinction between Configuration Items (CIs) and Assets. However, 4me adopts a streamlined approach, blurring these lines for user simplicity. In this framework, all CIs can be considered assets, simplifying the concept for end users and reducing complexity.

Unpacking the 4me CMDB Structure

At the core of 4me's configuration management capability is the Configuration Management Database (CMDB), structured into three layers:

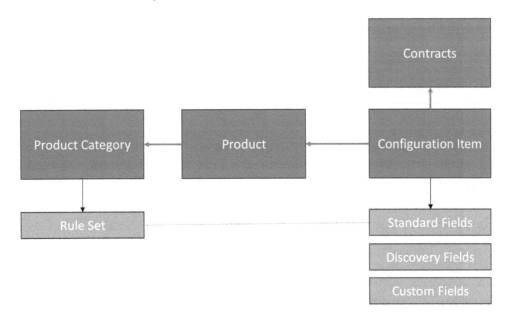

Figure 178: The three-layered architecture of the 4me CMDB.

1. **Product Categories**: This foundational layer categorizes the different types of CIs present in the environment. Categories can range widely, encompassing items from printers and routers to more unconventional items like vending machines, cars, and even life insurance policies. Each product category must be linked to a specific rule set, defining the applicable fields for CIs within that category. The following rule sets are available:
   - License Certificate
   - Logical Asset with Financial Data
   - Logical Asset without Financial Data
   - Physical Asset

- Server
- Software
- Software Distribution Package

These rule sets are instrumental in determining the specific fields that will be accessible for the configuration items within that category. For instance, a CI under the 'Server' rule set will likely include fields like 'RAM' and 'Number of Cores.' In contrast, a CI categorized under 'License Certificate' will have the 'License Type' field available, but not 'Number of Processors.'

2. **Products**: This layer specifies the models or variants within a Product Category. For instance, under the 'Computer – Laptop' category, you might define specific models like '*Microsoft Surface Pro 9 - 13"*'. For more unique categories like 'Dog,' breeds such as '*Chihuahua*' or '*Poodle*' would represent different products.
3. **Configuration Items (CIs)**: This is where individual items are recorded, such as a specific '*Microsoft Surface Pro 9 - 13"*' assigned to an employee or a poodle named 'Max'. Each CI in this layer is a tangible representation of the product and category it belongs to.

New 4me accounts come equipped with a set of predefined product categories, primarily IT-oriented. Users have the flexibility to adapt these to their needs by removing and adding product categories.

Configuration Items Associated with Users

In the realm of asset management, particularly for those assets where user association is vital, 4me allows linking configuration items directly to individual users. This relationship is used to select the specific persons who make use of the configuration item.

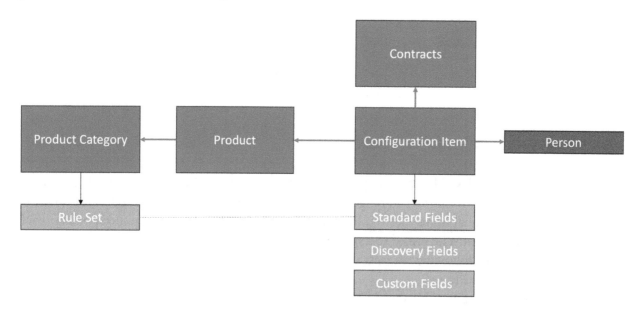

Figure 179: Configuration Items can be linked to person records.

This link between users and assets enhances visibility and accessibility across the platform:

- **Self Service Portal**: Users can easily view all the CIs they are currently using via the 'My Assets' feature. This personalized view ensures users are always aware of the assets at their disposal and can report issues or request support directly related to specific assets.

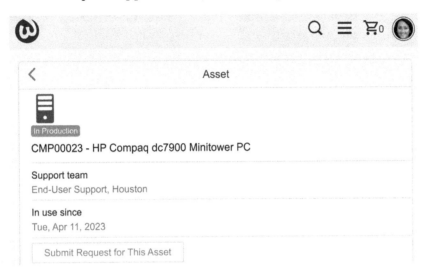

Figure 180: The My Assets view on the Self Service Portal.

- **Service Desk Console**: For service desk analysts, this user-CI relationship is equally useful. After accepting a call from a user, analysts can quickly view and identify which configuration items are associated with that individual: instead of navigating through services first, analysts can directly pinpoint and select the relevant configuration item.

Figure 181: The CIs of the user in the Service Desk Console.

Ownership of Configuration Items

Ownership is a critical aspect of configuration management, indicating the financial responsibility for each configuration item. The '**financial owner**' typically refers to the organization that has procured the CI.

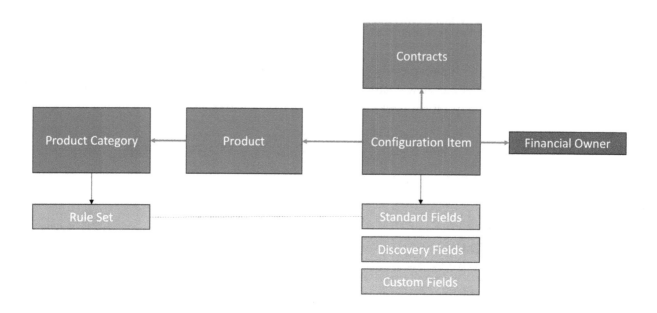

Figure 183: The financial ownership of a Configuration Item.

In the self-service portal, key contacts from an organization can access a comprehensive list of all CIs owned by their organization, including those under any subsidiary or descendant entities. This feature is particularly advantageous in scenarios where there's a distinct separation between the management and ownership of CIs, such as in customer-supplier dynamics. For example, when a customer organization has outsourced the management of certain assets to a Managed Service Provider (MSP) but retains ownership, this functionality provides key contacts with a transparent, real-time inventory of the assets under MSP management.

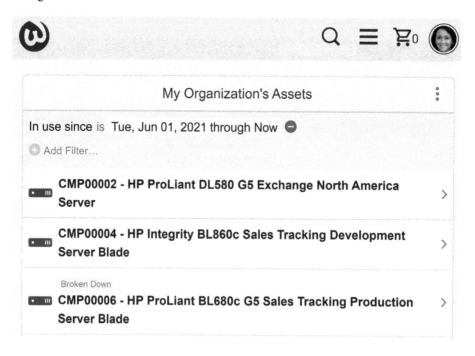

Figure 184: My Organization's Assets on the Self Service Portal.

Outsourcing of Configuration Management over a Trust

When a customer delegates the support of its configuration items (CIs) to a supplier operating within a separate 4me account, the process involves more than just creating a service and establishing an SLA for that service. The customer also wants to ensure that the supplier is performing the configuration management while the ownership remains with the customer. This scenario is facilitated through a specific account trust setting.

✅ Widget Data Center can assign support responsibility for CIs to us

   The support team(s) linked here can be selected by configuration managers of Widget Data
   Center in the configuration items that are registered in their account.

☐ Widget Data Center can see our configuration items

Figure 185: Assigning support responsibility for CIs over an account trust.

The supplier has the ability to activate the setting '***Trusted Account* can assign support responsibility for CIs to us**' within their account trust with the customer account. To maintain control over which of the supplier's teams the customer can assigned CIs to, the supplier can specify these teams in the trust with the customer account. Subsequently, the configuration manager on the customer's side can then proceed to assign the responsibility for some or all of its CIs, as outlined by the support contract, to one of these teams of the supplier organization.

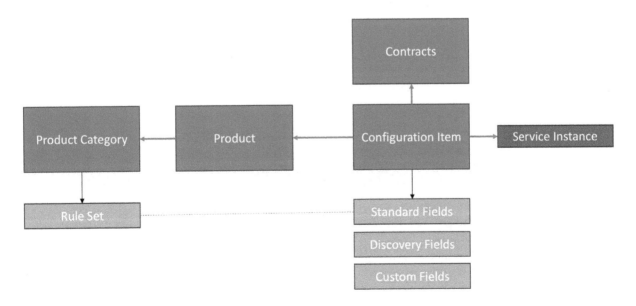

Figure 186: Physical CIs related to a Service Instance.

Mastering Service Infrastructures with 4me Configuration Management

The true power of 4me's configuration management functionality comes to the fore in the realm of complex service infrastructures - be it IT Operations overseeing data centers or Facilities Management maintaining multi-site technical systems. Such environments require a clear understanding of the interplay between various configuration items (CIs) and services, from warranty details to serial numbers and support contracts. This is the domain where 4me truly excels.

In 4me, physical CIs can be directly associated with specific service instances. This critical linkage ensures that each CI is clearly mapped within the service hierarchy, directly supporting and enhancing support processes. It's important to note that each physical CI is linked to only one service instance, establishing a clear line of responsibility to a designated support team. This clarity removes any ambiguity and streamlines support operations, ensuring that for every physical CI, there's a definitive support team accountable for it.

In contrast, a specific version of a software application may be running on several servers or laptops, which is why a software CI can be linked to several service instances.

Knowing these relationships between CIs and service instances is crucial for support specialists, providing them with invaluable insights:

- In the event of an incident affecting a specific service instance, specialists can swiftly identify potential problematic CIs.
- Before executing changes on a CI, they can assess the potential impact on business services via the service hierarchy.

The **Service Navigator**, accessible within a request from the Actions menu, offers a dynamic graphical representation of the service hierarchy and associated CIs.

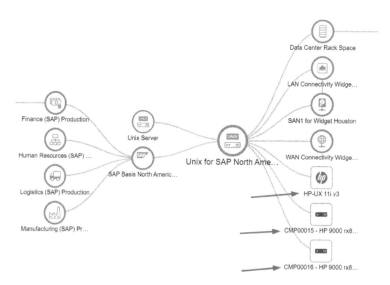

Figure 187: The Service Navigator revealing the service infrastructure and related CIs.

Software Asset Management (SAM) - Managing Software and Licenses

The 4me CMDB enables detailed management of software and their associated licenses. Distinctly, a software license and the software itself are treated as separate Configuration Items (CIs). The Software CI symbolizes the actual version of software installed on physical devices and can be connected not only to these devices but also to service instances. This linkage makes the software CI a visible component within the service hierarchy.

For example, typical software installed on a PC such as Chrome, Outlook, Word, Excel, and Project, when associated with the 'Personal Computing for Sales & Marketing' service instance, allows incidents related to these applications to be directly linked to the relevant software CI through the Service Hierarchy Browser, aiding significantly the incident management process.

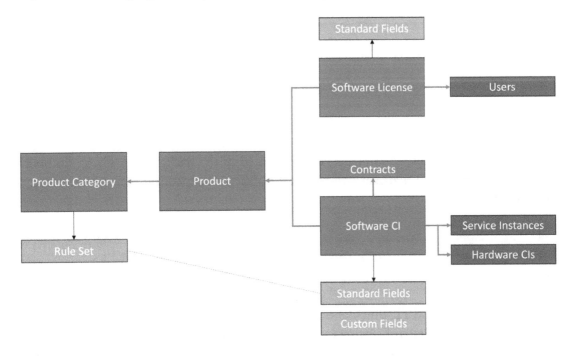

Figure 188: Software Asset Management in the 4me CMDB.

Licenses, conversely, denote the entitlement to use software. In scenarios like user-based licensing for Microsoft Project, individual licenses can be associated directly with person records, reflecting their usage rights. Generally, software products are delineated based on their versions; for instance, 'SQL Server 2019' and 'SQL Server 2022' might represent different software products. Corresponding software CIs could then be specified as 'SQL Server 2022.160.4105.2' or '2022.160.4100.1', mirroring the exact installed versions.

Bulk CI Updates

For configuration managers tasked with overseeing thousands of assets, individual updates to Configuration Items (CIs) are impractical. While comprehensive bulk updates to all 4me records are achievable through export/import functionality—details of which will be covered in a forthcoming chapter—configuration managers and account administrators have the ability to perform bulk CI updates directly from the Specialist Interface.

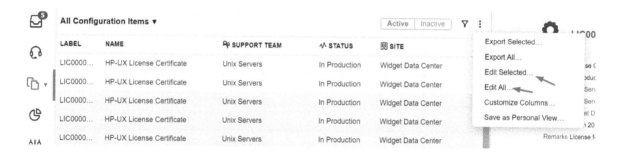

Figure 189: Bulk updating a series of selected CIs.

This bulk update feature operates as an asynchronous process, allowing the configuration manager to attend to other tasks while the updates are performed in the background. Once the bulk update completes, the configuration manager will receive a notification, ensuring they are informed and can verify the updates.

Optimizing Asset Management with QR Codes and Short URLs

In facilities management and IT, quick and accurate reporting of issues related to physical devices—such as vending machines, network printers, or projectors—is crucial. Implementing QR codes on these devices allows users to instantly scan with their smartphone and be directed to the self-service portal, automatically linking the correct asset to their request.

Figure 190: Creating a Short URL for a coffee machine.

The 4me platform simplifies this approach through the use of **Short URLs**. Within the Settings console, specialists can generate QR codes associated with specific services and configuration items. Considering the potential volume of assets, individually generating QR codes is impractical. Therefore, 4me offers the 'Reserve...' feature to configuration managers and account administrators for generating Short URLs and corresponding QR codes in bulk. The generated short URLs can then be exported for printing.

Once QR codes are affixed to the devices, the corresponding Short URLs can be linked to the respective configuration items. This method not only enhances the ease with which end users can report issues for these CIs, but it also improves reporting accuracy and significantly improves the efficiency of asset management.

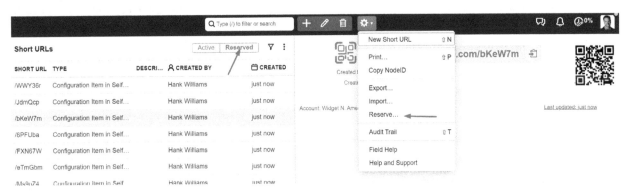

Figure 191: Bulk creation of reserved Short URLs.

CI Provisioning

In a typical IT environment, many thousands of physical devices and software items are managed. Such environments often employ system management tools, monitoring software, or endpoint management solutions. These tools 'discover' physical assets connected to the network, cataloging a wide range of technical attributes, including relationships between devices and installed software.

These systems are invaluable to enterprise service management systems like 4me, providing an inventory of the actual state of all assets. Rather than manually defining and managing these assets, it's more efficient to provision the CIs in 4me via integration. The 4me platform supports this with APIs for provisioning, as well as through numerous standard integrations with popular discovery tools.

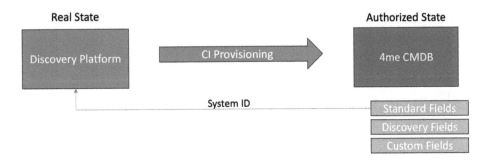

Figure 192: Discovery tool integration: Real state versus Authorized State.

Unlike many IT service management tools, 4me adopts a lean CMDB approach, limiting the number of standard fields on a CI to those relevant for support processes. For additional attributes, 4me employs a federated model. In this model, the '**System ID**' field of a CI record provides a link to the asset in the discovery tool, giving specialists direct access to detailed, real-time information about the CI's technical attributes.

While some technical attributes are crucial for support, they are not typically updated manually. Examples include '*lastSeenAt*' (the date and time the CI was last detected by the discovery tool) and '*operatingSystem*'. These fields are available out-of-the-box in 4me but are updated only through discovery tool provisioning and kept hidden when no value has been provisioned. Moreover, as discussed in upcoming chapters, additional custom fields can be added to meet specific organizational needs.

Automating Recurring Workflows for Maintenance

In contexts like IT and facilities, recurring workflows often involve the maintenance of physical assets, such as the annual servicing of air conditioning systems. Traditionally, this would necessitate the manual creation of a new recurring workflow template upon the deployment of a new configuration item.

4me simplifies this process by allowing workflow templates to be linked to products, allowing the recommended recurrence schedule to be defined at the product level. Once a configuration manager has linked a product to a workflow template in the product's 'Maintenance' section, a recurring workflow is automatically scheduled for each of the product's configuration items as soon as they are set to the status 'In Production'. This ensures that no maintenance task is accidentally forgotten.

Figure 193: Adding a workflow template to the maintenance section of a product.

Knowledge Management

4me incorporates Knowledge Management utilizing the principles of the **Knowledge-Centered Service (KCS)** methodology. This approach revolutionizes traditional knowledge management by seamlessly integrating it into the support process. In KCS, creating and updating knowledge becomes a natural component of daily activities, transforming problem-solving efforts into valuable knowledge assets.

Principles of KCS in 4me:

Reuse Over Create: In 4me, knowledge articles are intricately linked to the service-driven architecture. This integration ensures that relevant knowledge is readily accessible to users through the self-service portal or when interacting with the virtual agent. Moreover, these articles are contextually presented within the service hierarchy to provide proactive support during request resolution.

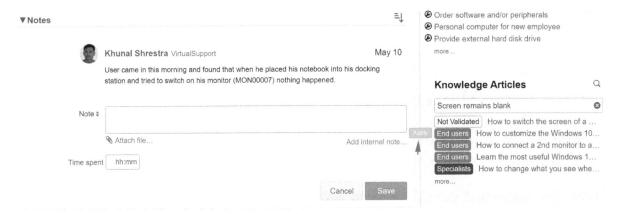

Figure 194: Knowledge articles available to be applied to a request in the service driven contextual view of the Service Hierarchy Browser (SHB).

Create Knowledge On-The-Go: 4me simplifies the creation of knowledge articles. Specialists can instantly transform solution notes into knowledge articles with just a click. Enhanced by AI, this process suggests content automatically, dramatically reducing the time needed to create knowledge articles while improving the quality of the information they provide.

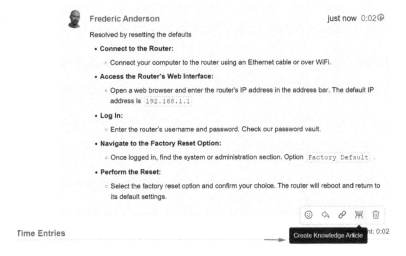

Evolve Content Based on Demand and Usage: The platform prioritizes knowledge articles based on their frequency of use, ensuring that the most beneficial resources are easily accessible. Users are encouraged to provide feedback, enabling continuous improvement of content. Furthermore, 4me's Search Phrases report identifies frequently searched terms that did not lead users to find the article they were looking for, guiding administrators and knowledge managers to fill content gaps effectively.

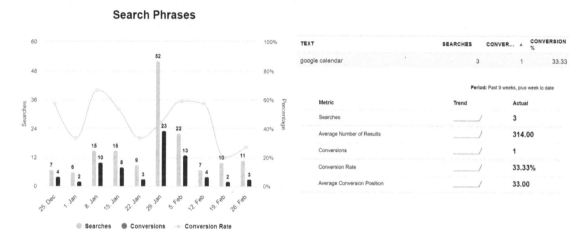

Figure 195: The Search Phrases report in the Analytics Console.

Service-Level Management

Understanding the Essentials

By now, you understand that the service hierarchy is the skeleton around which the service delivery operating model is configured. This service hierarchy is made up of the agreements established between the providers and their customers as defined by the service level agreements and the service offerings on which they are based. The service hierarchy makes it clear for specialists which underpinning service instance could be applied to a request to ensure that it is assigned to the right team for resolution. It also ensures that SLA response and resolution targets are measured correctly as requests are passed down the hierarchy. End users and specialists typically don't see, and don't need to understand, the complex calculations 4me performs to figure out the deadlines. End users have visibility into the resolution targets for their requests, setting clear expectations. Specialists are given specific target times, which prioritizes the work for them in their inbox.

However, *service level managers*, *service owners*, operations managers and even team leaders really need to understand this part of 4me because it helps them see where they can make services better. In this chapter, we'll break down how 4me's unique approach to service level management guarantees the most accurate SLA reporting and how it can help service providers understand and improve the support they provide for their services step by step.

Navigating Through a Real-Life Scenario

Let's examine a scenario that you can replicate in a demo environment: Randy Barton, a financial controller within Widget Europe's Finance department, uses the self-service portal to report an issue with the Enterprise Resource Planning (SAP) service. This system is critical to the business. Bert Jansen, the coordinator for the SAP Development team, reviews the incident and assigns it a 'Medium' impact level. He suspects the problem lies within the 'SAP Basis Europe Production (P47)' infrastructure and accordingly applies this child service instance, routing the request to the SAP Basis Support team in the Widget Data Center support domain account.

Grace Groupco, a member of this team, starts investigating the incident and deduces that it might be a configuration issue within the UNIX infrastructure. She applies the child service instance 'Unix for SAP Europe Production', directing the request to the Operations team. Ellen Brown, from the Operations team, identifies the problem by examining the log files of the CMP00011 HP 9000 server. She restarts the HP Serviceguard service and marks the request as completed. Once completed at the Widget Data Center, the request is reassigned back to Bert Jansen's SAP Development team in the Widget Europe, IT support domain account. Bert then confirms the resolution from his end and completes the request, which notifies Randy Barton that his request has been resolved.

This sequence illustrates a typical IT incident resolution involving multiple stakeholders across different teams and accounts. However, this raises questions from a service level management (SLM) perspective. If Bert Jansen delayed the final confirmation after Widget Data Center's Operations team resolved the issue, does this breach the SLA? And if so, who bears the responsibility?

Affected SLA Generation

The example above illustrates why it's not straightforward to simply state whether 'the' resolution target for a request in 4me was breached. Multiple parties, and multiple agreements between these parties, are involved:

- The Widget business, specifically the European Finance department, which has an SLA with Widget Europe IT for the SAP services.
- Widget Europe IT, which holds an **Underpinning Contract** (UC) with Widget Data Center for the SAP Basis service.

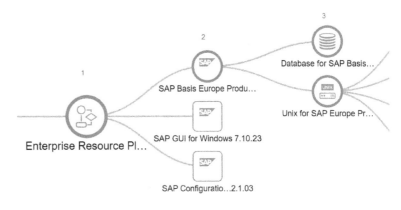

Figure 196: The Service Navigator's visualization of the service chain of the example.

- The SAP Basis support team, which maintains an **Operational Level Agreement** (OLA) with the Unix Server team concerning the Unix servers hosting the SAP Basis.

This scenario is a common example of how a Service hierarchy is needed both for getting requests passed to the correct teams and keeping track of the agreements between these teams. As a request moves through the hierarchy, an **Affected SLA (ASLA)** record is created for each applicable SLA. A section titled 'Affected SLAs' appears within the request details, listing the relevant SLAs for the support domain account that is looking at this section. In this case:

Bert Jansen of Widget Europe IT will see two affected SLAs:

- 'Standard Enterprise Resource Planning for Widget Europe, Finance', this is the SLA provided by Widget Europe's IT department which covers the requester.
- 'Premium SAP Basis for the SAP Production Instance of Widget Europe, IT', which is the underpinning SLA provided by Widget Data Center.

Conversely, Ellen Brown from the Widget Data Center will see these two affected SLAs:

- 'Premium SAP Basis for the SAP Production Instance of Widget Europe, IT', which is the SLA provided by Widget Data Center to Widget Europe's IT department.
- 'Gold Unix Server for the SAP Europe Production Instance', representing the OLA from the UNIX Servers team that covers the SAP Basis team.

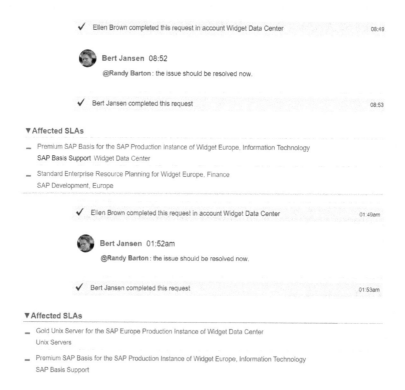

Figure 197: The same request with the affected SLAs seen in the Widget Europe, IT support domain account (top) and in the Widget Data Center support domain account (bottom).

In total, three ASLAs were generated in the above scenario. Therefore, questioning whether 'the' resolution target for a 4me request was breached is not entirely accurate. 4me can provide answers to more specific queries in this context:

- Was the SLA resolution target concerning the requester met or breached?
- Did Widget Data Center fulfill its underpinning SLA obligations for Widget Europe IT?
- Did the Operations team resolve the request in time for the SAP Basis team?

While investigating escalations or identifying systemic issues related to SLA target breaches, examining ASLAs on individual requests might be beneficial. However, the pursuit of service excellence should ideally begin from a more consolidated and higher-level perspective.

SLA Reports

The 'SLA Reports' section in the Analytics console is a crucial tool for analyzing SLA performance and understanding the interdependencies between services.

Consider a situation where Widget Europe, IT expresses concerns that Widget Data Center is not meeting

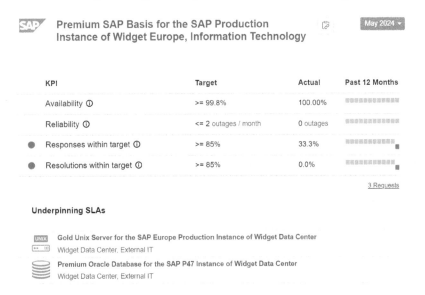

Figure 198: The report for the SLA 'Premium SAP Basis for Widget Europe, IT' gives insight in the service quality and that of its underpinning services.

its support targets for the SAP Basis service. Within the 'SLA Reports' section, a comprehensive overview of all SLAs provided by and to the support domain account is presented, highlighting any breaches with a red marker. This instant visibility also offers insight into any target breaches of underpinning SLAs, making it easy to drill down and find the provider that was the underlying cause.

For example, when examining the '*Premium SAP Basis*' SLA, it's possible to see if there are underlying issues with the two supporting services. This detailed breakdown helps determine whether a top-level breach is the result of failures lower down in the service hierarchy.

The Provider and Customer Reports

The '**Provider Reports**' section in the Analytics console is designed to offer a comprehensive look at how external service providers of a support domain account are performing. The 'Provider Reports' showcase all external providers with a detailed insight into the services and the activities provided, including the associated KPIs.

Figure 199: The providers of Widget Europe, IT.

For instance, within Widget Europe, IT's context, one can observe Widget Data Center listed as an external service provider. This entity offers a range of services, including SAP Basis, Business Intelligence, Directory Services and Email, among others. These reports provide detailed insights into each service offered by the external provider.

Figure 200: Widget Europe, IT, a customer of Widget Data Center.

Conversely, the '**Customer Reports**' section shows how well the provider organization is doing for its customers. This is where Widget Data Center can see if it is meeting its SLA targets for customers such as Widget Europe, IT. As a customer of Widget Data Center, Widget Europe, IT can review exactly the same performance metrics for Widget Data Center in the 'Provider Reports' section, because it is the service receiver. This reciprocal transparency ensures both parties are aligned on the performance metrics.

For managed service providers (MSPs), these customer reports are extremely valuable. They provide a snapshot of all clients, highlighting which targets have been missed. This real-time visibility into their performance allows MSPs to address issues proactively and maintain strong customer relations.

Figure 201: The reports that GigaTera Managed Services, an MSP in the demo environment, sees for all its customers.

Understanding ASLA Accountability

In the world of affected SLAs, understanding the Accountability field on an ASLA record is crucial. This field indicates whether the support team that is ultimately responsible for the targets specified in an ASLA record is expected to resolve the request, or whether this will be done by a team lower down in the service hierarchy. Looking back at our example, three teams were involved, generating three ASLAs. Suppose the initial two teams, the SAP Application and the SAP Basis support teams, efficiently met their response targets, but the UNIX team took excessively long to resolve the issue, leading to breaches in all three ASLAs. The question arises: should the first two teams be blamed?

In the 4me framework, the SAP Application and SAP Basis support teams are considered *accountable* but not responsible for the breach. Their ASLAs will indicate Supplier in the Accountability field, signifying their contribution to the solution without bearing direct fault. This differentiation is critical for management: if the end-to-end SLA for the SAP service is consistently missed, Widget Europe, IT holds the overall accountability. If repeated breaches are traced back to the SAP Basis service provided by Widget Data Center, then it's Widget Europe, IT's responsibility to seek corrective actions from Widget Data Center. Similarly, if Widget Data Center identifies that the Unix team's delays are causing the breaches, they should prompt the Unix team for improvements. In our example, the Accountability field of the UNIX team's ASLA would be set to **Provider**, pinpointing them as the party responsible for the breach.

Conversely, if Bert Jansen from the SAP Application team identifies the root cause as an incorrect installation parameter in the SAP GUI, which falls under the Personal Computing service, he would apply the *Personal Computing for Finance* service instance to the request. Should the Personal Computing team fail to timely resolve the issue, it's unjust to hold the SAP Application team accountable. They are no longer part of the service chain. Therefore, their ASLA's accountability would be marked as **SLA not affected**. An ASLA with accountability **SLA not affected** is excluded from resolution target calculations. Note, however, that such an ASLA will still be included in response target reports. In our example, the SAP Application team should have responded in time to the request to decide that another service instance was the affected one. To make it easy to identify ASLAs with the accountability 'SLA Not Affected', they are presented in strike-through text within the 'Affected SLAs' section of requests.

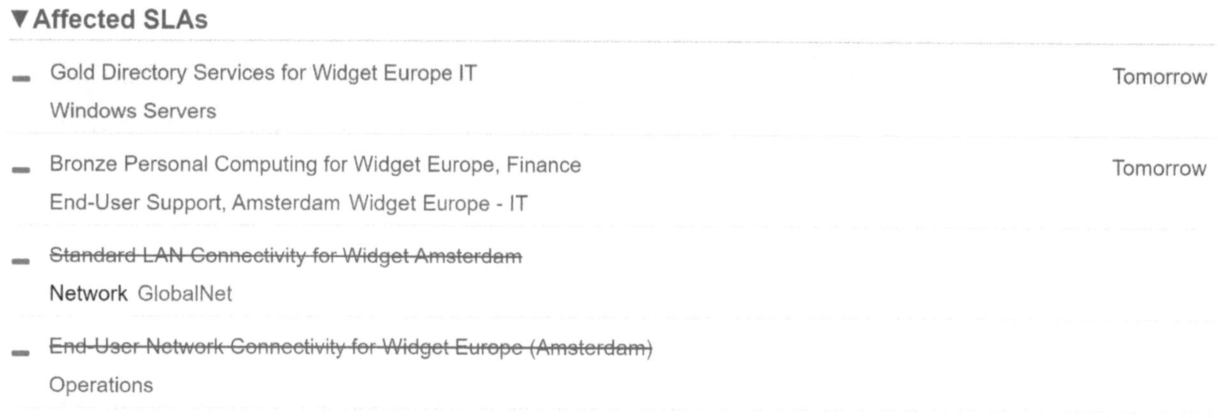

▼ **Affected SLAs**

— Gold Directory Services for Widget Europe IT   Tomorrow
   Windows Servers

— Bronze Personal Computing for Widget Europe, Finance   Tomorrow
   End-User Support, Amsterdam Widget Europe - IT

— ~~Standard LAN Connectivity for Widget Amsterdam~~
   Network GlobalNet

— ~~End-User Network Connectivity for Widget Europe (Amsterdam)~~
   Operations

Figure 202: ASLAs with accountability 'SLA Not Affected'

Creating SLA Dashboards

The creation of custom SLA Dashboards in 4me allows organizations to leverage and customize their service level analysis beyond the comprehensive out-of-the-box SLA reports available in the Analytics console. The foundational report for such dashboards is typically the '**SLA Resolution Targets Met and Breached**' report. However, interpreting this report without any contextual filters can be misleading because it is based on affected SLA records (ASLAs).

For instance, if a report initially shows 42 affected SLAs met and 26 affected SLAs breached, this doesn't directly translate to 42 requests having been completed within target out of a total of 68 requests. That's because multiple ASLAs can be generated for a single request.

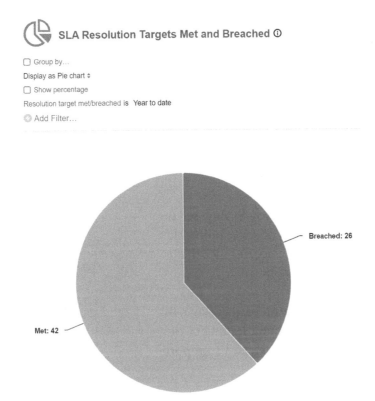

Figure 203: The SLA Resolution Targets Met and Breached without Filtering.

The Accountability and Support Team Filter

By making use of the '*Accountability*' and '*Support team*' filters, more detailed insights can be gleaned from this report. For instance, to assess how often the SAP Development team failed to meet an SLA resolution target when they were responsible for the resolution, you could apply the 'Support team' filter and group the report by 'Accountability'. The refined report would then display, for services where the SAP Development team is recognized as the support team, that four ASLAs were met, and two were breached. Notably, for all breached ASLAs, the support team served as the supplier—accountable but not responsible for the breach.

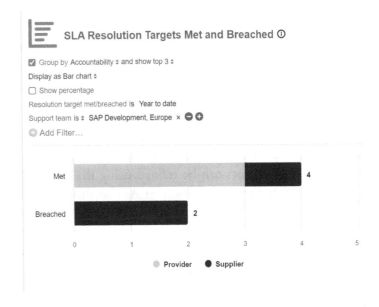

Figure 204: Adding the Support Team filter and Grouping by Accountability.

It's also important to note the difference between the 'Team' filter and the 'Support team' filter. The 'Team' filter pertains to the team to which the *request* (of the ASLAs) is assigned. This is the team that completed the request, hence all ASLAs under this filter will have their accountability set to 'Provider'. The Support Teams pertain to the teams of the ASLAs. Filtering on Support Team includes ASLAs with accountability set to 'Supplier' and 'Provider'.

Unraveling Process Disconnects: The Significance of 'SLA Not Affected' Accountability

When the accountability of an affected SLA is set to **SLA Not Affected**, it signifies that at some point, the associated request was linked to a service instance that is not part of the current service hierarchy.

Alternatively, it could mean that a team further down in the service hierarchy declined the request leading to the request being linked to a service instance, and a support team, higher in the hierarchy.

Both scenarios indicate potential issues: time wasted and a disconnect in the support process. Occasional occurrences are normal, but frequent, systematic instances suggest underlying problems, possibly necessitating updates to the service catalog or additional staff training. By applying the filter 'Accountability = SLA Not Affected' to the 'SLA Resolution Targets Met and Breached' report and grouping this report by service, these patterns can be identified and addressed.

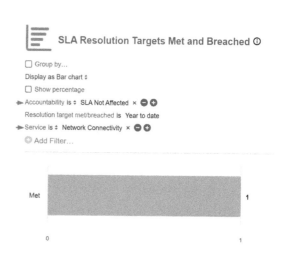

Figure 205: Filtering on Accountability SLA not Affected to reveal process inefficiencies.

Optimizing Customer SLA Reporting for Clear Insights

For enterprises, delivering service to the internal business, the ultimate measure of service success is the timeliness and effectiveness of issue resolution for their users. To obtain a focused view of support outcomes, SLA reports can be refined using the '**Requester covered = Yes**' filter. This adjustment ensures the inclusion of only those SLAs that directly cover end users, effectively omitting operational level agreements (OLAs) and underpinning contracts (UCs), which are more internally focused.

For a more detailed analysis, it is advisable to narrow down the report to a specific service. Furthermore, applying the 'Accountability' filter to remove 'SLA Not Affected' entries sharpens the focus on relevant SLA adherence, particularly for resolution targets. Choosing the 'Table view' format for these reports may enhance readability and facilitate a clearer understanding of the data.

Figure 206: Filtering on the 'Requester Covered' ASLAs.

Understanding Request-Based Customer SLA Reporting

The nature of Affected SLA records can sometimes lead to confusion, especially when comparing the number of registered and completed requests with actual SLA resolution metrics. As previously mentioned, a single request may be associated with multiple ASLAs, but a request might also not be linked to any ASLA at all. For example, a service desk analyst in a support domain account has the capability to register requests for any user within the directory account, regardless of whether that user is covered by a specific service. Consequently, such requests, lacking an associated SLA, do not generate an Affected SLA record and are treated as 'best effort' requests. These requests will not appear at all in ASLA-based reports.

This discrepancy means that when comparing Registered or Completed Requests reports with SLA Resolution Met and Breached reports for the same period, the numbers may not align due to the divergent bases of these

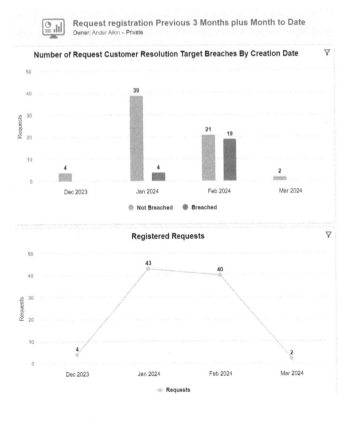

Figure 207: Using 'Request Customer Resolution Target' reports.

reports. To address this and align the data more closely, 4me offers request-based SLA reports such as **'Request Customer Response Targets'** and **'Request Customer Resolution Targets'**. These reports are based on the request records themselves, using only the customer ASLAs linked to each request. A **Customer ASLA** is defined as an affected SLA that covers the requester or, if the request originated from another 4me account, is associated with a customer organization of this account. In these reports, a request is marked as 'breached' if any linked Customer ASLA has been breached. In addition, 'best effort' requests, which lack an ASLA, are automatically classified as Non-breached.

Customer Satisfaction

Service delivery is so much more than resolving tickets in time. The best service is a service for which no tickets needed to be registered; a service without bugs, without incidents, so comprehensive and so intuitive that its users have no questions. Users require services that are available when they need them and that are so intuitive and fast that they do not leave them frustrated. An excellent service proactively provides the users all they need, even without asking for it. And this should all be provided against a reasonable cost.

So there is a lot more than SLA targets to judge customer satisfaction; a holistic view on how the services provided are perceived by the customer is required.

Embracing Moments of Truth in Service Management

The concept of 'Moments of Truth,' was introduced by Jan Carlzon in the 1980s. It highlights pivotal interactions that shape customer perceptions of a brand. This concept states that customer satisfaction with regard to a brand is determined by those short moments when you come into contact with the organization behind the brand. When you can convert a Moment of Truth into a positive outcome, you can turn dissatisfaction into customer satisfaction, which is a key success factor in building a successful business. In the context of service management, these moments are often encapsulated in the support tickets that customers raise. While a mid-sized support organization might face hundreds to thousands of these opportunities daily, the reality is that not every ticket leads to a critical moment. The challenge lies in identifying these critical moments and transforming those negative customer experiences into satisfied customers.

The 4me platform offers specialized tools to pinpoint and efficiently address these Moments of Truth. It empowers end users to easily express their dissatisfaction, capturing vital feedback with just a click. This immediate feedback mechanism ensures that service teams can quickly identify dissatisfied users.

Upon receiving a dissatisfaction alert, the *service desk manager* gets automatically notified, enabling a prompt response. Furthermore, the **'Requests with Dissatisfied Requester'** report in 4me provides a clear overview, showing the number of requests with which the requester was dissatisfied and tracking whether they are being addressed.

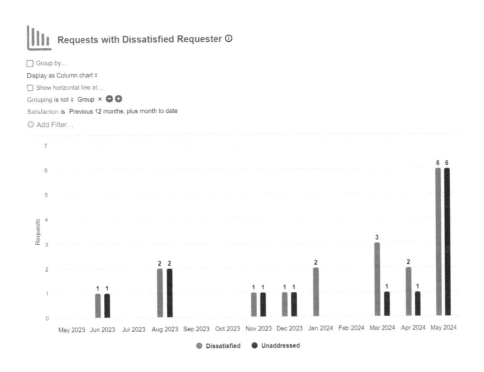

Figure 208: Identifying Moments of Truth with the 'Requests with Dissatisfied Requester' report.

The process you need to implement is simple: make sure that the *service desk manager* (or anyone of your choice) tracks all the dissatisfied responses. A good practice is to define a weekly recurring workflow to support this process. For each dissatisfied response, the service desk manager will determine the best way to conciliate the customer. In many cases, he or she will directly contact the customer: just listening will already remove some dissatisfaction. Once the customer is satisfied with the resolution, the service desk manager can set the satisfaction status of the request to 'Addressed', which will remove the request from the follow-up list.

By effectively addressing these Moments of Truth, the 4me platform facilitates a proactive approach to maintaining and enhancing customer satisfaction levels. However, the effectiveness of this approach largely depends on the interpersonal skills of the service desk manager. It's crucial to remember that at its core, service management thrives on personal interaction and empathy, making it fundamentally a human-centric endeavor.

Customer Surveys

Anyone involved in outsourcing may be familiar with the "watermelon effect": outwardly, everything appears fine (the green exterior), but underneath, there are problems (the red interior). This metaphor illustrates the discrepancy between service delivery KPIs, which may be green while customer satisfaction is red. To penetrate this facade and uncover the true state of service delivery, it's crucial to go beyond just tracking availability and support resolution times and delve into the real value provided to users.

4me enables organizations to create and distribute customer surveys, allowing for a deeper understanding of user satisfaction across various service aspects. In 4me's Settings console, in the 'Surveys' section, *account designers* and *administrators* can craft surveys with questions that can be rated (star rating) or open-ended (text response). These surveys can address all facets impacting customer satisfaction, including service functionality, usability, friendliness of support staff, and cost-effectiveness.

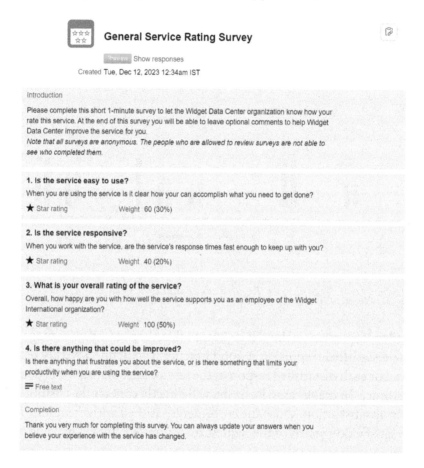

Figure 209: Creating customer surveys in 4me.

Users are prompted to complete surveys in the Self Service portal in the 'My Services' section, where they can provide ratings and feedback for the services they utilize. Additionally, shareable links and QR codes can be created in 4me to facilitate survey participation.

The gathered survey responses, along with their ratings and comments, are accessible in the 'Survey Responses' section of the Analytics Console. The Service Insight dashboard within the Analytics Console offers a comprehensive view, supplementing traditional service KPIs with survey results to provide a holistic perspective on service perception. This integration of feedback allows service delivery organizations to align their offerings more closely with user expectations, balancing service value with delivery costs.

By leveraging customer surveys in 4me, organizations can identify areas of dissatisfaction, enabling them to address the root causes and improve overall service quality. This approach not only slices through the watermelon effect but also fosters a culture of continuous improvement and customer-centric service delivery.

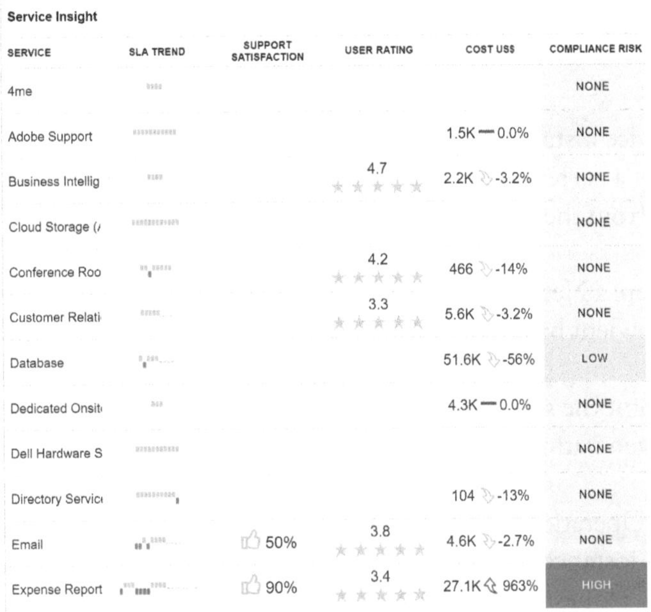

Service Insight

SERVICE	SLA TREND	SUPPORT SATISFACTION	USER RATING	COST US$	COMPLIANCE RISK
4me					NONE
Adobe Support				1.5K ▬ 0.0%	NONE
Business Intellig			4.7 ★ ★ ★ ★ ★	2.2K ⬊ -3.2%	NONE
Cloud Storage (/					NONE
Conference Roo			4.2 ★ ★ ★ ★ ★	466 ⬊ -14%	NONE
Customer Relati			3.3 ★ ★ ★ ★ ★	5.6K ⬊ -3.2%	NONE
Database				51.6K ⬊ -56%	LOW
Dedicated Onsit				4.3K ▬ 0.0%	NONE
Dell Hardware S					NONE
Directory Servic				104 ⬊ -13%	NONE
Email		👍 50%	3.8 ★ ★ ★ ★ ★	4.6K ⬊ -2.7%	NONE
Expense Report		👍 90%	3.4 ★ ★ ★ ★ ★	27.1K ⬈ 963%	HIGH

Figure 210: Service Insight provides a holistic view on services including customer support satisfaction and user ratings.

Event Management

Event management is the process dedicated to monitoring and addressing events within IT infrastructures or service environments. It is essential to note that while direct monitoring capabilities are not incorporated within the 4me platform, 4me excels in facilitating event escalation and response mechanisms. This becomes crucial when an event requires the intervention of support teams, necessitating the creation of an incident ticket within 4me.

The platform supports this through its straightforward Events API, detailed on the 4me developer site (https://developer.4me.com/v1/requests/events/). This API, which will be explored in more depth in Part III – Integrations of this book, enables the automated generation of incidents triggered by actionable events. Apart from the Events API, it is also possible to generate such incidents by having monitoring tools send structured emails to 4me. Ideally, the affected configuration item or service instance is already specified for these automatically generated incidents so that they get assigned to the correct team right away.

Moreover, by leveraging the service hierarchy within 4me, the necessary affected SLAs are generated for such events, tracing its implications right up to the business level, thus ensuring informed and targeted response strategies.

Affected SLA (ASLA) Generation

Within the 4me platform, affected service level agreement (ASLA) generation is a crucial feature for tracking and managing the impact of incidents within a service hierarchy. An ASLA is automatically added to a request whenever its service instance is updated by applying one of its child service instances.

In scenarios where a service instance is selected directly on the request form – and where the requester is not directly covered by a corresponding SLA - 4me dynamically generates ASLAs by identifying the most direct service path from the selected service instance to the requester.

Consider a situation where a Network Operations Center (NOC) operator, instead of using the Events API, manually logs an incident based on a monitoring alert. The operator would typically select a virtual user designated for monitoring purposes as the requester and navigate through the Service Hierarchy Browser (SHB) to pinpoint the service instance in which the issue resides. In doing so, 4me memorizes the traversed SLA path, generating ASLAs for each encountered SLA.

However, the Network Operations Center (NOC) operator could associate the new request directly with the affected service instance, without crawling through the SHB. In this scenario 4me calculates the shortest paths to the requester and generates ASLAs for all SLAs encountered along these paths. This feature becomes particularly beneficial when multiple business services rely on a single affected infrastructure component; 4me ensures visibility across all affected services, triggering a cascade of actions that aid in incident management. This functionality is particularly vital when an incident impacts a service instance that is foundational to multiple business services. For instance, consider a top-impact incident registered against a storage service instance, a common backbone for several business applications. Should this storage environment encounter an issue, it's not just one application that suffers but potentially several. Here, 4me's ASLA generation truly showcases its value. If, for example, this storage environment underpins five business applications, 4me is adept at generating an ASLA for each affected application. This systemic approach ensures that the full extent of an incident's impact is not just noted but made explicitly clear across all dependent services:

1. The Self-Service Portal and Service Desk Console clearly marks each service that is currently unavailable.
2. The Service Hierarchy Browser highlights the incidents across relevant business services, facilitating incident grouping and management.
3. The Service Navigator visually presents all impacted services, aiding specialists in understanding the broader impact and coordinating response efforts.

	Creating a "virtual" Monitoring User
Note that the ASLA generation depends on the requester. It is a good idea to create a virtual user, a 'Monitoring User' that is solely used by the Event API or by the operators to register incidents for events that require an action to be taken. Make sure that the monitoring user is covered by the SLAs for the principal business services.	

Event Management
ASLA Generation

Let's check the ASLA Generation in demo. In the following scenario, Howard Tanner will create an incident for an event that was detected on the SAN2 storage device which is managed by GigaTera Managed services. He will register this incident for a user from the Widget North America Sales & Marketing organization, Doc Abercrombie.

- Log in as howard.tanner@widget.com to Widget Data Center.
    - Go to the Service Desk Console.
    - Select Doc Abercrombie
    - Note that Doc is not covered by any service in Widget Data Center, the request form is displayed without the possibility to select a service.
    - Set the subject to 'Storage event' and the impact to 'Top'.
    - Link the request to service instance 'SAN2 for Widget Houston' and save.
    - Check the Affected SLAs section and notice that affected SLAs have been generated for the business applications Business Intelligence and Sales Tracking.
    - Go to the Actions menu and select the Service Navigator.
    - See how this event had an impact on the two service chains.

Note that no affected SLAs were generated for the business services *Sales Tracking Development* and *Sales Tracking Test*. That's because Doc Abercrombie has no coverage for these services. To get the full picture Widget Data Center could create a virtual monitoring user with a coverage for all the business services.

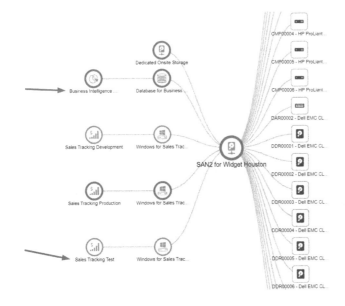

Figure 211: A monitoring event becomes visible in the Service Navigator.

4me + AI

AI as a Commodity

In 4me, AI isn't merely an add-on requiring extensive configuration, customization, or expensive licensing. Instead, 4me is pioneering the integration of AI as a standard feature across its platform to boost efficiency wherever possible. By the end of 2022, Generative AI had achieved a level of maturity previously unseen, and 4me wasted no time in harnessing this advanced technology, seamlessly weaving it into its existing framework. The results? Instant and remarkable improvements in service delivery and operations.

But why has 4me been so successful in swiftly and effectively implementing the latest AI technologies, outpacing other enterprise service management solutions? The key lies in the platform's service-oriented data structure, which provides the context an AI needs to offer exceptional support.

Customer Concerns on AI Integration

Although there is widespread agreement that generative AI can enhance the efficiency of service-oriented organizations, particularly in enterprise service management, there are legitimate concerns. Data privacy and security require special attention. Integrating AI could potentially expose and store personal identifiable information (PII) where it should not be, causing conflicts with compliance and privacy regulations. Additionally, blindly relying on AI might result in flawed or harmful decision-making.

4me's Secure Approach

4me has integrated AI cautiously, employing the AWS Bedrock generative AI stack. This integration adheres to strict guidelines:

- 4me systematically filters out all PII from data before sending it to the AI stack.
- Data remains within the geographical region of the 4me environment; for instance, data from the UK environment does not leave the UK. This local data handling principle applies equally to other environments like AU, CH, EU, and the USA.
- Data transferred to the AI stack is not utilized for AI training purposes.

These measures are in place under the data processing addendum (DPA) customers have with 4me and 4me in turn has with AWS, aiming to ensure that using AI within 4me aligns with data privacy compliance frameworks.

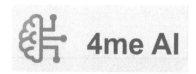

Figure 212: A clear Indicator of AI-generated content.

Another concern involves decision-making based on inaccurate AI-generated information. While 4me generally obtains reliable results from AI-generated content, errors can occur. To mitigate this, 4me highlights all AI-generated content with visual warnings and presents generated material as suggestions, leaving final approval to administrators or specialists. Awareness of AI's limitations is essential, regardless of the platform used. While halting AI integration is not feasible for organizations looking to maintain competitiveness, caution is advised.

Disabling AI in 4me

Currently, AI is turned off by default in the account settings. Organizations should make informed decisions regarding the use of AI in their daily operations. 4me provides a secure environment to trial and begin using AI, but it is vital to foster organizational awareness about AI's benefits and risks.

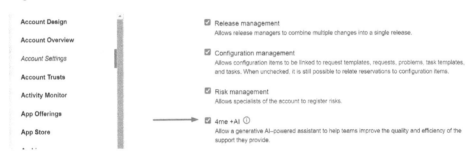

Figure 213: The account owner can enable or disable 4me + AI.

Actual 4me + AI features

4me's Auto Translation Feature

The 4me platform is designed to assist organizations in providing support to their internal and external customers in their native languages. Historically, offering multi-language support was a costly and labor-intensive task. However, with 4me, this has become significantly more accessible.

To facilitate the availability of customer-specific content—such as knowledge articles, email templates, service descriptions, fields on request forms, and the entire self-service portal—in multiple languages, 4me offers a Translation feature in the Settings console. This feature is accessible to *account administrators*, *service desk managers*, *knowledge managers*, and *service level managers*. Within the '**Translations**' section, all customer-specific phrases can be displayed for translation into more than 50 different languages. To simplify the process, a proposed translation is presented, which users can accept with a single click. Users also have the option to select multiple phrases and initiate an auto-translation in the background. However, it is highly recommended to review the translations for accuracy once they are completed.

An even greater advantage for supporting a fully multilingual environment is the near **real-time auto-translation** of notes provided by 4me. This functionality is particularly valuable in enterprise service management as it ensures that all users, regardless of their language proficiency, can understand and respond to support requests promptly. This capability enhances communication between teams and customers, reduces response times, and improves overall service satisfaction by ensuring that language barriers do not hinder the resolution of issues.

Generate Request Summaries

Certain requests, especially those associated with complex issues, can become extensive and lengthy. This situation poses a challenge and can reduce an organization's efficiency: a new team member assigned to the ticket might spend considerable time sifting through all the notes. This is precisely the situation where request summaries become invaluable. When a request accumulates at least five notes containing substantial text, 4me's AI capabilities can generate a concise summary of the request. This feature significantly reduces the time required for a team member to grasp the essentials of the request.

Empowering Knowledge Sharing with AI

4me leverages the Knowledge Centered Service (KCS) methodology, facilitating a hands-on 'create-as-you-go' approach for knowledge management. With the activation of 4me AI, the platform accelerates the creation of knowledge articles, transforming resolutions and answered queries into well-written knowledge article proposals in just a few seconds.

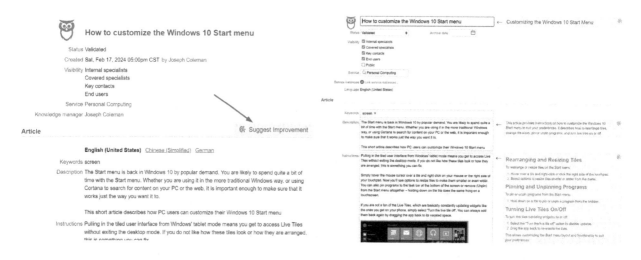

Figure 214: 4me AI can help a knowledge manager to improve a knowledge article.

Another directive of the KCS methodology is the 'Review when Reuse' principle, asking specialists to check the content of a knowledge article on each use. This process is also made easier by 4me AI by giving specialists access to the '*Suggest Improvement*' option in existing articles. This option triggers 4me's AI to propose a rewrite of the article.

Optimizing Customer Interactions with the Virtual Agent

The Virtual Agent, powered by 4me AI, represents a significant leap in automated customer service technology. By analyzing user chat messages, the Virtual Agent leverages data from the service hierarchy, including associated request templates and knowledge articles, to provide timely and relevant responses without the need for any human intervention.

Get Ready for the Revolution: The Future of AI in Service Management

The advent of Generative AI is set to revolutionize enterprise service management in ways we're just beginning to grasp. Imagine a world where the mundane and repetitive tasks are efficiently handled by AI, freeing up help desk agents from the tedious chore of transcribing user issues, classifying them, or puzzling over which team should handle a ticket. Instead, service desk analysts will evolve into knowledge managers, stepping in only where AI needs a human touch, and crafting and perfecting content in collaboration with AI to enhance the outcome of AI's future user interactions. This shift promises to make work more fulfilling, significantly boosting both the quality and efficiency of service delivery. With its service-driven architecture, the 4me platform is uniquely positioned to harness the full potential of AI, seamlessly integrating it into existing processes and setting a new standard in service management. Stay tuned to the 4me blog for a front-row seat to these groundbreaking developments and witness how AI is reshaping the future of service excellence. You ain't seen nothing yet...

Demo	4me + AI **Auto translation and Request Summaries**
Let's test 4me + AI in the demo environment. Ander Alkin, the administrator of the Widget Europe, IT account, will enable 4me + AI and add a note to a long request with auto-translated notes. • Log in as ander.alkin@widget.com to Widget Europe, IT. 　• Go to the Settings Console. 　• Select the Account Settings. 　• Enable 4me + AI. 　• Go the Records console and select Requests. 　• Check the urgent request # *704880 – Audit.* 　• Edit the request and add a note "*@Howard Tanner: can we get an update on this request. Our finance department needs this quite urgently.*"	

- Save the request.
- Check the notes from Arizona and Bert Jansen: click on the yellow Auto Translated indicator to show the original texts in Dutch and German.
- After some time, you might need to refresh the form a few times; a summary will be generated by AI for this request.

Figure 215: Auto Translation and a request summary generated by AI.

PART III

4me's Customizable Core

Beyond Basics: Elevating Your Service Management

Introduction

Embarking on Part III, we delve beyond the robust foundations and sophisticated, user-friendly functionalities of the 4me core. This journey is for those eager to tailor 4me more closely to their organization's unique needs. Whether you're looking to manage record types beyond the standard offerings, integrate custom self-service designs, tweak PDF layouts in approval workflows, or trigger tasks in external systems, this section delves deep into the realm of customization, ensuring that your 4me environment perfectly aligns with your specific requirements.

Customizing a platform can often feel like walking a tightrope, balancing between enhancing functionality and risking system integrity with future updates. However, 4me stands apart. Here, customizations don't compromise system performance or upgrade paths. With 4me, the worry of breaking your system with custom adjustments is a thing of the past. Weekly releases roll out smoothly, maintaining your tailored configurations intact and ensuring your platform's speed remains unrivaled. And the best part? You won't need to rely on costly consultants for these customizations. 4me empowers service management professionals to adapt and evolve their setup, ensuring that your platform remains as dynamic and responsive as your organization. Welcome to the flexible, fast, and fully customizable world of 4me.

Chapter 11 - Custom Collections and Custom Views

Introduction

Custom collections are invaluable when you encounter the need for record types not yet present in 4me and you will use custom views when existing records require presentation through finely tuned selection lists. Consider scenarios where users request new devices and must specify a Cost Center, or where the choice of a financial controller for workflow approvals is limited to a specific subset of personnel.

Custom Collections and Custom Collection Elements

Custom Collections and Custom Collection Elements significantly enhance the flexibility of 4me by allowing you to introduce bespoke record types tailored to your organization's specific needs. You can find Custom Collections and Custom Collection Elements as separate sections in the Settings console. *Account administrators* or *account designers* possess the necessary permissions to add or disable Custom Collections.

Key Attributes of a Custom Collection

- **Name**: This should be a descriptive title for your collection, such as "Cost Centers" or "SAP Transactions," that clearly identifies its purpose or content.
- **Picture** (optional): You can assign an avatar to visually represent your custom collection. This is particularly useful for quickly identifying different collections.
- **Reference**: A unique identifier for your Custom Collection within the 4me account structure. It is crucial for integrations and automation rules, ensuring a clear and unique reference. While it is automatically generated based on the collection's name, it can be customized for more precise identification.
- **Description** (optional): Offers a detailed explanation of the collection's purpose, aiding other administrators and designers in understanding its use.

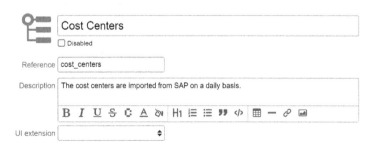

Figure 216: Account administrators and designers can add custom collection elements to 4me accounts via the Settings console.

- **UI Extension** (optional): A feature discussed in the next chapter. Attaching a UI Extension to a custom collection introduces additional fields to the Custom Collection Elements, akin to adding new columns to a database record for enriched data capture.

Adding Custom Collection Elements

After establishing a Custom Collection, the next step is to populate it with Custom Collection Elements, which represent the individual records. This action can be performed either by using the "Add Collection Element" button within a specific custom collection or directly from the Custom Collection Elements console.

- **Name**: A succinct name for the element is essential.
- **Description** (optional): Use this field to provide extra context or clarification, especially when the name alone might not be fully descriptive.
- **Reference**: Similar to the collection's reference, this unique ID within the 4me account structure is pivotal for seamless integrations and automation. It's crafted from the element's name but can be manually adjusted.
- **Information** (optional): For detailed narratives about what the element represents or how it should be used.
- **Attachments** (optional): To include additional documents or files relevant to the element.
- **Picture** (optional): Enables the attachment of an image to help users visually identify the element in a selection field.

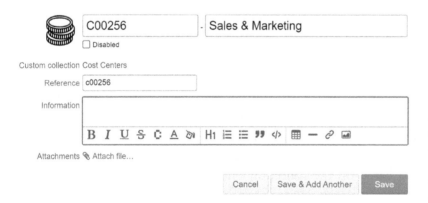

Figure 217: Account administrators and designers have the capability to populate a custom collection with multiple custom collection elements swiftly by utilizing the 'Save and Add Another' button.

Uploading Pictures: To add a picture to a collection or an element, enter Edit mode and select an image file using the picture icon.

Synchronization: For those managing custom collection elements externally, the Import API facilitates bulk updates, while the GraphQL API provides a solution for keeping elements synchronized in near-real-time with external systems.

Centralized Management and Support in Multilingual Environments

Custom collections can be created in all types of 4me accounts, including directory accounts. This functionality allows for centralized management and sharing of essential organizational elements, such as cost centers, across all support domain accounts within an enterprise.

In environments that support multiple languages, ensuring that customers can interact with 4me Self Service in their preferred language is crucial. Therefore, names and descriptions of custom collection elements can be translated via the "Translations" section in the Settings console. Here, 4me's auto-translation feature offers suggested translations, aiding in the process and ensuring clarity and accessibility for all users.

Custom Views: Bridging Records to UI Extensions

Custom Views are essential for incorporating both standard 4me record types and custom collection elements into UI Extensions, the feature for crafting custom forms on 4me. By defining a set of records as a Custom View, you effectively make this collection accessible in UI Extensions as a **Custom Suggest** field.

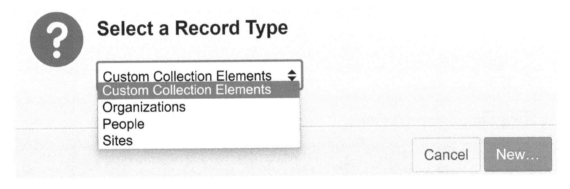

Figure 218: When creating a Custom View, a record type must be selected. In a directory account, only four record types are available: Custom Collection Elements, Organizations, People, and Sites.

Accessible via Account Settings, the Custom Views feature is available in both directory and support domain accounts. *Account administrators* and *account designers* can add, modify, or disable Custom Views as needed. Importantly, Custom Views related to custom collection elements defined in a directory account must also be created within that same account.

The process of creating a Custom View starts with selecting the record type. In directory accounts, the available record types are limited to custom collection elements, organizations, people, and sites. In contrast, a support domain account offers a broader range of available record types.

Key Fields in Custom View Creation

- **Name**: Provide a concise, descriptive name. This name is crucial for administrators or designers building the custom forms.
- **Reference**: Used by integrations and automation rules, the Reference field is automatically generated from the Name, employing lowercase letters and underscores for spaces.
- **State**: Typically set to "Enabled," this field determines the visibility of records.
- **Search Phrase**: This field filters records based on keywords found in their name or subject fields. For example, including "Joe" in a custom view of people records would filter for all individuals named Joe.
- **Metadata Fields**: In our upcoming discussions on UI Extensions, we'll delve into creating dynamic forms. Exposing fields like a person's manager through Metadata allows for their automatic display on forms.
- **Filters**: Narrow down the records included in the view, such as filtering people by their business unit.

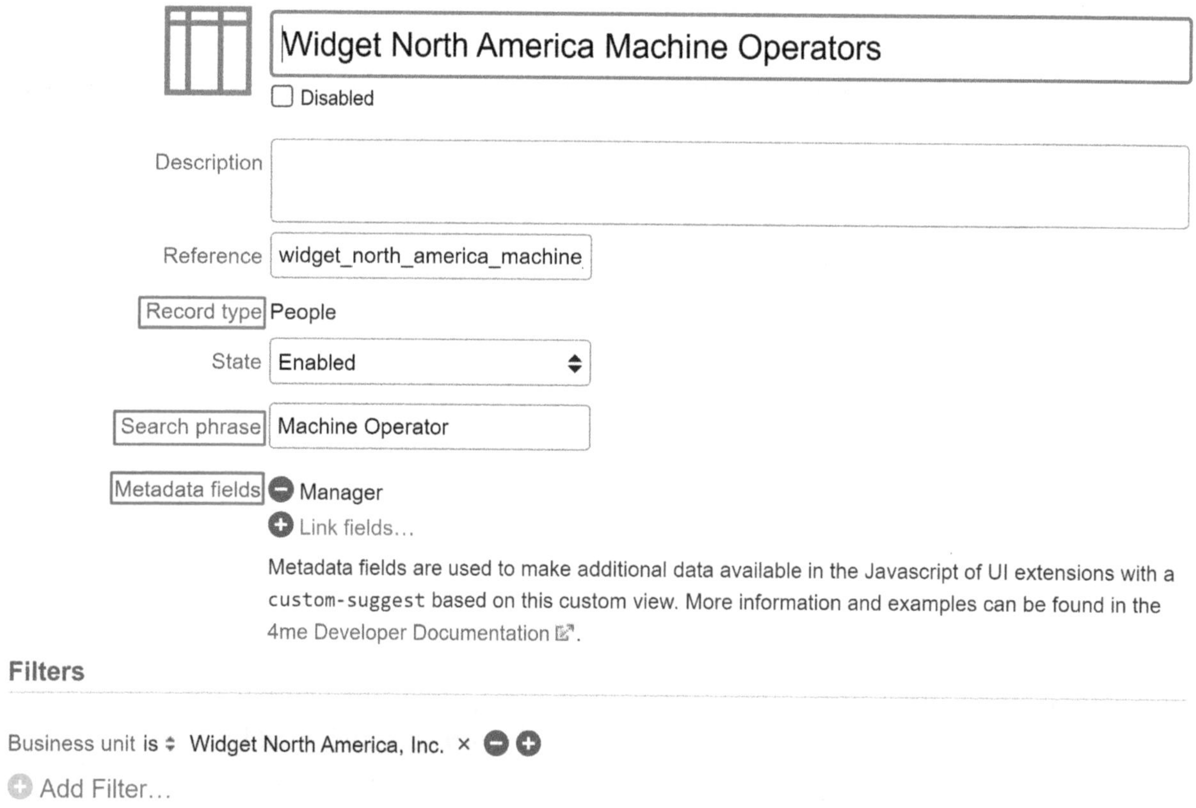

Figure 219: *The process of creating a Custom View begins with selecting the appropriate record type. Utilizing search phrases and applying filters refines and specifies the list of records to be included. Additionally, the Metadata fields option allows for the exposure of both standard and custom fields from the selected record to a UI Extension, thereby enriching the customization possibilities.*

Enhancing Custom Views for Configuration Items

To assist users in selecting a Configuration item on a form, it's important to offer a variety of search options. Users may prefer searching by the asset's label or name. Alternatively, they might only know the serial number or the (stock) location of the item. These search preferences are accommodated through the 'Search fields' attribute within a Custom View designated for the 'Configuration item' record type, ensuring users can efficiently find what they're looking for.

Search fields ⊖ **Label**
⊖ **Serial number**
⊖ **Site**
⊕ Link columns…

Figure 220: With the 'Search fields' feature in a Custom View for Configuration Items, you can specify which fields are available for searching. This enhances navigation through the list, making it easier to locate specific items.

Refining Custom Views for Custom Collection Elements

While it's not directly feasible to designate a custom collection as the record type for a Custom View, it is possible to link a Custom View to Custom Collection Elements. Such an approach, without the application of specific filters, would inherently include all custom collection elements across the board. This means that, in a scenario where you've established custom collections for diverse entities like Cost Centers, People, and Risks, a broad, unfiltered Custom View could inadvertently blend these distinct types together — a mix that's usually not practical.

To ensure relevance and coherence in your Custom Views, it's standard practice to employ a filter, specifically of the type 'Custom Collection,' when dealing with custom collection elements. Following the example provided, this method would lead to the creation of three distinct Custom Views, each refined through a filter targeting one of the custom collections: Cost Centers, People, and Risks, accordingly.

The power of Custom Views truly shines when you explore the possibility of including multiple custom collections within a single filter. This capability allows for the creation of Custom Views that are blends of various custom collections, introducing a remarkable level of flexibility and customization potential to your 4me environment.

Validating Custom Views with 'Show Underlying Data'

After crafting a custom view, it's vital for account administrators and designers to ensure that the view precisely captures the intended records. 4me facilitates this validation process by providing a practical feature: the 'Show Underlying Data' link. Accessible directly from the custom view, this clickable option unveils the records encompassed by the view, offering an immediate and clear inspection of whether the custom view's configurations accurately reflect the desired criteria.

Demo

Custom Views and Custom Collections
Exploring Custom Views in Widget Europe IT

Join Ander Alkin, the account administrator of Widget Europe IT, as we delve into the solution they've implemented for managing laptop replacements. When a user's laptop fails, it's crucial for specialists to quickly identify available replacements from stock. This scenario showcases how a custom view, tailored for this very purpose, streamlines the process through a UI Extension applied to a task template.

- Log in with ander.alkin@widget.com to the Widget Europe, IT account.
  - Navigate to the Settings console and select Custom Views.
  - Locate and choose the "*Laptops in Stock*" custom view.
  - Click on "*Show underlying data*" to display the filtered list of laptops.
  - You'll see a list of laptops, categorized as 'Computer – Laptop PC' and marked as in stock, demonstrating the effectiveness of the custom view in narrowing down options.
  - Observe the Serial Number and Location columns within the custom view. These columns are readily searchable due to their designation as Search fields in the custom view.

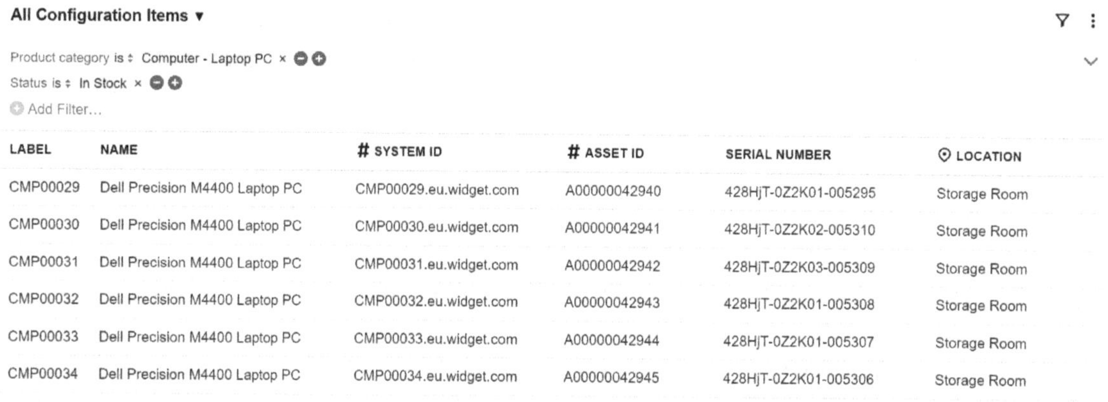

All Configuration Items ▾

Product category is ⇕ Computer - Laptop PC × ⊖ ⊕
Status is ⇕ In Stock × ⊖ ⊕
⊕ Add Filter…

LABEL	NAME	# SYSTEM ID	# ASSET ID	SERIAL NUMBER	⊙ LOCATION
CMP00029	Dell Precision M4400 Laptop PC	CMP00029.eu.widget.com	A00000042940	428HjT-0Z2K01-005295	Storage Room
CMP00030	Dell Precision M4400 Laptop PC	CMP00030.eu.widget.com	A00000042941	428HjT-0Z2K02-005310	Storage Room
CMP00031	Dell Precision M4400 Laptop PC	CMP00031.eu.widget.com	A00000042942	428HjT-0Z2K03-005309	Storage Room
CMP00032	Dell Precision M4400 Laptop PC	CMP00032.eu.widget.com	A00000042943	428HjT-0Z2K01-005308	Storage Room
CMP00033	Dell Precision M4400 Laptop PC	CMP00033.eu.widget.com	A00000042944	428HjT-0Z2K01-005307	Storage Room
CMP00034	Dell Precision M4400 Laptop PC	CMP00034.eu.widget.com	A00000042945	428HjT-0Z2K01-005306	Storage Room

Figure 221: The underlying data of a custom view.

Chapter 12 -
UI Extensions and Custom Fields

Introduction

Imagine a scenario where every detail, from a new employee's role to their IT equipment needs, is meticulously captured not in scattered notes but in structured, designated fields within an onboarding request. This chapter is your gateway to making that vision a reality. It's not merely about enhancing the data capture for tickets; it's an opportunity to enrich every record type, from configuration items to projects, with meaningful attributes that streamline processes, facilitate automation, and ensure seamless integration with adjacent systems. And the best part? Implementing UI Extensions and adding custom fields is surprisingly straightforward. No need for technical sorcery—just bring your creativity, common sense, and an eagerness to explore the insights in this chapter.

Introducing Custom Fields

To enhance the functionality of nearly every 4me record, including custom collection elements, you can incorporate additional fields known as Custom Fields. To understand the nature of Custom Fields, consider this enlightening exercise: An *account administrator* has the ability to export any record type, such as all requests or people records within an account, into a CSV or Excel file. Within these export files, a column labeled 'Custom Fields' will be present. This column contains all the custom fields that have been added to a record, organized into key-value pairs. However, without the necessary context, these key-value pairs can seem cryptic.

Subject	Custom Fields
Move desktop PC	[{"id":"move_from","value":"Room 119"},{"id":"move_to","\
Register new Widget product in SAP - Name: Plaximus	[{"id":"name","value":"Plaximus"},{"id":"toxic","value":false}
Register new Widget product in SAP - Name: ZZTOP	[{"id":"name","value":"ZZTOP"},{"id":"toxic","value":true},{"

Figure 222: In an Excel export of request records, you'll notice a single column labeled 'Custom Fields.' This column contains key-value pairs, with each pair comprising two strings: the 'ID' of the custom field and its corresponding 'Value'.

For example, an export might contain the following pairs:

- ID: manager, Value: 15520
- ID: description, Value: New projector
- ID: target_date, Value: 2027-01-24T09:00:00Z
- ID: avatar, Value: attachments/7/2024/03/19/10/1710848788.6908085-7/plaxiform.svg
- ID: urgency, Value: 2
- ID: cost_center, Value: 2689235

UI Extensions: Bridging Data and Meaning

At a glance, it's challenging to deduce the significance of these pairs. For instance, the pair {"id:"manager","value":"15520"} could hint at a 'Manager' field linking to a person with the 4me ID 15520, but this is speculative. This is where UI Extensions come into play. UI Extensions provide the necessary context for these custom fields, clarifying aspects such as the field's label (e.g., 'Approval Manager'), its visibility (internal, with access restricted to *specialists* or *administrators*), and its type (in this case, suggesting that '15520' is the ID of a person record, possibly John Doe).

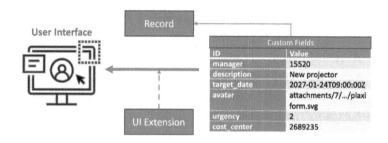

Figure 223: UI Extensions assign meaning to Custom Fields, which are fundamentally key-value pairs of two strings. They add necessary context and definitions, transforming raw data to actionable insights.

While UI Extensions ensure that data like a person's 4me ID is displayed as their actual name, they also guide the data entry process. When a user selects a person's name from a form, the UI Extension translates this selection into the corresponding 4me ID to be stored in the custom field.

Creating UI Extensions

Account administrators and *account designers* have the rights to create, modify, and manage UI Extensions directly within the UI Extensions section in the Settings console. Here's a closer look at the UI Extension creation process and the fields that need to be configured:

- **Name**: Crucial for accurately linking the UI Extension to its associated record, it should be clear and descriptive to avoid errors. Aligning the name with the subject of the related Request Template or Task Template is advisable.
- **Title**: Serves as the header for the UI Extension's section on the form, distinguishing it as a separate sub-section.

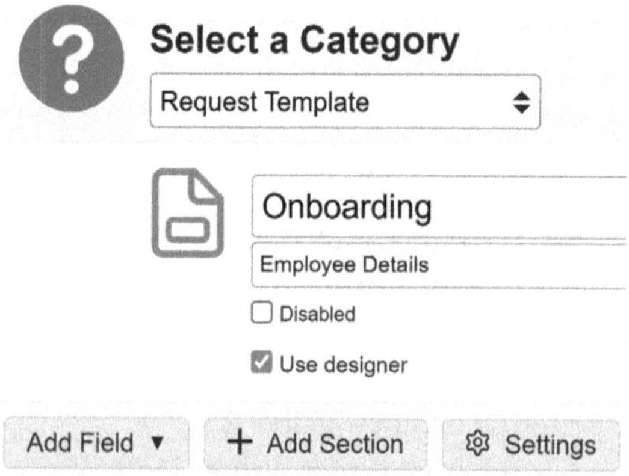

Figure 224: Providing a Name, a Title, a Category, and a Description on UI Extension creation.

Select a Category

Request Template
Request Template
Knowledge Article Template
Problem
Release
Workflow Template
Task Template
Project
Project Task Template
Service
Service Instance
Product
Product Category
Contract
Organization
Team
Person
Site
Custom Collection
SCIM User
App Offering

- **Category**: A crucial selection that specifies the record type to which the UI Extension is applied.
- **Description**: Provides additional details for administrators and designers, which can be particularly helpful when the purpose of the UI Extension isn't immediately evident from its name alone.
- **Check on complete**: This field option is specifically tailored for custom fields linked to ticket types, including request templates, problems, workflow task templates, and project task templates. It's an essential feature for ensuring that critical custom fields are updated before a ticket can be finalized. By enabling 'Check on Complete,' you prevent the completion of these tickets via mass updates without filling out mandatory custom fields. This helps maintain data integrity and ensures all required information is captured when resolving a ticket.

Figure 225: UI Extension categories.

The UI Extension Designer

Gone are the days when delving into HTML, CSS, and Javascript was necessary to create UI Extensions in 4me. While the classic UI Extension builder, enriched with an HTML snippet generator for adding form components, a CSS section for layout, and a Javascript section for dynamic behaviors, remains available for legacy purposes, today's 4me platform offers a far more intuitive alternative. The modern Graphical UI Extension Designer eliminates the need for technical expertise in web development languages, enabling you to achieve dynamic results and intricate layouts through simple configurations.

Form Structure and Layout

Creating a form starts with defining its structure. You can segment a form into multiple sections, each with its unique layout. Choose between a single-column or a multi-column layout to best suit your design needs. Responsive design principles ensure that multi-column layouts adapt flawlessly to various screen sizes, ensuring an optimal viewing experience across devices.

Adding the Components

Once the structure is set, populate sections with components or form elements. The Graphical UI Extension Designer offers a selection of approximately 20 component types, including familiar web form elements like checkboxes, email inputs, numeric fields, single-line texts, multi-line text areas, rich text fields, static texts, and select fields. Additionally, 4me-specific components like Custom Suggest and Team Suggest add a unique touch to your custom forms, aligning them closely with the 4me ecosystem.

Field Settings: Fine-Tuning Your Form Elements

Each component within the UI Extension Designer features a comprehensive suite of settings, allowing for precise control over each field's behavior and appearance:

- **ID**: Acts as the key in the key-value pair for custom fields, linking the UI Extension to the raw data within a record's Custom Fields column.
- **Label**: The visible field name on the form, which can be localized through the translation module for multilingual support.
- **Tooltip**: Provides additional information or guidance, appearing when the users hover over the field.
- **Show when empty**: Determines if a field should be visible when empty, particularly useful for checkboxes where an unchecked state ('false') is significant.
- **Hidden**: Designates a field hidden from the form, accessible only to automation rules and APIs, useful for storing information not intended for direct user interaction.
- **Required**: Marks a field as mandatory, ensuring users cannot submit the form without completing it.
- **Filterable**: Includes the field in the record's filter options, enhancing the ability to narrow down records in views and reports based on this field's value.
- **Searchable**: Adds the field's content to the search index, making records searchable by matching terms within this field.
- **Add to subject**: For custom fields on tickets, this feature automatically incorporates the field's value into the ticket's subject. For example, if a request template's subject is 'Onboarding,' specifying this setting for the custom field 'Name' adjusts the request's subject to 'Onboarding, Name = John Doe,' providing immediate context.
- **Internal**: Restricts visibility to *specialists*, *auditors*, and *account administrators* within the same account, concealing the field from end-users and external account specialists.

Adding Dynamics to UI Components

After configuring the fields, the next step is to bring your form to life by incorporating dynamics. For example, in an onboarding request form, if there's a checkbox for 'SAP Access,' you might want the 'SAP Access Roles' section to become visible only when this checkbox is selected.

Figure 226: : Defining the conditions to make a field required by utilizing the "Or" condition.

Dynamics can be applied to both fields and sections, in both edit and view modes, using conditions that determine when a field or section should appear or be hidden. In our example, the "SAP Access Roles" section would remain hidden unless the "SAP Access" checkbox is checked. A field can also be set as required based on specific conditions.

Attachments

Attachments play a vital role in various processes, enhancing the ability to share and review documents directly within tasks or requests. For example, in a Request for Proposal (RFP) process, a Managed Service Provider (MSP) may need to prepare and attach a proposal document, such as a PDF or Word file, to a task. This document can then be made available for review or approval in subsequent tasks. Attachment custom fields are designed to manage documents seamlessly within 4me.

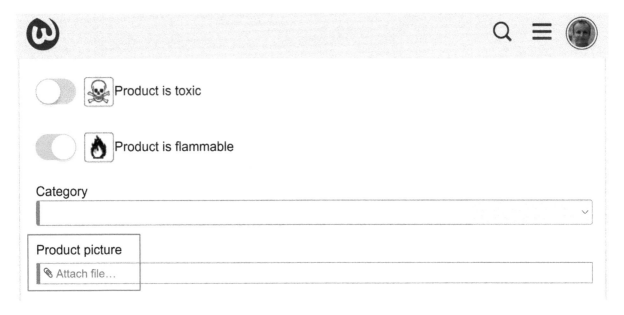

Figure 227: An "Attachment" custom field requires the user to add an attachment when registering a new product.

Attachment custom fields are versatile, offering configurations to meet specific process requirements. This includes setting attachments as mandatory or optional and defining rules regarding the number of attachments, including minimum and maximum limits.

The Google Maps Integration in 4me

4me offers a seamless integration with Google Maps, accessible through a free app available in the 4me App Store. To incorporate the Google Maps functionality into your UI Extensions, simply navigate to the App Store section within the Settings Console and install the Google Maps 4me app. You'll need a Google Maps API key, which is easily obtainable from Google. The Location component introduced by this integration allows the display of geographic locations directly within forms, using geographical coordinates. Moreover, this feature can be interactive, allowing users to specify a location themselves. A particularly convenient function is the ability to automatically pinpoint the user's current location, provided they grant permission. This capability proves especially valuable in scenarios where, for example, a municipal government wishes to empower residents to report local issues efficiently by marking the exact location on a map.

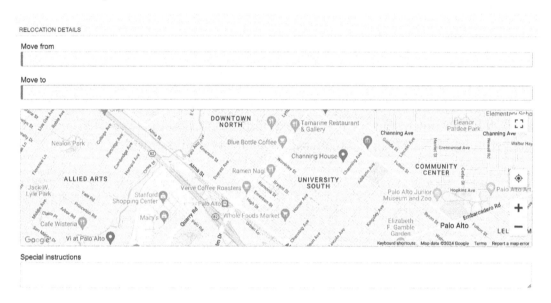

Figure 228: The Location component enables the inclusion of a Google Map within a form, offering an interactive and visual way to specify locations. This feature becomes accessible simply by activating the free 4me Google Maps app available in the 4me App Store.

Bringing Custom Views to Life with Custom Suggest Fields

Custom suggest fields in UI Extensions harness the capabilities of custom views, as discussed in the previous chapter. Once you've established a custom view, it becomes selectable within the custom suggest fields of UI Extensions. For instance, if you've created a custom view that displays all "Computer - Laptops" with "In Stock" status in the "Widget Amsterdam stock room," this custom view becomes an invaluable resource in your workflows.

Furthermore, custom suggest fields breathe life into the new record types—custom collection elements— you've added to your 4me configuration. By defining a custom view for your custom collection elements, filtered to display only "Cost Centers," you can seamlessly incorporate your organization's cost centers into your forms. It's important to note that when creating a UI Extension within a support domain account, like for a request template, you have the flexibility to choose custom views defined in both your support domain account and the directory account.

Creating Dynamic Selection Trees with Custom Suggest Fields

Linking custom collections to UI Extensions significantly boosts the functionality of your custom collection elements. This integration allows you to add custom fields to these elements, enriching them with more specific attributes. For instance, in Facilities Management, you might have a custom collection named "Buildings." Each building within this collection can be enhanced with custom fields such as "Number of Floors," "Total Area," and even a checklist of facilities like parking, cafeteria, and gym. You can also include a site suggest field to specify the site location of each building.

This enhancement paves the way for creating dynamic and dependent selection options within forms. Specifically, you can establish dependencies between custom suggest fields, where the selection in one field determines the available options in another, effectively forming a custom suggest tree.

Imagine an organization with multiple sites, each containing several buildings, and each building housing various rooms. To assist users in selecting a specific room in a request form, they would first choose a site, then a building within that site, and finally a room within the selected building.

To implement this, an account designer would create two custom collections ("Buildings" and "Rooms") and two custom views (assuming "Site" is already a foundational record in 4me). The "Buildings" custom collection would be linked to a UI Extension containing attributes of buildings, including a "Site" suggest field that is made filterable. Similarly, the "Rooms" custom collection would have a UI Extension, featuring at least one custom suggest field linked to "Buildings."

When adding a custom suggest field to a UI Extension, account designers can apply filters to establish dependencies on other custom suggest fields within the same UI Extension. This approach allows for the creation of custom suggest trees with multiple levels of branching. For example, selecting a site will limit the buildings suggest field to show only buildings within that site. Subsequently, choosing a building will refine the rooms suggest field to display only rooms within that selected building.

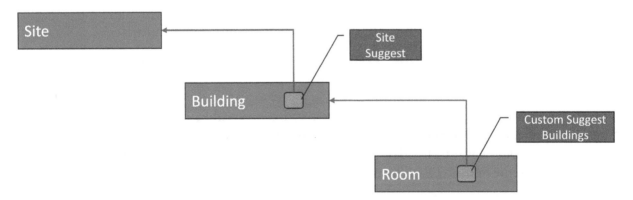

Figure 229: A Diagram of Custom Suggest Trees: This diagram illustrates the operation of custom suggest trees. The custom collection 'Buildings' is augmented with a UI Extension that includes a site suggest field, establishing a connection between buildings and their geographical locations. Likewise, the custom collection 'Rooms' integrates a UI Extension with a custom suggest field linked to buildings. This configuration highlights the hierarchical relationship, enabling users to dynamically narrow down their choices from site to building, and ultimately to a specific room.

| Demo | UI Extensions and Custom Fields
Unveiling the Magic of Custom Suggest Trees |

Dive into the digital world of Widget Europe IT and follow Randy Barton, the financial controller with a keen eye for detail, as he registers a new SAP issue using a standard request. This template is equipped with an intuitive custom suggest tree.

- Log in with randy.barton@widget.com at the Widget Europe, IT account.
  - Register a new request and select the *'Information Technology'* support domain.
  - Choose *Business Applications* and then *Enterprise Resource Planning (SAP)*.
  - Select the standard request *'Report an SAP issue or bug'*.
  - Check the available T-codes: there are many!
  - Choose the SAP System *'SAP FI – Financial Accounting'*.
  - Select a T-code: only those related to SAP FI are available now.

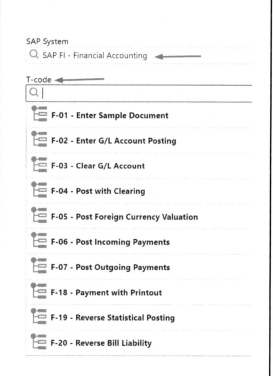

Figure 230: Example of a custom suggest tree.

Understanding Organization, Person, Site and Team Suggest Fields

The suggest fields for organizations, people, sites, and teams within UI Extensions offer dynamic functionality that adapts based on the user's contextual environment in 4me. These fields differ from custom suggest fields, which are based on predefined collections of records through custom views within the account structure of the UI Extension.

Key Insights on Organization, Person, Site and Team Suggest Fields:

- **Dynamic Content Based on User Context**: These fields generate their list of options dynamically, adhering to 4me's built-in access rules. This ensures that users only see records they're authorized to access. For example, end users typically can't access team records directly, meaning a Team suggest field would be empty for them. To show teams to end users, creating a custom view with a custom suggest field would be necessary.

- **Adherence to Account Structure**: The visibility of records within these suggest fields is limited to the user's specific account structure. An internal user will see individuals within their internal organization and those in linked external organizations. In contrast, an external user will only see individuals within their own external organization and its descendants. In the context of a supplier defining a person suggest field, an external user (e.g., a customer contact in a trusted customer account) will only see individuals from their own customer organization and descendants. This provides a tailored solution for scenarios where a customer contact needs to select a person from their own organization. This approach addresses the limitations of custom suggest fields based on custom views which are constrained to the account structure of the UI Extension.

- **Influence of Privacy Settings**: The End User Privacy settings can further restrict visibility within these suggest fields. In privacy-enabled accounts or organizations, users might not be able to see other users, even within the same organization, ensuring adherence to privacy standards.

UI Extension Categories

Template UI Extensions

Certain UI Extensions categories must be linked to a template, including:

- Request Template
- Workflow Template
- (Workflow) Task Template
- Project Task Template
- Knowledge Article Template

This means that for these record types each record can have its own set of custom fields, depending on the template that has been applied. A typical IT workflow for a non-standard change will have different custom fields than a standard workflow; a request for a new onboarding will require different custom fields than the standard request to replace a PC.

UI Extensions and Requests

Requests have the unique ability to span across multiple accounts, yet each request is anchored to a single request template, thereby linking it to a singular UI. This setup ensures that within the network of interconnected accounts, one is designated to define the UI Extension and, by extension, the custom fields for any given request. These UI Extensions can feature custom suggest fields that present a selectively filtered list of records.

The configuration of custom fields within UI Extensions, particularly whether they are marked as 'internal', directly influences their visibility. Custom fields not designated as internal are accessible across all accounts that can view the request, thus not restricted solely to *specialists*, *auditors*, and *account administrators* of the account where the request template/UI Extension resides.

For instance, an account may create a custom view featuring a filtered list of organizations within its structure, or compile all the cost centers of the organization into a custom collection and another custom view. These lists can then be incorporated as custom suggest fields within a UI Extension attached to a request template, making the detailed organizations and cost centers accessible in every request that utilizes this template. Such a setup is appropriate for trusted accounts directly associated with the originating account, where a contractual agreement ensures appropriate sharing of information between customer and supplier accounts.

However, the scenario changes when a request transitions to a secondary supplier outside the primary contractual framework. Given this supplier's absence of a direct contract with the initiating service delivery organization, it's imperative they do not gain access to the comprehensive list of organizations and cost centers from the original custom view.

address this, **UI Extension forms are designed to be editable only by users within directly trusted accounts**, ensuring data confidentiality within the service chain. Users from external accounts, not directly involved in the contractual relationship, will encounter the form in a view-only mode. They can see which organization or cost center has been selected but cannot access further details or explore the full listing. This safeguard is crucial for fields not marked as internal, as it maintains the intended level of visibility and confidentiality for shared data across the service delivery ecosystem.

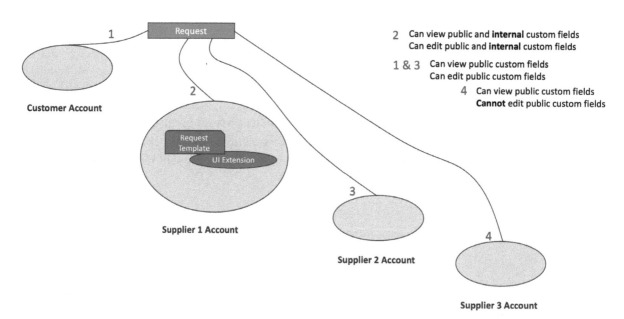

2   Can view public and **internal** custom fields
      Can edit public and **internal** custom fields

1 & 3   Can view public custom fields
      Can edit public custom fields

4   Can view public custom fields
      Cannot edit public custom fields

Request

Customer Account

Request Template

UI Extension

Supplier 1 Account

Supplier 2 Account

Supplier 3 Account

UI Extensions in Configuration Management

UI Extensions can be applied to both Product Categories and Products. Here's how they work:

- **For Configuration Items**: If you wish to add a custom field like 'Rack Address' to all Configuration Items categorized as physical servers, you should create a UI Extension for their *Products*. This UI Extension does not directly modify the products itself. Instead, it introduces custom fields to the Configuration Items associated with these products. After creating this UI Extension, link it to each product with the category 'Computer - Server' to ensure all relevant Configuration Items carry the custom field 'Rack Address'.
- **For Products**: Conversely, if your goal is to embed custom fields directly onto products (for example, adding a 'Form Factor' field with options like rack-mount, tower, or blade for server products), you must attach a UI Extension to the *Product Category*, not to the individual products. This UI Extension should be linked to the 'Computer - Server' product category, effectively adding the custom field to all server products under this category.

It's crucial to understand this distinction to avoid confusion: UI Extensions linked to products affect Configuration Items of those products, whereas UI Extensions linked to product categories add custom fields directly to the products.

Additionally, when configuration items are shared with support teams in trusted accounts, any 'internal' custom fields you create will only be visible to specialists, auditors, and account administrators of the account owning the Configuration Item or Product.

Universal UI Extensions: Enhancing Core Records

For a set of core record types the 4me platform allows for the application of a single UI Extension that spans universally across all instances within an account. This global approach ensures consistency and uniformity in data collection and presentation for:

1. Contracts
2. Organizations
3. People (Person records)
4. Problems
5. Releases
6. SCIM Users
7. Service Instances
8. Services
9. Sites
10. Teams

As a best practice, name the UI Extension after the generic category, for instance, you could name the UI Extension for Problems 'Problem,' making its purpose clear.

UI Extensions for Organizations Explained

When you create a UI Extension for 'Organization' records, it applies to organizations within the same 4me account as the UI Extension. Given the variety of organization types—internal, external, and trusted—understanding their distinctions is crucial.

- **Internal Organizations**: Originating from the directory account, these are linked to the organization's hierarchy within the directory account. Consequently, any custom fields for internal organizations must be defined within the directory account. Although visible in support domain accounts, these custom fields cannot be managed by support domain administrators or designers.
- **External Organizations**: These may be established in both directory and support domain accounts. Thus, a support domain account administrator has control over UI Extensions for external organizations only within their specific account.
- **Trusted Organizations**: Unique in nature, these organizations enter an account via SLAs with customers or service providers from the trusted account. While administrators of trusted account can create UI Extensions for their organizations, these custom fields remain exclusive to their account and are not shared externally. However, a UI Extension created in an account for the record type 'Organization' does extend to trusted organizations. This allows accounts to enrich trusted organization records with additional custom information, similar to standard fields like 'Financial ID' and 'Region'.

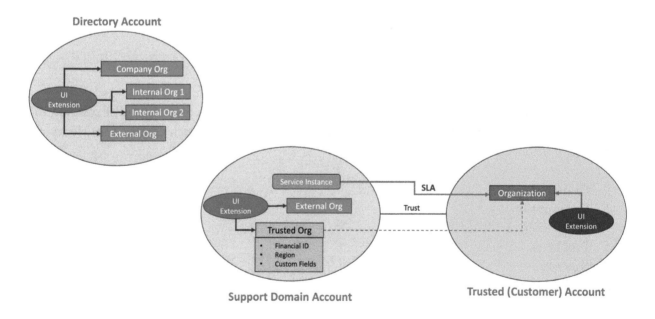

Figure 231: *It is possible to add custom fields to a trusted organization via the UI Extension in the account.*

UI Extensions for SCIM User Records

In a previous chapter, we introduced SCIM, the open and standardized protocol used in cloud software platforms to automatically provision user and group information from an Identity Provider (IdP) like Microsoft Azure Active Directory or OneLogin to 4me. This protocol supports a set of standard fields that one would expect to find on user and group records. Additionally, the SCIM standard provides a mechanism for IdPs and cloud applications to add extra custom fields to the standard set. 4me has implemented support for these extra custom fields, which can be defined by adding a UI Extension for SCIM User records. For more detailed information, please refer to the 4me developer site at https://developer.4me.com/v1/scim/users/#custom-fields-extension.

Chapter 13 - Automation Rules

Introduction

Imagine the process of replacing a user's broken computer: a standard request triggers a workflow that encompasses every step, from fetching a spare from stock and imaging and preparing the device, to delivery and the crucial final step—updating the CMDB. This update involves detaching the old computer from the user, marking it for repair, and linking the new one while setting it to 'In Production.' If all necessary information is systematically captured within your 4me setup, why resort to manual updates?

Enter the realm of 4me automation rules. These powerful tools can replicate almost any action a specialist performs through the Specialist Interface, automating workflows and updating data based on your specific criteria. The best part? Creating these automation rules is a breeze with 4me's low-code environment. You don't need to be a developer; you just need a solid grasp of 4me's architecture—knowledge you've been building as you've progressed through this book.

Dive into this chapter to explore how automation rules can transform your operational efficiency, streamline your processes, and allow your team to focus on what truly matters. Welcome to the efficient, automated world of 4me.

Understanding Automation Rule Types

In 4me, specialists interact with various record types through the Specialist Interface, typically engaging with ticket types like requests, problems, workflow tasks, or project tasks. Others might focus on configuration items, workflows, or projects, updating and editing these records as needed. Think of automation rules as specialized workers, each dedicated to a specific record type, streamlining tasks that specialists handle manually.

There are three main categories of automation rules:

- **Generic Automation Rules**: These rules apply broadly to record types such as requests, problems, tasks, configuration items, people, and risks. They act like specialists focused on automating actions related to these records.

Request Automation Rules ▼

✓ Request Automation Rules

Request Template Automation Rules

Problem Automation Rules

Workflow Automation Rules

Task Automation Rules

Workflow Template Automation Rules

Task Template Automation Rules

Project Task Automation Rules

Project Template Automation Rules

Project Task Template Automation Rules

Configuration Item Automation Rules

Person Automation Rules

Risk Automation Rules

SCIM User Automation Rules

Figure 232: The Automation Rules menu in the Settings Console with a view for each type of automation rules.

- **Template Automation Rules**: Linked specifically to templates like request templates, task templates, workflow templates, project task templates, and project templates. They trigger only when an action occurs on a record associated with their respective template.
- **SCIM User and SCIM Group Automation Rules**: These are designed for integrating SCIM (System for Cross-domain Identity Management) records with 4me, facilitating automatic mapping and updates between SCIM users and groups and 4me's people, organizations, and sites records.

Creating and Managing Automation Rules

Account designers and *account administrators* can create, update, and disable automation rules through the 'Automation Rules' section located in the Settings Console. For those interested in establishing template automation rules, like request templates or task templates, a dedicated 'Automation Rules...' option is available from the Actions menu.

Crafting Workflow Template Automation Rules

You can define a workflow template automation rule directly from a workflow template. To do this, select your desired workflow template and then choose the 'Automation Rules...' option from the Actions menu. This setup allows the automation rule to monitor events occurring within any workflow linked to this specific workflow template.

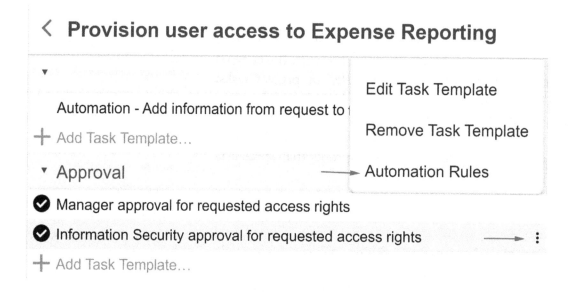

Figure 233: Creating a workflow template automation rule on a task template from the Gantt Chart view of the workflow template.

Additionally, a workflow template automation rule can be specifically associated with a task template within the workflow template. This specialization allows the rule to focus on events related to tasks derived from the selected task template within workflows associated with the overall workflow template.

To setup this type of rule, navigate to the Gantt Chart of the workflow template, locate the desired task template, and select 'Automation Rules...' from the ellipsis menu next to the task template name.

Task Template vs. Workflow Template Automation Rules

While it's possible to link a *workflow template automation rule* to a specific task template, you might wonder why not always opt for a *task template automation rule*. The choice between the two depends on the context and requirements of your automation objectives:

- **Task Template Automation Rules** are active across any workflow that incorporates the task template. This universality is advantageous when the same task template is used across multiple workflows and the automation doesn't require context from the surrounding workflow structure.
- **Workflow Template Automation Rules**, on the other hand, are preferable for automations that involve interactions with or references to other tasks within the same workflow. If your automation needs to access or modify information in tasks related to the same workflow template, then opting for a workflow template automation rule offers the necessary context and specificity.

In essence, when deciding which type of automation rule to use, consider the scope and context requirements of your automation. If the automation tasks are specific to the workflow's context, choose workflow template automation rules. For broader, task-specific automations that apply across multiple workflows, task template automation rules might be the more effective choice.

Breaking Down the Elements of an Automation Rule

Automation rules within 4me are comprised of four key components. Here's a closer look at the structure of an automation rule:

Figure 234: The four elements of an automation rule: a Trigger, Expressions, Conditions and Actions.

- **Trigger**: The trigger serves as the starting point for an automation rule. It listens for specific events related to a designated record type, such as the creation of a record ('On create'), the addition of a note ('On note added'), or updates to certain attributes ('On update of ...'). These triggers initiate the automation process in motion when the specified event occurs.
- **Expressions**: Before an automation rule can execute its actions, it often requires some preparatory steps or data retrieval. This is where expressions come into play. For example, to update the Configuration Management Database (CMDB) based on a task's completion, expressions are used to gather the necessary configuration item records.
- **Conditions**: Conditions determine whether the actions of an automation rule should be executed. They evaluate to true or false based on the current state or attributes of the record. Continuing with the CMDB update example, an automation rule might only proceed with its actions if the task's status changes to 'Assigned'.
- **Actions**: The core of the automation rule, actions define what the rule will do once triggered and conditions are met. Actions could range from updating record fields, such as changing the status of a configuration item, to sending an email notification.

Low Code

In this chapter, we explore automation rules, illustrating concepts through code snippets to demonstrate how to construct them. However, it's important to note that memorizing the syntax of these snippets isn't necessary. The design of the automation rules interface in 4me offers intuitive guidance, providing suggestions and selectable options as you define expressions, conditions, and actions. For example, within an automation rule for requests, as soon as you type 's' while defining an expression, the interface displays all request attributes starting with 's' for easy selection.

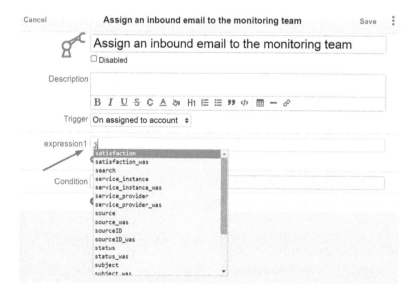

Figure 235: Within an automation rule for requests, as soon as you type 's' while defining an expression, the interface reveals all request attributes beginning with 's'.

Mastering automation rules hinges on a solid understanding of 4me's fundamental record architecture. For instance, when creating an automation rule for a task template and aiming to reference an attribute from the initiating request, it's crucial to recognize the task's link to its workflow record. Given that a workflow can be associated with multiple requests, the first in the series is typically your target. Additionally, a thorough understanding of the available actions and operators is essential. These are the topics we'll cover next, equipping you with the knowledge to effectively navigate and utilize 4me's low-code environment for automation rules.

Automation Rule Actions: Crafting the Final Touch

In automation rules, actions represent the culminating step of creation, yet they are often the first consideration during design. Initially, you outline the 'when'—your triggers and conditions—and then pinpoint the 'what'—the actions to be executed. This foundational planning guides the subsequent detailing of expressions, gathering necessary data to define conditions and enable actions. Therefore, before venturing into expressions, let's explore the capabilities automation rules offer. Available to you are five distinct types of actions:

1. Updating records,
2. Appending notes,
3. Dispatching emails,
4. Triggering another rule after a delay,
5. Initiating a webhook.

Let's delve into each action type now.

Figure 236: The five available action types in an automation rule.

Update Actions

Update actions have two main components: the target record and the type of action to be performed.

Target Record Selection

The default target is the '`current record`' to which the automation rule is linked. For instance, in a request template automation rule, this would be the individual request; for a CI automation rule, it's the configuration item. However, through expressions, you can extend beyond the default, enabling updates on related or even unrelated records by overriding the '`current record`' choice.

Choosing the Update Type

The next component is selecting the Update type, which is crucial for specifying the nature of the update. For straightforward attributes, such as a record's status, a 'Set' action is sufficient. As you begin typing in the attribute field you wish to update 4me suggests available fields. Next enter the "=" operator and select an applicable value from the list.

```
Update          current record
Add             status = completed
```

Automation Rule 1: Automation Rule for Updating Request Status.

> **Tip**
>
> A smart approach when crafting automation rules is to first mimic the desired actions manually via the Specialist Interface. This hands-on trial helps confirm whether an action is feasible directly through 4me's interface. If you find an action unachievable this way, it likely won't work via an automation rule either, and you might need to consider setting up an integration for the desired outcome.
>
> This process is also invaluable for identifying precisely which fields require updating. For example, when marking a request as completed, you'll notice that updating the status to 'Completed' necessitates specifying both a completion reason and a note. Therefore, your automation rule should encompass these three updates to avoid execution failures.

Handling Multi-Value Fields

Fields like those linking multiple CIs to requests can also be updated. These list are called **Arrays** in an automation rule. We'll delve into managing arrays with expressions later. To modify multi-select fields, you have three action types: Add, Remove, and Clear. The Add action is to add an item or multiple items to the list.

```
Update          current record
Add             stock_ci to cis
```

Automation Rule 2: Add a CI (Configuration Item) to the multi-select field cis (configuration items) on a request.

The Remove action lets you eliminate a specific item from a multi-select field, whereas Clear empties the entire array.

```
Update        current record
Remove        stock_ci from cis
```

Automation Rule 3: Remove a CI (Configuration Item) from the multi-select field cis (configuration items) on a request.

Add Notes

The 'Add Note' action stands out for its simplicity and effectiveness in automating communication. Like the Update action, this function requires you to select a target record, typically defaulting to the current one being worked on. The Add Note action includes the ability to attach files to notes. For request records specifically, there's the added flexibility to mark a note as internal.

The inclusion of a rich text editor empowers you to craft well-formatted notes, while the integration of named expressions through the "{{" notation adds a layer of dynamic content. For instance, embedding an organization's name retrieved from a named expression 'organization_name' is as straightforward as inserting {{organization_name}} into your note. Clicking on the curly bracket icon in the toolbar unveils a list of all available named expressions.

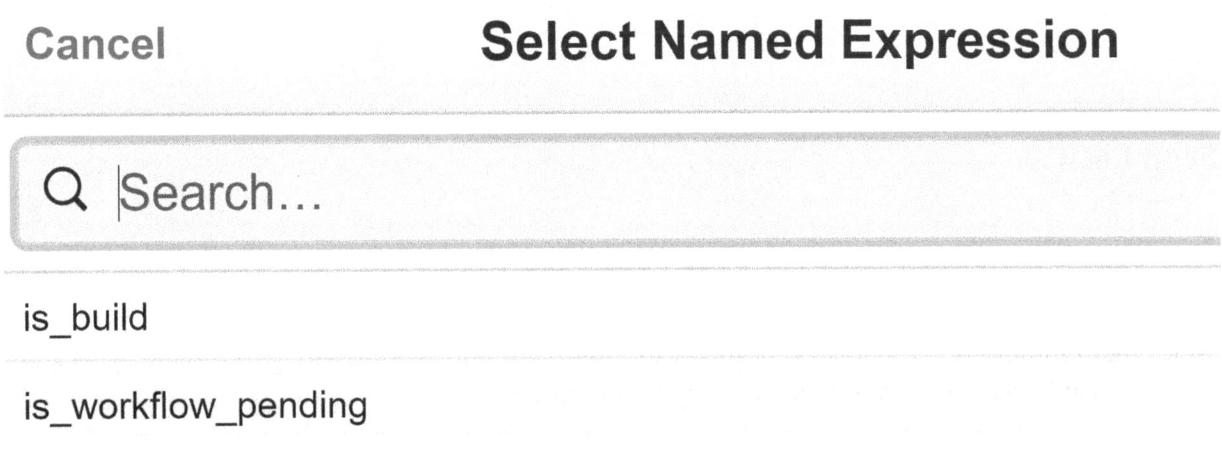

Cancel   **Select Named Expression**

Q Search…

is_build

is_workflow_pending

Figure 237: Selecting a Named Expression by clicking on the {{ action in the toolbar of the Add note section.

Furthermore, the ability to mention individuals directly in notes, akin to a specialist's capability, is retained here. For automation rules, the mention functionality in the toolbar facilitates the selection of individuals from within the account. To achieve dynamic person selection in your notes, incorporate the individual's person record as a named expression, prefixed with the "@" symbol.

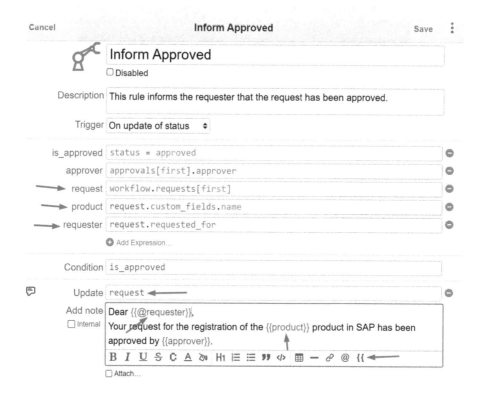

Figure 238: The 'Add note' action provides a rich text editor in which Named Expressions can be embedded, including a 'mentioned user'.

Send Email

In a previous section, we discussed how 4me's core functionality enhances communication by enabling the sending of emails directly from various records capable of holding notes. This feature supports a wide range of interactions, from healthcare organizations communicating with government agencies to retail companies liaising with suppliers and logistics partners.

Building on this foundational capability, 4me offers the added advantage of sending emails through automation rules. For example, imagine a service delivery organization using 4me that collaborates with a supplier not on the 4me platform. The supplier requires any tickets from the service delivery organization to be submitted via a structured email to their ITSM system's email address. This process can be streamlined and automated with 4me's 'Send Email' action in automation rules. Thus, whenever a request is assigned to the supplier's service instance within 4me, an automation rule can automatically trigger and dispatch the necessary email.

It's a best practice to create a tailored email design for these automated communications sent externally. You'll want to carefully craft the header and footer of the email to ensure it aligns with your organization's branding and communication standards. Keep in mind that the email will appear as a note on the ticket, and any replies to these emails will also be attached to the ticket, provided the email policy in the account settings permits this. In the example of communicating with the supplier, an automation rule of type 'Request' can process the email reply from the supplier's ITSM system to extract the ticket ID and populate the 'Supplier Request ID' field with this ID.

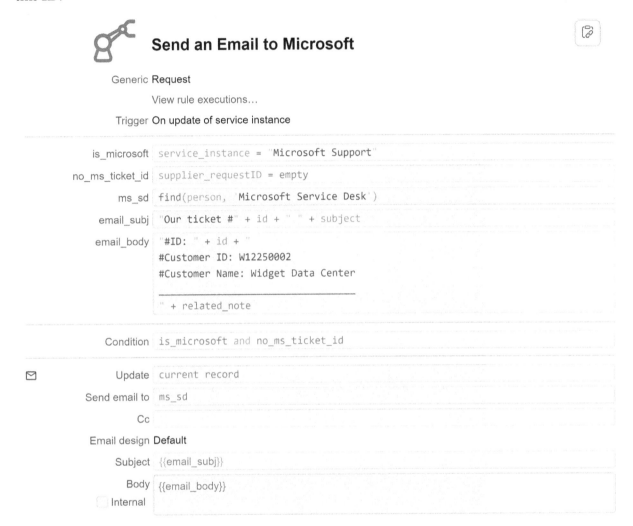

Send an Email to Microsoft

Generic **Request**

View rule executions…

Trigger **On update of service instance**

is_microsoft	service_instance = "Microsoft Support"
no_ms_ticket_id	supplier_requestID = empty
ms_sd	find(person, "Microsoft Service Desk")
email_subj	"Our ticket #" + id + " " + subject
email_body	"#ID: " + id + " #Customer ID: W12250002 #Customer Name: Widget Data Center _____ " + related_note
Condition	is_microsoft and no_ms_ticket_id
Update	current record
Send email to	ms_sd
Cc	
Email design	**Default**
Subject	{{email_subj}}
Body	{{email_body}}
☐ Internal	

Figure 239: The" Send an email" action. The email is sent to the email addresses of the person records in the TO: and CC: fields. The contents of the Subject and Body can be constructed with named expressions.

Start an Automation Rule with a Delay

When a task awaits approval, the workflow pauses until the required approval is received. Yet, delays can occur—perhaps the approver missed the initial notification or is unable to respond due to unforeseen circumstances, such as illness, without designating a delegate for their approvals. This can result in tasks remaining in a 'Waiting for approval' state indefinitely. To address this, sending reminders to the approver or even automatically escalating the approval to another user after a set period can be effective strategies. This is where automation rules with delays become invaluable.

First, define the delayed action in an automation rule using the 'After delay' trigger. Then, create another automation rule that specifies when to execute the 'delayed' automation rule through a 'Delay action'. Here, you simply set the duration of the delay—be it in seconds, minutes, hours, days, months, or years—and select the automation rule with the 'After delay' trigger in the Start field. You can also specify a particular date and time for the action to occur. Using a named expression with an exact date-time value changes the 'After...' statement to an 'At...' statement.

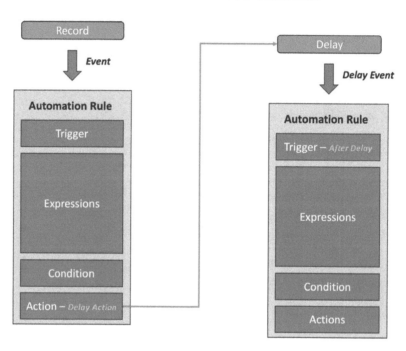

Figure 240: Starting an automation rule with a delay involves two steps. First create an automation rule with the trigger 'After delay.' Next, set up another automation rule to initiate this first automation rule after a specified delay.

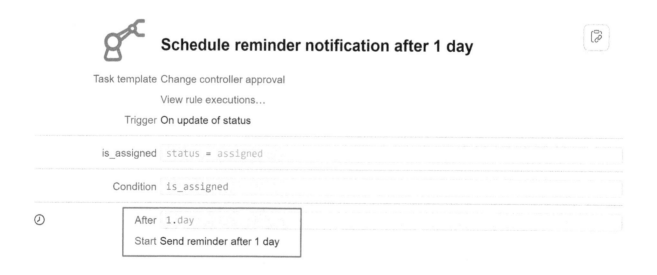

Figure 241: The 'Approval Reminder' automation rule will be started after one day.

Recurring Execution of Automation Rules

Expanding on the concept of sending reminders for approval tasks, imagine you want to send daily reminders instead of a one-time alert. Transforming the existing automation rules setup in a loop is quite simple. By adding an action to the second automation rule that triggers itself again after 24 hours, you establish a recurring loop.

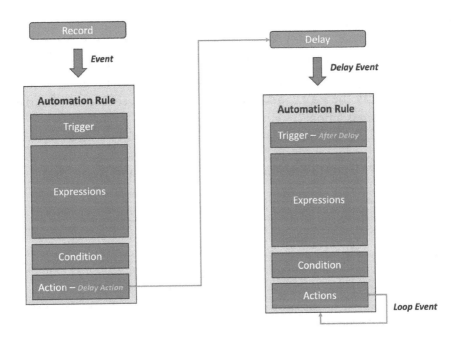

Figure 242: The delayed automation rule can start itself to create a loop.

However, it's crucial to include conditions to break this loop to prevent endless reminders. For instance, the loop should only continue if the task's status remains 'Assigned.' To safeguard against infinite loops, 4me incorporates several built-in protections: a loop is capped at a maximum of 120 executions, and an automation rule can be executed no more than once per day.

Figure 243: An automation rule starting itself with a delay creating a loop.

Start a Webhook

Imagine an enterprise where employees can request access to an Expense Reporting service via 4me Self Service. This process uses a workflow template with two task templates, creating a two-step workflow: manager approval followed by access implementation. The real innovation comes when, upon managerial approval, access to the Expense Reporting system is automatically granted through automation. The upcoming chapter on integrations will explore various methods for establishing such integrations, all of which will likely require triggering a webhook at some point.

To set this up, your first step is to establish the webhook with the event type 'automation_rule'. After successfully creating and verifying the webhook, you can select it in the automation rule's 'Call' field. Then, you'll specify the Payload, which is essentially a collection of variables the integration needs to execute the desired action.

Figure 244: This automation rule calls an integration to provide access rights to a user to the Expense Reporting application, by triggering a webhook. The name of the person, the employee ID and the required access level are defined as named expressions and added to the payload.

Automation Rule Expressions

Automation Rule Expressions: Mastering Operators

Named expressions serve as the foundation of automation rules, laying the groundwork for conditions, actions, and ultimately, the execution of these rules. They play a crucial role in various tasks, such as evaluating conditions to determine if an action should proceed, identifying records for action execution, preparing content for notes and emails, updating record attributes, and populating webhook payloads with necessary data.

While many automation rules are straightforward, there are instances where complex logic and a deeper understanding of the available operators are required. These operators allow for the creation of detailed expressions that precisely define the behavior of automation rules.

To tackle advanced automation needs, a comprehensive list of operators and their applications can be found in the 4me online help documentation, available here: https://help.4me.com/help/automation_ rule_operators/. This resource is invaluable for those looking to expand their knowledge and capabilities within the 4me platform. As we continue, we'll delve into some of these operators in detail, providing insights into their practical applications and how they can enhance your automation rules.

Assignments

At the core of every automation rule is the 'current record'—the specific record that triggers the rule through a particular event. This fundamental concept allows for direct access to the record's fields within the automation rule. The user-friendly interface of the automation rule editor intuitively lists all accessible fields, making it straightforward to incorporate them into your rule.

To allocate a field's value to a named expression, the process is straightforward. You'll define your named expression on the left side of the equation and assign the desired field's value on the right. For example, if you're looking to capture the 'Category' attribute of a request within a variable, your expression might look like this:

```
my_category       category                          In an automation rule of type Request
                                                     the named expression my_category is
                                                     set the category of the request
```

Named expressions are **case-sensitive**. To maintain clarity and prevent potential mix-ups, a best practice is to consistently define all named expressions using lower-case letters. This approach helps avoid confusion that can arise from mixing lower-case and upper-case characters.

4me predefines a set of **regular field names** for use in these rules. To prevent any overlap or confusion, the system restricts the use of these reserved names for your custom named expressions. If you attempt to use a reserved name for a named expression, 4me will automatically prepend an underscore (_) to your named expression to differentiate it. You can start your named expression with the keyword my_ to avoid this behavior.

The Transition Tracking with _was Fields

Automation rules are activated by specific events on associated records, such as a change in a ticket's status. Understanding how a record changes—the transition it undergoes—is crucial for certain automation rules. For instance, if an automation rule is triggered by the "On update of status" event, it may be necessary for the rule to execute only if the status changed from "Waiting for Customer" to "Assigned".

To facilitate this, 4me provides not only the current value of a field but also its previous value before the update occurred, using the _was suffix. For the given example, both status and status_was fields are available to the automation rule.

Defining Conditions – Comparison Operators

The most common operator is the Equality operator, which can be preceded with the not (!) operator.

is_assigned	status = assigned	The named expression **is_assigned** will be set to true when the status of the record is "Assigned".
is_not_assigned	status != assigned	The opposite, the named expression becomes trues if the status is nor assigned.

In scenarios where you need to compare more than one value, defining an **Array** becomes invaluable. An Array is essentially a list of values enclosed in square brackets. For example, [assigned, accepted, in_progress] represents an array of possible statuses. The 'Contains' operator, symbolized by in, allows you to check if a given value matches any within the array. For instance, to verify if a ticket's status is either 'Accepted' or 'In Progress', you would employ the following expression:

is_picked_up	status in [accepted, in_progress]	The named expression **is_picked_up** will be set to true when the status of the record is "Accepted" or "In Progress".

To enhance automation rules' logic, you might need to ascertain if a field is unfilled or if a record is linked. This is achievable with the **is_blank** and **is_present** operators. For instance, consider a scenario to notify the knowledge manager whenever a knowledge article is linked to a request with an archive date set in the past.

In the request automation rule, the process begins by identifying if a knowledge article is associated with the request. Following this, the automation rule checks if the knowledge article's archive date is defined. Named expressions are utilized to evaluate these conditions:

my_ka	knowledge_article	Get the knowledge article related to the request.
ka_found	my_ka is_present	If a knowledge article is found, this named expression is true.
ka_archive_date	my_ka.archive_date	Get the Archive Date of the knowledge article.
no_archive_date	ka_archive_date is_blank	Check whether an archive date has been defined.

Note that the `is_blank` and `is_present` operators are the inverse of each other.

- `".is_blank => True` and `".is_present => False`
- `'value'.is_blank => False` and `'value'.is_present => True`
- `[].is_blank => True` and `[].is_present => False`
- `[value].is_blank => False` and `[value].is_present => True`

Conditional Operators

Conditional operators are essential tools for defining the execution conditions of automation rules. By using comparison operators, you can create Boolean named expressions that evaluate to either true or false. These expressions serve as the foundation for specifying the rule's conditions, allowing the automation to execute based on specific criteria. The conditional operators and, or, and the negation operator not enable the combination and inversion of these Boolean expressions within the Conditions section of an automation rule.

For instance, revisiting the previous example concerning knowledge articles and archive dates, the automation rule's conditions could incorporate these operators to precisely determine when the rule should activate. This might involve verifying that a knowledge article exists (`ka_found`) and confirming that its archive date is both present and in the past (additional condition not shown here for simplicity). A basic outline of such conditions, incorporating conditional operators, could appear as follows:

| Conditions | ka_found and not no_archive_date | Only execute the automation rule when a knowledge article is found and when the knowledge article has an archive date |

Navigating Through Records

To create effective automation rules in 4me, it's essential to understand the structure and relationships between records. While the automation rule designer interface provides suggestions for accessible record fields, a comprehensive understanding of how records interconnect is vital for accurately navigating and utilizing related records. A key area of focus, particularly since many automation rules are triggered by tasks linked to task template or workflow template automation rules, involves understanding the relationships starting from a task. Here's a brief overview of these relationships:

- **Tasks and Workflows**: A task is directly associated with a single workflow, which can be easily accessed in a task automation rule.
- **Predecessors and Successors**: A task may have multiple preceding and succeeding tasks, outlining the sequence of activities within a workflow.
- **Workflow and Requests**: A workflow might be linked to several requests, adding complexity when accessing specific request information.

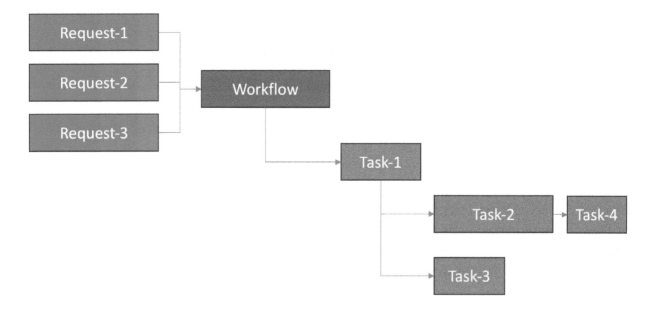

A common automation rule requirement is to fetch data from the Requester related to the initiating action. Typically, the Requester is the "Requested for" user of the primary request linked to the workflow. Here's how to navigate from a task to its relevant request and onto the Requester's details:

request	`workflow.requests[first]`	workflow is an exposed field on a task. Take the first request of all requests related to the workflow.
requester	`request.requested_for`	Get the person record of the Requested For person.
requester_name	`requester.name`	Get the name of the person record.

Note that in the provided code snippet, the named expressions `request` and `requester` represent specific 4me records. These named expressions can be used for specifying target records in the Actions part of an automation rule. If there's a need to update the request record or the person record of the requester, you can simply use `request` or `requester` to override the default `current_record` specification in your actions.

In a task automation rule, when you need to identify another task within the same workflow, you have two methods at your disposal. The first method involves leveraging the 'predecessors' or 'successors' relationships. For example, in the provided diagram, Task-4 is a successor to Task-2. Thus, an automation rule targeting Task-2 can pinpoint Task-4 using a named expression like this:

task_4	successors[first]	The successors field is an array. So you need to specify which element in the array you need, even when the array only consists of one element.

Alternatively, the second method gets the list of all tasks related to the workflow and utilizes the name of the task template directly within square brackets. Suppose the Task-4 template is named 'Update the CMDB'; you could then locate this task with the following approach:

task_4	workflow.tasks["Update the CMDB"]	Get the array of all tasks in the workflow. Next specify the task based on the name of the task template.

Similar to using `first` as a keyword to access the first element in a list, `last` serves to access the last element. Alternatively, `1` can be used to denote the first element, and `-1` for the last. Additionally, it's possible to reference a task directly by its 4me ID within expressions. For instance, using `workflow.tasks[#2555698]` retrieves the task associated with the task template having the 4me ID `2555698` within a workflow. However, it's important to note that automation rules incorporating direct 4me ID references may be less intuitive to understand due to the abstract nature of numerical IDs.

Add a New Task to a Workflow

In dynamic workflows, where tasks are contingent upon specific criteria, it's common practice to include all potential task templates within the workflow template initially. Depending on the outcome of criteria evaluation, tasks may be automatically set to 'Cancelled' through automation rules. An alternative approach, however, is to refrain from adding certain task templates to the workflow template and instead dynamically insert tasks based on those templates as needed through automation rules. This flexibility is enabled by the **new** operator, which requires specifying the record type (in this case, 'task') and the task template by name.

For example, to create a new task based on the 'Prepare a security badge' task template, you might use the following expression:

sec_badge_task	new(task, "Prepare a security badge")	A new task record is created based on task template "Prepare a security badge".

Once created, this new task can be integrated into the workflow's task array with an action like:

```
Update          workflow
Add             sec_badge_task to tasks
```

Furthermore, by specifying the successors or predecessors for this new task, it can be seamlessly incorporated into the workflow schedule, and its status updated accordingly. For instance, the following example illustrates setting an existing task, identified by update_cmdb, as a successor to the new task and assigning it a status of 'Assigned':

```
Update          sec_badge_task
Add             update_cmdb to successors
Update          sec_badge_task
set             status = assigned
```

Finding Unrelated Record Types

Accessing records that don't have a direct link to the initiating record in an automation rule can be essential for certain operations. There are three primary methods for locating these unrelated records, each with its unique use case:

Using the `find(record_type, search_key)` Operator: This operator is designed to retrieve a single record based on a specific key, such as the record's 4me ID or other identifiers that vary by record type (e.g., label or name for CIs, name, primary_email or supportID for person records). It's important to note that if the search key isn't unique, the first matching record encountered will be returned. For example, to fetch the person record for Microsoft Service Desk, one might use:

ms_support support	find(person,"Microsoft Service Desk")	**Finds the person record named "Microsoft Service Desk".**

Using the `find_all(record_type, search_key)` Operator: Contrary to the `find()` operator, `find_all()` returns an array of records that match the search criteria. It's particularly useful when you're not looking for a unique identifier but a common attribute among several records. For instance, to find all CIs named "HP Compaq dc7900 Minitower PC":

hp_minitowers	find_all(ci,"HP Compaq dc7900 Minitower PC")	**Gathers an array of CIs named "HP Compaq dc7900 Minitower PC".**

Be mindful that there's a limit of 250 records for the results returned by `find_all()`.

Using the `search(record_type, search_key)` Operator: Similar to a full search in the Specialist Interface, search() allows partial matches and is akin to a broad query across a specified record type. Unlike find_all(), search() doesn't require an exact match to return results. For example, a search for "HP Compaq" in CIs would return all items containing these terms in their name, up to a maximum of 50 records:

`hp_compaq_cis`	`search(ci,"HP Compaq")`	Fetches a list of CIs where "HP" or "Compaq" appear in the name.

Understanding Arrays

Arrays returned by the find_all() and search() operators often require an additional selection layer. 4me automation rules offer a multitude of operators to process arrays effectively.

The Select and Detect Operators

The Select() and Detect() operators are essential tools for refining the set of records returned by a query in your automation rules. These operators enable you to filter a list of records based on specific attribute values.

Using the Select() Operator:

Suppose you have retrieved an array of Configuration Items (CIs) named "HP Compaq dc7900 Minitower PC," but you are only interested in those with a status of "Broken Down." To achieve this, you can use the `Select()` operator as follows:

`hp_minitowers`	`find_all(ci,"HP Compaq dc7900 Minitower PC").select(status = broken_down)`	Gathers an array of CIs named "HP Compaq dc7900 Minitower PC" with status "Broken Down".

If further filtering is required, such as finding those "Broken Down" CIs located in a specific area like the "Stock Room 1st floor," you can chain multiple `Select()` operators:

`hp_minitowers`	`find_all(ci,"HP Compaq dc7900 Minitower PC").select(status = broken_down).select(location = "Stock Room 1st floor")`	Gathers an array of CIs named "HP Compaq dc7900 Minitower PC" with status "Broken Down" and located in the stock room on the 1st floor.

Using the Detect() Operator:

In scenarios where only the first matching record is needed from a filtered list, the `detect()` operator becomes valuable. It functions similarly to chaining the `select()` operator with the `[first]` index but simplifies the process by directly returning the first record that meets the criteria:

my_hp_minitower	`find_all(ci,"HP Compaq dc7900 Minitower PC").select(status = broken_down).delect(location = "Stock Room 1st floor")`	Gathers the first CI out of an array of CIs named "HP Compaq dc7900 Minitower PC" with status "Broken Down" and located in the stock room on the 1st floor.

The Map Operator

The `map()` operator is an invaluable tool within 4me's automation rules, when the goal is to transform a list of records into a list of specific attributes from those records. This operator enables you to extract a particular attribute from each record in a collection, resulting in an array of those attribute values. Consider the previous scenario where you're interested in just the Asset IDs. To accomplish this, the map() operator can be applied as follows:

hp_minitowers	`find_all(ci,"HP Compaq dc7900 Minitower PC").select(status = broken_down).select(location = "Stock Room 1st floor"). map(assetID)`	Gathers an array of Asset IDs of CIs named "HP Compaq dc7900 Minitower PC" with status "Broken Down" and located in the stock room on the 1st floor.

The Count, Empty, Any and All Operators

The **count, empty?, any?**, and **all?** operators can be used for evaluating the results of queries and making decisions based on those results.

Count Operator:

The count() operator is used to determine the number of records within an array, which is particularly useful when the size of the result set is a factor in decision-making processes.

Example:

nr_hp_minitowers	`find_all(ci,"HP Compaq dc7900 Minitower PC").select(status = broken_down).select(location = "Stock Room 1st floor").count`	The number of CIs named "HP Compaq dc7900 Minitower PC" with status "Broken Down" and located in the stock room on the 1st floor.

Empty? Operator:

The empty? operator checks whether an array is empty and returns a Boolean value (true or false).

Example:

no_hp_minitowers	find_all(ci,"HP Compaq dc7900 Minitower PC").select(status = broken_down).select(location = "Stock Room 1st floor").empty?	This named expression will be 'true' when the array is empty.

Any? Operator:

The any? operator is used to determine if any records in an array meet a specified condition, returning true if at least one record matches the condition.

Example:

any_in_stock	find_all(ci,"HP Compaq dc7900 Minitower PC").select(status = broken_down).select(location = "Stock Room 1st floor").any?	This named expression will be 'true' if at least one HP minitower is found with status "Broken Down".

The any? operator accepts an argument. This means that the previous code can even be shortened like this:

any_in_stock	find_all(ci,"HP Compaq dc7900 Minitower PC").select(status = broken_down).any?(location = "Stock Room 1st floor")	The any? operator accepts a select statement as an argument.

All? Operator:

The all? operator checks if all records in an array satisfy a given condition.

Example:

all_status_ok	find_all(ci,"HP Compaq dc7900 Minitower PC").select(location = "Stock Room 1st floor").all?(status = "in_stock")	Check whether all the HP computers in the stock room on the first floor have the status "in Stock".

Custom Fields in Automation Rules

Custom fields in 4me are stored as key-value pairs within the custom_fields attribute of a record. These custom fields are vital for extending the data stored about records beyond the standard fields provided by 4me. However, when it comes to automation rules, accessing these custom fields directly is not as straightforward as accessing standard fields.

Consider an array of key-value pairs that might represent custom fields for a record:

- manager: 15520
- sites: [56889,56894]
- description: New projector
- target_date: 2027-01-24T09:00:00Z
- avatar: [Attachment link]
- urgency: 2
- cost_center: 2689235

For end-users, UI Extensions play a crucial role in making these custom fields meaningful and user-friendly, whether in the Self-Service Portal or the Specialist Interface.

When dealing with automation rules, custom_fields is recognized as an attribute of records, including the current record involved in the automation rule. Yet, the automation rule builder does not automatically suggest specific key-value pairs within custom_fields. It is the responsibility of the automation rule designer to know the IDs (keys) of the custom fields, which can be found within the UI Extensions, and to manually specify these when accessing or modifying their values.

For instance, to access the value of the custom field with the key 'manager':

manager_id	custom_fields.manager	The value of the custom field with key = 'manager' is set in the named expression 'manager'

However, this value is treated as a string within the automation rule and does not inherently carry the attributes of a person record it may reference. To convert this string value into a meaningful reference to a person record, the find() operator can be employed:

manager_id	custom_fields.manager	The value of the custom field with key = 'manager' is set in the named expression 'manager_id'
manager	find(person,manager_id)	Turn the named expression in a person record.
manager_name	manager.name	Once the named expression is a person record the automation rule gets access to the attributes.

Similar to single-value custom fields, multi-select custom fields store arrays of 4me IDs. Consider a custom field named sites that is a multi-select field and contains an array of 4me IDs like ['56889', '56894']. This array represents the IDs of two sites within the 4me platform. However, to an automation rule, this value is just a string representation of an array. To effectively utilize the 4me IDs stored within a multi-select custom field, we can employ the find_all operator.

For example, to retrieve the names of the sites identified by the IDs within the sites custom field, the following steps can be taken:

`site_ids`	`custom_fields.sites`	The value of the custom field with key = 'sites' is set to an array of 4me IDs
`site_names`	`find_all(site,site_ids).map(name)`	When the array of 4me IDs is provided as an argument to the find_all operator all records will be retrieved.

Utilizing Custom Collection Elements in Automation Rules

Custom collection elements are managed similar to the way custom fields linked to 4me records are handled. This involves dealing with both single-select and multi-select custom suggest fields that reference custom collection elements.

Single-Select Custom Suggest Fields

For single-select custom suggest fields, the field stores the unique 4me ID of the selected custom collection element. To retrieve the actual custom collection element based on its ID, you can use the `find()` operator:

`cc_id`	`custom_fields.cost_center`	Retrieve the 4me ID of the custom collection element.
`cc`	`find(custom_collection_element,cc_id)`	Get the custom collection element record.
`cc_name`	`cc.name`	Get the name of the custom collection element.

Multi-Select Custom Suggest Fields

When dealing with multi-select custom suggest fields, these fields store an array of IDs, each representing a distinct custom collection element. To access the corresponding records for all IDs within the array, the `find_all()` operator is employed:

`cc_ids`	`custom_fields.cost_centers`	Retrieve the 4me IDs of the custom collection elements.
`ccs`	`find_all(custom_collection_field,cc_ids)`	Get the array of custom collection element records.
`cc_names`	`ccs.map(name)`	Get the names of these custom collection elements.

Utilizing Ternary Operators in Automation Rules (If, Then and Else)

Ternary operators provide a concise way to perform conditional operations within automation rules. They enable setting values based on conditions using a compact syntax, which is particularly useful for defining logic that assigns a value to a named expression based on a condition. The ternary operator is composed of three parts, hence the term "ternary."

Syntax and Operation

The basic structure of a ternary operator in an automation rule is as follows:

```
named_expression          condition then expression1 else expression2
```

- condition: This is a Boolean expression that evaluates to either true or false.
- expression1: This expression is assigned to the `named_expression` if the condition is true.
- expression2: This expression is assigned to the `named_expression` if the condition is false.

Example Scenario: Determining Cost Impact

Consider a scenario where you need to determine the `cost_impact` based on a `budget` amount, with three possible impact levels: 'low', 'medium', and 'high'.

- Low Budget Condition: If the budget is less than $1,000, the cost impact is considered 'low'.
- High Budget Condition: If the budget exceeds $10,000, the cost impact is considered 'high'.
- Otherwise, the cost impact defaults to 'medium'.

Using ternary operators, the logic can be implemented as follows:

`low_budget`	`budget < 1000`	Define a low_budget boolean.
`high_budget`	`Budget > 10000`	Define a high_budget boolean.
`cost_impact`	`'medium'`	Default value setting.
`cost_impact`	`low_budget then 'low' else cost_impact`	If the budget is low, set the cost_impact to low, else leave it to the previous value.
`cost_impact`	`high_budget then 'high' else cost_impact`	If the budget is high, set the cost_impact to high, else leave it to the previous value.

In this structure, `cost_impact` is initially set to 'medium'. The ternary operator then evaluates `low_budget` and `high_budget` conditions to adjust `cost_impact` accordingly. If neither condition is met, `cost_impact` remains 'medium'.

Note Manipulation

The Related Note

Given that multiple notes can be attached to a single ticket—making `notes` an array-type field—navigating these notes becomes essential in specific automation scenarios. A prime example is when an automation rule must act upon the rejection of an approval task, possibly requiring the replication of the note detailing the rejection reasons.

Automation rules in 4me operate asynchronously, introducing a level of unpredictability regarding the sequentiality of notes. While one might be tempted to retrieve the most recent note with the expression `notes[last]`, assuming it to be the relevant note for the triggered event, this approach lacks certainty due to the asynchronous nature of rule execution.

To address this challenge, 4me introduces a specialized field within automation rules—**`related_note`**. This field represents the note created concurrently with the event trigger, ensuring that the automation rule references the precise note relevant to the specific event it's responding to. Utilizing `related_note` rather than `notes[last]` is more than just a recommendation; it's a best practice for ensuring accuracy in automation rule actions that depend on note content.

Exploring String Operators

4me automation rules feature a comprehensive set of operators for string manipulation, facilitating the modification and analysis of string values within automation rule expressions. The 4me online help section provides an extensive overview of these operators. Below are some particularly useful string operators:

Commonly Used String Operators

- **size, length**: Returns the count of characters within a string.
- **strip**: Eliminates any leading and trailing whitespace from the string.
- **squeeze**: Removes consecutive duplicate spaces, leaving only single spaces.
- **reverse**: Reverses the order of characters in the string.
- **upcase**: Converts all characters in the string to uppercase.
- **downcase**: Converts all characters in the string to lowercase.
- **swapcase**: Inverts the case of each character in the string from lower to upper or vice versa.
- **empty?, blank?**: Returns true if the string is empty or contains only whitespace.
- **present?**: Returns true if the string includes characters other than whitespace.

Advanced String Functions

- **split()**: Divides the string into an array of substrings based on a specified separator, which can be a direct string (e.g., ' ') or a regular expression (e.g., /[,|]/).

- **slice(,)**: Extracts a substring from the string starting at a specified index. If the length parameter is omitted, it returns all characters from the starting index to the end of the string.
- **replace(,)**: Searches for a specific string or regular expression within the string and replaces it with a new specified string.

Simple Email-Based Integrations with Supplier Service Management Systems

While not suitable for business-critical or sensitive data integrations, simple email-based integrations can offer a cost-efficient solution for scenarios involving a limited number of tickets exchanged between partners. Building such integrations via email can be accomplished with automation rules within a few hours, as opposed to the days often required for API-based integrations.

Utilizing the 'Send Email' action, it's straightforward to configure an automation rule that forwards an email to a supplier's service management system, initiating a new ticket. Challenges arise when attempting to coordinate additional communications and ticket closures between the systems. This scenario requires four specific automation rules:

1. **Ticket Creation**: An automation rule using the 'Send Email' action to notify the supplier's service management system, thereby creating a new ticket.
2. **Capture Supplier Ticket ID**: When the supplier's system creates a ticket, it sends an email back to 4me, which is appended as a note to the corresponding 4me ticket. An automation rule, triggered by the 'Note Added' event, parses this note to extract the supplier's ticket ID, updating the 'Supplier Request ID' field in 4me.

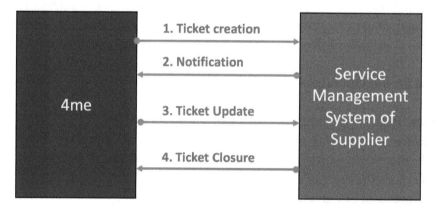

Figure 245: The automation rules in an email-based integration.

3. **Forwarding Notes to Supplier**: Upon adding a new note to a 4me ticket, another automation rule sends an email to the supplier, including the note and the 'Supplier Request ID', ensuring the supplier's system appends the information to the correct ticket.
4. **Ticket Completion**: When the supplier resolves the ticket, a closure notification email is sent back to 4me and added as a note. An automation rule, again triggered by a 'Note Added' event, searches the note for a phrase indicating closure to automatically complete the ticket in 4me.

For this process to function smoothly, it's imperative that both the customer and supplier agree on email formats to ensure mutual systems can correctly process and respond to messages. The critical task for automation rules 2 and 4 is accurately identifying and capturing specific phrases:

- Automation Rule 2: Extracts the supplier's ticket ID.
- Automation Rule 4: Identifies the closure phrase.

Using Regular Expressions (RegEx) to Identify Patterns in Notes

4me automation rules utilize Regular Expressions (RegEx) to search for specific patterns within notes, enabling the precise extraction of information. While Regular Expressions offer powerful and flexible searching capabilities, they can be daunting due to their complex syntax, especially for those without prior experience. Enlisting a developer's help or OpenAI might be necessary to formulate effective RegEx patterns tailored to your integration's requirements.

Consider a scenario where the ticket ID from a supplier's service management system follows a specific format, such as INC-X(n), where X(n) represents a sequence of numbers (e.g., INC-00588 or INC-100555558). The objective is to extract this ticket ID from a note and utilize it within the automation rule. The following example demonstrates how to achieve this, setting a named expression based on the ticket ID's presence:

```
note_text       related_note.text.replace(/\n/,' ')

ticket_id       note_text.replace(/.*Ticketid (INC-[\d]+).*/,'\1')

id_found        ticket_id starts with 'INC'
```

First of all, all line terminators (symbol = \n) are removed from the note text with the **replace** operator. We need to remove line terminators because the matching patterns in RegEx ignore line terminators. Now, let's break down the regular expression and the replace operation:

1. **Regular Expression: `/.*Ticketid (INC-[\d]+).*/`**
   - `.*`: This part will match any sequence of characters (except for line terminators) at the beginning of the string until it finds the specific pattern that follows.
   - `'Ticketid'`: Matches the literal string "Ticketid ". This part looks for the occurrence of "Ticketid " in the string.
   - `(INC-[\d]+)`: This is a **capturing group** that matches the pattern for a ticket ID.
     - `INC-`: Matches the literal string "INC-".
     - `[\d]+`: Matches one or more digits (\d is a shorthand character class that matches any digit). The square brackets define a character class, and the plus sign indicates one or more occurrences of the class.
   - `.*`: Matches any sequence of characters) following the ticket ID pattern. This part will match any sequence of characters after the ticket ID until the end of the string.
2. **Replacement: `'\1'`**: Refers to the first **capturing group** in the regular expression. In this case, it's the `(INC-[\d]+)` part, which captures the ticket ID.

3. **Operation**: This operation searches the note_.text string for the pattern specified by the regular expression. If the pattern is found, it **replaces** the entire string with just the part that was captured by the first capturing group, effectively isolating the ticket ID (e.g., "INC-1234") and discarding the rest of the original string.

Automation Rules for Attachment Management

As previously discussed, custom fields of the Attachment type play a significant role in various processes. For instance, in a Request for Proposal (RFP) process, a Managed Service Provider (MSP) may need to prepare a proposal document, attaching it to a workflow task in formats like PDF or Word. Subsequently, these documents might need to be available for review or approval in later tasks. The transition of attachments from one task to another can be automated through the use of automation rules.

Attachments within 4me are uniquely identifiable through their access paths, which are stored within the Attachment custom field. When dealing with multi-attachment fields, these paths are stored as an array. While automation rules treat the content of these custom fields as strings or arrays without intrinsic meaning, the values of a custom field of type attachment can be copied to another custom field of type attachment with the same settings . However, when intending to append these attachments to a note, the automation rule requires a conversion of these paths into recognizable attachment references. This can be achieved using operators such as **find(attachment, access_path)** for single attachments or **find_all(attachment, [access_path1, access_path2])** for multiple attachments.

Here is an example that demonstrates capturing the attachment paths from two custom fields, converting them into arrays of attachment references, and then amalgamating these arrays for use in a note:

```
avatars        design_task.custom_fields.avatars
designs        design_task.custom_fields.designs
avatar_files   find_all(attachment,avatars)
design_files   find_all(attachment,designs)
all_files      avatar_files + design_files
```

Date and Time Manipulation

4me incorporates two predominant standards for managing date and time:

- **RFC 2822 Format**: Utilized for presenting date-time values in a user-friendly manner, this format specifies the day, date, and time zone succinctly (e.g., "Tue, Apr 02, 2024 08:00 UTC"). By including the time zone and using a format that sidesteps confusion between American and European date formats, RFC 2822 is ideal for display purposes in notes and audit trails.

- **ISO 8601 Format**: Known for its straightforward numeric representation, ISO 8601 (e.g., "2024-04-02T08:00:00Z") is favored in software development, databases, and international contexts for its ease of sorting and clear distinction of date components. 4me leverages ISO 8601 for storing date-time values in custom fields, providing a standard that is both precise and widely recognized.

When dealing with automation rules, it's important to note that date-time values retrieved from custom fields are treated as strings. To utilize date-time operators effectively on these values, they must first be converted into date-time objects using the **to_date_time** operator, as shown in the example:

```
date_time_object        custom_fields.my_date_time.to_date_time
```

The pre-defined date-time value of *now* and *today* represent the current date and time, adjusted to the time zone settings of the account. Note that *now* is a date-time and *today* is a date record.

Date-time Operators

Automation rules in 4me offer a comprehensive set of operators for working with date-time values, enabling precise time calculations and comparisons:

- **Relative Time Calculations**: Operators like **2.seconds.ago**, **1.minute.ago**, **2.hours. ago**, **1.day.ago**, **1.week.ago**, **1.month.ago,** and **1.year.ago** calculate specific time intervals before the current time.
- **Future Time Calculations**: Similarly, expressions like **1.second.from_now** and **planned_ duration.hours.from_now** calculate future times based on the current moment.
- **Time Component Extraction**: **now.year**, **now.day_of_week**, and **now.is_monday** extract specific components or check conditions related to the current date and time.
- **UTC Conversion**: **now.utc** converts the current time to the Coordinated Universal Time (UTC) timezone.
- **Time zone conversion**: **now.in_time_zone(person.time_zone)** converts a date-time record to the specified time zone, for example, the time zone of the person. A specific timezone can be specified, for instance **updated_at.in_time_zone('Amsterdam').**
- **Duration Calculation**: **duration(created_at, now)** calculates the duration, typically in minutes, between the **created_at** timestamp and the current moment **(now)**.

Adding a date-time Value to a Pay Load

When a date-time record is added to a note, an automation rule will convert it to the RFC 2822 Format. However, when adding a date-time record to a payload, it is often required to use the ISO 8601 format. This can be done with the **iso8601** operator.

```
iso8601_format          created.iso8601
```

Looking for the Next Time Slot

Automating scheduling within defined work hours is crucial in many processes, and 4me supports this through the use of Calendars and time zones. Calendars in 4me can define work hours, such as 'Monday through Friday, 9:00am until 5:00pm.' However, it's important to note that Calendars themselves do not include time zones; when used, especially in automation rules, the relevant time zone must be specified.

To schedule an event or task within the constraints of a Calendar, the `target_at` operator is used in automation rules. This operator calculates a future date-time within the specified Calendar's hours, considering a given duration from a starting date-time. The syntax for this operation is as follows:

```
target_time   calendar.target_at(date_time_record, duration, time_zone)
```

For example, if a workflow requires an action to be performed within 2 working days, simply adding 48 hours (or `2.days.from_now`) might not accurately reflect working hours, as it would not account for weekends or holidays. Instead, using the `target_at` operator with a specified Calendar and time zone ensures the calculated `target_time` falls within actual working hours. Here's how it could look:

```
work_cal      find(calendar,' Monday through Friday, 9:00am until 5:00pm')
time_zone     support_team.working_hours
target_time   work_cal.target_at(now, 2.days, time_zone)
```

Deep Dive into SCIM Automation Rules

With System for Cross-domain Identity Management (SCIM) enabled on the 4me platform, three default automation rules are automatically generated: one for SCIM User Records and two for SCIM Groups. The SCIM User automation rule is designed to map attributes from SCIM user records to corresponding fields in 4me person records, while the SCIM Group automation rules associate SCIM Group records with either 4me Organizations or Sites. Although these out-of-the-box automation rules offer a basic setup, there's flexibility to either add new SCIM User or SCIM Group automation rules or to refine the existing ones for tailored field mappings and extensions.

Characteristics of SCIM Automation Rules

- Each SCIM automation rule is associated with a specific 4me record type—SCIM User records or SCIM Group records.

- Unlike generic automation rules that may cater to a broader spectrum of events, SCIM automation rules specifically focus on the lifecycle of SCIM records within the 4me platform, offering two distinct trigger events to choose from:
  - **Create**: This trigger activates when a new SCIM record is created.
  - **Create or Update**: This more encompassing trigger ensures the automation rule is executed not just when a SCIM record is newly created but also whenever existing SCIM records undergo any modifications.

A unique feature of SCIM automation rules is their ability to retroactively apply changes across all existing SCIM records upon an update to the rule itself. This ensures that any modifications to the automation rule's logic or mappings are consistently applied across the board.

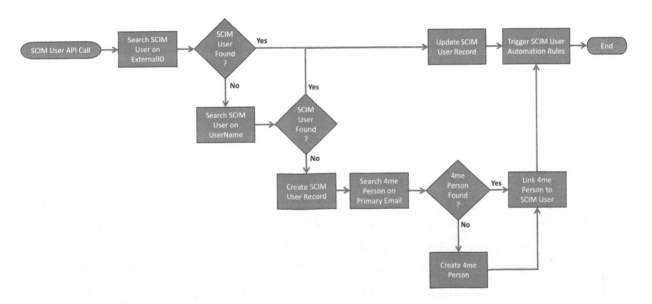

Figure 246: The logic in 4me when a SCIM User API call is received.

	To re-execute SCIM User or SCIM Group automation rules for all SCIM records, simply incorporate an additional expression into the rule. Saving the rule subsequently triggers it across all existing SCIM records, ensuring comprehensive application of any adjustments made.

SCIM User Automation Rules in Action

When an Identity Provider (IdP) triggers a SCIM User API request for provisioning a user, 4me orchestrates the creation or update of a SCIM User record, aligning it with a corresponding 4me person record based on criteria like `userName` or `externalID`. Here's the step-by-step process:

1. Search for an existing SCIM User record by `externalID`.

2. If found, update this SCIM User record. If not, proceed to the next step.
3. Search for a SCIM user record matching the `userName`.
4. If found, update this SCIM User record. If not, create a new SCIM User record.
5. On creation of a new SCIM User record, search for a 4me person record by primary email address.
6. If a corresponding 4me person record is located, link it to the new SCIM User record.
7. If not found, create a new 4me person record and establish the link.
8. Activate SCIM automation rules based on creation or update triggers.

This methodology offers flexibility, notably allowing the use of an IdP's unique user ID (e.g., Azure Active Directory's ObjectID) instead of an email address. The IdP's unique user ID should be mapped to the SCIM User field `externalID`. In such a setup the SCIM User record will be identified by this unique user ID. This is beneficial for scenarios where an email address may change, ensuring continuity in the user's 4me record by leveraging the stable unique ID. The `externalID` is also mapped to the 4me user `AuthenticationID` to align it with the SSO setup.

The crux of the SCIM integration lies in the automation rules activated post-record creation or update, particularly focusing on updating person records in 4me. The assignments within these rules kickstart with identifying the primary email:

`userName_is_email`	`userName contains '@'`	Is userName an email address ?
`primary_email`	`userName_is_email then userName else nil`	If username is an email address assign it to primary_email, else set primary_email to nil (empty).
`scim_primary_email`	`emails.select(primary = true) [first].value`	Pickup the first email address from all scim email addreses defined as the primary email address.
`primary_email`	`primary_email then primary_email else scim_primary_email`	If primary_email is not nil don't modify it, else set it to the scim_primary_email.
`primary_email`	`primary_email then primary_email else emails[first].value`	If primary_email is not nil don't modify it, else set it to the first of all scim email addresses.

Adjusting the user's name order or format might necessitate edits in the following section, ensuring the 4me name field reflects the desired structure:

`name`	`userName_is_email then displayName else userName`	If userName is an email address then use the displayName, else use the username.
`name`	`name then name else formatted`	If the name is still empty use the SCIM field formatted
`given`	`givenName`	
`family`	`familyName`	
`name`	`name then name else "{{given}} {{family}}"`	If the name is still empty thenconcatenate the givneName and familyName
`name`	`name then name else person.name`	If the name is still empty then use the person.name

In the default SCIM User automation rules, certain fields are designed to retain their existing values in 4me when the corresponding SCIM payload comes through empty. This approach is particularly noticeable with fields like the job title. Here's how it's managed:

`job_title`	`title`	The SCIM field title
`job_title`	`title` then `title` else `person.job_title`	If the SCIM job_title is empty keep the title of the 4me person record

Linking the SCIM Provisioned User to an Organization and Site

Ensuring person records are accurately linked to the correct organization and site is crucial in 4me, impacting SLA coverages and automatic task assignments. Maintaining this information within the Identity Provider (IdP) and leveraging SCIM for provisioning is a best practice. Let's delve deeper into this mechanism:

The default SCIM provisioning within 4me relies on two specific fields for mapping:

- **Organization**: This SCIM field determines the 4me organization linked to the person record.
- **Department**: This field identifies the corresponding 4me site for the person record.

Should direct mapping via these fields not be possible, 4me turns to SCIM Groups for resolution. While IdPs manage user memberships across various SCIM Groups, 4me's approach does not create new organizations or sites from these groups. Instead, SCIM Group provisioning focuses on generating SCIM Group records and associating them with pre-existing 4me organizations and sites. Therefore, it's necessary to manually establish organization and site records within 4me.

Once SCIM Groups are linked to either an organization or site in 4me, they receive a classification—either 'organization' or 'site'. This categorization is then utilized in the SCIM User automation rule to accurately assign users. For instance, the SCIM User automation rules filters through a user's SCIM Groups, isolating those classified as 'organization' and selecting the first group as the user's organization. A parallel method is employed for determining site affiliations.

The default SCIM Group Automation Rule looks like this:

`search_result`	`find(organization, displayName)`	Lookup a 4me organization based on the name of the Group
`org4me`	`organization.id` then `organization` else `search_result`	When the SCIM Group record is already linked to an organization the organization is already known. Else the 4me organization is the one found in the lookup (search_result)
`orgName`	`displayName`	We keep the displayName from the SCIM Group to eventually update the 4me organization

Condition	Org4me	The automation rule only runs when a 4me org is found (a new one or the already known one)
Update	current_record	
Set	organization = org4me	When the SCIM Group was not yet linked to a 4me org, it will now be linked to the 4me org.
Update	current_record	
Set	classification = 'organization'	The SCIM Group is now classified as an organization
Update	org4me	When the SCIM Group was already linked to a 4me org, the name of the 4me org is updated with the diaplayName of the SCIM Group
Set	name = orgName	

Based on the values in the SCIM User organization field and subsequently, the SCIM Groups with the classification 'organization', the 4me person will be linked to the organization org4me as set in the following automation rule snippet:

org4me	find(organization, organization)	Lookup a 4me organization based on the name of the SCIM org
organization_group	groups.select(classification = 'organization')[first]	Lookup the first SCIM Group of category 'organization'
org4me	org4me then org4me else organization_group.organization	If the org4me is still empty, set it to org of the SCIM Group
org4me	org4me.disabled then nil else org4me	If the org4me is disabled, set it to nil
org4me	org4me then org4me else person.organization	If org4me is empty keep the actual org of the person record
org4me	org4me then org4me else account.organization	If org4me is still empty (= when it is a new person record without an organization) then the org of the 4me account

Deeper Understanding of Automation Rules

Who Executes Automation Rules?

Automation rules in 4me operate as if they were actual users, executing actions under specific roles:

- **Workflow-Related Automation Rules**: Actions related to workflow tasks and the workflows themselves are executed as if by the workflow's designated manager. This ensures these rules have the authority to manage workflows as expected.
- **Project-Related Automation Rules**: Similarly, automation rules for project tasks and projects act in the capacity of the project manager, allowing full management of project-related tasks.
- **Generic Automation Rules**: Automation rules that apply to requests, problems, configuration items, people records, and risks, are run as the *account owner* with elevated permissions meaning

that (temporarily) all possible roles (in the current account) will be assigned to the owner so that user has full access in the account, including in strong privacy accounts.

This design typically allows automation rules to execute their intended actions without the need for additional role assignments. However, there are exceptions to consider. For example, if an automation rule associated with a task needs to update a configuration item (CI), it is essential to ensure that the workflow manager also possesses the Configuration Manager role.

Caution is advised when automation rules complete or cancel tickets, as they might inaccurately attribute actions to real individuals like account owners or managers, potentially causing confusion in ticket histories and reports.

To mitigate this, a recommended practice is to establish a virtual "Automation" team with an "Automation User" as its sole member. Utilizing this virtual user for automated ticket completions clearly distinguishes automation actions, maintaining clarity and avoiding misattribution. For instance, to automatically complete a request while attributing actions to a designated virtual user, you can define the following sequence of actions within your automation rule:

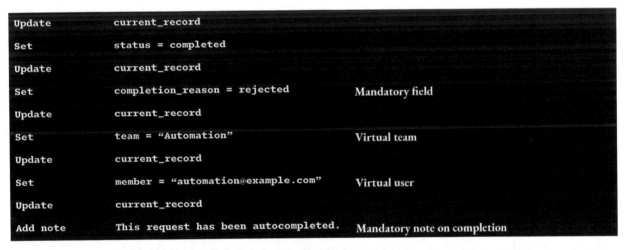

Update	current_record	
Set	status = completed	
Update	current_record	
Set	completion_reason = rejected	Mandatory field
Update	current_record	
Set	team = "Automation"	Virtual team
Update	current_record	
Set	member = "automation@example.com"	Virtual user
Update	current_record	
Add note	This request has been autocompleted.	Mandatory note on completion

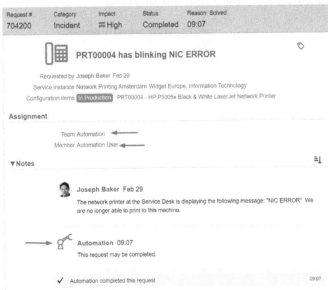

Figure 247: Autocompletion of a request by an automation rule. The team and member are set to a virtual automation team and virtual user.

The Asynchronous Nature of Automation Rules

Automation rules in 4me operate asynchronously to maintain the platform's performance. These rules are assigned to background worker queues that process the tasks as they are received. To efficiently manage high demand periods, 4me dynamically activates additional worker queues. Typically, automation rules execute within a few seconds.

However, it's crucial to consider the asynchronous execution in certain scenarios. For instance, consider a workflow that includes an evaluation task followed by an approval task requiring consent from both the service owner and the workflow manager. If a budget defined in a custom field during the evaluation is below 1000 USD, the service owner's approval isn't needed.

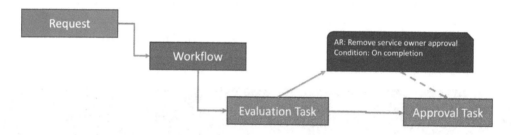

Figure 248: A wrong approach: the service owner will receive an approval notification which will probably be canceled upon responding.

You might consider configuring an automation rule to remove the service owner's approval upon completing the evaluation task. However, this approach could result in a suboptimal outcome: the service owner receives an approval notification but, due to the rule's delayed execution, discovers the task has already been canceled when they respond.

To circumvent this issue, introduce an automation task template between the evaluation and approval tasks in your workflow template. Employ three specific automation rules for this task:

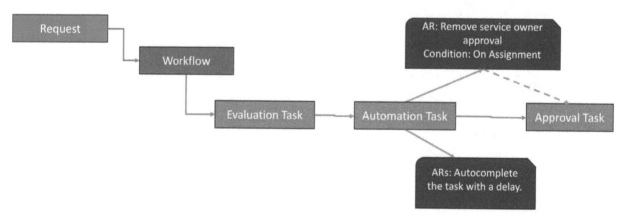

Figure 249: A correct approach is to define an automation task in between the evaluation and approval tasks.

1. An autocompletion rule with a delay trigger.
2. Upon assignment of the automation task, trigger its delayed autocompletion, setting a minimal delay of 2 seconds.
3. Concurrently, assess the budget from the preceding task. If it's under 1000 USD, remove the service owner from the subsequent approval task.

This setup prevents the service owner from ever receiving an unnecessary approval request. Task templates of category 'Automation' don't require an assignment team and are tailored for such scenarios. Consider creating automation task templates equipped with the autocompletion rules defined as task template automation rules. These automation rules will be reused in every workflow template in which the automation task template is added. You can then incorporate specific workflow template automation rules directly into these workflow templates.

Automation Rule Chains

Automation Rule Chains in 4me are created whenever a record is updated or created. These chains coordinate the sequence for triggering, evaluating, and executing automation rules in response to changes. Here's how it unfolds:

1. **Rule Retrieval**: Identifies automation rules triggered by the record's update or creation.
2. **Expression Evaluation**: Calculates expressions for all triggered rules.
3. **Conditional Execution**: Evaluates and executes actions for rules when their conditions are met. When these automation rules update another record, new triggers can arise. This process repeats steps 1-3 until no new triggers are found.
4. **Loop Prevention**: Rules that have executed within the last 23 hours and whose actions were previously applied within the same Automation Chain are excluded to prevent infinite loops.
5. **Execution Continuity**: Continues until no new triggers arise, concluding the chain.

Key Points to Note:

- **Field Values**: If multiple rules within the chain modify the same field on the same record, the final value is determined by the last rule executed.
- **System Error Handling**: A system error in any part of the chain causes the entire chain to fail, displaying the error across all affected rules!
- **Import API Exclusion**: Records updated via CSV import are not evaluated by automation rules.
- **Delayed automation rules rescheduling**: Automation rule actions that invoke a delayed automation rule will remove any prior schedules for the delayed rule and reschedule the delayed automation rule.
- **Concurrent execution of automation rules** will **not** happen in case the automation rules are triggered from the same group of records (e.g. tasks in the same workflow). They are executed sequentially to prevent multiple updates on the same record to happen at the same time leading to race conditions. This does mean that when a lot of rules are triggered on the same group of records, it may take some time before all of them are executed.

Managing Automation Rules

Monitoring Automation Rule Executions

In 4me, automation rule executions are critical to ensuring seamless operations. While notifications alert administrators to failures, a proactive and organized approach involves regular monitoring through the "Automation Rule Executions" section. Accessible via the Settings Console, this feature is tailored for account administrators to oversee automation rule performance.

Figure 250: The 'Automation rule executions with errors' provides a list of all failed automation rules. All details related to the execution are included.

Key Features:

- **Dedicated View for Errors**: The Automation Rule Executions with Errors view is designed to be meticulously monitored, aiming for no entries in a well-maintained production environment.
- **Comprehensive Record Details**: Each execution record offers an in-depth look into the rule's operation, including trigger timing, expression and condition evaluations, executed actions, and detailed error information if failures occur.

Regularly reviewing the "Automation Rule Executions with Errors" view helps in identifying and rectifying issues promptly, maintaining the integrity of automated processes. It is advisable to setup a recurring workflow for this purpose.

Efficient Debugging of Automation Rules

Debugging automation rules during their initial setup can often lead to encountering issues. While the Automation Rule Executions with Errors view is a comprehensive source for identifying such issues post-implementation, accessing the automation rule execution details directly from the record that triggered the automation rule can be more practical during the debugging phase. This direct access is facilitated through the Actions menu of a record, which, upon the triggering of an automation rule by a record, will offer the Automation Trail option.

Figure 251: The Automation Trail on a request.

The Automation Trail provides a clear and informative overview of the automation rule's triggers, marking successful executions with a green checkbox and failures with a red cross. Clicking on an automation rule execution within the Automation Trail presents the automation rule chain, these are all the automation rules that have been triggered by the same event on the record. This view offers valuable insights, especially considering that a failure in any part of the chain leads to the failure of all automation rules within that chain. In this view, every automation rule is represented by a circle around the automation rules' avatar. Red indicates an issue. Clicking on these circled avatars directs you to the detailed record of the automation rule's execution.

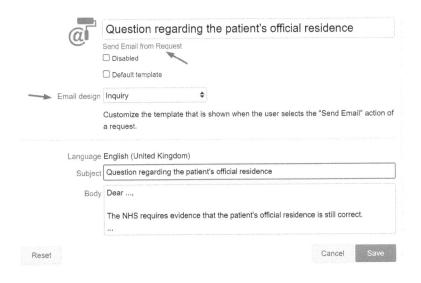

Figure 252: The Automation Rule Chain on a record. Click on the individual automation rules to get the automation rule execution records.

Tip

To ensure high performance, 4me does not retain the intermediate values of named expressions during an automation rule's execution. What is captured in the automation rule execution record are the final outcomes of these named expressions. A good strategy is to assign a unique named expression to each line in your rule.

Chapter 14 -
Integrations: Unleashing Connectivity

Introduction

In the dynamic world of enterprise service management, the pinnacle of optimization lies in seamless integration. Why wait for manual access provisioning to an IT platform when it can be instantaneous upon approval? Imagine a Managed Service Provider effortlessly generating and dispatching invoices for the prior month's services, directly from 4me to their billing system, or monitoring systems that autonomously alert 4me, spawning incidents for immediate attention by the appropriate support team. Consider the ease of automatically updating 4me out-of-office records based on holiday and sickness data for more accurate resource planning. Integrations offer myriad opportunities to elevate organizational efficiency and enhance the user experience. From the inception of service management projects to ongoing improvement initiatives, integrations should be a part of it.

The best part? 4me was conceived with openness at its core, ensuring an integration-friendly environment. Whether your integration requirements are straightforward or complex, 4me provides the tools and flexibility needed to bring your integration visions to life. Dive into this chapter to explore how 4me can become the nexus of your organization's IT ecosystem, facilitating seamless interactions and data flows between diverse systems and services. Let the journey of integrating for excellence begin!

The Fundamental Pillars of 4me Integrations

At the heart of bi-directional integrations between the 4me platform and other platforms lies a crucial intermediary—the integration platform. This platform acts as the orchestrator, managing the flow of data and events between 4me and the external systems. Here's a breakdown of the basic components that make this possible:

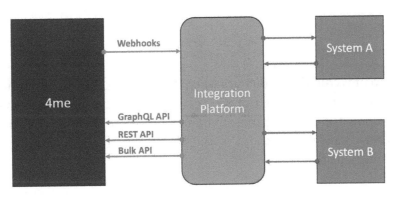

Figure 253: A bi-directional integration is based on outbound webhooks to and inbound API calls from the integration platform.

Webhooks in 4me:

4me utilizes webhooks as the primary mechanism to send real-time notifications about events within its environment. When specific events of interest occur in 4me, these webhooks are triggered, sending a signal out to the integration platform.

Integration Platform's Role:

On the receiving end, the integration platform is set up with webhook listeners. These listeners are on the lookout for the signals sent by 4me's webhooks. Once a webhook is received, the integration platform processes this data, potentially translating it into actions or updates in another system or back into 4me itself.

Updating 4me from the Integration Platform:

Integration is a two-way street. Just as 4me can send out information via webhooks, the integration platform can also send updates back to 4me. This is achieved through 4me's trio of open APIs:

- **GraphQL API**: Offers a flexible and efficient approach to querying and updating data, allowing for precise and tailored data exchanges.
- **REST API**: Provides a straightforward, resource-oriented way to interact with 4me. The syntax of REST API is less complex than that of GraphQL, offering simplicity but at the cost of reduced flexibility.
- **Bulk API**: Specially designed for handling large volumes of data, it's the go-to option when you need to create or update records in bulk within 4me.

4me Outbound: Webhooks

Account administrators can manage webhooks directly from the Webhooks section within the Settings console. The essence of a webhook lies in its simplicity, necessitating just a name, an event to watch for, and a destination URI—the latter acting as the endpoint for the integration platform's webhook listener.

Generic Webhook Events

Choosing the right event is crucial, as it dictates when the webhook springs into action. 4me's extensive list encompasses numerous record types and their specific events. For instance, a webhook related to a task can be activated upon its creation, changes to its members, notes addition, status updates, and more. Each trigger dispatches a standard payload, ensuring the receiver gets the record's essential identifiers, like the 4me ID and the node ID.

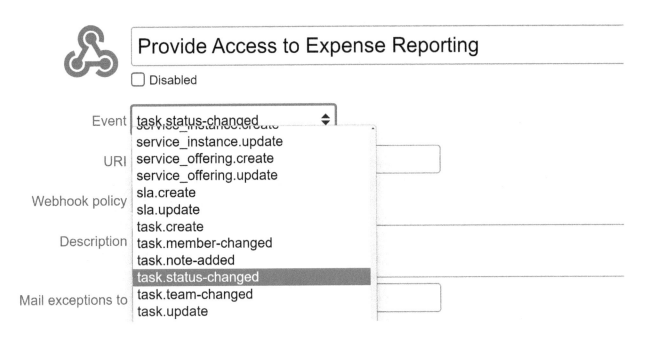

Figure 254: Defining a webhook in the Settings console. Each webhook is related to an event type.

Automation Rule Webhook Events

A unique webhook event type is the automation rule event. As discussed in the chapter dedicated to automation rules, triggering a webhook is one of the actions available within automation rules. This approach grants a more granular control over when webhooks are activated and what information they carry (= customized payload). However, it can introduce some complexity by dispersing the integration logic between automation rules in 4me and the external integration platform — a scenario that might present challenges, especially when the roles of 4me designer and integration specialist do not overlap.

<table>
<tr>
<td>
Tip</td>
<td>Deciding between utilizing generic event-driven webhooks and those initiated by automation rules is a pivotal design decision. Opting for the latter necessitates thoughtful planning around the payload. Establishing a standardized payload for all webhook calls triggered by automation rules could significantly ease integration management.</td>
</tr>
</table>

Secure Validation of Webhook Endpoints

In a world where data integrity and security are paramount, 4me's webhook verification process plays a critical role. Immediately after a new webhook is established, 4me proactively sends out a verification signal—`webhook.verify`—to the specified endpoint. This verification message includes a callback parameter essential for confirming the endpoint's ownership. This safeguard ensures that webhooks remain dormant until their legitimacy is confirmed.

Fortifying Webhooks with Policies

Webhook policies add an additional layer of security to the data exchange process. These policies stipulate a signing algorithm that 4me utilizes to authenticate the payload of each webhook request. This authentication mechanism empowers the recipient to ascertain the genuineness of the payload, ensuring it's directly from 4me and not an imposter.

Within the "Webhook Policies" section under Settings, administrators can define and manage these policies. Notably, a single policy can encompass multiple webhooks. Upon saving a new policy, there's a singular opportunity to download its public key. This key is vital for the receiving end to decrypt and verify the integrity of the payloads.

Webhooks Built for Robustness

For webhooks to function seamlessly, a response within the 200-299 range, indicative of successful communication, is expected promptly. Given the 10-second timeout limitation of a 4me webhook, it's crucial for any prolonged processing on the integration platform to occur asynchronously, ensuring immediate response to the webhook call while background tasks continue as needed.

Handling Webhook Failures

In the event of a webhook failure, 4me's robust infrastructure initiates a meticulously structured retry mechanism, characterized by an exponential backoff strategy. This approach moderates the frequency of retry attempts, escalating from once per minute in the initial phase to less frequent attempts, culminating in a temporary suspension of the webhook after prolonged downtime of more than 4 hours. This intelligent system aims to mitigate potential server overload, providing a balanced attempt to re-establish connection without overwhelming resources.

A special email address can be added in the `Mail exceptions to` field of a webhook. 4me sends exception emails to this email address and to all account administrators upon failure and subsequent recovery of webhook operations. This proactive communication ensures that administrators and support are well-informed about the webhook's status, allowing for timely interventions when necessary and avoiding unnecessary troubleshooting efforts post-recovery.

The Webhook Deliveries Console: A Diagnostic Tool

The Webhook Deliveries, a section in the Settings console available for *administrators*, offers a detailed log of webhook activities. This feature not only aids in tracking the success and failure of webhook deliveries but also provides insight into the retry mechanisms in action. By examining this console, administrators can dissect each webhook's journey, identifying patterns or anomalies that may indicate underlying issues. When the delivery failed, the administrator can click on the Redeliver button to send its payload again.

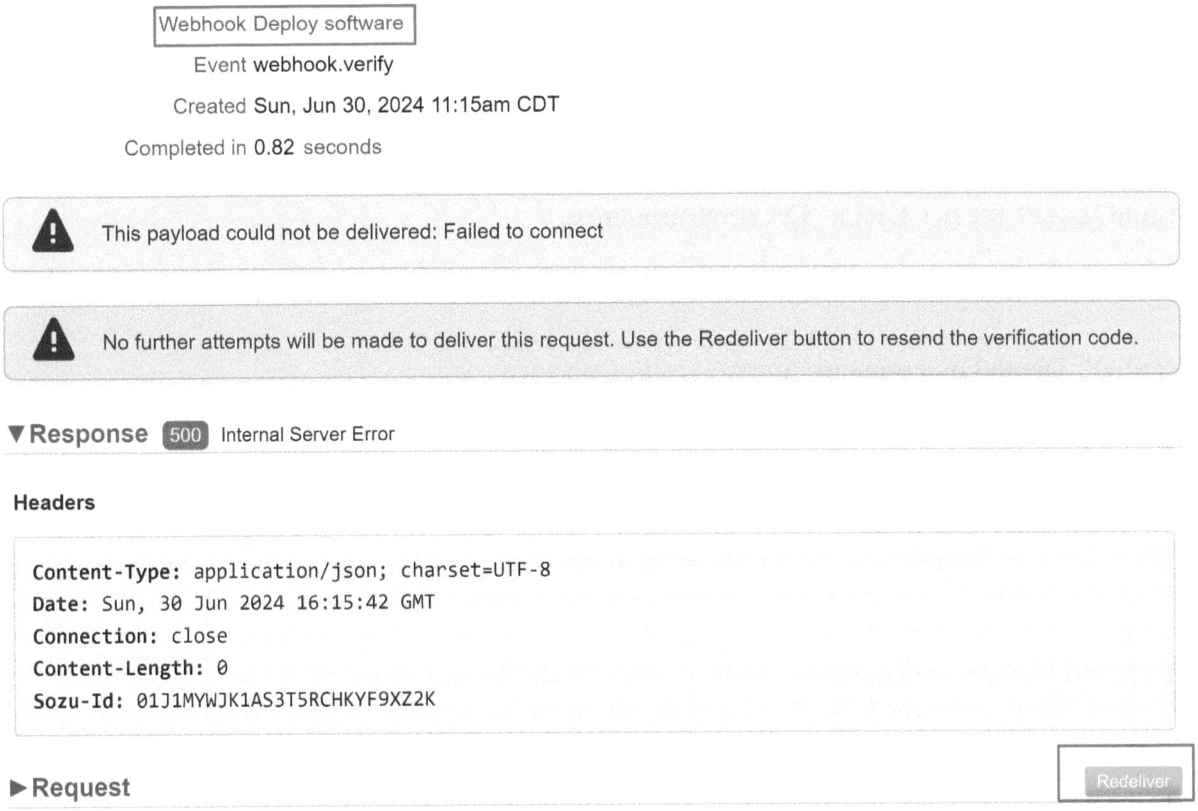

Webhook Deploy software

Event **webhook.verify**

Created **Sun, Jun 30, 2024 11:15am CDT**

Completed in **0.82** seconds

⚠ This payload could not be delivered: Failed to connect

⚠ No further attempts will be made to deliver this request. Use the Redeliver button to resend the verification code.

▼ **Response** `500` Internal Server Error

Headers

```
Content-Type: application/json; charset=UTF-8
Date: Sun, 30 Jun 2024 16:15:42 GMT
Connection: close
Content-Length: 0
Sozu-Id: 01J1MYWJK1AS3T5RCHKYF9XZ2K
```

▶ **Request**

Redeliver

Figure 255: The Webhook Deliveries console with the possibility to redeliver a webhook call.

4me Inbound

End-points, Service URLs and Accounts

Integrating with the 4me platform requires clear answers to two foundational questions right from the start:

1. Target Environment: Where are the updates headed?

The destination of your integration efforts—be it a QA environment in the US or a production environment in the EU—is determined by the end-point specified in the service URL of your API call. These URLs not only define the geographical location but also the environment type (production or QA), ensuring your integration hits the right spot. Here's a concise guide to the service URLs for both the GraphQL and REST APIs across different environments and regions:

GraphQL API Service URLs - Production Environments:

- Australia: `https://graphql.au.4me.com/`
- Europe: `https://graphql.4me.com/`
- Switzerland: `https://graphql.ch.4me.com/`
- UK: `https://graphql.uk.4me.com/`
- US: `https://graphql.us.4me.com/`

GraphQL API Service URLs - QA Environments:

Similar structure as production, but replace `.4me.com/` with `.4me.qa/` for the respective region.

GraphQL Demo Environment: https://graphql.4me-demo.com/

REST API Service URLs:

Follows the same regional and environmental structure as GraphQL, but with base URLs like `https://api.<region>.4me.com/v1` for Production or `https://api.<region>.4me.qa/v1` for QA environments.

REST API Demo Environment: `https://api.4me-demo.com/v1`

The **Bulk API**, built on the REST API foundation, further extends this with /import and /export paths appended to the base REST API service URL.

Demo Environment Specifics: Multiple demo instances reside under the demo environment. The bearer-token in your API call dictates the specific demo instance your call addresses.

2. 4me Account Identification?

Similar to a user logging in to a specific account, such as the Widget Data Center or Widget International, every API call operates within a specific 4me account context. This critical detail is conveyed through a mandatory header in your API call:

```
x-4me-Account: <accountID>
```

4me Inbound API Rate Limiting

Rate limiting is an essential strategy employed by cloud services, including the 4me platform, to ensure fair usage, uphold system stability, prevent misuse, and effectively manage platform load. This strategy involves regulating the number of requests that an integration can send to either the GraphQL API, REST API or Bulk API within a specified period.

All inbound integrations to 4me, regardless of the API being used, must be designed to handle the **429 Too Many Requests - Rate Limit Exceeded** status code appropriately. This status code indicates that the rate limit has been surpassed. Upon receiving this code, the integration should adhere to the "`Retry-After`" header found in the 429 response. This header specifies the number of seconds the integration must wait before it can safely retry the request.

Failure to comply with 4me's rate limiting can lead to stringent measures to safeguard the platform. Automated systems are in place to detect non-compliance, resulting in the potential blocking of all traffic from the offending integration's IP addresses. This is a critical security measure intended to protect the 4me platform against Distributed Denial of Service (DDOS) attacks.

The GraphQL API and REST API

The 4me platform is arguably the fastest enterprise service management solution available, which is why effective and efficient resource use is paramount for 4me. This principle underscores the recommendation to use the GraphQL API over the REST API for data queries and updates within 4me accounts. While both APIs offer comprehensive functionalities, as detailed on the 4me Developer Site (https://developer.4me.com) and through the hands-on training available in the 4me Learning Center (https://learning.4me.com/training/), the GraphQL API stands out for its flexibility and efficiency.

The primary advantage of GraphQL lies in its ability to tailor responses to exact needs, enabling clients to specify precisely which fields to include. This granularity reduces unnecessary data transfer. Furthermore, GraphQL's capability to navigate through record structures in a single API call significantly enhances efficiency. For example, retrieving the manager and their substitute of the organization tied to the requester of a request can be achieved in one GraphQL query, whereas multiple calls would be necessary with REST API.

This emphasis on GraphQL reflects a strategic direction aimed at maximizing resource efficiency. While both APIs currently offer similar functionalities, the commitment to further develop and extend GraphQL underscores a future-focused approach to API design. In contrast, the REST API, although still fully supported, will not be the focus of major new investments.

The Bulk API

When thousands of records must be exported from or imported in a 4me account, the GraphQL API and REST API, would hit the rate limits which could lead to unacceptable long time slots to process all the records. In these scenario's the Bulk API must be used. Basically the Bulk API is based on the import or export of csv files. The format of these csv files is published on the 4me developer site (see https://developer.4me.com/v1/import/#type).

Understanding the Source and Source ID fields

When integrating data into 4me from external systems, the 'Source' and 'Source ID' fields play a crucial role in tracking the origin of each record. The Source field should capture the name of the external system while the Source ID field should contain the unique identifier of the record within that external system. For instance, if you're importing cost centers from SAP FI into 4me, you would specify 'SAP FI' as the 'Source' and use the SAP-specific unique key as the 'Source ID'. This practice becomes particularly significant during Bulk API imports, ensuring that if a record with matching 'Source' and 'Source ID' already exists in the 4me account, it gets updated instead of creating a duplicate.

Understanding 4me ID and Node ID

The 4me ID is a human-readable identifier assigned to every record in 4me, unique within each specific environment, such as US Production or UK QA. The 4me ID is displayed on nearly every record form and is included in the URL when accessing a record directly. For instance, the URL https://widget-it.us.4me.com/requests/111 references the request with the 4me ID of 111 in the widget-it account within the US production environment. On the other hand, the node ID serves as a machine-readable identifier for each record. A node ID is unique across all 4me environments. For queries and updates, the GraphQL API is based on the node ID. To facilitate the work of developers and support specialists, 4me has included a convenient feature: by selecting a record, the 'Copy NodeID' option becomes available.

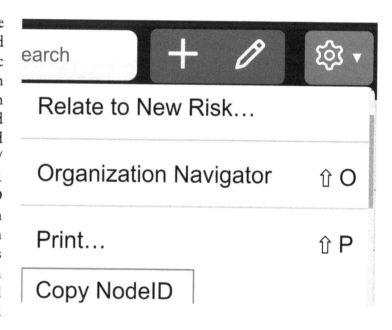

Figure 256: Copy the node ID of a record.

Tip — A 4me node ID is actually a Base64 encoded string. If you copy a node ID from a 4me record and decode it using one of the many free online Base64 decoders, you'll uncover that a node ID is composed of the environment, the record type, and the unique 4me ID.

The Integration Field on a Contact Record of a Person

The `Integration` field within a person's contact records in 4me serves as a safeguard for data consistency between 4me and external systems. Contact records store various details like phone numbers, email addresses, and messaging identifiers. While users and administrators can normally update these details manually in 4me, setting the 'Integration' flag to true for a contact record locks these details from being altered through the 4me interface. This ensures that any updates must be made within the originating external system, maintaining data integrity. Additionally, during imports, contact records marked with the 'Integration' flag as true are automatically deleted and replaced with the imported details. This mechanism simplifies the integration process by eliminating the need for complex scripts to manage discrepancies between 4me contact records and those in external systems, particularly for deleted or absent records in the latter.

Integrating with Discovery Tools for CI Provisioning

A Configuration Management Database (CMDB) with thousands of configuration items (CIs) is virtually unmanageable through manual updates. Integration with discovery tools emerges as the optimal solution to automate this process. While some discovery tools, such as Lansweeper or Microsoft's Intune, offer standard integrations with 4me, unique requirements or the absence of a standard integration necessitate the development of custom integrations. For handling large volumes of records, though the bulk import API is an option, 4me provides a more tailored approach through the GraphQL mutation known as `discoveredConfigurationItems`. This mutation addresses the complexity of 4me's CMDB three-tier architecture, encompassing product categories, products, and CIs themselves. A `discoveredConfigurationItems` request allows for the transmission of comprehensive CI data, including Product Categories, Products, and even CI-CI relationships, in a singular API call. Furthermore, this approach optimizes API utilization by grouping discovered CIs into batches (up to 100 items), significantly reducing the number of required API calls. For detailed guidance on implementing this mutation, refer to 4me's developer site at https://developer.4me.com/v1/import/discovery_tools/.

Secure Authentication via Bearer Tokens

For integrations with 4me, secure authentication is achieved by adding a bearer token to the Authorization header:

```
Authorization: Bearer <oauth-token>
```

The management of these bearer tokens is based on the **OAuth 2.0 Authorization framework**. OAuth 2.0 bearer tokens are designed with a finite lifespan and can be revoked anytime, offering a robust security layer. Their temporal limitation means that, even if compromised, they provide a narrow window of vulnerability before expiration. Additionally, bearer tokens are tailored with specific scopes and permissions, limiting integrations to essential operations, and thereby minimizing risks if tokens were to be compromised.

For development and testing phases, 4me permits authentication via **Personal Access Tokens** for convenience. These can be created within the 4me Specialists console under 'My Profile', followed by the 'Personal Access Tokens' section. It's crucial to assign appropriate permissions by specifying the necessary scopes for your API interactions. Nevertheless, for production environments, reliance on personal access tokens is discouraged, reinforcing the preference for OAuth 2.0 bearer tokens to uphold stringent security standards.

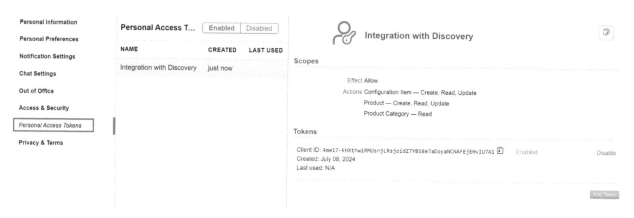

Figure 257: A specialist can create personal access tokens.

How OAuth 2.0 Works

For an application on the Integration Platform to initiate a GraphQL or REST API call to 4me, it requires a bearer token. This token is acquired through the OAuth Client Credentials Grant flow. In the initial step, the application requests a temporary bearer token from 4me by sending an access token request. This request is a REST API call that must include a **client_id**, a **client_secret**, and the **grant_type** parameter set to **client_credentials**. For example, in the US production environment, the access token request would be made to:

```
POST https://oauth.us.4me.com/token
```

After acquiring the bearer token, the application can then proceed with making API calls to the 4me platform. It's important to note that the bearer token has a lifespan of 1 hour. Attempts to use an expired bearer token will result in a 401 Unauthorized response from the server.

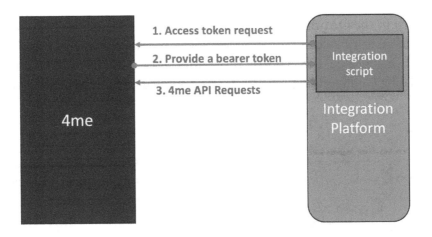

Obtaining a Client ID and Client Secret: OAuth Applications

To set up an integration with 4me, an integration script on the Integration Platform requires a token that consists of a **Client ID** and **Client Secret**. These credentials can be generated by a 4me account administrator. To do this, navigate to the 'OAuth Applications' section within the Settings console. It's important to give the OAuth application a descriptive name, ideally indicating the external IT system involved in the integration. Choose the *Client Credentials Grant* for the Grant Type.

The next step involves defining the scope of the application's access to 4me. Specify which records the application can access and the level of access (create, read, update, etc.) needed for those records.

Upon registering the OAuth application, the following occurs:

- A Token is generated. A token consists of a **Client ID** and a **Client Secret**. The Client ID uniquely identifies the token and is always visible. The **Client Secret** is shown just once. Make sure to copy it immediately, as it cannot be retrieved later (though a new token can be generated if necessary).
- A **4me person record** for the OAuth application is created without a primary email address. This user cannot be mentioned, nor can it log in, as it exists solely for integration purposes. Initially, it's assigned all roles available in the account for convenience, though these can be adjusted as needed. For instance, for certain integrations it is required to grant specialist access to a trusted account.

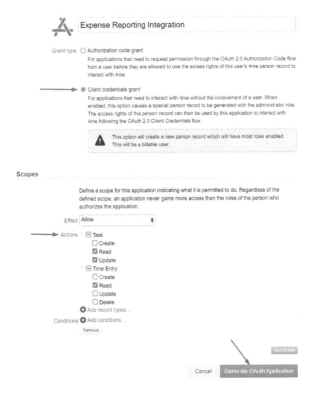

Figure 258: Creating an OAuth application allows you to specify exactly what the integration can see and do in the Actions section.

The defined Actions in the OAuth application, along with the roles assigned to the application user, form a dual layer of security. Access by the integration is contingent upon both the allowed actions and the user roles being aligned. For example, if the integration user does not have the Configuration Manager role, updating Configuration Items (CIs) is prohibited, even if the action to create and update CIs is permitted.

 The OAuth 2.0 Authorization framework, as implemented on the 4me platform, offers robust security for integrations. However, ensuring security is as much about adherence to best practices as it is about leveraging technology effectively. To maintain a high security standard, consider the following guidelines:

1. **Secure Transmission and Storage**: Always protect the security of your tokens. Avoid sending the client ID and client secret together and opt for secure communication methods over email for sharing the client secret with the application owner.
2. **Regular Token Rotation**: Establish a policy for regular token rotation, ideally at least once a year. 4me's recurring workflows can facilitate this process. Rotating tokens is straightforward: when you expire a token (and generate a new one), the old token remains valid for an additional month, providing ample time to update the integration script with the new token details.
3. **Integration User Roles**: Fine-tune the roles assigned to the integration user. If the administrator role is unnecessary, remove it to add an extra layer of security.
4. **Minimal Access Rights**: Avoid granting blanket access rights through OAuth applications. Start with minimal necessary access and only expand permissions as required for the integration's functionality.

Choosing the Right Integration Platform

Selecting the right integration platform is a crucial step in developing your strategy. There's no universal "best" integration platform; the optimal choice often hinges on your organization's existing tools and preferences. If your organization already employs an integration platform, it's likely the most appropriate starting point for your integration project.

For organizations without an existing solution, there's a wealth of **Integration Platform as a Service (iPaaS)** options to consider. Some prominent platforms include AWS App Integration Services, Azure Integration Services, Dell Boomi, IBM App Connect, MuleSoft Anypoint Platform, SnapLogic, and Workato. This list is not exhaustive nor a ranking but showcases some well-established solutions. iPaaS platforms excel in facilitating seamless communication and data exchange between diverse applications, largely due to their extensive libraries of standard connectors to various apps and databases.

Using 4me SDKs

While crafting API requests using GraphQL or REST is straightforward, following the respective API's specifications, the preparation of these requests—including setting all headers and parameters for an HTTP request—can be tedious. This is where **Software Development Kits (SDKs)** come into play, simplifying the process by consolidating common parameters and providing easy-to-use functions. These SDKs can transform what would be multiple lines of code into a single function call, enhancing development speed, code readability, and manageability.

4me offers two SDKs available for free:

- **Ruby SDK for 4me**
  - Source code on GitHub: https://github.com/code4me/4me-sdk-ruby
  - Ruby Gem: https://rubygems.org/gems/4me-sdk/
- **.NET SDK for 4me**:
  - Source code on GitHub: https://github.com/code4me/4me-sdk-graphql-dotnet
  - On NuGet: https://www.nuget.org/packages/Sdk4me.GraphQL

Workato iPaaS embedded in the 4me Ecosystem

In the 4me ecosystem, the Workato iPaaS solution stands out. Renowned for its low-code platform, Workato boasts a comprehensive library of over 1000 connectors, seamlessly linking well-known business applications and data sources. Through a collaborative effort with Workato, 4me has unveiled a dedicated Workato 4me connector. With this 4me connector the creation of robust connections between diverse IT systems and 4me is very much simplified.

The 4me Workflow Automator: Simplifying Integration While Safeguarding Data Privacy

The adoption of a new iPaaS platform within an organization raises crucial considerations, notably additional licensing costs and data privacy implications. Integrating an iPaaS solution means data processing occurs on an additional platform, posing challenges for organizations striving to comply with stringent data protection regulations, such as the GDPR. This necessitates a Data Processing Agreement (DPA) with the iPaaS provider to ensure data privacy and security.

Addressing these concerns, 4me has joined forces with Workato to launch the **4me Workflow Automator**. This feature fully integrates Workato's capabilities with the 4me platform, eliminating the need for separate Workato licenses. Integrations crafted within the Workflow Automator environment utilize 4me service credits, offering a streamlined and cost-effective solution. Furthermore, signing a DPA with Workato becomes unnecessary. The Workflow Automator's complete integration into the 4me platform means it is encompassed by 4me's existing DPA.

To activate their 4me Workflow Automator, customers can contact their local 4me partner.

OAuth - Authorization Code Grant

Consider this scenario: an organization uses 4me's time tracking features for recording specialists' support activities while also employing a separate time registration application for all employees. Each week on Friday evening, employees are required to log their activities and corresponding time spent in this external application. For specialists already tracking their time in 4me, manually transferring their logged support hours to another system can be cumbersome and redundant. Ideally, they want an automated solution that real-time populates their weekly support time into the external time tracking system when completing their timesheets.

This seamless integration is achievable through the OAuth - Authorization Code Grant flow.

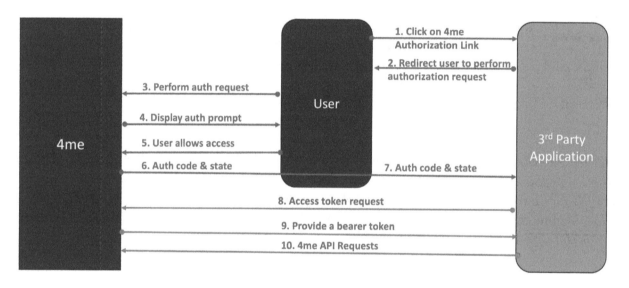

Figure 259: The Authorization Code Grant flow shares similarities with the OAuth Client Credentials flow in steps 8, 9, and 10, where the third-party application requests an access token from 4me. However, earlier in the process, a user must grant the third-party application permission to access 4me using their credentials.

This process places the user at the intersection of the third-party application and 4me. It initiates with the third-party application requesting authorization from 4me, which then asks the user to approve sharing their data with the third-party application. Approval by the user grants the application the ability to request an access token from 4me, enabling the necessary data queries. Once authorization is given, it's recorded within 4me, streamlining future interactions by bypassing the initial user approval step. Users can manage and revoke application permissions anytime within their 4me profile settings.

Like with OAuth Client Credentials Grant, the third-party integration requires a Client ID and Client Secret, generated by a 4me account administrator. For this workflow, the Grant Type should be set to Authorization Code Grant.

The Events API

As discussed in the chapter on 4me's core processes, the Event Management process focuses on monitoring and managing events within IT infrastructures or service environments. Although 4me itself does not include direct monitoring features, it can be seamlessly integrated with external monitoring solutions through the Events API. Detailed documentation is available on the 4me developer site (https://developer.4me.com/v1/requests/events/).

The Events API enables the generation of requests, typically incidents, in response to actionable monitoring events, facilitating a straightforward, uni-directional interaction that doesn't necessitate an Integration Platform. Monitoring solutions can either directly issue a REST API Event request or send a structured email to 4me. While the API requires only the subject field as mandatory, it's highly advisable to also specify the source (identifying the monitoring system), include a note (with the generated alert), and mention the affected configuration item (CI).

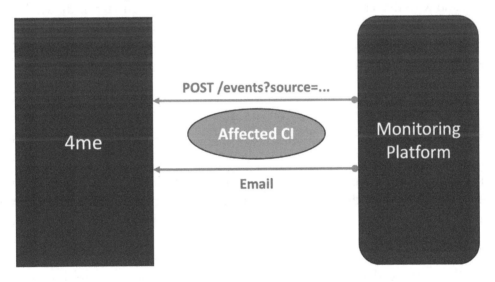

Figure 260: Integration with monitoring platforms via the Events API or via structured emails.

Identifying the Configuration Item

Specifying the affected CI is pivotal for effective event management. If the CI is a hardware component linked to a service instance, 4me automatically associates both the CI and the service instance with the newly created request. This ensures accurate ticket assignment to the appropriate support team and the generation of relevant affected SLAs, tagging the business services that are impacted with a red bullet on the self-service portal.

The challenge lies in specifying a CI without using its unique 4me ID or node ID, which the monitoring solution may not know. Instead, the CI's label (or name, for software CIs) can be utilized. If the monitoring tool also serves as a discovery tool that provisions CIs to 4me, it should set the source and source ID fields in 4me to the monitoring platform's name and the CI's unique ID within that system, respectively. This way, the Events API request can include just the CI source and CI source ID, enabling 4me to accurately identify the affected CI.

Using the Email API

Monitoring solutions often have the capability to issue structured emails in response to events. 4me's inbound email interface can process these emails effectively by utilizing tags to populate request fields. For instance, the affected CI can be denoted using the tag #ci: PRT00001, or if referencing the source system and ID, the tags #ci_source: LogicMonitor and #ci_sourceID: 0554488888 can be employed.

It's essential that the FROM email address sending the event notifications be associated with a person record in 4me, and with the service desk analyst role assigned. The requester of the service (Requested for) can be specified using the #requested_for tag; in its absence, the system defaults to using the sender of the email. To facilitate effective SLA generation and ensure incidents are linked to critical business services, the Requested for user should be covered by the relevant business services.

Event Matching

A common challenge when integrating monitoring solutions with service management systems is the risk of incident storms—where the same event triggers hundreds of redundant tickets, overwhelming support teams. To address this, 4me incorporates advanced event matching mechanisms to ensure efficient incident management.

When an email is received that matches the criteria of an existing open request—specifically the same account, source, requested_for, service_instance, and CI—within 24 hours of the request's creation, a new request is not generated. Instead, the content of the email is assessed for addition as a new note to the ongoing request. This process is finely tuned to avoid note duplication: a note is added only if it contains new attachments or its text differs from that of any prior note in the request. Blank notes or those with identical text that lack attachments do not result in any update to the request.

In instances where the service_instance parameter is omitted, 4me identifies the relevant service instance via the linked CI before proceeding with event matching. Similarly, if an email lacks the CI parameter, event matching still prevents the creation of a new request if the subject, account, source, and requested_for parameters match those of an open request from the last 24 hours.

The APP Store

4me's App Store is a treasure trove of standard integrations accessible directly within the platform's Settings Console. Account administrators can effortlessly enhance their 4me environment by installing apps that require minimal configuration. Popular standard integrations include:

Single Sign-On and SCIM Connectors: Streamline user provisioning and authentication processes.

Google Maps App: Enrich UI Extensions with location-based custom fields.

Lansweeper App: Automate CI provisioning for an up-to-date CMDB.

Figure 261: The 4me App Store. Technology partners can add their integrations to the app store via the App Builder Framework.

The App Builder Framework

Beyond the ready-made solutions, the 4me App Store is open to innovations from 4me technology partners, allowing them to share their standard integrations with the wider 4me community. Partners can utilize the App Offerings feature to introduce their integrations to customers directly in the Apps section.

Developers looking to dive into creating apps for 4me can find rich resources and example offerings in the App Builder Framework on GitHub (see: https://github.com/code4me/4me-app-builder-nodejs).

Initially, App Offerings crafted by a partner are exclusive to the developer's environment, ensuring thorough testing before widespread release. Upon successful validation, offerings can be published, making them available across trusted accounts and broadening the integration possibilities for all 4me users.

Chapter 15 - Self Service Design

Introduction

Every 4me account boasts a self-service portal, the gateway for users to effortlessly access support. Within a directory account structure, the portal on the directory account serves as the ultimate hub where employees can navigate a wide array of enterprise services—from resolving HR queries and reporting facility issues to booking company cars or ordering IT assets through the web shop.

The self-service portal's appearance is not just a matter of aesthetics; it represents the initial impression for new employees and a constant touchpoint for all users seeking support. Beyond the sleek, out-of-the-box designs offered by 4me, there lies the potential to infuse the portal with your organization's unique colors and branding, or even to craft an entirely new and bespoke self-service experience.

This chapter delves into the nuances of self-service design within 4me, equipping you with the knowledge to customize and create a portal that resonates with your organization's identity. Prepare to transform your self-service portal into a place where employees are not just visitors but engaged participants in your support ecosystem.

The Media Library: Essential for Your Self-Service Portal

Completing a Self-Service Design requires the right images, logos, and fonts. 4me's Media Library serves as the centralized storage area for these necessary multimedia contents. Whether it's for enhancing your self-service portal or adding visual appeal to PDF designs the Media Library provides the essential tools.

Available through the Settings console, the Media Library in the directory account is open to directory account administrators and designers. In support domain accounts it extends its access to all specialists.

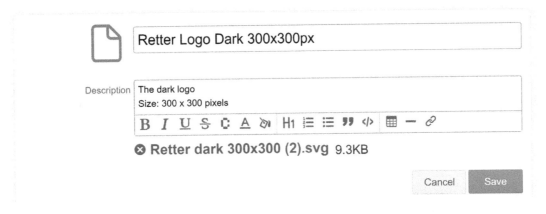

Figure 262: The Media Library: it is good practice to add the size of the images and some clear description to the media files.

Uploading is straightforward: assign your media file a name, provide an optional description, and upload. A unique public URL is automatically generated for each uploaded item, facilitating seamless integration into your projects. The platform allows for file replacement while maintaining the original URL, making it easy to keep your content current.

Prerequisites for Customizing a Self-Service Design

To effectively customize the self-service design, a fundamental understanding of HTML and CSS is essential. For those aiming to modify the default designs, basic familiarity with these technologies is sufficient. However, crafting your own self-service design from scratch demands a more comprehensive knowledge of both HTML and CSS.

If you're not yet acquainted with HTML and CSS, or if you're looking to bolster your skills, we highly recommend starting with the following tutorials available at MDN:

- For HTML: https://developer.mozilla.org/en-US/docs/Learn/HTML
- For CSS: https://developer.mozilla.org/en-US/docs/Learn/CSS

Additionally, to ensure you're working with the most advanced features and the latest design capabilities, make sure to utilize the latest version of the self-service design platform in 4me. *Account administrators* can enable this version through the Self-Service Settings in the Settings console. Always verify you're using this updated version for the best customization experience.

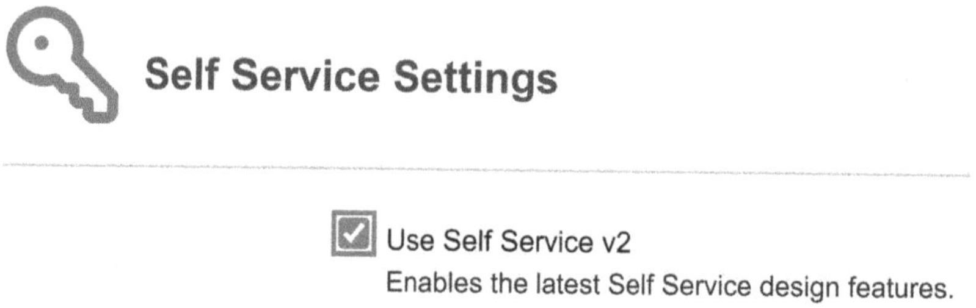

Self Service Settings

☑ Use Self Service v2
Enables the latest Self Service design features.

Figure 263: Make sure the latest version of Self Service is checked in the Self-Service Settings.

The Self-Service Portal:

Essential Components and Design Choices

Navigating the Self-Service Portal

The 4me Self-Service Portal is designed for efficient user navigation, enabling quick access to required services or relevant information. The portal layout is straightforward, featuring a home page that serves as the initial point of interaction for users. This home page typically includes a prominent 'New Request' button, HTML components for versatile content presentation, dynamic widgets such as a list of recent knowledge articles, and direct access to support chat or a virtual agent if available.

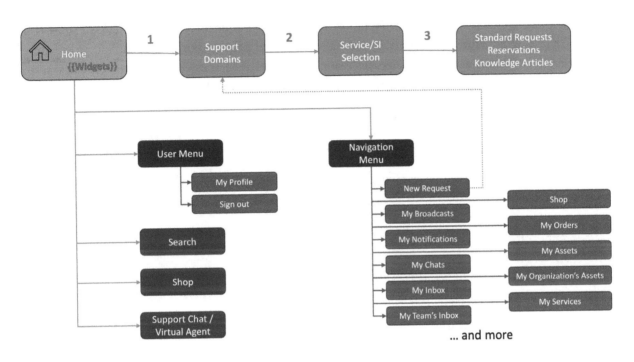

Figure 264: A site map of the 4me self-service portal.

The persistent header on every page offers consistent access to the User Menu, a comprehensive Search feature, and the Shop, ensuring essential tools are always within reach. Additionally, the global navigation menu, which can be integrated into the header or placed as a separate column on the left, facilitates access to all major sections of the portal.

A key element of the portal's navigation is the 'New Request' pathway, which guides users through a hierarchical selection process—from choosing a support domain to selecting specific services or service instances, and ultimately to a request template, reservation, or knowledge article.

The Building Blocks of the Self Service Portal

Every 4me self-service portal is built from several core components, understanding these components is crucial when designing or customizing your portal:

- **Header**: A consistent element across all pages, offering immediate access to key sections and tools.
- **Footer** (Optional): A section for additional information or links, present on every page.
- **Navigation Menus**:
    - **Global Navigation Menu**: Can be integrated into the header or placed in the sidebar,

providing broad navigational capabilities across the portal.
- **User Menu**: Located within the header, this menu is tailored to individual user settings and options.
- **Main Content Area**:
  - **Self-Service Homepage**: Refers to the main landing page of your self-service portal. Fully customizable, allowing for a tailored welcome experience.
  - **Self-Service Subpage**: Refers to all lower level pages, in other words, pages that are not the homepage. Currently, the main content area of these pages offer no customization options, though future updates may expand this capability.

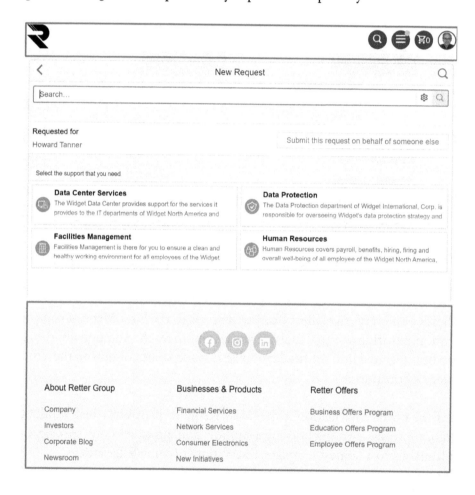

Figure 265: In the default Retter design, both the header and an optional footer appear on every page of the self-service portal. The header integrates the general navigation and user menus. The main content area on this page is preset and not open for customization.

As you begin to envision your self-service design, consider how each of these elements will be implemented and interact within your portal. Exploring the various default self-service designs provided by 4me can offer valuable insights and inspiration. Below is a summary of how the global navigation menu has been defined in some default self-service designs:

Design	Global Navigation Menu
gigatera	Header, full screen hamburger menu that slides in from the right
globalnet	Sidebar, fixed
ultramax	Header, a centered drop down menu. The hamburger menu is in a protruding area in the header bar
retter	Header, conventional hamburger/drop down menu
virtualsupport	Sidebar, fixed
wdp	Sidebar, collapsible
widget	Sidebar, fixed
wna-hr	Sidebar, fixed

Figure 266: Design choices in the 4me default designs.

The Home Page Sections

Creating an inviting and functional home page for your 4me self-service portal involves careful planning and consideration of user needs. The home page can be structured into multiple sections, with the flexibility to configure multiple columns per section. Ensure your design is responsive, allowing the layout to seamlessly adapt to different device screen sizes for an optimal viewing experience on all devices. Note that all standard 4me designs are already responsive.

The content within these sections can range from custom HTML to dynamic 4me components, such as:

- A list of the most recent knowledge articles,
- A carousel slider for current broadcast messages,
- Quick access buttons for key actions like reporting a security incident.

4me's self-service content dynamically adjusts based on the user, displaying menu items, broadcasts and knowledge articles relevant to the roles of the user and to the services the user has access to. This customization is facilitated by the Self-Service Design Composer, which allows for easy integration of these dynamic elements into your design.

As you draft your home page design, explore the variety of default designs available within 4me. These can serve as a foundation or inspiration for your portal. Opting for an existing design can simplify the customization process, allowing you to focus on incorporating your brand's visual elements and color scheme with minimal technical effort.

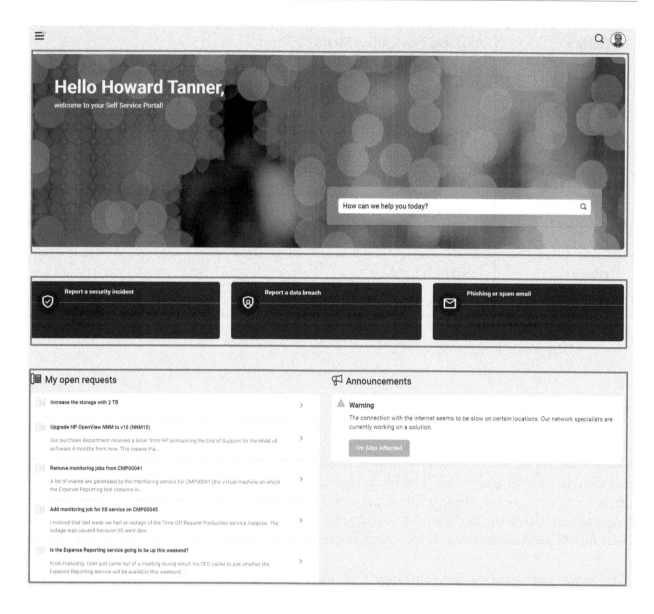

Figure 267: The wdp design features three sections on the home page, each capable of housing multiple columns. These columns automatically adjust or collapse to fit smaller screens. Within each section, various components such as menu item buttons, record lists, dynamic widgets (e.g., Broadcasts), and static HTML content can be incorporated for a customized user experience.

Designing Your Self-Service Portal

The Self-Service Design editor is divided into four main tabs:

- **HTML**: Where you add and organize the components of your web pages.
- **CSS**: Used to style and customize the appearance of your portal.
- **Fonts**: Ensures text consistency across various platforms and devices.
- **Global Settings**: Houses the overarching design settings.

Starting with Fonts and Global Settings is recommended when creating your design. This approach ensures a consistent base before adding components with the HTML section and customizing styles in the CSS section.

The Fonts

To ensure text displays consistently across different platforms and devices, the 4me self-service design supports the Web Open Font Format (WOFF). Include the public URLs for both WOFF 1.0 and WOFF 2.0 font files in the Fonts section, using the standard format:

```
@font-face {
  font-family: 'outfit';
  font-style: normal;
  font-weight: 400;
  src: url(,https://…/outfit-400.woff2') format(,woff2'),
       url(,https://…/outfit-400.woff') format(,woff');
}
```

If WOFF files are not available via a public URL, they can be uploaded to the media library of your 4me account. Please note that to enable uploading of **.woff** and **.woff2** files to the media library, the account owner must include these file extensions in the 'Allowed Extensions' list found on the Security settings page of the account.

Global Settings Overview

This section provides options for customizing the overall appearance and functionality of the self-service portal:

- **Background Image**: Select an image from the media library to serve as the background for sub-pages. Future updates may introduce further customization options, such as color schemes for sub-pages.
- **Show Support Chat**: Enable the display of a support chat button on the self-service portal for users eligible for this feature.

The HTML Tab

The HTML page is composed of four potential main sections, each serving a distinct purpose in the layout:

1. **<self-service-header>…</self-service-header>**: This section is fundamental as it creates the header, which is consistently visible across all pages of the portal, ensuring a uniform navigational experience.
2. **<self-service-nav>…</self-service-nav>**: This optional section is dedicated to the global navigation menu. If your design necessitates a left-pane positioning for the global navigation menu across the self-service pages, it should be encapsulated within this tag. Alternatively, the global navigation menu can be integrated into the header as a subsection.
3. **<self-service-homepage>…</self-service-homepage>**: This tag is crucial as it encapsulates the main content of the home page, serving as the centerpiece of your self-service portal design. It is where users are greeted with key information, resources, and navigational options upon their arrival.
4. **<self-service-footer>...</self-service-footer>**: This optional section allows for the addition of a footer, which, when utilized, appears on all portal pages. The footer can be used to display additional information, links, or disclaimers consistently throughout the self-service experience.

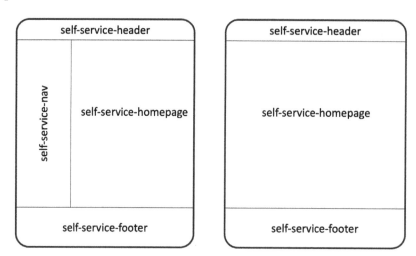

Figure 268: The core layout components of a 4me self-service design.

Component (node)	Required?	Visibility
self-service-header	true	Homepage + subpages
self-service-nav	true	Homepage + subpages
self-service-footer	false	Homepage + subpages
self-service-homepage	true	Homepage

Liquid: The Basis for Data Content Generation

Before exploring the Self-Service Design Composer and its suite of components, it's crucial to grasp the mechanics behind dynamic content creation, powered by Liquid. Liquid is an open-source template language crafted by Shopify, designed to inject data into HTML templates dynamically. This functionality is essential for creating a self-service portal that not only looks appealing but also adapts to display user-relevant information in real-time.

Consider the scenario where you wish to showcase a list of the most-viewed knowledge articles on the homepage. The content displayed here needs to be dynamic, as the list might be long for users with extensive service coverage, yet non-existent for new users without any interactions. Moreover, the titles of these knowledge articles could vary greatly in length. Ensuring that the homepage layout remains consistent and visually appealing, regardless of these variables, requires a dynamic approach to content management.

This is where Liquid comes into play, offering:

- **Objects**: Objects contain attributes used to display dynamic content on a page. They are denoted by double curly braces: `{{ }}`. For example, `{{ knowledge_article.subject }}` would display the subject of a knowledge article.
- **Tags**: Tags create the logic and control flow for templates. They are enclosed in curly braces and percent symbols: `{% %}`. Tags can be used for loops, conditionals, and variable assignments. For example `{% if list.latest.knowledge_articles.size > 0 %}` ... `{% endif %}` would include a "Latest Knowledge Articles" section if there is at least 1 'latest knowledge article' found.
- **Filters**: Filters modify the output of Liquid objects. They are used within an output tag and are separated by a pipe symbol: `|`. For example, `{{ knowledge_article.text | truncate: 140 }}` will truncate the text of a knowledge article to its first 140 characters.

While the Self-Service Design Composer incorporates Liquid controls into its components, eliminating the need for in-depth syntax knowledge, understanding Liquid's basics enhances your ability to tailor the self-service portal to meet specific organizational and user requirements.

Self-Service Design Composer

The Self-Service Design Composer in 4me equips you with a comprehensive suite of components to elevate the design and functionality of your self-service portal. To discover these components, simply press CTRL-k. You'll then be presented with an array of options to enrich your portal, including:

- Lists
- Counts
- Variables

- Navigation
- Widgets

Diving Deeper into Lists

One of the key components, Lists, allows you to dynamically display various records directly within your self-service design. Available lists include:

- Assets
- Broadcasts
- Inbox
- Knowledge Articles
  - Lates Knowledge Articles
  - Most Viewed Knowledge Articles
- Requests
  - Completed Requests
  - Open Requests
- Request Templates
  - Latest Request Templates
  - Most Applied Request Templates
  - My Recently Used Request Templates

Adding a list to your design injects an HTML snippet, powered by Liquid, to dynamically render the selected data. For example, incorporating the "Most Viewed Knowledge Articles" list translates to the following snippet being added to your design:

```liquid
{% if list.popular.knowledge_articles.size > 0 %}
  <ul>
    {% for record in list.popular.knowledge_articles limit: 5 %}
      <li>
        <a href="{{ record.url }}">
          <i class="ii icon-knowledge-article"></i>
          <h5>{{ record.subject }}</h5>
          <p>{{ record.text | truncate: 140 }}</p>
          <div>Views: {{ record.count }}</div>
        </a>
      </li>
    {% endfor %}
  </ul>
{% endif %}
```

Count

The 'Count' component plays a crucial role in enhancing the interactivity of the self-service portal by dynamically checking conditions or displaying counts relevant to the user's interests. It adeptly returns the count of items in various lists. Available counts include:

- Approvals
- Assets
- Broadcasts
- Completed Requests
- Inbox
- Navigation Menu Unread Count
- Notifications
- Open Requests
- Project Tasks
- Requests
- Requests Waiting for Me
- Watchlist

A notable application of this component is the 'Navigation Menu Unread Count'. For menu items like 'My Notifications' and 'My Inbox,' it tallies the number of unread notifications or tickets yet to be accepted. When the count is above zero, indicating pending items, you can adapt the navigation menu visually to prompt user attention. Here's how you can implement it:

```
{% if count.navigation_menu > 0 %}

    <span class="navigation-menu-badge"></span>

{% endif %}
```

Variables

The variables expose contextual information that can be useful for the user. The list is still limited and may be extended with other variables in the future:

- The account name
- The username
- The job title of the user

The username and the job title for example, are typically used in the upper part of the user menu:

```
<span class="user-info-name">{{ user.name }}</span>
<small class="user-info-position">{{ user.job_title }}</small>
```

Navigation

The following components are available:

- **Navigation Menu Toggler**: Often represented by a hamburger menu icon, this component allows users to reveal or conceal the navigation menu items with a simple toggle action.
- **Navigation Menu**: The primary container that houses individual navigation menu items, providing a structured menu for accessing various sections of the portal.
- **Single Navigation Menu Item**: To display and control a single navigation menu item. Note that the Navigation Menu dynamically generates all navigation menu items.

The global navigation menu can be situated within the header or along the sidebar of the portal. The positioning and behavior of the global navigation menu are determined by the **data-nav-variant** custom data attribute of the `<self-service-nav>` element, which enables various display modes on a wide screen. The `data-nav-variant` custom data attribute can get the following values:

- dropdown
- aside
- aside-fixed
- full-screen

Some examples:

- **Global Navigation Menu in the Header**: To integrate the navigation menu within the portal's header, include both the navigation menu toggler and the navigation menu within the header section. Use **data-nav-variant="dropdown"** for the navigation menu to enable a dropdown functionality or **data-nav-variant="full-screen"** for a full-screen menu.
- **Global Navigation Menu Collapsible in the Sidebar**: For a collapsible navigation menu positioned in the sidebar, place the navigation menu toggler within the header and add the global navigation menu as a separate section in the HTML page. Assign **data-nav-variant="dropdown"** to the navigation menu for collapsible behavior.
- **Global Navigation Menu Fixed in the Sidebar**: To establish a fixed navigation menu in the sidebar, render the navigation menu toggler invisible and include the global navigation menu as a distinct section in the HTML page. Set **data-nav-variant="aside-fixed"** on the navigation menu for a fixed display.

Widgets

Widgets in 4me's self-service portal are dynamic components that enhance user interaction and provide key functionalities. Below is an overview of each widget and recommendations for their implementation:

- **Broadcast Carousel**: Integral for communicating important announcements from any of the support domain accounts. It's recommended to always include the Broadcast Carousel in the main section of the home page, as it automatically hides when there are no relevant broadcasts for the user.
- **Color Mode Picker**: Allows users to switch between light and dark modes, offering a personalized experience. Including a Color Mode Picker is suggested for a contemporary and user-centric portal design, but keep in mind that supporting both modes increases the need for thorough testing and adds complexity.
- **Search Widget**: A critical component for any home page, enabling users to easily find the information or services they need. Placing the Search widget prominently, often alongside a welcoming message like "How can we help you today?", is considered best practice.
- **Shopping Cart**: When a 4me shop is accessible to users, integrating the Shopping Cart icon in the header ensures users have easy access to their cart at any time.
- **User Menu**: An essential part of the header, providing users with quick access to their profile, settings, and other personal options.
- **User Menu Toggler**: A clickable button, usually represented by the user's avatar or initials, that toggles the expansion or collapse of the User Menu. This widget enhances navigation efficiency and user experience by making personal options readily accessible.

The CSS Tab

The content of the header, footer, and the main section of the home page is defined in the HTML; how it all looks like comes from the CSS. A fundamental aspect of the 4me self-service design philosophy is providing minimal CSS out of the box, which gives you full control over the look and feel of your homepage. However, this level of control means that more effort is required to achieve a high-quality design from scratch. To help alleviate this challenge, the provided demo designs offer excellent starting points that adhere to the latest best practices in web design.

Please note that the content and layout of the self-service homepage, header, footer, and sidebar are fully customizable. However, the content and layout of the main section of the self-service subpages within the portal cannot be altered.

Ensuring Encapsulation with Shadow DOM

4me's self-service design is safeguarded from unintended CSS conflicts on subpages by using a Shadow Document Object Model (DOM). This encapsulation ensures that custom CSS applied to the self-service portal does not interfere with the default styles of subpages, and vice versa, preventing unexpected styling overlaps.

Ensuring Style Consistency with CSS Variables

CSS custom properties, or variables, which you'll encounter at the beginning of the CSS section are of great help to ensure style consistency. These variables serve as a central repository for reusable values across your CSS, facilitating a consistent look and feel throughout the self-service portal.

Here's an example snippet from the CSS Variables section:

```
/* ------ CSS Variables ------------------------------ */
:host {--radius: 7px;
       --radius-inner: 5px;
       --radius-round: 50%;
       /* More variables */
```

For instance, brand color variables might be defined as follows:

```
/* ------ CSS Variables ------------------------------ */
:host { …
        --color-brand-150: #7fc3d6;
        …
```

These variables are then utilized within specific CSS rules, such as button styling:

```
/* ------ Widget Button ------------------------------ */
.widget-btn.brand-100:hover {
  background-color: var(--color-brand-150);
}
```

Furthermore, CSS variables are dynamically adjusted based on the selected color mode (e.g., light or dark), including different branding elements like logos:

```
:host([data-color-mode='dark']) {

  --color-text-100: #dee4ec;

  --color-text-200: #b3b9c2;

  --brand: url(https://.../brand-dark.png);
```

This dynamic adjustment ensures that elements like the brand logo, often a part of the global navigation menu, seamlessly integrate with the user's chosen color scheme. By defining these elements as variables, the design can automatically apply the appropriate assets based on the current color mode.

The adaptability to be aligned across a variety of devices is achieved using of media queries and CSS custom properties that tailor your design to different screen sizes. A notable section of the CSS variables in 4me's self-service design is dedicated to these adjustments.

Media queries are utilized to apply different sets of CSS rules based on the screen's width, allowing for a responsive design that adjusts to the viewer's device. These are encapsulated within the **@media** rule, specifying the conditions under which the enclosed CSS should be applied. For example:

```
@media (min-width: 1400px) {

  :host {

    --nav-width: 300px;

    --space-horizontal: var(--space-xl);

  }

}
```

In this snippet, CSS custom properties are set for screens with a minimum width of 1400 pixels. The **--nav-width** property, for example, determines the width of the navigation bar, and **--space-horizontal** defines the horizontal spacing within the portal, drawing from another **variable --space-xl** that has been defined in the previous section.

Leveraging Browser Developer Tools for Design Adjustments

Browser Developer Tools are invaluable resources for web developers and designers alike, offering a suite of functionalities to inspect and interact with the structure and styling of web pages. These tools are integrated into most modern browsers and are instrumental in examining the HTML and CSS of any webpage, allowing for on-the-fly modifications and troubleshooting.

For example, in Google Chrome, Developer Tools can be accessed by pressing **Ctrl+Shift+I** (Windows) or **Command+Option+I** (Mac). One of the core features of these tools is the ability to inspect individual elements on a webpage. By right-clicking on any part of a page and selecting "Inspect," you can immediately zero in on the relevant HTML and CSS.

```
.widget-item-block-header h2 {                           design.css:778
    color: ■ var(--color-section-block-title);
    font-size: var(--section-block-title-size);
    font-weight: var(--font-weight-medium);
    margin-block-end: var(--space-md);
}
```

Figure 269: Inspecting a button on the self-service reveals the CSS variables that have been applied.

Upon selecting an element, the Developer Tools will display its associated CSS properties, including any CSS variables defined in the self-service design. If you're working on refining the styling of a component, such as a button, and need to understand or alter its visual properties, this direct insight into the applied CSS is incredibly useful.

In the 4me Self Service Design editor, an embedded search functionality simplifies the process of working with CSS variables. Once you've identified a CSS variable of interest through browser developer tools or your inspection process, the next step is to trace how this variable is defined within the 4me CSS page.

```
119
120     --color-search: rgba(170, 239, 158, 0.8);
121     --color-on-search-input: #343a40;
122     --color-search-input: var(--color-white);
123     --color-on-search-btn: #343a40;
124     --color-search-btn: var(--color-white);
125     --shadow-search-focus: rgba(0, 0, 0, 0.1);
126
127     --color-user-menu-btn: #343a40;
128     --color-user-menu-btn-hover: var(--color-brand-1
```

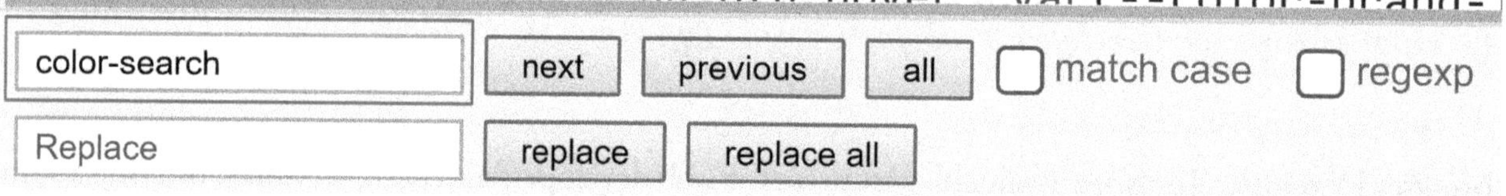

| color-search | | next | previous | all | ☐ match case | ☐ regexp |
| Replace | | replace | replace all | | | |

Figure 270: The search and replace feature in the 4me Self Service Design editor can be activated by pressing CTRL+F.

To activate the search feature, simply press **Ctrl+F** within the editor. This action opens a search and replace tool located at the bottom left corner of the editor, providing a straightforward means to locate specific CSS variable definitions or any other elements within your CSS code.

Ensuring Accessibility in Self-Service Designs with ARIA Attributes

In ensuring accessibility, 4me is committed to complying with the Web Content Accessibility Guidelines (WCAG). The platform's out-of-the-box self-service designs are crafted and regularly evaluated to meet these standards. When customizing an existing self-service design or creating a new one, it's crucial to maintain this commitment to accessibility.

For instance, the **sr-only** class is a staple in default designs, designed to make specific content accessible exclusively to screen readers—hence the abbreviation 'sr'. This class strategically hides visual content from sighted users while ensuring it remains fully accessible to those using screen readers. It's especially valuable for incorporating descriptive texts or labels. These elements enrich screen readers' navigation and comprehension of page structures without overcrowding the visual interface for sighted individuals.

A key aspect of adhering to accessibility standards involves the use of ARIA (Accessible Rich Internet Applications) attributes, a set of specifications from the World Wide Web Consortium (W3C) that enhance web accessibility. ARIA plays a pivotal role in the 'Robust' principle of WCAG by providing additional semantic details to assistive technologies like screen readers.

Key uses of ARIA attributes include:

- **Role Attributes**: These attributes specify the type of UI element to assistive technologies. For instance, when designing your self-service portal, incorporating attributes like **role="menu"** and **role="menuitem"** helps in identifying the element's function.
- **Properties**: These attributes offer more details about an element. Coupling role="menu" with attributes like **aria-label="User Menu" or aria-label="Navigation Menu"** clearly communicates the menu's purpose.

Demo

Self-Service Design
Revamping Widget's Homepage: A Colorful Transformation

Imagine stepping into the digital workshop of Widget, Inc., where the default home page gleams with potential:

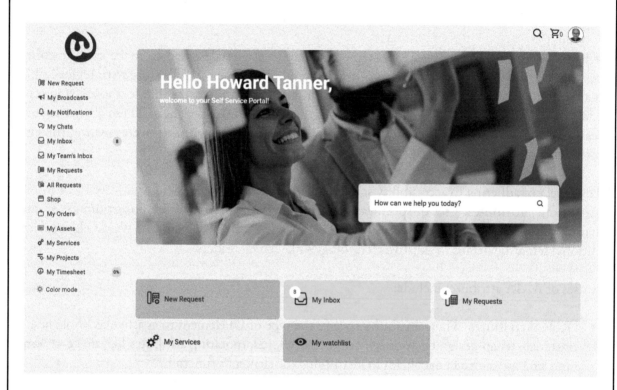

Figure 271: The widget design with the old branding colors.

But change is afoot. The marketing wizards have woven a new palette into the company's brand tapestry:
- Accent colors:
  - Bright blue: #007BC7
  - Bright green: #8BC027
- Secondary colors:
  - Mid gray: #a6adb0
  - Dark gray: #33333

Enter Howard Tanner, the digital craftsman. Tasked with infusing these colors into the homepage, Howard aims to paint the search bar and left buttons with bright blue's vibrancy, drench the middle buttons in bright green's energy, and cloak the right-most button in mid gray's calm. A challenge? Perhaps. But with his tools ready, Howard dives into action.

First of all, Howard will use the inspector to check the CSS code on the home page for these elements.

Armed with insights, Howard embarks on a creative spree in the CSS style sheet:

```
self-service-search {
    background-color: ☐ var(--color-search);
    border-radius: ▶ var(--radius);
    padding: ▶ var(--space-responsive);
}
```

```
--color-brand-100: #007BC7; /* -- bright blue --- */

--color-brand-200: #8BC027; /* --- bright green --- */

--color-brand-300: #a6adb0; /* --- mid gray --- */
```

Still in the CSS, he sets the color-search variable to the color-brand-100:

```
--color-search: var(--color-brand-100);
```

Finally, Howard turns his attention to the HTML canvas. Each button is delicately brushed with its designated color-branding class, a testament to Howard's meticulous handiwork. And just like that, job done!

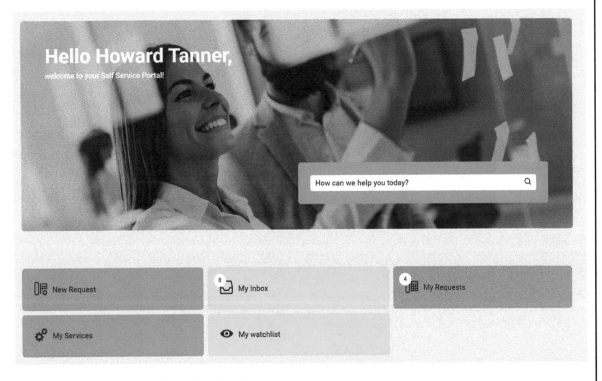

Figure 272: Modifying the colors of the widget design.

Chapter 16 - PDF Designs

Introduction

4me facilitates a variety of scenarios requiring managerial approval, from steering group decisions in project management to substantial orders placed within the 4me shop. In each case, the manager's decision is informed by detailed PDF documents, linked directly to the task at hand. Additionally, the scheduled KPI dashboards are bundled in PDF files based on a specific PDF design. These documents serve as comprehensive references, allowing for informed decisions.

While the default PDF designs for workflow summaries, project summaries, and dashboard reports in 4me are both aesthetically pleasing and informative, the real power lies in customization. This chapter will guide you through creating bespoke PDF designs tailored to specific needs, enabling you to refine both the content and the presentation of these crucial documents.

The Essentials of PDF Design Customization in 4me

The "PDF Designs" section, accessible from the Account Settings, offers account administrators and designers the capability to tailor PDF documents for a variety of purposes, including approval requests and monthly report distribution. A PDF Design is structured into HTML and CSS pages, with HTML focusing on content arrangement and CSS on aesthetic presentation. Elements such as images, logos, and fonts can be integrated from the media library.

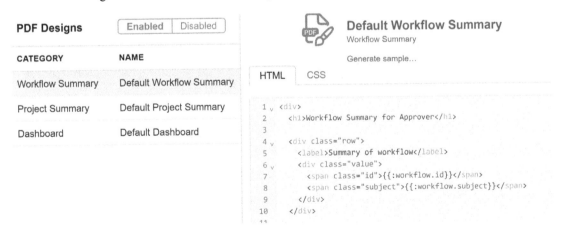

Figure 273: The section on "PDF Designs" is equipped with three default PDF designs tailored for Workflow Summaries, Project Summaries, and Dashboards, providing a solid starting point for customization.

Unlike Self-Service Design, PDF Designs are inherently simpler due to the absence of navigational elements and menus. The content structure found in default PDF Designs serves as an excellent starting point for customization, possibly requiring only minor adjustments or additions. From a layout perspective, the inclusion of a company logo might be all that's needed to tailor the document to your brand. A fundamental understanding of HTML and CSS is essential, but for most cases there will be no need for advanced web design expertise.

HTML - The Content

Just as dynamic content creation is essential for self-service design, PDF design also benefits from one-time dynamic content generation. For example, a workflow summary might require injecting task details into an HTML template dynamically. To achieve this, 4me leverages the JsRender framework for dynamic content generation within PDF designs. JsRender operates on principles similar to those of Liquid, which is employed in self-service design, but it's tailored for PDF content creation. JsRender is an open-source, lightweight framework detailed at https://www.jsviews.com/#jsrapi.

With JsRender, dynamically adding content to HTML is straightforward using the `{{:object.field}}` syntax. For instance, in a PDF design for a workflow summary, the workflow object becomes accessible, just as a project object would be in a project summary. Consequently, to include the subject of a workflow in a PDF design, you would use the following statement:

`{{:workflow.subject}}`

To make it easy, the PDF Design editor provides pop-up suggestions: when adding the curly brackets {{, it will for example suggest ":", "if, "for", and "unless"; when entering ":", it will suggest "now", "workflow", and "recipient"; finally, when entering "workflow.", it will suggest the exposed workflow fields.

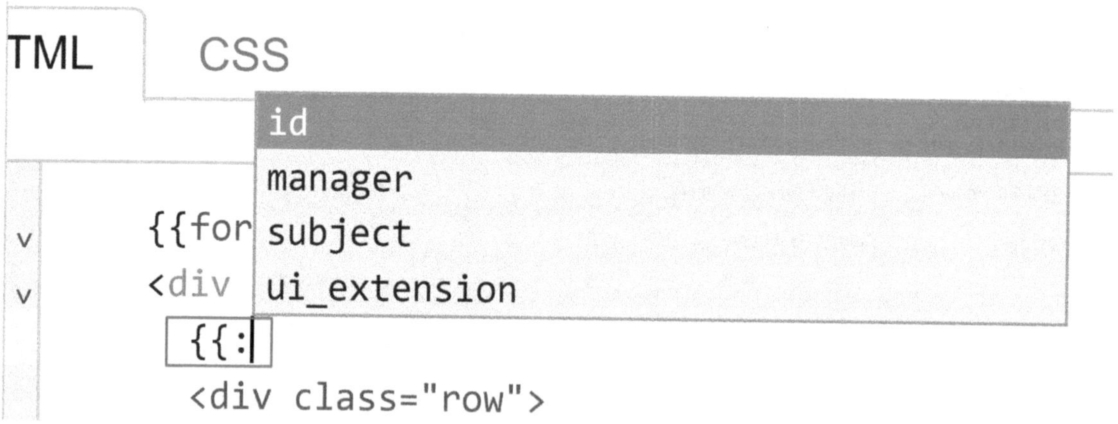

Figure 274: The PDF Design editor provides pop-up suggestions.

An essential field often included in PDFs is `recipient`—the person for whom the PDF is generated. This is coupled with `now` to indicate when the PDF was generated. However, it's important to remember that you can't use the recipient variable directly in the HTML for the PDF, as `recipient` is an object and the PDF requires strings. Therefore, you would use `{{recipient.name}}` to include the recipient's name. For instance, the beginning of the default workflow summary contains:

```
<div class="row">

  <label>Generated for</label>

  <div class="value">

    <span class="recipient">{{:recipient.name}}</span>

    <span class="postfix">{{:now}}</span>

  </div>

</div>
```

This code snippet, styled with the default CSS, generates the following PDF:

Workflow Summary for Approver

Summary of workflow: #1727 Expense Reporting Release r12.4.2
Generated for: Howard Tanner, Sun, Jun 30, 2024 11:59am CDT

Figure 275: This image showcases the PDF output, emphasizing the 'Generated for' line. This line dynamically incorporates the recipient's name and the current date and time using the recipient.name and now variables.

Conditional Statements and Loops

Mastering the art of dynamic content within PDF designs hinges on effectively using conditional statements and loops. These tools breathe life into your documents, ensuring each PDF is tailored and relevant:

- The `{{if condition ...}}` ... `{{/if}}` construct allows content to appear only when a specific condition is met, adding a layer of decision-making to your design.
- With `{{for objects}}` ... `{{/for}}`, you can iterate over a list, applying template content to each item. This is perfect for listing related records like requests or problems.
- `{{unless condition}}` serves as a filter within loops, including only those objects that meet a specified criterion.

Note that entering a `{{for}}` loop changes the context. Initially, `{{:}}` tags expose fields related to the workflow. Once inside a loop, these tags dynamically shift to present fields related to the current item in the loop, such as a request or problem.

Let's check the default workflow summary. A workflow might be associated with several requests and problems. Integrating these records into your summary necessitates the use of conditions, loops, and the unless statement. The initial check—using conditional blocks—determines if there are any linked requests or problems by verifying that **workflow.requests.length** or **workflow.problems.length** are greater than zero. A loop then iterates through all requests and will display the request ID, the request subject and the requester. However, a 'request group', the request type that bundles a number of 'grouped requests', doesn't have a requester. So, we will not include request groups in the overview by defining an **unless** statement based on the **grouping_key** field.

The following snippet from the default workflow summary PDF design illustrates this approach:

```
{{if workflow.requests.length || workflow.problems.length}}

  <section>

  <h2>Created For</h2>

  {{for workflow.requests}}

  {{unless grouping_key == 'group'}}

      <!-- HTML content goes here -→

    {{/unless}}

  {{/for}}

      <!-- Additional HTML content -→

  {{for workflow.problems}}

  {{/for}}

  </section>

{{/if}}
```

Created For

Request #699510:	Add an approval delegate via the app	
Requested for:	**Bobby Baird**	
Request #699610:	Load cost centers from SAP on a daily basis	
Requested for:	**Bobby Baird**	

Figure 276: The request overview in a workflow summary.

Going up the data hierarchy

Within a loop, the current object is the 'data context', and within that context you only have direct access to the fields of the current object. However, JsRender provides mechanisms to reach beyond this immediate scope:

- **Accessing Parent Data**: When the need arises to refer to a field in an object one level up the hierarchy, use **{{:#parent.field}}**. This notation breaks out of the current context to access a parent object's field.

- **Accessing Root Data**: For scenarios requiring a leap back to the top-level object, `{{:~root.root_object.field}}` navigates directly to any field within the root object, bypassing intervening levels.

As an example, in the default workflow summary a list of workflow implementation tasks is included. But the list doesn't specify the member to whom the task is assigned. Let's modify the default workflow summary to display the member name assigned to each task, mark it with a dash ("-") if unassigned, and highlight the name in bold if the task is assigned to the PDF's recipient. The following code snippet elegantly accomplishes this:

```
{{for workflow.tasks}}

    <!-- Other HTML content goes here -→

    <div class="row">

      <label>Member</label>

      <div class="value">

        {{if member}}

          {{if member.id == ~root.recipient.id}}

            <strong>{{:member.name}}</strong>

          {{else}}

            {{:member.name}}

          {{/if}}

        {{else}}

          -

        {{/if}}

      </div>

    </div>

    <!-- Other HTML content goes here -→

{{/for}}
```

Implementation

Task #21357:	Upgrade Ubuntu from v9.04 to v9.10 on CMP00048
Impact:	Top - Service Down for Several Users
Member:	**Howard Tanner**
Planned start:	Wed, Jul 03, 2024 02:00pm CDT
Completion target:	Wed, Jul 03, 2024 04:00pm CDT
Duration:	about 2 hours

Figure 277: Displaying task member assignments in the workflow summary, with the member's name highlighted in bold when the task is assigned to the recipient of the PDF.

CSS: Layout and Styling

Testing and Debugging PDF Designs

The objective of CSS is to add layout and styling to the HTML structure. This includes adjusting font sizes, colors, spacing, and other design elements to match your organizational branding and content presentation needs. Refining the CSS styling of PDF designs typically involves a cycle of trial and error to achieve the desired appearance. To facilitate this design refinement process, the 4me PDF Design editor offers an on-the-fly PDF generation feature.

By clicking the "Generate sample..." link, you can choose a specific workflow, project, or dashboard depending on your PDF design's category. Be aware that this option is not available for an *account designer* without the *specialist* role; the account designer doesn't have access to these records.

The Generate sample window also presents two format options: PDF and HTML. For ongoing design adjustments, selecting the HTML option allows you to leverage your browser's Developer Tools for rapid experimentation and testing. This approach is invaluable for making swift design modifications and assessing their immediate effects on the document's layout and aesthetics. Conversely, generating a sample in PDF format is ideal for final reviews, as it accurately represents the appearance that the recipient will encounter.

Adding Fonts for PDF Design Precision

Gaining full control over your PDF layout includes specifying the fonts used in the document. Like self-service design, fonts can be uploaded to the media library and incorporated in the CSS page using the @ font-face at-rule. For instance:

```css
@font-face {
    font-family: 'roboto';
    font-style: normal;
    font-weight: 400;
    src: url('https://… /roboto-400.woff2') format('woff2'),
      url('https://…/roboto-400.woff') format(,woff');
}
```

After uploading your font files, integrate the font into your document styling. For example:

```
body {
    font-family: Roboto, sans-serif;
    font-size: 1.2rem;
    line-height: 1.4;
}
```

This approach ensures that your generated PDFs maintain a consistent appearance, closely aligned with your branding and design preferences.

Using a Table Layout for Enhanced PDF Design

Tables might not be ideal for self-service designs due to their lack of scalability on smaller devices like smartphones, but they can be quite useful in PDF designs. Incorporating a table layout can significantly improve control over element visibility across pages, especially for adding headers or footers that recur on every page, such as logos.

Here's how you can implement this:

1. Enclose the entire HTML content of your PDF design within a `<table>` element, including a `<tbody>` for the main content.
2. To create a repeating header, insert a `<thead>` element at the beginning of the table. Place the content you wish to appear at the top of every page inside this section.
3. For a repeating footer, include a `<tfoot>` element at the beginning of the table, adding content that should appear at the bottom of every page.

To ensure these elements display correctly across pages in your PDF, add the following CSS:

```
thead {
    display: table-header-group;
}
tfoot {
    display: table-footer-group;
}
```

Using Flex Layout

Now, imagine you want to add the company logo and the title of the PDF design in the table header, with the logo positioned on the left and the title on the right side within a table cell. You can use

CSS Flexbox for a simple and effective solution. First, you'll need to wrap your image and text in a container (a <div>, for example) that you can then apply Flexbox styling to. Here's how you could adjust your HTML:

```html
<thead>
    <tr>
      <td>
        <div class="content-container">
          <img src="https://.../logo.png">
          <h1>Workflow Summary for Approver</h1>
        </div>
      </td>
    </tr>
</thead>
```

Then, apply the following CSS:

```css
.content-container {
  display: flex;
  align-items: center;
}

.content-container img {
  margin-right: 10px;
}
```

In this CSS:

- **display: flex;** turns the .content-container into a flex container, making its children (the **<img>** and the **<h1>**) flex items. By default, flex items are laid out horizontally, which aligns with your requirement.
- **align-items: center;** vertically centers the flex items within the container. This is useful if your table cell has more height than your content and you want the logo and text vertically aligned in the middle.
- **margin-right: 10px;** on the **<img>** element adds some space between the image and the text, making it visually separated and more readable. You can adjust this value as needed.

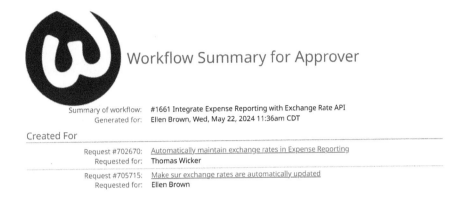

Summary of workflow:	#1661 Integrate Expense Reporting with Exchange Rate API
Generated for:	Ellen Brown, Wed, May 22, 2024 11:36am CDT

Created For

Request #702670:	Automatically maintain exchange rates in Expense Reporting
Requested for:	Thomas Wicker
Request #705715:	Make sur exchange rates are automatically updated
Requested for:	Ellen Brown

Figure 278: The workflow summary in a table format. The header with the logo will be visible at the top of each page.

PART IV

The Complete Service Management System

Expanding the 4me Universe

Introduction

Welcome to the next stage of your journey with 4me. In Part III of this book, you've ventured through the customization layer built atop the 4me core, adjusting 4me's configuration to perfectly align with your organization's unique processes and procedures. You've experienced how the 4me core acts as an unchangeable backbone, supporting your organization's service-driven operating model. This steadfast foundation fosters effortless collaboration across internal and external organizational boundaries, enabling solid and transparent reporting regardless of customization levels.

As we delve into Part IV, we'll explore the array of additional functionalities that 4me offers beyond its core capabilities. From comprehensive risk management to dynamic project management, from an intuitive reservations module to a fully-featured webshop, 4me evolves into a holistic enterprise service management solution, fulfilling every expectation you might have from such a platform.

As you venture into this part of the book, you'll discover that these aren't standalone modules requiring separate licenses. Instead, they are intrinsic parts of the 4me package, waiting to be activated and utilized. Embedded deeply in the 4me philosophy, these features extend the core principles you're already familiar with, without forming technical silos. They are designed to integrate seamlessly into a service-driven operating model, offering straightforward configuration for immediate utility. Prepare to experience why 4me is celebrated as the fastest enterprise service management platform on (planet) earth, where every added functionality enriches your experience without compromising speed or efficiency.

Chapter 17 - Time Tracking and Cost Management

Introduction

4me's approach to time tracking is notably user-friendly. It integrates seamlessly into the daily workflow of specialists, making it a natural part of ticket management. However, activating time tracking from the outset is not just a procedural step; it's a strategic move, especially on the 4me platform. Time tracking forms the bedrock for efficient resource planning, a critical aspect of any enterprise service management ecosystem. Beyond resource planning, time tracking serves as a crucial component of comprehensive cost management. Given that a significant portion of service costs is attributable to specialist activities, time tracking effectively completes this segment of the cost management puzzle.

For Managed Service Providers (MSPs), initiating time tracking from day one is almost a given. The necessity of this functionality extends beyond mere operational metrics to the core of customer billing and charging practices. Specialists within MSPs understand the critical nature of accurate time tracking, recognizing its direct impact on the financial health of their services. They'll find the time tracking features on the 4me platform refreshingly straightforward, facilitating a smooth transition into regular use.

Conversely, in enterprise and corporate settings, where services are delivered internally, the introduction of time tracking requires a more nuanced approach. It's essential to accompany this implementation with thorough organizational change management, ensuring that all team members grasp the importance of time tracking, understand its usage, and recognize the personal and collective benefits. This chapter will delve into the specifics of implementing time tracking effectively, covering both the 'how' and the 'why' to ensure a clear understanding and successful adoption. Let's start by unpacking how time tracking operates within the 4me environment.

Understanding Time Entries in 4me

Time entries form the core of time tracking in 4me. Essentially, a time entry quantifies the time spent on an activity, measured in minutes. In the user interface, time is displayed in an hh : mm format, though users can input time directly in minutes. For example, inputting "75" automatically converts to "01 : 15".

A time entry not only records the duration of time spent but also addresses three critical questions: Who spent the time? When was it spent? and What was accomplished?

- **Who Spent the Time?** This is determined by the **Person** who logs the time entry.
- **When Was the Time Spent?** The 'When' is detailed by the '**Date**' and '**Start At**' fields. It is automatically filled when a time entry is registered, but can be adjusted afterward if necessary.

- **What Has Been Done?** This is defined by the activity associated with the time spent.

Assignment vs. Allocation Time Tracking

There are two primary ways to report time spent:

- **Assignment Time Tracking**: Time associated with specific tickets - requests, problems, (workflow) tasks, or project tasks.
- **Allocation Time Tracking**: Used for activities not directly tied to a ticket, like training, meetings, or travel. This form of tracking utilizes Time allocations and can include descriptive details for audit purposes or clarity.

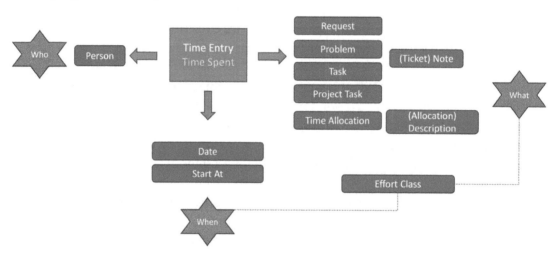

Figure 280: A time entry answers 3 questions: 'Who?', 'When?' and 'What?'.

Effort Classes and Their Role

Effort classes provide additional context to time entries, clarifying when and what activities were performed. They're particularly useful for indicating work done outside normal business hours or specifying the nature of the task (e.g., regular duties versus overtime work). For MSPs, effort classes help categorize activities by their billing rates when one person has multiple skills can perform multiple roles, such as software development and software architecture.

Other Time Entry Fields

Beyond those already discussed, time entries in 4me feature numerous additional fields. For a detailed overview, refer to the time entry record documentation in the GraphQL and REST API sections on the

4me developer site (https://developer.4me.com). Certain fields are particularly relevant for the billing and charging processes; these will be explored further in the next chapter.

An interesting aspect of a time entry is the '**Team**' field. Specialists may be part of multiple teams across various accounts, and for accurate reporting, 4me needs to allocate time entries to the correct team. This allocation is automatically determined when a specialist submits a time entry for a ticket, based on the context. For example, if the request is associated with a service instance and the specialist is a member of that service instance's first-line support team, the 'Team' field in the time entry will be set to this specific team.

The User Experience with Time Tracking in 4me

In 4me, every user has the capability to track their time, extending this functionality to the self-service portal for end users. Typically, end users don't handle tickets, except when they're involved in approval or project tasks, meaning they often engage in Allocation Time Tracking. The Self-Service Design can be customized to include the 'Time spent today' widget, directing users to a calendar view where they can log time entries for any day or compile a weekly summary. Clicking on the '+' symbol allows them to choose a time allocation and fill in pertinent details.

Figure 281: The 'Time spent today' widget on the self-service portal.

For specialists, the '**Time spent today**' feature becomes available in the specialist UI once time tracking is activated in their profile. Just like end users, specialists can also utilize this feature for Allocation Time Tracking, allowing them to log time spent on non-ticket related activities such as training sessions, meetings, holidays, and other overhead activities. However, specialists predominantly work within tickets, and 4me has optimized this process for ease of use. When editing a ticket to add a note, specialists can (or should) record the time spent and select an effort class if needed. The system aids efficiency

Figure 282: When registering time on a ticket, 4me makes some useful suggestions.

by suggesting possible durations based on the user's current activities, such as the time elapsed since the record was first accessed or since the day's first activity. This method of recording time as work on a ticket is performed provides a precise overview of how time is allocated across support activities, significantly surpassing the accuracy of retrospective time reporting methods, which often rely on flawed memory recall at the day's or week's end.

The Management Perspective

Management Insights into Timesheets

Every individual on the platform can access their own timesheets via the (My) Timesheets section, available in both the Self-Service Portal and the Analytics console for specialists. Most users can only view their personal timesheets.

However, *Account administrators* and *financial managers* have broader access, allowing them to view timesheets across a range of users.

Directory account administrators and those holding the *financial manager* role within the directory account have the capability to oversee timesheets for all users linked to organizations defined in the directory account.

Similarly, *administrators* and *financial managers* within a support domain account can access timesheets for users of the organization of the account, including all descendant organizations. Moreover, they have access to the timesheets of the users of external organizations defined within the support domain account. For example, in a demo environment where the Widget Data Center account is associated with an organization of the same name, which in turn has three child organizations, a financial manager in the Widget Data Center account can review the timesheets of all users belonging to these organizations.

Figure 283: A financial manager in the Widget Data Center support domain account has access to view the Timesheets (available in the Analytics console) of all individuals associated with the Widget Data Center organizations and their descendants.

Also, the *managers* and their *substitutes* of the organizations are granted enhanced access to timesheets, enabling them to peruse time entries for all users of their managed organizations.

Time Spent on Tickets

Once Assignment Time Tracking is enabled, the 4me platform offers detailed insights into the time spent on tickets in the Time Entries section. The time spent is consolidated by person. By selecting an individual's time spent, users can access a detailed list of that person's time entries.

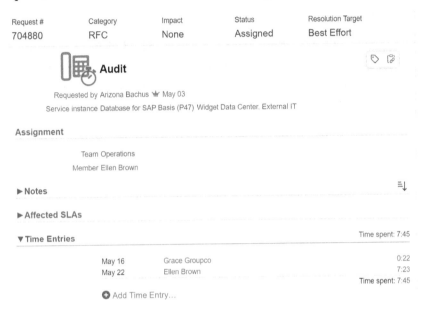

Figure 284: Example of time spent in the Time Entries section on request.

Additionally, when workflow tasks and project tasks are assigned to individuals from a trusted account, their time spent can also be shared.

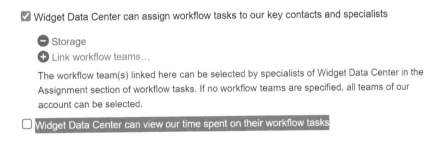

Figure 285: The supplier account can allow the customer to see their time spent on the customer tasks assigned to them.

This sharing capability is controlled through the following two settings on a trust:

- '*Trusted Account* can view our time spent on their workflow tasks'
- '*Trusted Account* can view our time spent on their project tasks'

To ensure privacy and comply with data protection regulations, time entries from a trusted account are presented in a non-clickable format, preventing the disclosure of personal information. This feature is particularly beneficial in collaborations with suppliers working on a time and materials basis on workflows or projects, allowing workflow managers or project managers from the customer to verify the supplier's reported time on their workflows and projects directly within 4me.

Time Spent on Workflows

In the Time Entries section of a workflow record, a consolidated view of the time spent is provided. This view encompasses not only each related workflow task but also associated requests and problems. Furthermore, the workflow summary offers a comparison between the **Total Planned Effort** and the **Actual Effort**, which represents the total time spent across all related records.

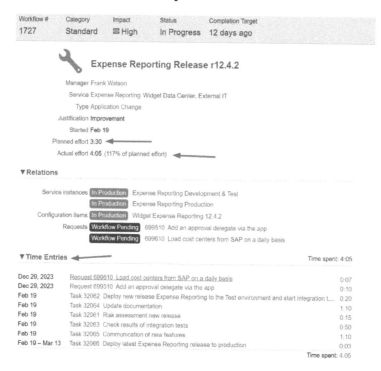

Figure 286: The consolidated view on time spent on a workflow, including the deviation from the consolidated Planned Effort (budget).

This feature holds particular significance for Managed Service Providers (MSPs). It enables them to define planned effort both for customer requests and tasks within the related workflow, representing the total budget allocated for a customer's request. By comparing the actual time spent across all records to the total planned effort, MSPs can readily identify any deviations from the budget.

Time Spent Reports

Beyond individual workflow insights, 4me's reporting capabilities extend to offer aggregated views of time spent versus budgeted time across multiple requests and workflows.

One particularly useful report is the '**Time Spent on Requests and Related Workflows**,' available for both open and completed requests. This report displays on the X-axis different ranges of consolidated time spent and on the Y-axis the number of requests within each time spent range. Filtering this report by a specific workflow template can highlight outliers—requests where the time spent significantly exceeds expectations. Additionally, a wide variance in time spent on similar requests could indicate a lack of standardization in execution, often pointing to potential quality issues.

A companion report shifts the focus towards budgetary analysis, specifically the total planned effort versus actual effort for workflows and their related requests and problems. The reports '**Actual Versus Planned Effort for Workflows and Related Requests and Problems**' for both open and completed workflow highlight significant deviations between budgeted and actual efforts. For MSPs, this insight is crucial for evaluating the financial health of their request fulfillment process.

Each 4me account includes an extensive range of reports dedicated to tracking time spent and the costs associated with it, but these are initially turned off. As we'll explore in a later section dedicated to organizational

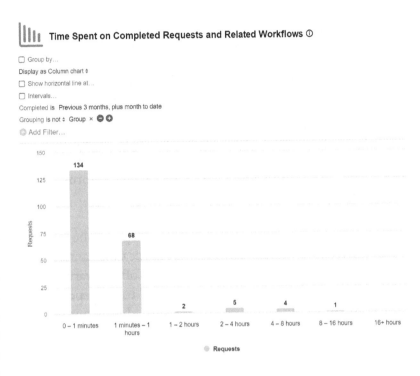

Figure 287: The report 'Time Spent on Completed Requests and Related Workflows' allows the identification of outliers.

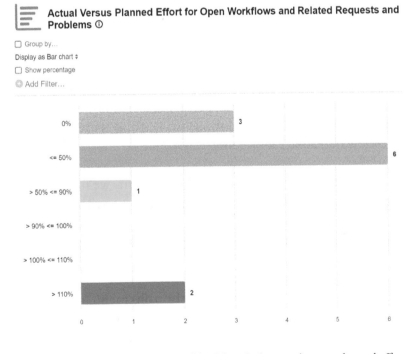

Figure 288: Evaluating the financial health with the actual versus planned effort reports.

change management, it's vital to approach time tracking with caution, particularly regarding performance measurement.

Emphasizing individual or team performance based solely on time spent can lead to skewed and unreliable time entries. When personnel perceive their performance is judged by the amount of time logged, there's a significant risk of time tracking data being manipulated, undermining the integrity of information critical for making informed management decisions.

Thus, activating and utilizing time spent reports should be approached with thoughtful communication and a strategic mindset. Additionally, the platform offers a variety of reports focusing on the costs incurred due to time spent, which are accessible exclusively to account administrators and financial managers for good reason.

Reports

TITLE
Cost of Time Spent
Cost of Time Spent by Customer
Cost of Time Spent by Person
Cost of Time Spent by Project
Cost of Time Spent by Service
Cost of Time Spent by Service Instance
Cost of Time Spent by Team
Time Spent
Time Spent by Customer
Time Spent by Person
Time Spent by Project
Time Spent by Request Category
Time Spent by Service
Time Spent by Service Instance
Time Spent by Team
Time Spent by Time Allocation
Time Spent by Time Allocation Group
Time Spent on Completed Requests
Time Spent on Completed Requests and Related Workflows
Time Spent on Open Requests
Time Spent on Open Requests and Related Workflows

Figure 289: Each 4me account includes a large collection of reports related to time entries, time spent and the cost of time spent. By default, these reports are disabled, but they can be enabled by an account administrator.

The 4me Resource Planning View

The Resource Planning view stands out as a potent utility within the 4me platform, designed to offer all specialists an account-wide perspective on resource availability versus demand. This tool is not only beneficial for individual specialists but also for teams and skill pools, providing a comprehensive overview of resource allocations.

In the chapter ahead on Project Management, we'll delve into how project managers can leverage this view to streamline resource management within project contexts. The Resource Planning view ensures a holistic approach; for instance, if a specialist is part of multiple teams or involved in several projects, the tool aggregates resource demands from all these engagements, offering complete visibility.

Accessible through the Actions (gear button) menu in the Inbox or within the Analytics console, the Resource Planning view is an invaluable asset for optimizing resource allocation and ensuring project and task demands align with available capacities.

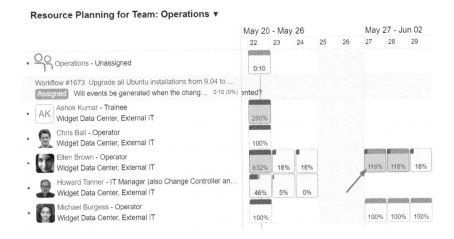

Figure 290: The Resource Planning view, accessible via the Actions menu in the Inbox, offers a comprehensive overview of resource demand compared to resource availability within a team. Instances of over-allocation are immediately identifiable, facilitating efficient resource management.

Understanding Resource Demand vs. Resource Availability

The Resource Planning view calculates an allocation percentage for each individual and each calendar day, revealing the balance between resource demand and availability. An allocation percentage over 100% indicates that demand exceeds availability, signaling potential resource allocation issues.

Here's a breakdown of how this calculation works for workflow tasks (the calculation is similar for project tasks):

- **Resource Demand**: This is represented by the total allocated hours for workflow tasks within a specified period, with the minimum period being one day.
- **Allocated Hours for Workflow Tasks**: These are determined based on the team's work hours, the task's planned or actual start date, remaining effort, and planned duration.
  - **Workflow Schedule**: Indicates the intended start or actual start date of a task.
  - **Remaining Effort**: Calculated as the planned effort minus any actual time spent on the task.
  - **Task Completion Target**: Derived from the team's work hours and the task's planned duration, indicating when the task is expected to be completed.
  - **Allocation Percentage**: The ratio of remaining effort to planned duration, indicating how much of the task is expected to be completed each day.
  - **Allocated Hours per Day**: For each day within the task's start and completion target, the platform calculates available hours. The number of allocated hours per day is then determined by multiplying the allocation percentage by the day's available hours.

The Resource Planning view provides some nice features:

Box Details Explained: The gray bar at the top of each box visually represents the work assigned to an individual. The darkest gray portion indicates planned project work. A slightly lighter gray shows planned change work. The lightest gray represents time allocations. Clicking on a box opens a detailed view. The header on the detailed view shows the Period, Active Hours, Allocated Hours, and Allocation %. Below, you'll find a list of all planned activities for the resource within the specified period. Clickable entries allow for adjustments to the planned duration directly from this view.

Person	Period	Active Hours	Allocated Hours	Utilization
Ellen Brown	May 27	8:00	9:17	116%

Allocation Details

Project #7497 Digital Operations Center (DOC)	**1:17**
Task #24500 Set up production environment	1:17
Mon, May 20, 2024 03:10pm CDT – Thu, May 30, 2024 11:10am CDT	

Time Entries	**8:00**
Time Off - Vacation	8:00

Figure 291: Opening a box in the Resource Planning view reveals the specifics behind the over-allocation. A 116% allocation indicates Ellen Brown is on holiday, impacting her available working hours.

Resource Assignment Details: Expanding a person's row reveals all activities planned for them, alongside each activity's planned duration and its allocation percentage. Absence of an allocation % suggests no defined planned effort, leading to potential overallocation due to 4me defaulting remaining effort to equal planned duration.

Figure 292: Expanding a row in the Resource Planning gives a complete overview of all planned activities.

Team and Skill Pool Rows: Teams and skill pools have their workload represented by boxes indicating unassigned tasks' requested hours in absolute numbers rather than percentages. This design helps resource managers gauge the volume of work pending assignment.

Drag and Drop for Efficient Resource Planning: Workflow and project managers can redistribute work by dragging tasks from unassigned team or skill pool queues to individuals or from one individual to another. This does not apply to approval tasks, which cannot be reassigned via drag and drop.

Addressing the Work Backlog: If a task's completion target is past due, its allocated hours accumulate in the "Today" box, highlighting the backlog of overdue work clearly in the Resource Planning view.

As of now, the Resource Planning view does not account for the unplanned workload associated with requests and problems. However, the integration of 4me with artificial intelligence (AI) technologies presents promising avenues for future enhancements. AI capabilities could enable the platform to accurately estimate the planned effort for requests by leveraging the context of services and analyzing historical data. Additionally, by utilizing the target dates specified by the affected SLAs, it may become feasible to incorporate requests and problems into the Resource Planning view.

Time Tracking and Cost Management
Use the Resource Planning view

Ellen Brown, the Operations Team Coordinator at Widget Data Center, faces an unexpected challenge. The application development team's expert, Frank Watson, is out sick, and this week's deployment of the Expense Reporting release is at risk. How can Ellen ensure the release still goes out on time? Let's dive into how she leverages the Resource Planning view in 4me to find the team member with the best availability to take over the task.

- Ellen logs in as ellen.brown@widget.com to the Widget Data Center account.
  - **Navigate to the Task**: She proceeds to the Records console to find task #32066, titled "*Deploy latest Expense Reporting release to production.*"
    - Edit the Task Details:
    - Ellen edits the task, setting "*Start no earlier than*" to the upcoming Friday at 09:00 am.
    - She assigns the task to the Operations team and saves her changes.
  - **Checking Availability**:
    - Back in her Inbox, Ellen sees the task but needs to confirm who's available on Friday morning.
    - She clicks on the Actions menu (gear button) and selects Resource Planning.
    - Ellen chooses "Resource Planning for Team ..." and selects the Operations Team.
    - Expanding the Operations team line by clicking the arrow on the left, she spots the still unassigned workflow task.
  - **Assigning the Task**: Ellen finds a team member with no allocations on Friday morning by hovering over the task and then drags and drops it onto their row.

FLSA Reports and Time Tracking

Time tracking plays a crucial role in evaluating the performance of a service desk within an account. In the Analytics console, under the First Line Support Agreement (FLSA) reports, there's a section dedicated to **Service Desk Activity**. For any given month, this section showcases key performance indicators, such as first call resolutions, and updates and completions of requests. These metrics are derived from time entries, making time tracking essential for their accuracy. Without enabling time tracking, these crucial figures reflecting service desk efficiency will not be available.

KPI	Target	Actual	Past 12 Months
Pickups within target ⓘ	>= 85%	100.00%	
● First call resolutions ⓘ	>= 40%	30.00%	
Service desk only resolutions ⓘ	>= 50%	60.00%	
Service desk resolutions ⓘ	>= 60%	80.00%	
Rejected solutions ⓘ	< 10%	0.00%	

Service Desk Customer Satisfaction

👍 **50%**   👍 2 Satisfied
👎 2 Dissatisfied
67% Response rate

Service Desk Activity ⓘ	Count
Registration of new requests completed on first call	3
Registration of new requests not completed on first call	3
Updates of existing requests	1
Completion of existing requests	1
Totals	**8**

Figure 293: The numbers in the Service Desk Activity section of the First Line Support Agreement (FLSA) reports in the Analytics Console are based on time entries.

Integrating 4me's Time Registration with Other Systems

There's often a requirement to export time entries from 4me, such as exporting time spent outside business hours to a payroll system for overtime payment. These integrations are relatively straightforward, as time entries, like all other records, are accessible via 4me's APIs (GraphQL, REST API, and Bulk export/import). Because performing a 4me API call always requires the specification of the target 4me account, it's important to understand one key rule: time entry records are stored within the user's organizational account, typically the directory account.

Tip

For effective resource planning, it's crucial to account for unavailability due to holidays and sick leave. These time allocations should be integrated and accessible. However, to streamline processes and enhance user experience, avoid requiring users to register their holidays in multiple systems. Instead, develop an integration between 4me and your HR platform to seamlessly register holiday time and sick leave.

Setting Up Time Tracking

Enabling time tracking in 4me is a straightforward process that can be completed in three key steps, with only the final step being mandatory:

1. **Defining Effort Classes (Optional)**: This step is not required but can help differentiate the types of work performed.
2. **Defining Time Allocations (Optional)**: While not essential, this step allows for tracking of time spent not related to tickets.
3. **Defining Time Sheet Settings**: This crucial step is required to activate and configure the time tracking functionality.

Defining Effort Classes

Effort classes are not required for all setups. In corporate environments, particularly those with support domain accounts serving internal users, effort classes are primarily employed to distinguish between activities completed during standard business hours versus those conducted outside these times.

Tip	**Understanding the 'Start At' Field versus Effort Classes** While you might consider using the 'Start At' field of a time entry to determine if an activity occurred outside normal business hours, remember that this field is automatically populated when a time entry is created. Specialists recording their overtime on the following day will need to manually adjust this field, which could lead to inaccuracies. Therefore, opting to use effort classes to categorize activities by time of day—such as distinguishing between standard office hours and overtime—can be a more effective strategy.

Determining the Right Account for Effort Class Definitions

Effort classes can be established within either the directory account or the support domain accounts, depending on the operational context and specific requirements.

In the Directory Account: This setup is ideal for scenarios where the application of effort classes is tied to the user's organizational affiliation. This setup allows effort classes to be associated with the timesheet settings specific to the user's organization, commonly seen in corporate environments. For example, IT departments may frequently engage in overtime activities and therefore require the use of effort classes, whereas HR departments might not typically log hours beyond standard business times.

In the Support Domain Account: This approach is more suited for contexts where effort class selection is linked to contractual terms, typical of Managed Service Providers (MSPs). Here, effort classes correspond to the profiles stipulated within service contracts. By attaching these effort classes to service offerings, the appropriate effort class becomes accessible in alignment with the relevant SLA. This methodology aligns closely with contractual obligations and service delivery metrics. More details on this approach will be explored in the subsequent chapter.

The Fields of an Effort Class

An effort class consists of the following attributes:

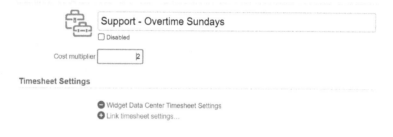

- **Name**: Choose a clear and descriptive name for each effort class. This name is what users will see and select when they log their time, so it should clearly convey the nature of the work or conditions under which the work was performed.

Figure 294: Defining effort classes. It is not possible to link the effort class to a skill pool in a directory account.

- **Cost Multiplier (optional)**: Important for accurate cost management. Time spent outside normal business hours is probably more expensive. This cost is calculated by multiplying the normal cost by this specific cost multiplier. This figure relates to the internal cost to be allocated to the service provider organization, not the price billed or charged to clients.
- **Linked Timesheet Settings**: By associating an effort class with specific timesheet settings, that effort class becomes selectable for individuals whose organizational timesheet settings align.
- **Skill Pool (optional)**: This option becomes accessible only when skill pools are established within the account. Only those specialists that belong to the skill pool will get the effort class as an option. Note that in a directory account, this field remains unavailable, as skill pools cannot be defined there.

Defining Time Allocations

If you aim to have users log all their working hours, time allocations are essential. These are particularly useful for gaining insight into overhead costs inherent in every organization. Moreover, time allocations aid in resource planning by accounting for non-ticket activities like holidays, sick leave, and training within resource calendars. Initially, the key step is to catalog the variety of non-ticket-related tasks.

Avoid Over-Engineering

Simplicity is key when creating your list of time allocations. An overly extensive list can impede efficiency and potentially compromise data accuracy, as users might be prone to selecting an incorrect category. To mitigate this, consider including a universal time category, such as 'Other,' to cover all uncommon scenarios.

Determining the Right Account for Time Allocations

Time allocations should be set up within support domain accounts. This enables account administrators in these specific domains to create time allocations tailored to their own area of support, which may not be applicable to specialists in other domains.

For standard time allocations that are common across different support domains, such as 'Vacation' or 'Medical Leave,' it's a sound practice to centralize their management in a single support domain account. Typically, this would be the account tasked with overseeing enterprise service management within the corporate structure.

The Fields of a Time Allocation

- **Name**: Ensure the name is clear and straightforward so that it is easily recognizable by your employees.
- **Organizations**: Time allocations must be linked to specific organizations. Only members of these designated organizations can select these time allocations when logging new time entries.
- **Group**: To manage a lengthy list of time allocations effectively, they can be categorized into groups. This organization aids users in locating the correct time allocation and can simplify reporting. For instance, creating a 'Time Off' group for all non-working time allocations is practical.

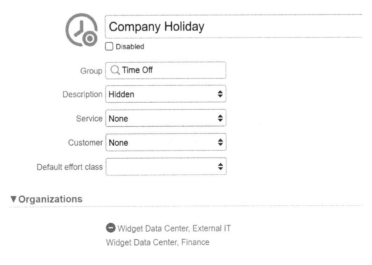

Figure 295: A Time Allocation must be defined in a support domain account.

- **Description**: For certain time allocations, providing additional details could be beneficial. For example, for the "Training" time allocation, it can be useful to know which training the user attended. This field can be configured as 'Hidden', 'Optional', or 'Required' based on the need for this detail.

- **Service and Customer**: For certain service-related activities, there may not be a specific ticket available to register the time spent. For example, a customer success organization might hold regular meetings with their customers, for which a dedicated time allocation could be created. For such time allocations, it is beneficial to break down the time spent by customer and service. The 'Service and Customer' fields can be set to 'Hidden', 'Any', or 'One of the Following', allowing employees to specify which services or customers are related when logging a time entry.

- **Default Effort Class**: In the case of a time allocation used for customer success meetings, it would not be appropriate to choose an overtime effort class. This setting allows you to predefine the most applicable effort class for each specific time allocation.

Defining Timesheet Settings

Initially, time tracking is turned off in a new 4me account. To activate time tracking, simply set up a Timesheet Setting record and associate it with the organizations whose members should start tracking their time.

Determining the Right Account for Timesheet Settings

Timesheet Settings should be established within the account where the organizations of the individuals needing time tracking are located. In corporate settings, this is typically the directory account. However, if a support domain account manages external organizations, such as contractors, and requires them to track time, Timesheet Settings for these external members must be configured in the support domain account.

Configuring Timesheet Settings: Key Fields Overview

The initial setup involves deciding between enabling **Assignment Time Tracking**, **Allocation Time Tracking**, or both. Assignment Time Tracking allows specialists to log time spent on tickets. To ensure detailed documentation of activities, the '**Require Note**' option mandates an accompanying note for each time entry on a ticket.

For Allocation Time Tracking, organizations may want employees to account for their entire workweek. The '**Notify people when their timesheet is incomplete**' option triggers a 'Monday' notification for any user who hasn't logged the expected workweek hours. Customize the notification message through the '*Past Week Incomplete*' email template in the Timesheet Settings account. Ensure this template is active for effective communication.

Allocation Time Tracking settings include:

- Normal workday and workweek hours.
- Options for users to record workday and workweek **overtime.**
- Preferences for logging time on allocations, either as a **percentage** of the workday or in **absolute hours**.
- Minimum and maximum time that can be logged on an allocation, ranging from 5 minutes to 4 hours, or in percentages from 12.5% to 100% of a workday.

Effort classes, if defined in the account, can be associated with Timesheet Settings. You can set default effort classes for each ticket type and time allocation, with the flexibility to specify different default effort classes for individual time allocations.

The final step is linking Timesheet Settings to **Organizations**, which specifies which users are governed by these settings.

Figure 296: Defining Timesheet Settings and linking these settings to organizations. These Timesheet Settings will apply to all the people of the associated organizations.

Organizational Change Management

The introduction of time tracking within an organization can raise concerns among employees regarding autonomy, privacy, and perceived productivity scrutiny. Addressing these concerns effectively is vital to ensure that time tracking is embraced as a tool for enhancing operational efficiency rather than strict oversight.

Successful implementation relies on building trust and transparency through thoughtful organizational change management. Consider the following guidelines to alleviate concerns and emphasize the benefits of time tracking:

1. **Clarify Purpose and Benefits**: Clearly communicate the objectives behind time tracking and its benefits for both the organization and its employees. Whether it's for more accurate billing, identifying overtime, or better resource allocation, highlighting these goals demystifies the process. Emphasize benefits like preventing burnout, ensuring equitable work distribution, and uncovering workflow inefficiencies to address the "What's in it for me?" question.

2. **Dispel Misconceptions**: Reassure staff that time tracking is not a surveillance tool. Make it clear that it's not intended for micromanagement or as the sole metric for performance evaluation. Emphasize understanding patterns and making informed decisions on workload and resource management, not individual activity scrutiny.

3. **Develop a Comprehensive Communication and Training Plan**: Invest in interactive sessions to explain the system, address concerns, and gather feedback. A tailored communication strategy for managers and team leaders is essential, as they play a crucial role in promoting the time tracking system.

4. **Incorporate Time Tracking in Onboarding**: To maintain the culture of time tracking, integrate it into the onboarding process for new hires, emphasizing its importance and the organization's commitment to a balanced and efficient work environment.

5. **Adhere to Golden Rules for Time Tracking**:

   - Establish and communicate clear guidelines.
   - Avoid directly linking time tracking to performance reviews.
   - Ensure transparency of time tracking data.
   - Encourage daily timesheet updates for accuracy.
   - Avoid tracking minutiae to maintain a meaningful and manageable process.

By proactively addressing potential concerns and highlighting the benefits of time tracking, organizations can cultivate a culture where time tracking is seen as a valuable tool rather than an intrusive measure. This approach not only alleviates fears but also enhances the overall acceptance and effectiveness of time tracking in achieving operational excellence.

Service Cost Tracking

In a service-driven environment, effective cost tracking requires a detailed breakdown of service costs. This detailed approach enables management to pinpoint where costs are highest and where potential savings could be made. Service costs can generally be divided into three main categories:

1. **Time Spent**: The majority of costs in service-oriented environments arise from the time employees spend on service-related tasks.
2. **Assets Required**: The physical or digital assets needed to deliver the service.
3. **Supporting Services**: The additional services required to ensure the main service is effectively delivered to end-users.

Time Spent

Traditional time-tracking methods, such as weekly timesheets assigned to cost centers, often lack the detail needed to truly understand the costs associated with specific service activities. Moreover, these methods can be prone to inaccuracies due to the inherent flaws of weekly time reporting.

The introduction of Activity-Based Costing (ABC) in the late 20th century offered a more nuanced view of cost allocation by closely analyzing activities and their cost drivers. This approach enabled organizations to gain a clearer understanding of the true costs of their products and services. However, the complexity of gathering detailed activity data has hindered its widespread adoption.

The 4me platform, with its user-friendly time tracking features, simplifies this process. It allows organizations to adopt a Service-Based Costing approach, offering a granular understanding of service-related costs, moving beyond the limitations of traditional cost tracking methods.

The diagram below outlines the key components of a Service-Based Costing model, correlating each component with its corresponding records in 4me. At the far right are the cost objects—Services in 4me terms—along with their associated service providers. The Service Provider field on the Service record identifies the organization responsible for providing the service. To the left, you'll see the activities tied to delivering a service, including tickets and, where applicable, time allocations (e.g., a service owner meeting with customer representatives).

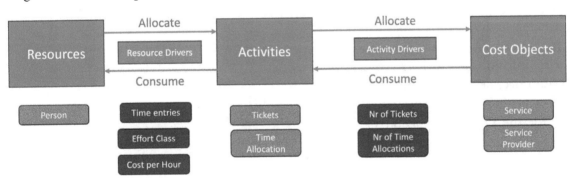

Figure 297: Service-Based Costing in 4me, via the time spent added to service related activities.

On the far left of the diagram, we identify the resources involved in service delivery. These resources, typically the employees or contractors, log their time spent on various service-related activities. 4me can calculate the cost associated with this time spent if the **cost per hour** is specified in the personnel records. Moreover, by employing effort classes, additional costs incurred from overtime are also factored in.

Assets

For the second cost component, assets play a pivotal role in the delivery of enterprise services. These assets range widely, from office furniture (like desks and chairs leased by the Facilities department) to software licenses acquired by the IT department for enterprise resource planning (ERP) services. While some asset-related costs are expensed immediately—fully attributing the purchase amount to the service—larger purchases often undergo depreciation over time. Consequently, these capital expenditures gradually contribute to the service costs across their useful life. Similarly, leased equipment costs are distributed throughout the lease term, ensuring accurate monthly service cost reporting. Maintenance and support contracts are also evenly allocated over their duration to reflect true service expenses.

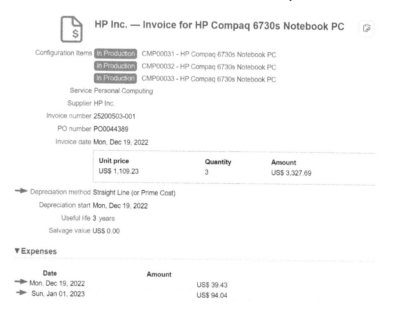

Figure 298: A configuration item is linked to a service instance, a support contract and a purchase invoice.

Within the 4me platform, essential assets for service delivery are meticulously recorded as configuration items (CIs) in the configuration management database (CMDB). These CIs are directly linked to the services they enable, facilitating a comprehensive approach to service cost tracking. Each CI can be associated with purchase invoices, detailing crucial financial information such as the purchase price, depreciation method, and depreciation period. This setup allows for the precise calculation of monthly amortization costs associated with each asset.

Furthermore, CIs can be tied to support/maintenance contracts and lease agreements, with these contracts themselves linked to specific invoices. This connection delineates the costs of contracts in relation to the CIs they encompass.

Figure 299: The purchase invoice specifies the depreciation parameters and the cost that will be expensed over the months of the depreciation period.

Supporting Services

The third critical component influencing service cost within an enterprise is associated with supporting or underpinning services. These services are integral to the delivery and functioning of primary business services, representing both internal and external contributions to service infrastructure.

4me's architecture is designed with this complexity in mind, featuring a robust service hierarchy or service chain. This framework meticulously outlines the interconnections between business services (those directly provided to customers) and supporting services. These supporting services may either be internal (managed within the same 4me account) or external (supplied through trusted 4me accounts or external providers).

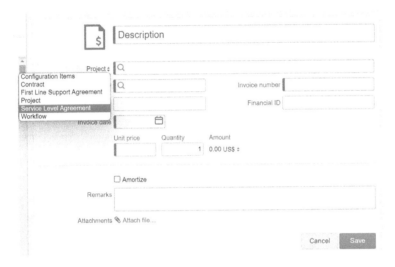

Figure 300: It is possible to link the invoice of a supplier to an SLA in 4me.

These external suppliers will send an invoice for their supporting services. These invoices can be registered in 4me and linked to the Service Level Agreement. The expenses related to the invoice will be allocated to the main service.

Service Insight Reporting

Specialists with the financial manager role have the capability to comprehensively review the costs associated with all services provided within a 4me account. This is facilitated through the "**Service Insight**" report, accessible within the Analytics console. The report's Cost section provides a monthly breakdown of service costs, distinguishing between the costs associated with time spent and other expenses.

These expenses are calculated from invoices linked either to the assets necessary for service delivery or to the Service-Level Agreements (SLAs) of supporting services. The report allows for in-depth exploration, offering users the ability to drill down into both time spent and expenses for a granular analysis of a service's cost structure.

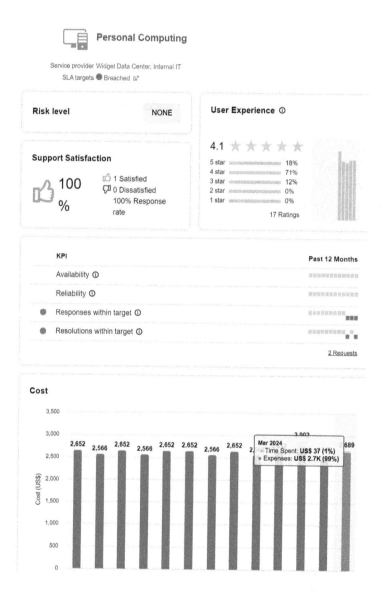

Figure 301: Service Insight provides a detailed insight of the Service Costs.

Chapter 18 - Charging and Billing

For Managed Service Providers (MSPs), billing isn't just a process; it's their lifeline. Effective billing practices are what keep an MSP afloat, distinguishing between merely surviving and thriving. After all, the ability to bill services accurately and profitably is what enables growth and ensures sustainability. Billing extends beyond mere financial transactions; it's also about efficiency and nurturing customer satisfaction. Errors or disputes in invoicing not only cause operational headaches but can also significantly dent customer trust. MSPs strive for invoicing that is timely, accurate, and, importantly, transparent.

In our exploration of the 4me platform, we've uncovered its prowess in delivering precise service-based costing. However, 4me doesn't stop there; it goes a step further by laying down the foundation for precise and streamlined service-based billing.

It's essential to note, however, that 4me isn't designed to replace your financial system. The creation and management of outgoing invoices, along with their integration into the general ledger, remain within the MSP's financial ecosystem. What 4me aims to provide is a reliable source of data reflecting the services rendered to customers. It ensures both the service provider and the customer have a clear, factual basis for the invoicing process. By adding specific fields to the service catalog, 4me equips service providers with all the necessary details to accurately feed the Billing Integration. This integration, between 4me and the MSP's financial system, generates invoices for services and activities performed.

Join us as we explore how 4me supports this critical aspect of MSP operations, enhancing both efficiency and client satisfaction.

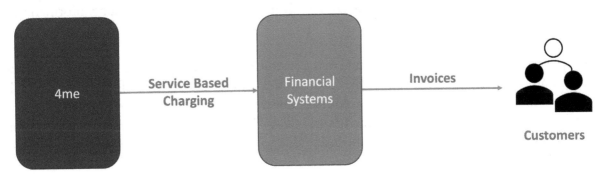

Figure 302: 4me generates service-based charging data for an MSP's financial systems, enabling the creation of customer invoices.

Understanding Service-Based Charging Data Requirements

Service-based charging data forms the backbone of an MSP's invoicing process, rooted in the specifics outlined within customer contracts. These contracts detail the billing and payment terms, shaping the foundation for generating invoices. Key elements include:

- **Payment Schedule**: Specifies the timing and frequency at which payments are due.
- **Fee Structure and Schedule**: Outlines the method for calculating fees, encompassing fixed fees, time-and-material billing, or a combination thereof.
- **Billing Structure/Policy**: Organizes and manages the billing process.
- **Rate Card**: Provides a comprehensive listing of rates for various service components or work types.

These billing and payment terms often vary from one customer contract to another, complicating the invoicing process. For example, decisions on invoicing for time-and-material requests within the month of service or upon request completion can differ based on customer-specific agreements.

4me is designed to navigate this complexity. The platform's flexibility is driven by the use of unique IDs for performed activities. These IDs can be linked to corresponding records in financial systems, allowing MSPs the flexibility to either leverage 4me's built-in fee and rate calculations or to rely on their financial systems to determine invoicing fees based on the activities logged in 4me. This dual approach ensures that regardless of an MSP's specific needs or the complexity of their billing arrangements, 4me offers a seamless and efficient pathway to accurate service-based charging.

Foundations of Billing: Requests and Time Entries

In 4me, activities are recorded through four primary ticket types: requests, problems, (workflow) tasks, and project tasks. Requests originate directly from customers, while the other ticket types are not directly linked to customer records. Therefore, the request serves as the initial key component for service-based charging. The second critical element is the time spent, documented in time entry records. Once billing is configured, 4me automatically includes comprehensive billing information in the time entries.

Time spent on requests can be directly related to the customer of the request. Time spent on (workflow) tasks and problems can be traced back to the customer through the relationship of the workflow or the problem with the corresponding customer request. However, it's worth noting that time entries related to problem management are often excluded from billing. This is because problem management aims to reduce incident frequency, providing intrinsic value to the MSP and, by extension, the customer, without direct charges.

Also project tasks of projects for external customers typically link back to the customer through the relationship of the project with a customer request (a 'demand'). But project billing, distinct from monthly service charges, usually adheres to milestones defined in the customer charter rather than a regular billing cycle.

This all means that in most environments the billing integration only needs to export requests and time entries. The integration can ignore the time entries related to problems and projects. And the time entries on workflow tasks will get their billing info from the first request related to the workflow.

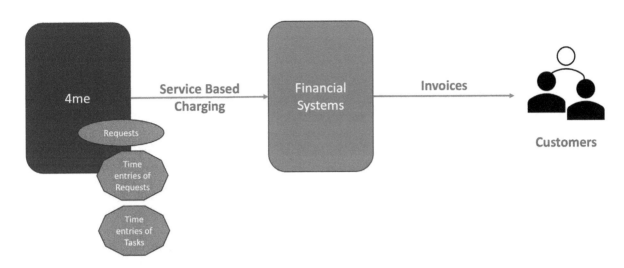

Figure 303: The billing integration needs requests and time entries on requests and workflow tasks.

Understanding the Billable SLA

In the billing process facilitated by 4me, the concept of the Billable Service Level Agreement (SLA) plays a pivotal role. As a request traverses the service hierarchy or service chain, it might engage multiple teams, encompassing both internal shared services and external suppliers. Each step in this journey generates affected SLAs that are associated with the request.

Because the SLAs for these supporting services are shared between multiple customers with different contracts and different billing and payment terms, it makes no sense to define billing info to these SLAs. When it comes to billing, only the SLA that encapsulates the contractual agreement with the customer— **the Billable SLA**—carries the necessary billing information for that customer. Each time a time entry is added to a request 4me will check if an affected SLA can be found for a Billable SLA. The information from the Billable SLA will be added to the time entry. This works in the same way for time entries added to workflow tasks. 4me will check if the (first) request related to the workflow has an affected SLA for a Billable SLA and again, the information of that Billable SLA will be added to the time entry of the task.

It's crucial to note that a request may span across multiple 4me accounts. In each account, the request can be associated with a distinct Billable SLA. When a specialist records a time entry, the Billable SLA referred to is the one from the account of their team.

A Billable SLA in 4me is distinguished through specific indicators within the SLA's financial details that underscore its billing relevance. These include:

- An Agreement ID specified in the SLA's Financial Details section, or
- Activity IDs in the SLA's Financial Details, or
- Effort classes associated with the service offering of the SLA.

Let's explore how this works.

Defining Financial IDs

When a time entry is processed by the billing integration, four main questions need to be answered.

1. Who is the customer?
2. What is the customer contract?
3. What was the activity performed?
4. What is the rate to be applied?

4me will answer these questions by adding unique financial IDs to the time entries. These financial IDs should relate to the relevant records in the MSP's financial system to generate correct invoices.

Identifying the Customer

Each time entry in 4me automatically includes the customer's name along with the unique 4me ID of their organization. To further streamline the billing process and ensure accuracy, organizations can assign a unique Financial ID to each customer record. While not always necessary for billing integrations— since the contract ID typically suffices to identify the customer— implementing Financial IDs is considered best practice. This approach helps eliminate any potential confusion that might arise from having multiple organizations with similar names.

Figure 304: Adding a Financial ID to a customer organization.

Identifying the Customer Contract

The cornerstone of the billing process is the accurate identification of the customer contract. A unique ID for the customer contract can be assigned within the financial details section of an SLA by a financial manager. This **Agreement ID** is intended to correspond directly to the record of the customer contract within the MSP's financial system. The Agreement ID is added to the time entries on requests and workflow tasks.

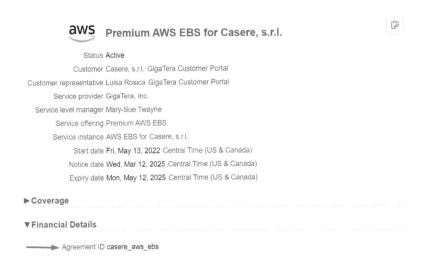

Figure 305: The Agreement ID, representing the customer contract, can be added to the Financial Details section of an SLA.

Identifying the Activity

In 4me, the basic unit for an activity performed for a customer is a request. As explained in the previous section, the request forms the basis for customer billing. The type of activity that is performed determines the billing method. For example, incidents may be covered by the standard monthly service fee, while a routine request like restoring a backup may incur a fixed price fee.

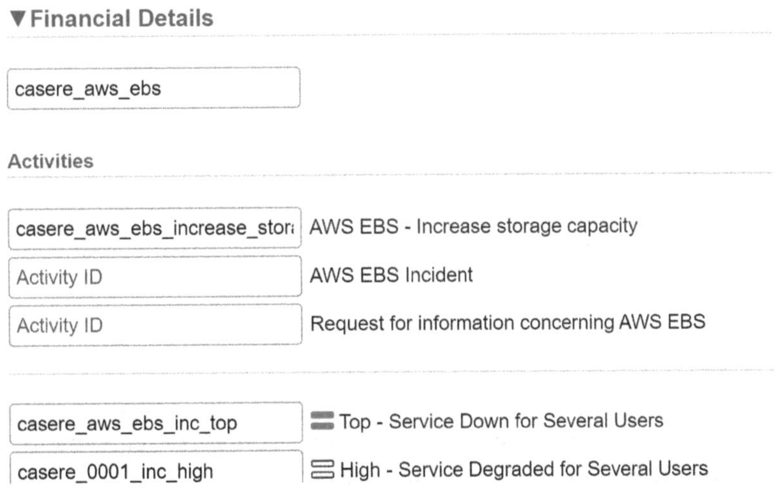

> ▼ **Financial Details**
>
> casere_aws_ebs
>
> **Activities**
>
> | casere_aws_ebs_increase_stor: | AWS EBS - Increase storage capacity |
> | Activity ID | AWS EBS Incident |
> | Activity ID | Request for information concerning AWS EBS |
>
> | casere_aws_ebs_inc_top | ▬ Top - Service Down for Several Users |
> | casere_0001_inc_high | ▤ High - Service Degraded for Several Users |

Figure 306: Defining Activity IDs in the Financial Details section of an SLA.

The activity type of a request can be identified at two levels. Firstly, there are standard requests, which are made available in a service contract when a request template is associated with a service offering. Additionally, there are three generic activity types: an Incident with four possible impact levels (Top, High, Medium and Low), a Request for Information (RFI), and a Request for Change (RFC).

In the Activities section of the Financial Details within a Service Level Agreement (SLA), a unique **Activity ID** can be assigned to each activity type. These Activity IDs are listed beginning with the standard requests followed by the generic activity types. This structure allows for the definition of separate billing fees for incidents based on their impact level. For instance, higher impact levels may require faster response times or support during non-standard working hours, resulting in additional expenses that an MSP may want to charge at a higher rate.

It's crucial to note that the Activity ID for standard requests takes precedence over the Activity IDs for generic requests. For instance, if a standard service request for RFIs is assigned Activity ID 1 and the generic RFI is assigned Activity ID 2, the Activity ID 1 will be added to the time entries whenever the standard request is applied.

Identifying the Rate

When it comes to charging an activity based on time and material, the billing integration must identify the appropriate rate. This is achieved through Effort Classes.

In the previous chapter on time tracking, we discussed how Effort Classes can be defined either in a directory account or in support domain accounts. When an Effort Class is defined in a directory account and linked to the timesheet settings of an organization, all specialists within the organization receive the same Effort Class, regardless of the customer or service provided. While

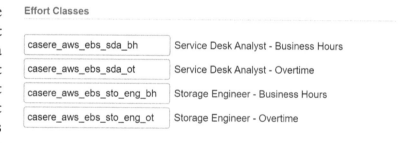

Figure 307: When Effort Classes are linked to a service offering, they appear in the Financial Details section of the associated SLAs. Financial managers can then assign Rate IDs to these Effort Classes.

this setup works well for corporate environments serving internal customers, Managed Service Providers (MSPs) require a more flexible approach. Each customer contract may necessitate its own list of profiles and customer-specific pricing related to these profiles. Thus, MSPs typically define Effort Classes in support domain accounts and link them to specific service offerings.

Similar to standard requests, once an Effort Class is associated with a service offering, it is displayed in the Effort Classes section of the Financial Details within a Service Level Agreement (SLA). Financial managers can then assign a **Rate ID** to these Effort Classes.

Tip

Consider **linking effort classes to skill pools** as a best practice. This limits choices and reduces errors when specialists register time. For instance, if a system architect is associated with the skill pool 'System Architects' and the effort class 'System Architect' is also linked to that skill pool, only specialists belonging to that skill pool will have the 'System Architect' effort class as an option.

The Billing Integration

Once the Agreement ID, Activity IDs, and Rate IDs are specified in the customer SLAs, the 4me platform will enhance time entries with this essential data. These IDs should correspond to unique records in the MSP's financial system. By combining the exported requests and time entries with financial records, the billing integration will compile a list of all activities performed for a customer, facilitating the generation of customer invoices.

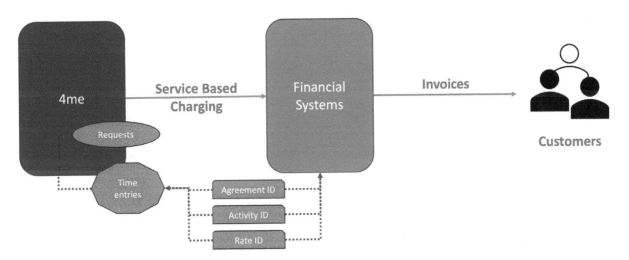

Figure 308: Once the financial IDs are defined in the customer SLAs, 4me will enrich the time entries with the Agreement ID, Activity ID, and Rate ID, allowing the billing integration to compile a customer invoice.

Defining Pricing and Rates in 4me

4me allows MSPs to directly set up pricing policies and define both profile rates and fixed price rates for activities. This is particularly useful for MSPs that operate with standardized contracts, enabling them to automate the calculation of charge amounts that are then added directly to time entries.

Pricing information is inputted into the **Standard Service Request Activity Rates** and **Activity Rates** sections of the Financial Details of Service Offerings. These sections list all associated activities, placing standard requests at the forefront. For each activity, the **Charge Type** is designated as either:

- **Included**: The activity is covered by the monthly service fee and requires no separate billing.
- **Fixed Price**: A set charge for the activity is defined in the Rate field.
- **Time & Material**: Billing is based on the actual time spent, with rates determined by the profiles (effort classes).

For activities billed on a Time & Material basis, the **Effort Class Rates** section allows for the specification of hourly rates for each effort class tied to the service offering. Once established, 4me automatically calculates the charge for these activities, annotating time entries with both the Charge Type and the Charge.

Figure 309: In the Financial Details section of a service offering, pricing info can be added to activities and effort classes.

This setup enables MSPs with standardized contracts to utilize a set of common service offerings across all customer SLAs. For unique cases where customer rates deviate from standard, bespoke service offerings can be easily created.

Charging and Billing
Discover GigaTera Managed Services Billing

Join us as we delve into the billing process at GigaTera, a Managed Service Provider (MSP) known for its expertise in managing AWS cloud storage solutions. GigaTera has leveraged 4me's billing integration capabilities to streamline their invoicing process. In this demo, we'll showcase how comprehensive billing information is seamlessly integrated into a time entry. Watch as Sarah Hendricks from the service desk manages a storage capacity upgrade request from GigaTera's client, Casere. Follow along as Sandra Store, GigaTera's diligent account administrator, verifies that Sarah's time entry captures all necessary billing details.

- Login as sarah.hendrix@gigatera.com to the GigaTera Managed Services account.
  - Navigate to the service desk console.
  - Enter 'Casere' as the customer name.
  - Select Key Contact 'Luisa Rosica'.
  - Choose the service 'Cloud Storage (AWS)'.
  - Select 'AWS S3 for Casere, s.r.l.'.
  - Pick the standard request 'AWS S3 – Increase storage capacity'.
  - Add a note specifying that 4012 GB need to be added.
  - Enter time spent as 00:01.
  - Select the effort class 'Service Desk Analyst – Business Hours'.
  - Save the entry.
  - Log out.
- Login as Sandra.store@gigatera.com to the GigaTera Managed Services account.
  - Select the request from Luisa Rosica.
  - Expand the Time Entries section.
  - Click on the time entries from Sarah Hendrix.
  - In the list with the time entries, there is just one time entry. Click on the time entry to see the details.
- Result: The time entry provides all the billing details.

 705711 AWS S3 - Increase storage capacity

Type	Request
Start	Wed, May 22, 2024 01:48pm CDT
Person	Sarah Hendrix
Organization	GigaTera, Inc.
Team	Service Desk
Time spent	0:01
Effort class	Service Desk Analyst - Business Hours
Cost	US$ 1.67
Service	Cloud Storage (AWS)
Service instance	AWS S3 for Casere, s.r.l.
Service level agreement	Premium AWS S3 for Casere, s.r.l.

Customer	Casere, s.r.l.
Agreement ID	casere_aws_s3
Rate ID	casere_aws_s3_sda_bh
Activity ID	casere_aws_s3_increase_storage_capacity
Charge type	Fixed Price
Charge	US$ 50.00

Figure 310: The time entry provides all the details for the billing integration to generate invoices.

The Billing Process

Locking Time Entries

4me provides users the flexibility to modify their time entries, simplifying the process of correcting errors. Managers and their substitutes also have the capability to adjust timesheets as needed. However, for organizations utilizing these timesheets for billing purposes, securing the recorded time at a certain point becomes essential. This is where timesheet locking comes into play, establishing a cut-off period beyond which modifications are restricted. It's important that this period is communicated clearly to all involved parties to ensure alignment.

In 4me, timesheets for a specified past week or month can be locked for all the people of an entire organization or for individual employees within an organization. To lock timesheets at the organization level, you must be designated as the *manager* or *substitute manager* of that organization. *Directory account administrators* have the authority to lock timesheets for all users across all organizations.

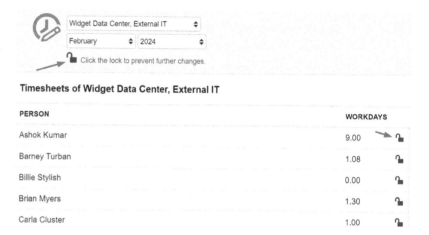

Figure 311: The manager of an organization can lock the timesheets of the past month for all users in the organization.

 **Tip**

Timesheet locking can be automated, offering two significant advantages: firstly, it allows for the enforcement of a precise cut-off date; secondly, it enables locking not only for entire weeks or months but also for specific days. For guidance on implementing this through automation scripts, refer to the 4me developer site at https://developer.4me.com/v1/timesheets/#lock-dates.

Making Corrections to Locked Timesheets

Once a timesheet date is locked, no changes can be made to any time entries for that particular day, not even by *managers* or *substitute managers*. Timesheets are usually locked shortly before generating invoices, executing payroll reports, or conducting internal chargebacks to ensure data integrity during these critical financial processes.

However, if errors are discovered after locking, the *directory account administrators* have the capability to address these inaccuracies. Instead of altering the original time entry, corrections are made by creating a new time entry of the "Correction" type. This entry can either subtract from (negative value) or add to (positive value) the original time, without modifying the original entry itself. These correction entries then need to be accounted for in the billing process, potentially leading to the issuance of credit notes or additional invoices to rectify the original billing based on the corrected timesheets.

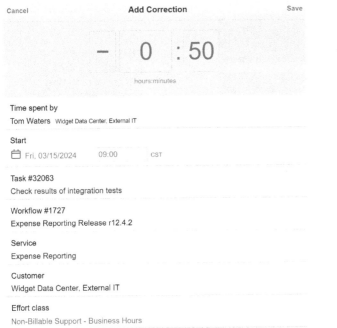

Figure 312: A time entry correction is a new time entry of type 'Correction' with a negative or positive time spent value.

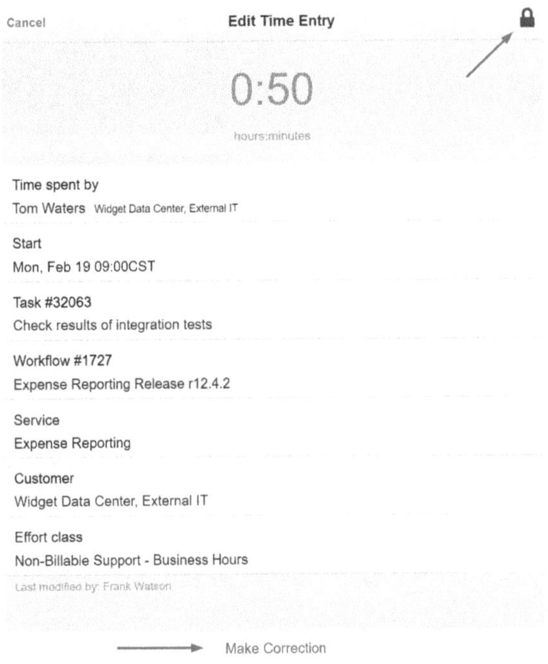

Figure 313: A directory account administrator can make corrections to a locked time entry.

The Billing Process – A Best Practices Approach

Incorporating a quality control setup into the billing process through 4me's timesheet locking functionality is a best practice for Managed Service Providers (MSPs). Accuracy in invoicing is key to avoiding disputes and the operational challenges of rectifying incorrect bills. Most billing errors can be mitigated by initially generating pro forma invoices for review by account managers and/or team leads for accuracy. Once quality control checks are complete, timesheets are locked via the billing integration, and final invoices are generated and dispatched to customers.

Additionally, it's important to consider periodic updates to pricing, a common scenario given that many customer contracts span several years with annual price adjustments.

Updating pricing in the financial system and/or 4me can be time-consuming and isn't a task that can be completed overnight. It's likely that new records will need to be created in the MSP's financial system, necessitating updates to financial IDs in 4me during this transition. Meanwhile, specialists continue to log time, raising the question of how to ensure that time entries logged during this transition period carry the correct billing information.

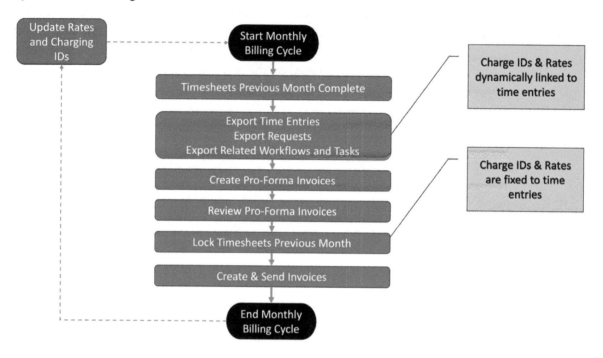

Figure 314: A best practices approach for billing, including quality control and a grace period to update pricing info.

4me's billing functionality is designed to accommodate these pricing updates. As long as time entries remain unlocked, billing information is dynamically retrieved from Billable SLAs and service offerings. Once time entries are locked, their billing information is fixed and cannot be altered. This feature allows for a billing process that effectively handles pricing updates. For example, consider a scenario where pricing updates are due at the beginning of a new year. Initially, the focus would be on generating and internally approving draft invoices for December of the prior year. Following approval, time entries for December are locked in 4me, fixing the billing information on those records. Final invoices can then be sent out to customers. Subsequently, new pricing updates can be applied without affecting the locked time entries of the previous year, giving the service provider a grace period of a few weeks to complete these updates before starting the billing cycle for January in early February.

Chapter 19 -
Unlocking the Power of 4me Reservations

Introduction

Imagine a world where securing a company car for your next business trip, or reserving a projector for your upcoming presentation is as easy as clicking a button. Welcome to the realm of 4me Reservations, where convenience meets efficiency.

Across various business units, assets critical for day-to-day operations and special events are frequently shared among users. Facilities management teams juggle meeting rooms, company vehicles, and parking spaces, while IT departments may offer laptops or projectors on a temporary basis. Meanwhile, sales and marketing teams require materials and resources to create standout booth displays for industry events.

The 4me platform transforms how these assets are accessed and managed, providing a seamless and straightforward solution to publish available assets directly on the Self-Service Portal. End users gain the power to make reservations with ease, transforming a potentially complex process into a few simple clicks.

But the magic doesn't stop there. With 4me's integrated workflow functionality, support organizations can orchestrate a full reservation process, encompassing necessary pre- and post-reservation tasks. This ensures not just a reservation, but a complete experience, tailored to meet the demands of both the service provider and the user.

Figure 315: A user making a reservation on the self-service portal.

Dive into the world of 4me Reservations and discover how this powerful feature can streamline asset management, enhance user satisfaction, and drive efficiency across your organization.

Registering Assets for Reservation

In 4me, any asset available for reservation is recorded as a Configuration Item (CI). The initial step involves ensuring that all assets eligible for reservation are cataloged properly by a configuration manager. When you want the users to find assets according to certain criteria, you will need to add some custom sfields to the products. For instance, when enabling the reservation of company cars, custom fields, such as seat number and transmission type (automatic or manual), might be beneficial. It's also advisable to link these CIs to specific sites (locations where the assets are stationed) and service instances (identifying the support team that manages the assets) if reservations are to span across multiple locations.

Creating Reservation Offerings

Reservation offerings, accessible via the Records console, are defined and managed by *account administrators* and *configuration managers*. Begin by assigning a distinct Name to each reservation offering, such as "Company Cars @ Widget Headquarters (New-York)".

Linking Assets to Reservation Offerings

Next, associate the reservation offering with one or more CIs – the actual assets made available. If the reservation offering pertains to a specific location, like cars available at a New York site, linking the CIs to that site beforehand simplifies the setup: one can filter the available CIs on their site.

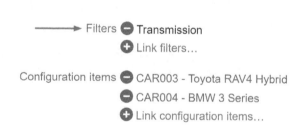

Any CI attributes including the filterable custom fields like car transmission can be set now as filters. This will allow users to make specific selections.

Figure 316: Adding CIs with a filter to a reservation offering.

Defining Reservation Parameters

In the reservation offering setup, you need to specify the conditions and restrictions for asset reservations:

- **Calendar and Time zone**: Set availability times for the reservation slots, for instance aligning with business hours and excluding holidays.

- **Initial Status**: Define whether approvals or checks are needed before confirming reservations. Notifications are sent for status updates from Pending to Confirmed, and for reservation conclusions.
- **Min/Max Duration**: Establish the allowable reservation lengths.
- **Multi-day**: Decide if reservations can extend beyond a single day.
- **Step Duration**: Define the calendar's time increments for user selections.
- **Preparation Duration**: This field is used to define the buffer period required to prepare an asset before it can be used again. For example, when a user reserves a temporary laptop, the IT team may need time to configure the system according to the user's needs. The 'Preparation duration' sets the minimum time needed by the support organization to prepare the laptop between two consecutive reservations. This ensures the asset is ready and fully functional for the next user.

Figure 317: The reservation parameters in the Reservation Offering.

- **Minimum Advance Duration**: This field determines the lead time required for a reservation. For instance, if a user needs to arrange catering for a meeting, this request typically requires advance planning. The 'Min. advance duration' specifies the minimum amount of time needed between making the reservation and the actual reservation date. This ensures all necessary preparations, such as food orders, are completed on time.
- **Maximum Advance Duration**: This parameter controls how far in advance a reservation can be made. For assets that are in high demand, such as a popular meeting room or a company car, users might attempt to secure these assets well ahead of time. While this ensures availability, it can lead to long-term blockage of resources that might not actually be needed, leading to inefficient asset utilization. Setting a 'Max. advance duration' helps prevent excessive advance bookings, ensuring more users have access to these resources and preventing the reservation calendar from being filled months in advance with speculative bookings.
- **Instructions**: This field guides the user and explains the reservation process of the organization, the use and conditions of the equipment, or any other instructions that the user might need.
- **Reservations are private**: By default, users can view details of existing reservations made by others within the Reservations Calendar. An example of how this transparency can be beneficial is if there's a single 12-seat meeting room booked during a desired time slot, one might contact the individual who made the reservation to negotiate an alternative, such as switching to a smaller available room, thus bypassing support intervention. However, if confidentiality around who made a reservation is crucial, the 'Reservations are private' option allows for hiding this information, ensuring sensitive details remain undisclosed.

Setting Up Recurring Reservations

For activities such as a weekly onsite project team meeting, it may be beneficial to secure the meeting room in advance through recurring reservations. Activating the '**Allow repeat**' feature within the reservation settings enables this, but it also necessitates specifying the '**Maximum advance duration**'—a crucial parameter determining the end date for the sequence of bookings. This duration should be set within a range of 1 day to 1 year. Though presented in hours, this field can accept values like '365d' for 365 days or '52w' for 52 weeks, offering flexibility in scheduling.

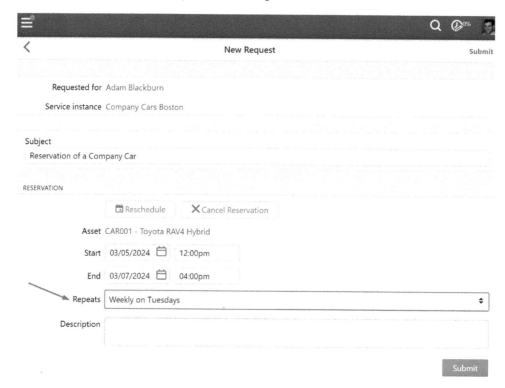

Figure 318: A user creating a recurring reservation.

Upon submitting a reservation request, users can opt to make their booking recurring by choosing an appropriate pattern from the 'Repeats' dropdown menu. The first three selections following 'No repeat' provide suggestions based on the initial chosen date, while the 'Custom...' option allows users to tailor the frequency and duration of their reservations to their specific needs.

The Request Template

Once the various reservation offerings, such as catering services, are defined, the next step involves linking these to specific request templates. This process ensures that the robust functionalities of the 4me core framework are seamlessly integrated into the reservations system. In practice, when a user books a service—like catering for an event—this action generates a corresponding request.

To facilitate this, the request template should be labeled under the 'Reservation' category. When a particular service, like catering, is chosen, the linked reservation offerings become selectable within the request template.

Enhancing User Experience with UI Extensions

You can enhance the reservation request template with UI Extensions to gather more detailed information from the requester. For example, for a catering reservation, the template could include fields for specifying dietary restrictions or allergies. This tailored approach ensures all user needs are considered and addressed.

Streamlining Approvals and Tasks with Workflow Templates

Linking a workflow template to the request template can streamline approvals and outline essential tasks, such as pre-event setup and post-event cleanup. This template could also include steps for sending an invoice to the requester post-event, ensuring all administrative tasks are covered.

Automation for Efficiency

Automation rules can significantly streamline this process. For example, in the case of catering reservations, an automation rule could automatically set the reservation's status to 'Confirmed' once the catering order has been confirmed.

Maximizing Flexibility in Asset Reservations:

Service Offerings, Service Instances, and Request Templates

The 4me platform's reservation module showcases exceptional flexibility. This versatility is attributed to three critical elements: reservation offerings, service instances, and request templates. These components work in tandem to tailor the reservation process to the unique needs of diverse user groups and assets, from laptops and meeting rooms to company cars and catering services.

Consider an IT department with five laptops available for temporary use. Developers are permitted to borrow a laptop for up to two weeks, whereas other staff members are restricted to one-day loans. This scenario necessitates the creation of two distinct reservation offerings, each linked to the same five laptops, to cater to the different needs of developers and non-developers.

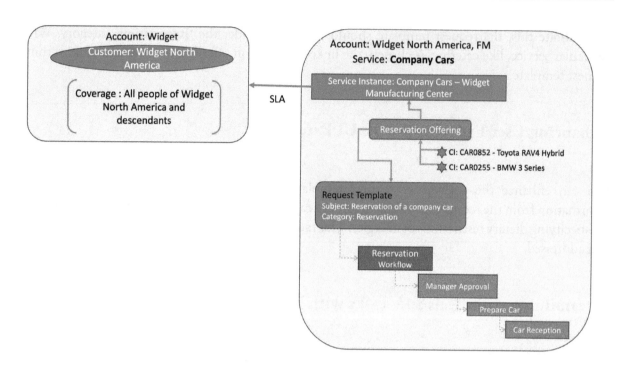

Figure 319: The relationships between the reservation offerings, the service instances, and request templates offer a lot of flexibility when setting up reservations in 4me.

Now you need to make sure that the correct reservation offering is provided to the right user groups:

- **Separate User Groups via Service Instances**: Two service instances could be established: "Personal Computing for Non-developers" and "Personal Computing for Developers," with each linked to a single, universal request template. By matching the SLAs to the appropriate user groups, individuals gain access to the suitable reservation offerings based on their coverage.
- **Single-Service Instance with Varied Offerings**: Alternatively, you might opt for one service instance—"Personal Computing"—paired with two distinct service offerings. This approach involves creating two SLAs tailored to the respective user groups. Furthermore, this method requires developing two request templates, each linked to its respective reservation offering and service offering.

If reservation management differs between user groups (developers versus non-developers), utilizing two separate service instances, each with its unique support team, could be the most effective strategy. This setup allows for the dynamic assignment of the support team based on the service instance associated with the reservation, eliminating the need to specify an assignment team within the request template.

Should distinct workflows be necessary for each group's reservations (and to avoid creating a single dynamic workflow), the second option with different request templates for each group becomes the preferable solution.

The Specialist Perspective: Reservation Records

Once a user registers a reservation, both a 'Request' and a related 'Reservation record' are generated. These reservation records are accessible to all specialists and can be managed by configuration managers and account administrators. They have the authority to modify the status of a reservation, cancel a reservation, or alter the timeslot of a reservation as needed.

The End User Experience: Using iCalendar

In addition to receiving notifications for their reservations, users can view all their bookings through the '**My Reservations**' feature available on the self-service portal.

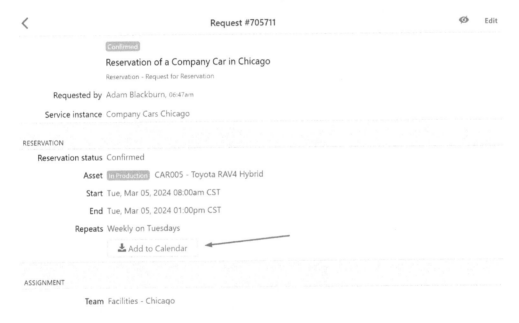

Figure 320: The 'Add to Calendar' option on a reservation record.

The 4me platform enhances user convenience by attaching an **ICS file** to each reservation, accessible via the "Add to Calendar" button. An ICS file (standing for iCalendar file) is a globally-recognized calendar format compatible with various calendar programs, including Microsoft Outlook, Google Calendar, and Apple Calendar. This integration allows users to easily import their reservations into their personal calendars. Moreover, the ICS format supports recurring events, enabling users to effortlessly incorporate recurring reservations into their calendars with just a few clicks.

Demo

4me Reservations
Reservation of a Company Car

Welcome to the vibrant world of Widget Facilities in North America, where a dynamic fleet of company cars awaits at our four strategic locations: Boston, Chicago, Houston, and New York. Imagine a crisp Tuesday morning in Chicago, and we find Adam Blackburn from the Manufacturing Department gearing up for a crucial task—a weekly quality control meeting with one of their esteemed suppliers.

Adam's mission is clear, but there's a twist! He needs a reliable set of wheels from the company fleet, not just once, but every Tuesday morning. Let's dive into our demo environment, where the plot thickens: currently, our Chicago car reservation system doesn't accommodate the saga of recurring bookings.

Enter our hero, Hank Williams, the dedicated account administrator for Widget North America's Facilities Management. It's up to Hank to navigate the settings and steer our tale towards a happy ending by enabling the recurring reservation feature. Join us as we embark on this journey, transforming the way Widget empowers its team, one car reservation at a time.

- Log in as hank.williams@widget.com to Widget N. America – FM.
  - Go to the Records console - Reservation Offerings.
  - Select and edit 'Reservation of a Company Car in Chicago.'
  - Check the 'Allow repeat' option. Set the Maximum advanced duration to 20w.
- Login as adam.blackburn@widget.com to Widget International.
  - Register a new request.
  - Select Facilities Management.
  - Select Company Cars.
  - Select Company Cars Chicago.
  - Select 'Reservation of a Company Car in Chicago.'
  - Choose a slot for the next Tuesday from 08:00 am to 01:00 pm. Click on Continue.
  - Select Weekly on Tuesdays.
  - Set the End date.
  - Save.
  - Go to My Reservations.
  - Click on the reservation for the company car.
  - Zoom out in the reservation calendar.

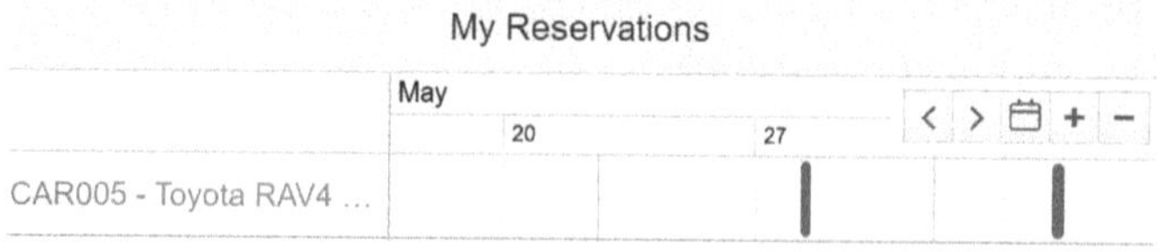

My Reservations

May
20   27   < > 🗓 + −

CAR005 - Toyota RAV4 ...

Figure 321: Adam Blackburn checks the recurring reservation.

Check that a reservation has been made on every Tuesday.

Chapter 20 - Risk Management

Introduction

In the quest for organizational resilience, risk management stands as a beacon, guiding companies through the murky waters of uncertainty. By proactively identifying, analyzing, and mitigating risks, organizations safeguard their future, turning potential pitfalls into steppingstones for success.

The integration of risk management within the 4me platform enhances how organizations uphold governance, risk management, and compliance (GRC). Imagine a world where your risk register doesn't just exist; it thrives within the secure confines of 4me. This isn't just about managing risks; it's about mastering them.

Why choose 4me for this mission? Firstly, 4me is not just a platform; it's your ally in embedding robust controls straight from compliance frameworks into the fabric of your operations. With its powerful recurring workflows and insightful dashboards, 4me transforms theoretical frameworks into practical, actionable strategies. And when audit time comes, breathe easy—4me's audit capabilities shine, offering crystal-clear transparency and incontrovertible evidence of your compliance diligence.

But that's not all—integrating the Risk Register within your GRC support domain in 4me doesn't just centralize your efforts; it elevates them. This harmonious integration ensures that every risk, every control, and every compliance activity reside within a single, secure, and meticulously-audited environment.

Moreover, the enhanced risk management functionality in 4me extends its reach to the external forces shaping your organization—your vendors and managed service providers (MSPs). By linking risks directly to supplier organizations or the services they render, 4me not only fortifies your supplier management process but also enriches vendor management and the SIAM service integrator function.

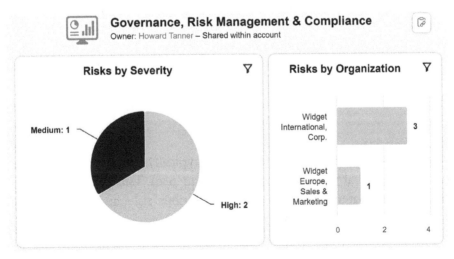

Figure 322: Adding risk reports on a dashboard in a GRC support domain account.

Activating Risk Management

Initially, risk management functionality is turned off by default in a 4me account. Technically speaking, introducing risk management into an organization is straightforward: the account owner simply needs to activate Risk Management within the 'Account Settings' section of the Settings console. However, before flipping that switch, it's crucial for an organization to establish a clear policy and structured process for risk management. This is precisely why the feature is not enabled from the outset.

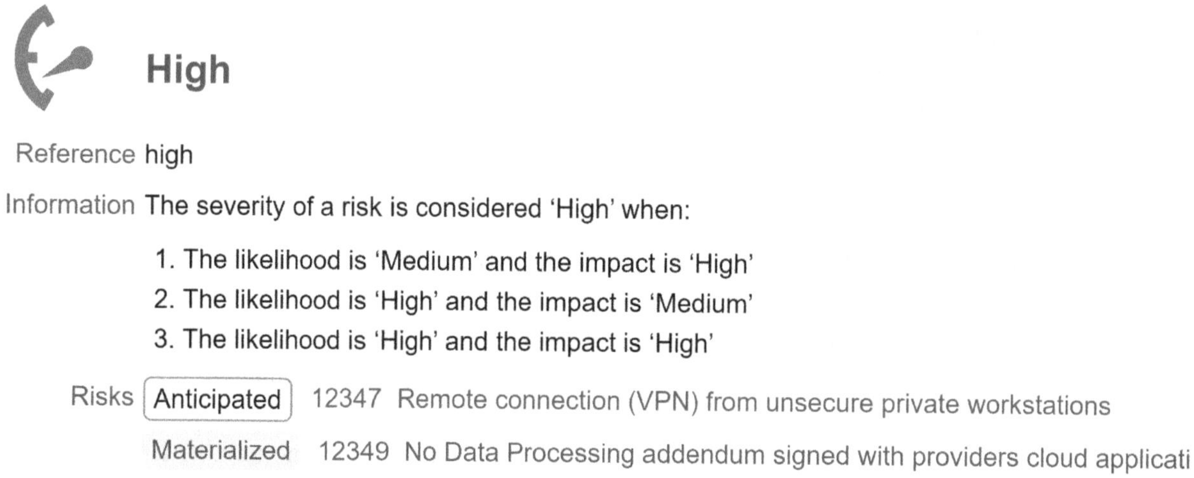

 High

Reference high

Information The severity of a risk is considered 'High' when:

1. The likelihood is 'Medium' and the impact is 'High'
2. The likelihood is 'High' and the impact is 'Medium'
3. The likelihood is 'High' and the impact is 'High'

Risks Anticipated   12347 Remote connection (VPN) from unsecure private workstations

Materialized   12349 No Data Processing addendum signed with providers cloud applicati

Figure 323: Risk severities in the Widget Data Center account. Check how the risks with this severity level are displayed on the form.

Once risk management is activated, a new segment titled '**Risk Severities**' appears within the Settings console. Pre-populated with four default risk severities, this area paves the way for defining the gravity of risks as recorded in the Risk form. *Account administrators* have the flexibility to modify these default settings, tailoring the 'Severity' field of the Risk form to better fit the organization's specific needs. They can introduce additional severity levels or deactivate existing ones to align with their risk assessment criteria. Furthermore, the 'Risk Severities' section is equipped with drag-and-drop functionality, allowing for swift reordering to establish a logical hierarchy of severities.

Risk Assessment

Risk severity within risk management frameworks is typically assessed by evaluating two primary components: likelihood (probability) and impact (consequence). This assessment is crucial for helping organizations identify the potential threats posed by various risks and prioritize mitigation efforts effectively. Here's a breakdown of these components:

- **Likelihood** (Probability): This factor evaluates the probability of the risk event occurring within a given timeframe.

- **Impact** (Consequence): This component assesses the potential severity of the damage or negative effects that the risk event could cause if it were to occur. Impact can encompass financial loss, health and safety consequences, reputational damage, or other organizational objectives.

Once the likelihood and impact are assessed, they are collectively used to determine the overall severity level of the risk using a **risk matrix** (also known as a risk assessment matrix or risk map). In the 4me platform, this matrix is facilitated through a UI Extension. Activating risk management within 4me introduces a 'Risk UI Extension' to the account, which integrates a 'Risk Assessment' section into the risk form.

The embedded JavaScript within this UI Extension, which automatically updates the 'Severity' field based on selections made in the Likelihood and Impact fields, can be updated and aligned with the organization's specific risk matrix logic.

Risk
Risk

| View | HTML | **JavaScript** | CSS |

```
1   var $ = ITRP.$;              // jQuery
2   var $extension = $(this);    // The UI Extension container with custom HTML
3
4   var $likelihood = $extension.find('#likelihood');
5   var $impact = $extension.find('#impact');
6   var $residual = $extension.find('#residual_risk');
7   var $status = ITRP.field('status');
8   var $severity = ITRP.field('severity');
9   var $mitigation_target_at = ITRP.field('mitigation_target_at');
10  var $closure_reason = ITRP.field('closure_reason');
11
12  // Mapping from likelihood and impact to Reference field value of a Risk Severity.
13  // For example: likelihood 'low' and impact 'high' maps to severity 'medium'.
14  // Make sure to adjust this mapping when the Reference field value is updated.
15  var mapping = {
16     low:    { low: 'low',    medium: 'low',    high: 'medium' },
17     medium: { low: 'low',    medium: 'medium', high: 'high'   },
18     high:   { low: 'medium', medium: 'high',   high: 'high'   },
19  };
```

Figure 324: The 'out-of-the box' UI Extension for the record type Risk includes logic to calculate the risk level.

For organizations yet to establish their risk matrix, the default UI extension and associated options for the 'Severity' field offer a solid foundation to start from.

Managing Risks in 4me

Risk Registration

Once risk management is enabled in 4me, all *specialists* will gain access to the 'Risks' section within the Records console. This feature empowers every specialist to contribute to their organization's risk register, promoting a culture of risk awareness crucial for capturing and addressing risks promptly as they arise.

Specialists register new risks directly from the Records console. When adding a risk, it's important to assign a risk manager—the individual accountable for mitigating or reducing the risk's impact. Additionally, the risk should be associated with any relevant elements such as a project, a service, or an organization that might be affected by the risk.

Moreover, specialists have the flexibility to initiate a risk entry from within the project, service, or organization records by selecting the 'Relate to New Risk' option from the Actions (gear icon) menu.

Risk Lifecycle

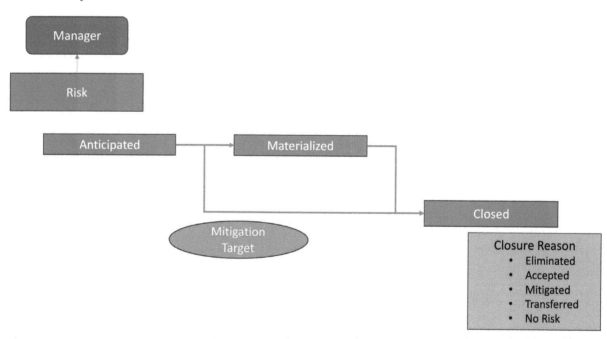

Figure 325: The lifecycle of 4me's risk record.

Once a risk is logged, the designated risk manager, who could be a compliance officer, a project manager, or another responsible individual, assumes responsibility for reviewing, reassessing, and defining necessary mitigation actions. Their primary goal is to transition a newly identified risk, initially marked with the

'**Anticipated**' status, towards a '**Closed**' status. It's crucial to understand that in 4me, 'Closed' does not imply the risk no longer exists; rather, it indicates that the risk no longer requires active management due to acceptance, mitigation, or transfer.

Within 4me, one of the key tools in risk management is the 'Mitigation Target' field. By setting a clear mitigation target, the organization establishes concrete objectives and timelines for addressing significant risks. This helps ensure that high-severity risks are prioritized and dealt with in a timely manner.

The risk manager assesses and decides on the appropriate actions to mitigate or eliminate the risk. Should actions be required, they can initiate them by generating new requests within 4me. To maintain a coherent timeline and clear association, links to these requests, along with related problems, changes, or project items, can be annotated within the risk's notes. This ensures a comprehensive chronological trail is available, showcasing the measures taken to shield the organization from potential harm.

A noteworthy status within the risk lifecycle is '**Materialized**'. This status signifies that the anticipated risk has escalated into an actual **issue**. This categorization is particularly prevalent in project management contexts, where risk registers often evolve into combined risk and issue logs.

Chapter 21 - 4me Project Management

Introduction

In today's fast-paced work environment, operations teams often find their specialists navigating between support tasks and project engagements. These two areas come with distinct objectives and timelines. In the support domain, targets are typically short-term, driven by Service-Level Agreements (SLAs) and support contract terms, with failure to meet these targets potentially resulting in penalties. Conversely, in projects, long-term milestones are set which, if not met, can have substantial financial implications.

The tension between the resource demands of these two spheres can lead to significant challenges. Specialists might struggle to meet SLA requirements due to their commitments to project tasks, or project milestones could be delayed because of urgent support issues. This resource tug-of-war often results in both support and project tasks suffering from reduced quality and delays. Managing and balancing the unpredictable resource demands from support alongside the stringent planning requirements of projects is complex, especially when projects frequently demand more resources than initially anticipated.

Addressing this resource conflict demands between support and project tasks is a key driver behind the integration of project management functionalities into the 4me platform. While 4me doesn't directly resolve resource shortages, it offers visibility into resource demands and assignments, facilitating better management and allocation. By consolidating both domains on a single platform, 4me aims to provide a clearer overview of resource availability and needs, enabling more informed decision-making and prioritization.

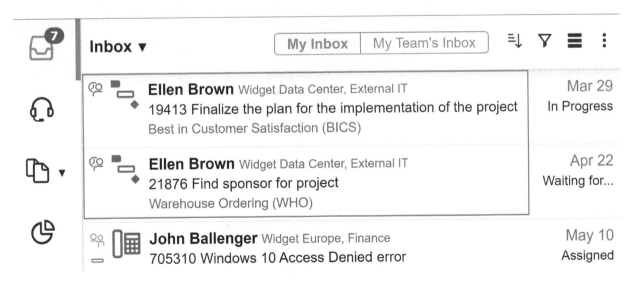

Figure 326: The specialist gets a consolidated view of support tasks and project tasks in the inbox.

Incorporating project management within the 4me platform offers numerous benefits beyond just resolving resource clashes. For project managers, project plans become interactive and dynamic entities.

Upon initiating a project and crafting a schedule, tasks begin to automatically appear in the inboxes of assigned project team members. The inherent communication and collaboration features of the 4me platform foster real-time, efficient interactions among project members, managers, and other necessary stakeholders. This approach transforms project plans into 'living' entities that adapt and respond in real time, enhancing engagement and responsiveness.

Furthermore, the integration of project management into 4me enriches the experience for specialists. With all actionable tasks centralized in one inbox, there's no need to sift through emails or toggle between different platforms. This consolidation helps specialists manage their workload more effectively, ensuring they stay on top of both project tasks and support duties.

The integration also facilitates a seamless demand management process, laying the groundwork for identifying and defining new projects directly within the platform. This streamlines the transition from conceptual demand to actionable project plans, ensuring a cohesive approach from start to finish.

Moreover, the project management features in 4me are designed to be cost-effective. There are no additional licensing fees to access these robust project management tools. While project managers do require a specific user license, project tasks can be assigned to any user without necessitating additional licenses, making this an economically-advantageous solution for managing projects within the service delivery framework.

Understanding the Project Management Structure within 4me

Delving into the heart of 4me's project management, we find the project record as the central component. Illustrated below, a project in 4me is segmented into various **phases**, each containing a structured schedule of tasks, akin to what one may encounter within workflow management.

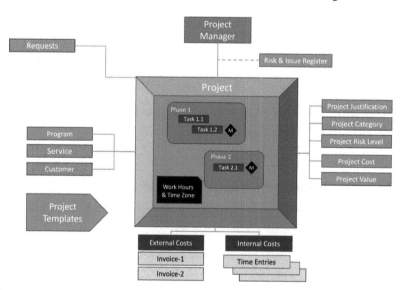

Figure 327: The 4me project, project fields, and related 4me records.

This familiarity in design means those accustomed to navigating workflow schedules in 4me will find a similar intuitive interface when constructing a project schedule using the **Gantt chart**. Project tasks can be added, and relationships between them, such as task predecessors and successors, are clearly defined, ensuring a logical flow of project activities.

Integrating Project Management with the Enterprise Service Management Framework

Project management in 4me isn't an isolated feature but rather an integral part of the broader enterprise service management framework. At the core of every project is the **Customer** or sponsor, whose needs and objectives drive the project's inception. Equally important is the **Service** aspect; projects are typically undertaken to enhance an existing service or to introduce a new one within the organizational landscape.

Initially, especially when a project aims to develop a new service, it can be associated with a generic **Project Management Office (PMO) service** within 4me. This PMO service serves as a financial placeholder, accounting for the investment into potential new initiatives, whether they come to fruition or not. Often, this PMO service covers the initial costs related to project exploration and planning.

As projects progress, especially those focused on establishing new services, they naturally transition into the operational phase. Here, the newly developed service is incorporated into 4me's service catalog. This transition is crucial for a seamless handover to support teams, ensuring that new services are fully integrated within the platform for ongoing management.

The initiation of a project within 4me usually originates from one or more initial **requests**, often referred to as '**demands**', directed to the PMO. These demands set the foundation for project objectives and are pivotal in the formal initiation and approval process of new projects, aligning them with organizational strategies and priorities.

Key Elements and Attributes of a 4me Project Record

A 4me project is characterized by several key attributes that define its scope, risks, and potential benefits. These attributes form the foundation of the project's planning and execution stages:

- **Program**: Every project may be part of a larger program, aligning it with broader organizational goals and strategies.
- **Project Assessment Attributes**: During the initial assessment phase, critical information is gathered to evaluate the project's viability. This includes:
  - **Project Category**: Often reflective of the project's size and scope.
  - **Project Risk Level**: An evaluation of potential challenges and obstacles the project may face.
  - **Estimated Value**: The anticipated benefits or outcomes the project aims to deliver, which could be financial gains, efficiency improvements, or other organizational benefits.

- **Cost Estimates**: Preliminary estimates of internal and external costs associated with the project. This early-stage financial assessment is crucial for budgeting and resource allocation.

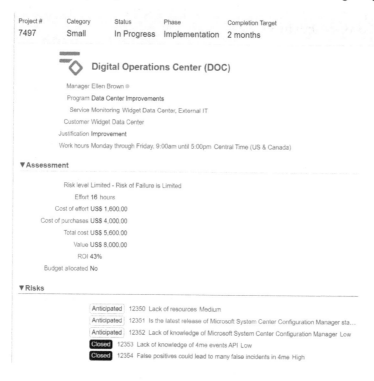

Figure 328: A project record in 4me.

- **Project Templates**: To ensure a consistent and structured approach to project initiation, planning, and project closure, project templates can be utilized. These templates standardize the process, ensuring that all necessary assessments are conducted and documented.
- **The Project Manager's Role**: The project manager stands at the helm of the project, responsible for crafting the initial schedule and steering the project towards its objectives. Their responsibilities extend beyond scheduling, encompassing active **risk and issue** management to navigate the project through potential hurdles and ensure its success.
- **Cost and Time Tracking**: As the project progresses, tracking mechanisms are put in place to monitor both external and internal costs. This is typically done through the logging of:
    - **Invoices**: Documenting external expenses related to the project.
    - **Time Entries**: Capturing the time invested by project team members, which reflects internal cost contributions.

Project Management Activation in 4me

Activating project management within your 4me account requires the *account administrator* role and can be accomplished effortlessly; it requires the execution of three well-defined steps. Here's a concise guide to set the stage for efficient project management:

- **Define Project Categories**: Go to the Settings console and establish your project categories. Categories often reflect the scale of the project, such as Small, Medium, or Large. Utilize the Description field to delineate clear criteria for each category, often based on the anticipated number of workdays required or the estimated total cost. Categories are instrumental in aligning with your organization's project management protocols, such as determining the composition of the steering committee based on project size.

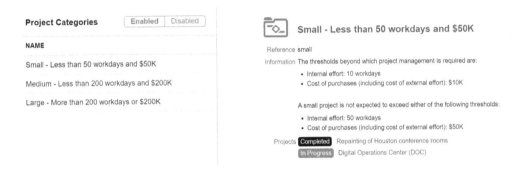

Figure 329: Project Categories in the Settings Console.

- **Set Project Risk Levels**: Just like categories, project risk levels are configured in the Settings console. Common classifications include Limited, Moderate, and Significant. It's essential to clearly document how each project's risk level is determined. Furthermore, your project management policy should detail the necessary approvals, such as who must sign off on the project plan, based on the identified risk level.

Figure 330: Project Risk Levels in the Settings Console.

- **Assign the Project Manager Role**: The final step is to designate the project manager role to at least one specialist within your 4me account.

After these steps are completed, you'll notice a new Projects section within the Records console, equipped with Project, Project Tasks, Project Templates, and Project Task Templates menu options. While enabling the project management feature is a swift process, typically achievable in under five minutes, the key to success lies in having a solid policy and clear definitions in place beforehand.

The Lifecycle of a Project

The Demand Management Process

Every project begins with an idea or initiative. While many ideas are valuable, not all are viable or align with the company's strategic goals. Also, it's important to distinguish between what constitutes a true project need versus what might be resolved through a simpler, non-standard change. This evaluation is the essence of the demand management process.

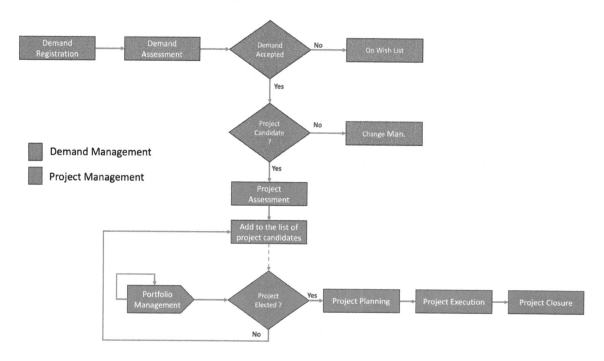

Figure 331: A typical demand management process.

In the 4me platform, integrating demand management within request management is practical and efficient. Typically, user-generated demands become requests assigned to the Portfolio or Project Management Office (PMO) for initial assessment. The process delineated ensures only viable demands, which cannot be addressed through standard operational changes, progress to detailed project assessment.

Bid Management for MSPs

The scenario differs for Managed Service Providers (MSPs). In this context, requests might extend beyond the scope of current managed services agreements, encompassing proposals for new projects or expansions of service. These requests, whether originating from the customer or an internal account manager, trigger the involvement of a pre-sales or bid team. This team's role is to comprehensively evaluate the request for proposal, developing a project plan and proposal accordingly. The project only moves forward upon the customer's approval, transitioning from a potential opportunity to an actionable plan.

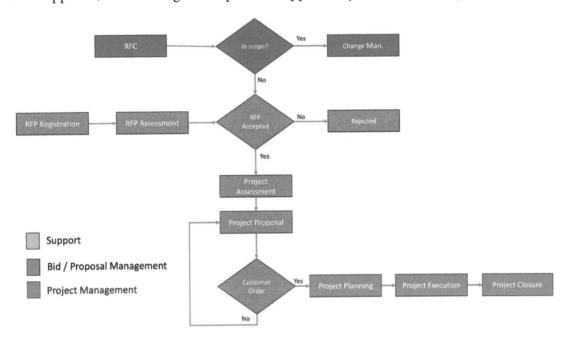

Figure 332: Integration of the bid management process for MSPs.

4me Project Management
Transitioning from Request to Project

Imagine this scenario: Howard Tanner receives an urgent notification that the HP NNM software currently installed requires an immediate upgrade due to end-of-support issues. Recognizing the complexity and the need for structured execution, Howard determines that this situation warrants more than just a non-standard change; it calls for a full-fledged project. He submits a request and entrusts it to Ellen Brown, a dynamic project manager known for her efficiency and problem-solving skills at Widget Data Center. Let's follow along as Ellen takes charge:

- Log in as ellen.brown@widget.com to Widget Data Center.
  - Check the inbox.
  - Select the request "*Upgrade HP OpenView NNM to v10 (NNM10)*".
  - In the Actions menu (gear button), select "*Relate to a New Project...*".
  - Select Program: *Data Center Improvements*.
  - Select Customer: *Widget Data Center*.
  - The Service is already filled in: it is the service of the request.
  - Select Justification: *Compliance*.
  - Save.
That's all it takes to create a new project from a request.

Initiating a New Project

From Demand to Project Creation

While initiating a new project directly from the Records console in 4me is straightforward, a best practice is to generate a project from an existing request. This request usually stems from a Demand or a Request for Proposal. By selecting the "Relate to a New Project" option in the Actions menu of a request, a new project record can be seamlessly created. This method ensures that vital details like Service and Customer information are automatically transferred from the request to the new project.

Setting Up the Project Basics

Upon initiating a project, it is essential to specify certain foundational elements:

- **Program**: this is the group of related projects to which the project belongs. Often programs are defined based on strategic objectives or organizational goals to be achieved. The program is the broader category under which the project falls.
- **Justification**: The primary reason for the project's inception, which could range from Compliance to Expansion or Improvement. This outlines the project's purpose and its alignment with organizational goals.

Furthermore, selecting the appropriate Calendar for **Work Hours** and the associated **Time Zone** is crucial, as it influences the scheduling and planning of project tasks. For example, if a project task with an 8-hour duration commences on a Friday at 4 PM, considering standard work hours from 9 AM to 5 PM, Monday to Friday, the task will logically conclude by Monday at 4 PM.

Initially, certain project attributes, such as the project category and specific details within the Assessment section, may remain undefined. At this early stage, it's acceptable to leave these fields blank, allowing for flexibility as the project's scope and requirements become clearer.

By default, the "**Project Work Hours**" and "**Time Zone**" settings align with the work hours and locale of the first team to which the project manager belongs. Typically, project managers are part of the Project Management Office (PMO) team. It's advisable to ensure that the PMO team's "Work Hours" and "Time Zone" accurately reflect the standard working hours of the project team members. However, these default "Work Hours" and the associated "Time Zone" for a project can be overwritten if necessary.

Project Assessment and Utilization of 4me Project Templates

After a project has been officially registered, the crucial phase of project assessment commences. This stage involves critical evaluation elements, such as identifying the project's potential value and estimating both internal and external costs. Additionally, it is imperative to determine the project's risk level and categorize the project. All these steps should be executed in strict adherence to the organization's established project management policy and methodology. Renowned methodologies like Prince2 and PMI provide a structured approach and terminology for this assessment phase.

The Role of 4me Project Templates

Project templates within 4me serve a similar purpose to workflow templates by offering a structured schedule of pre-defined project tasks. Creating these templates follows a process akin to workflow templates; however, a significant distinction exists. Unlike workflow templates that generate an entire workflow, project templates are utilized to enhance an existing project, adding predefined tasks and phases to it. Importantly, a single project can incorporate multiple project templates, contrasting the one-to-one correspondence between a workflow and its template.

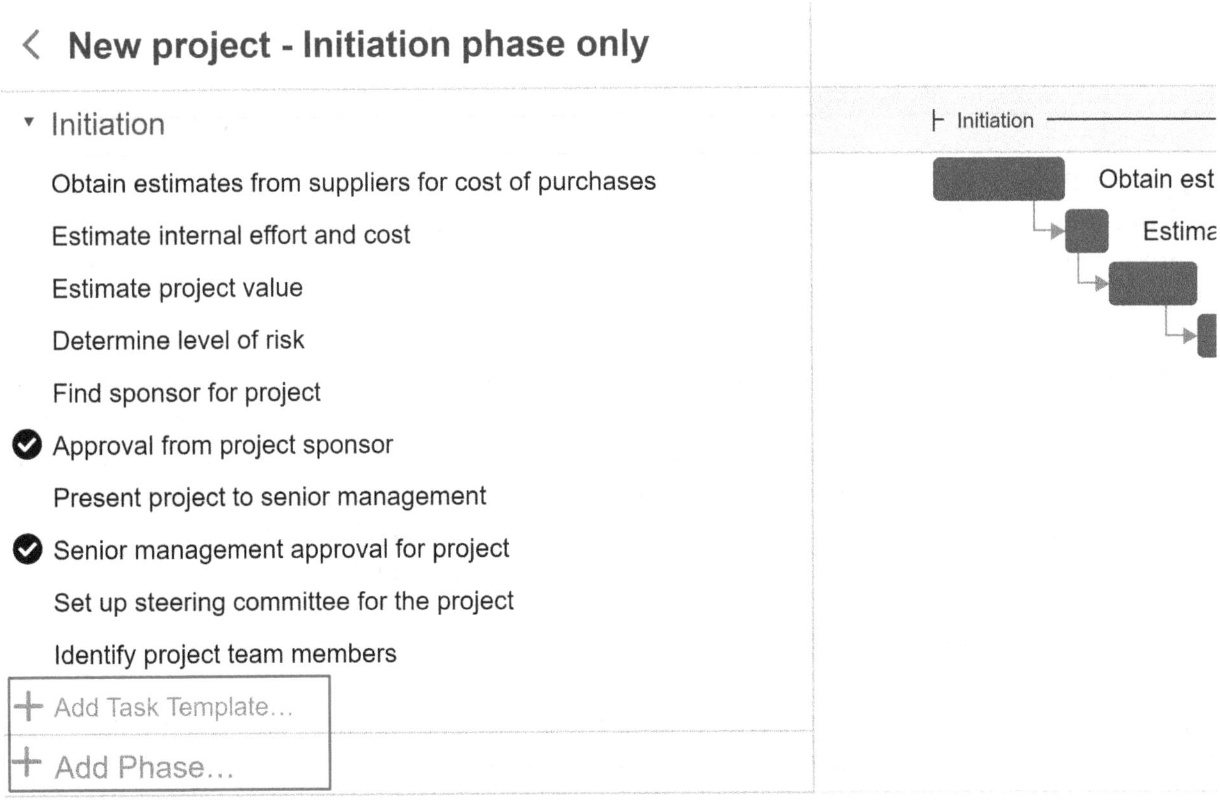

Figure 333: Example of a project template for a project initiation.

The Building Blocks: Project Task Templates

In 4me, project task templates are categorized into Activity, Approval, and Milestone:

Activity project tasks: This category mirrors the structure of a workflow implementation task, including instructions, note fields, and settings for note behavior upon task completion ('Optional' or 'Required'). A defining feature of project task templates compared to workflow task templates is their assignment flexibility; tasks can be allocated to individual users, including end users, without specifying a team. Yet, when designing project templates, project members are often unspecified at the onset. 4me provides options to dynamically assign tasks to roles like the Project Manager or the Service Owner, ensuring relevant tasks are directed to appropriate stakeholders. For broader assignments, tasks may be linked to specific teams or skill pools, such as assigning architectural review tasks to the "System Architects" team or financial validation tasks to the "Financial Controllers" skill pool.

Refined Task Assignment in 4me Projects: When defining assignments within a project, specifying both a team and a skill pool for a task can refine and restrict the assignment process. For example, if a task is allocated to the "Windows Servers support" team, incorporating the "Senior System Engineers" skill pool as part of the assignment ensures that only the most experienced and qualified team members are tasked with the responsibility.

Approval Project Tasks: These tasks align with the structure of workflow approval tasks, providing a platform to establish a virtual steering committee. Managed Service Providers (MSPs) can assign an approval task to the customer to validate project milestones and facilitate the invoicing process tied to those milestones.

Milestones: In 4me, a milestone is characterized by its simplicity, typically consisting of just a Subject and, optionally, a Note field. These milestones denote significant events within the project timeline, such as the completion of a major project phase. This could either add immediate value or resolve an existing challenge affecting other projects. For MSPs, milestones can also indicate when invoicing should occur. Once the project commences, milestones adhere to their initially scheduled dates. Importantly, project managers receive notifications when milestones are achieved or missed.

Planned Duration and Planned Effort

On the Activity and Approval project task templates a 'Planned duration' must be specified. This field is essential and used by the 4me platform to calculate the project schedule. Once the 'Planned duration' is defined, you need to specify the 'Planned effort,' which is vital for tracking the project cost and schedule. Since a task can be assigned to multiple users, the planned effort must be defined for each assignment.

- Time Tracking Activation: Even if time tracking isn't enabled in a 4me account, it will become available for project tasks, as project management cannot proceed without a comprehensive overview of time spent.
- Duration Adjustment: For tasks extending over weeks, leveraging the Gantt chart's drag functionality provides an intuitive method to outline the duration, with 4me auto calculating the total hours.

Project Schedule Development

Once the project record is created, the project manager can embark on constructing the project schedule. This is facilitated through three primary action buttons found in the project's top bar: the Gantt Chart, Task Assignment, and Resource Planning views.

Gantt Chart console: In the project's Gantt chart view, project managers can apply project templates which are typically utilized for standard project phases, such as assessment, initiation, or closure. In specific sectors like building and construction, templates may also be crafted for the implementation phase. However, the unique nature of other projects might require the project manager to directly insert phases, activity, and approval tasks into the Gantt chart.

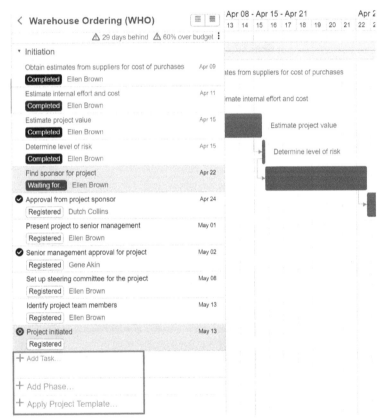

Figure 334: The Gantt Chart console of a project.

When you apply a project template to an existing project, the phases from the template are duplicated into the project. If a phase with the same name already exists, the new tasks will be integrated into that pre-existing phase. To circumvent this and ensure distinct phases for different segments of your project, such as 'build-1', 'build-2', etc., simply double-click on the existing phase name to rename it. This strategy allows for the application of the same template across multiple, uniquely named phases.

Task Assignment console: Proceeding to the Task Assignment console, the project manager can add all necessary assignment records, including teams, skill pools, and individual project members. These resources are conveniently dragged and dropped onto corresponding tasks. Initially, during the project schedule setup, member assignments are typically restricted to the assessment and initiation phases, with broader team and skill pool assignments allocated for later stages.

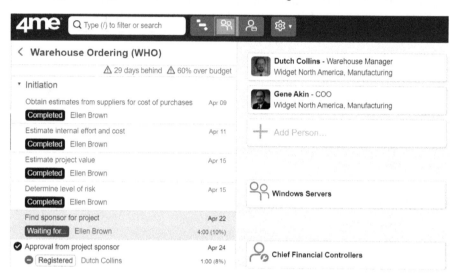

Figure 335: The Task Assignment console of a project.

Resource Planning console: The final step involves navigating to the Resource Planning console. Here, defining the Planned Effort for each task is crucial. Tasks lacking designated planned effort are easily identified in the sidebar by their lack of a percentage indicator, meaning that all hours are yet to be allocated as planned effort. In phases where project members are directly assigned, Resource Planning offers a visual representation of potential resource conflicts, considering assignments from other projects and tasks. Conversely, for tasks delegated at the team or skill pool level, the tool displays overall demand.

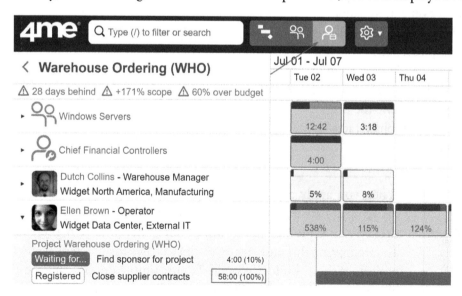

Figure 336: The Resource Planning console. Tasks without a % still need a planned effort.

Project Portfolio Management

After completing the project assessment, projects become candidates for selection. In many corporate settings, there's typically an annual or semi-annual review conducted by a management committee to decide which projects will proceed for the upcoming year.

The 4me platform aids this decision-making process with two insightful dashboards located in the Portfolio Management section of the Analytics console:

- **Bubble Chart Analysis**: This dashboard visualizes the candidate projects on a bubble chart, where the X-axis represents the estimated value of each project, and the Y-axis indicates the risk level. Projects are shown as bubbles, with their size (radius) illustrating the Return on Investment (ROI). Ideally, projects positioned in the lower-right quadrant with larger bubbles are the most favorable candidates for selection.

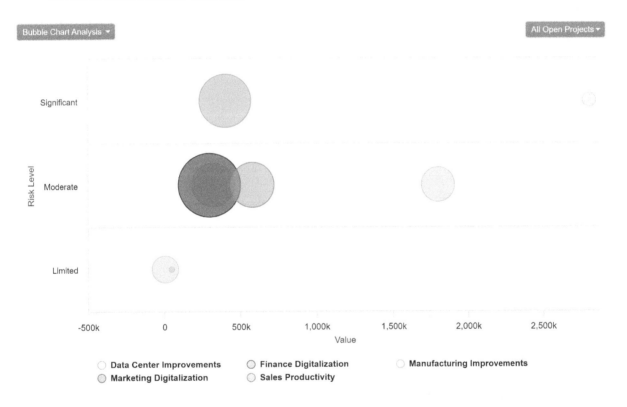

Figure 337: Project portfolio management - the Bubble Chart Analysis dashboard.

- **Waterline Overview**: This dashboard presents candidate projects in a tabular format, detailing their Category, Risk Level, effort costs, purchase costs, total costs, and Value.

Within the Waterline Overview, users can 'drag' project candidates above the 'waterline' to simulate investment costs and resource requirements for selected projects. Summing up the allocated investment costs helps in budget planning and prioritization. Once decisions are finalized, marking the 'Budget Allocated' field for selected projects will remove them from these dashboards, signaling their transition from candidates to active projects.

Waterline Overview ▾
All Programs ▾

Project	Category	Risk Level	Effort	Cost of Effort	Cost of Purchases	Total Cost	Value	ROI	
Data 2020 Data Center Improvements	Large	Moderate	4,000 hours	US$ 400,000	US$ 600,000	US$ 1,000,000	US$ 1,800,000	80%	⋮
Digital Marketing (DiMa) Marketing Digitalization	Large	Significant	800 hours	US$ 65,000	US$ 60,000	US$ 125,000	US$ 400,000	220%	⋮
Digital Operations Center … Data Center Improvements	Small	Limited	16 hours	US$ 1,600	US$ 4,000	US$ 5,600	US$ 8,000	43%	⋮
Above waterline: 3 projects			**4,816 hours**	**US$ 466,600**	**US$ 664,000**	**US$ 1,130,600**	**US$ 2,208,000**	**95%**	
Best in Customer Satisfact… Data Center Improvements	Medium	Moderate	720 hours	US$ 72,000	US$ 61,000	US$ 133,000	US$ 320,000	141%	⋮
Warehouse Ordering (WHO) Manufacturing Improvements	Large	Significant	3,200 hours	US$ 320,000	US$ 2,315,000	US$ 2,635,000	US$ 2,800,000	6%	⋮
COBIT Certification (CoCert) Data Center Improvements	Medium	Limited	400 hours	US$ 40,000	US$ 10,000	US$ 50,000	US$ 50,000	0%	⋮
Mobile Salesforce Tablets … Sales Productivity	Large	Moderate	420 hours	US$ 42,000	US$ 190,000	US$ 232,000	US$ 580,000	150%	⋮
Expense Reporting V12 Finance Digitalization	Medium	Moderate	700 hours	US$ 70,000	US$ 0	US$ 70,000	US$ 297,000	324%	

Figure 338: Project portfolio management - the Waterline Overview.

Project Follow Up

Project Management Essentials: Tracking Cost, Schedule, and Scope

The core of project management methodologies is encapsulated in the well-known project management triangle, representing the balance between cost, schedule, and scope. These elements outline the quality of the deliverables, each influencing the other. Project managers often navigate between these constraints to maintain project quality.

A distinguishing feature of the 4me project management functionality is its real-time tracking capability of these three crucial dimensions. In each project, the left-top bar displays these dimensions, providing immediate visibility into the project's health. This information stems from the project baseline, which records and tracks data for every project task.

The baseline feature includes a 'Show Baseline' action, integrating baseline data directly into the Gantt chart. This empowers project managers with clear insights into which specific tasks are contributing to any deviations from the planned cost, schedule, and scope, facilitating informed decision-making and corrective actions.

Figure 339: The Project Management Triangle.

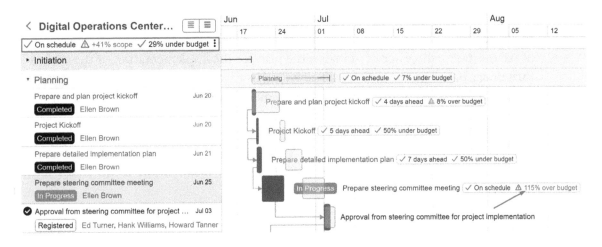

Figure 340: The project baseline details visible on the Gantt chart.

How it Works - Earned Value Management

The 4me platform integrates **Earned Value Management (EVM)**, a sophisticated project management technique designed to objectively assess project performance and progression. What sets 4me apart in project management is its user-friendly and real-time execution; neither project team members nor managers need to delve into the complexities of EVM. The platform simplifies the process by automatically generating and displaying results. For a practical understanding of how EVM functions within 4me, we recommend exploring the following demo scenario.

	4me Project Management **Tracking Cost, Schedule, and Scope**

Meeting with Ellen Brown, the dynamic project manager at Widget Data Center, we find her steering the Digital Operations Center (DOC) project with a mission to seamlessly integrate Microsoft's OpManager within the center. However, Ellen encounters challenges with the existing project plan: vital tasks, such as project management during implementation, are notably absent. Moreover, she's keen to leverage the expertise of Microsoft's Subject Matter Experts for the setup. Let's see how Ellen revises the project schedule and how these modifications impact the project's baseline:

- Log in as ellen.brown@widget.com to Widget Data Center.
  - Check the inbox: it includes a project task *"Prepare steering committee meeting."*
  - In the project task, CTRL+ Click on the project record (or go to the Records console and select projects) to open the *Digital Operations Center (DOC)* project.
  - Open the Gantt Chart (click on the icon in the top bar).
  - Check the actual baseline in the top-left bar; it appears satisfactory.

- In the implementation phase, add a new task: "Project Management."
- Make this task a successor of "Finalize the plan for the implementation of the project" (just drag a line from this task to the new task).
- Adjust the duration of the "Project Management" task to span over the entire project (just drag the right side of the task to project's end).
- Proceed to *Task Assignment*. Select the second action button in the top bar to open this view.
- Assign Ellen Brown to the new "Project Management" Task.
- Click on "Add Person..." and type Microsoft to find all (external) users from Microsoft. Select *Jamie Styx*.
- Assign Jamie Stux to the '*Setup production environment*' task.
- Define the effort required for these activities.
- Click on the Resource Planning view.
- Check Ellen Brown's resource availability: she is overbooked.
- Click on the little arrow before Ellen Brown. Note that the Project Management task doesn't have a percentage, indicating that the estimated planned effort equals the planned duration, explaining the overbooking. Click on the task and fill in the Planned effort field with 16:00 hours. Save the task and confirm that the resource planning now looks appropriate.
- Return to the Inbox.
- Edit the project task "*Prepare steering committee meeting.*"
- Add 2:00 hours to the Time spent field.
- Note that all Planned effort has been consumed now; since the task is not finished, specify the *Remaining effort*. Enter 1:00 hour and save.
- Next, Ellen prepares a presentation for the steering committee, requiring an additional hour of her time. Edit the task again, set the status to Completed, and add the extra hour in the Time spent field.
- Go back to the Project record.
- Check the Baseline: you have introduced scope creep, and the budget alignment is compromised.
- Display the baseline on the Gantt chart.
- Note that the "*Prepare steering committee meeting*" is 40% over budget.

Earned Value Management (EVM) is fundamentally intuitive. Consider a straightforward example: imagine a project focused on constructing a 100-meter wall. The worker is expected to build at a rate of 1 meter per hour, equating to a total estimated effort of 100 hours. If, at the halfway point, the worker reports having worked 50 hours, the project manager gains limited insight without evaluating the work's physical progress. However, if the worker estimates an additional 150 hours to complete the task, the situation becomes clearer. In this scenario, only 25 meters, or 25% of the wall, are complete, indicating a 100% budget overrun, as 25 meters should have been achieved with 25 hours of work. Moreover, if the project's initial schedule anticipated these 25 meters to be finished four days earlier, a schedule delay is also evident.

In 4me, as project members log their activity and record time spent, the platform automatically calculates the estimated **remaining effort**, factoring in the total planned effort and time already expended. Here, project members are prompted to review and possibly adjust the proposed remaining effort by 4me, ensuring a more realistic forecast. This figure must be provided in hours rather than percentages to avoid the common trap of overly optimistic '80% complete' scenarios, which often overlook detailed finishing tasks like testing, documentation, and administration. This precise and real-time feedback is invaluable for the project manager, shifting from typical weekly updates to continuous, dynamic monitoring. It embodies a crucial project management principle: significant cost and schedule variances are often detected early, requiring substantive measures for correction.

Understanding the EVM baselines

The calculations for earned value require a baseline. This is essentially a snapshot of the project schedule at a certain point, detailing when tasks were originally expected to be completed. In 4me, these baselines are generated automatically whenever a new project phase commences, eliminating the need for project managers to manually create or adjust baselines.

Baseline Creation and Management: A baseline takes on the name of the project phase that initiated its creation. By default, a project's progress—covering budget, schedule, and scope deviations—is measured against the initial baseline. However, project managers have the flexibility to adjust this in the project settings, choosing which baseline should be used for comparison purposes.

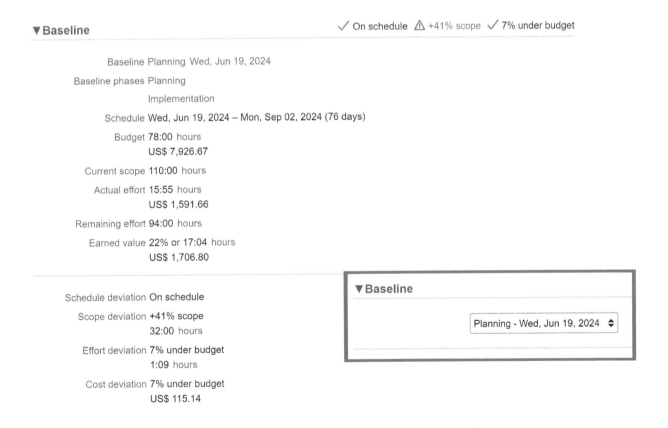

Figure 341: Project baseline selection.

Baseline Constraints: For a baseline to be created, task assignments must be clear, meaning all necessary information must be filled out. In the Gantt chart, any tasks lacking vital details are marked with an orange exclamation symbol. Should a project phase conclude with the succeeding phase unable to commence due to incomplete information, the project status shifts to **Progress Halted**, prompting a notification to the project manager.

Managing Scope Changes: It's common in many projects for the scope to evolve, leading to the addition of new tasks. These changes, once incorporated into the project plan, will manifest as scope deviations from the original baseline. Upon endorsement of the new scope and budget by the steering committee, it's advisable to start a new project phase, perhaps titled "Implementation plan – Scope V2." This strategy allows the project manager to monitor the project against this updated baseline while retaining the option to compare progress with the original expectations.

As a sidenote, when clicking on the baseline record, 4me provides the details of the baseline, including typical Earned Value Management graphs. This feature offers in-depth insights into the project's performance metrics and variations from planned values.

The Project Management Office (PMO) Perspective

For monitoring all projects within an organization's portfolio, a Project Management Office (PMO) can craft specialized dashboards using the extensive range of reports available. However, 4me particularly highlights two ready-made reports beneficial for PMO analysis:

Portfolio Insight Dashboard

Accessible from the project records console, the "Portfolio Insight" dashboard offers a comprehensive view of all active projects within the 4me account. For accounts with strict privacy settings, it displays projects relevant to the logged-in user. Each project is detailed with metrics crucial for project assessment:

# ID	SUBJECT	◎ TARGET	COST	EFFORT	SCOPE	SCHEDULE
7499	Expense Reporting V12	Aug 12	⚠ 30% over budget	⚠ 11% over budget		⚠ 11 days behind
7497	Digital Operations Center ...	Sep 03	✓ 7% under budget	✓ 7% under budget	⚠ +41% scope	✓ On schedule
7345	Warehouse Ordering (WHO)	Jul 23	⚠ 60% over budget	⚠ 60% over budget	⚠ +171% scope	⚠ 28 days behind
4021	Best in Customer Satisfact...	Aug 23	⚠ 75% over budget	⚠ 75% over budget		⚠ 53 days behind

Figure 342: The Portfolio Insight dashboard, one of the available views in the project section in the records console.

- **Target**: Displays the expected completion date based on current progress.
- **Cost**: Indicates the variance from the projected budget.
- **Effort**: Shows any deviations from the planned labor input.
- **Scope**: Highlights whether there has been an expansion or reduction in project scope.
- **Schedule**: Assesses whether the project is lagging or leading its planned timeline.
- **Risk**: Reports the highest risk severity associated with the project.

The Project Calendar

The "Project Calendar" is a particularly valuable dashboard for PMOs needing to scrutinize inter-project dependencies or potential scheduling conflicts. This tool is accessible within the Analytics console under the '**Project Calendar**' section.

Upon accessing, the Project Calendar illustrates the timeline of ongoing project phases within the chosen date range. By default, the display is set to 'Projects Managed by Me,' but alternatives include 'All Projects' and 'Projects for My Team's Services.' Users have the flexibility to apply filters for a more tailored view, focusing on specific projects defined by selected attributes.

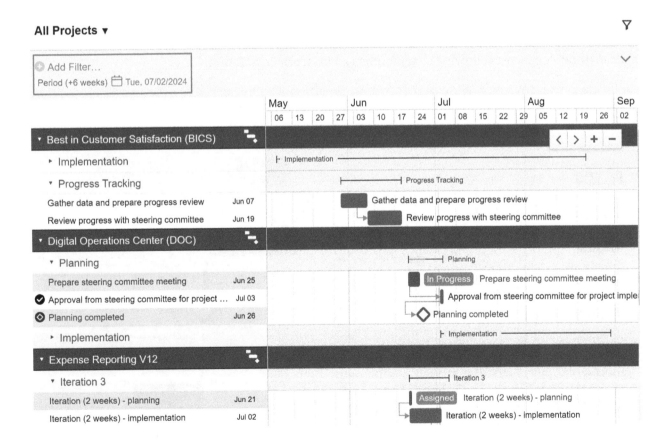

Figure 343: The Project Calendar in the Analytics console, with an overview of all project activities in a 6 weeks' timeslot.

The interface allows for the expansion or contraction of project details or phases by clicking on them within the left-hand section of the screen. Expanding the phases reveals a granular view that includes all associated project tasks, enhancing the analysis depth. Like other calendar views within 4me, users can navigate through time via the < > buttons and adjust the view scale using the + – controls. The integrated Gantt chart icons adjacent to project titles enable quick transitions to the Gantt chart view for any chosen project. Selecting any task from the calendar will open it in edit mode for further examination or adjustments.

Agile Project Management

A common question arises when exploring 4me's extensive project management capabilities: How does it accommodate agile project management? In 4me, agile project management is facilitated by structuring iterations within a project template. This allows a project to integrate iterations into a comprehensive plan. The Earned Value Management (EVM) baseline further supports agile practices by providing a burndown chart, assisting project managers in tracking the remaining budget across various sprints or iterations over time.

However, embracing an agile methodology goes beyond merely adapting project plans to include iterations. Agile encompasses a broader spectrum of practices and principles aimed at enhancing collaboration, flexibility, and iterative progress. For those eager to delve deeper into leveraging 4me for agile methodologies, the following chapter offers an in-depth exploration.

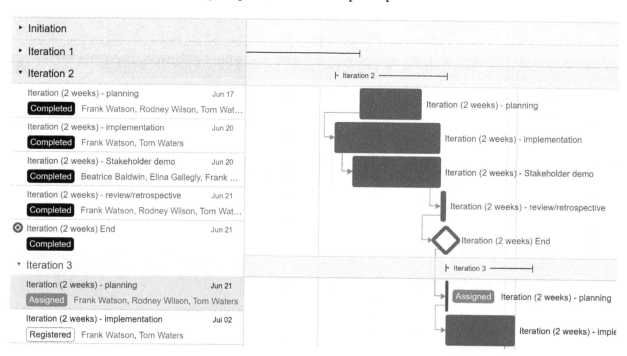

Figure 344: A project plan with multiple iterations.

Chapter 22 - Agile and Scrum

Introduction

Rewind to the early 2000s: the software development landscape faced significant challenges. Beyond the infamous dot-com bubble burst, a more pressing issue emerged—the alarming failure rate of software projects. Budgets swelled, timelines extended, and yet, the output often fell short of expectations. This, despite rigorous adherence to established project management methodologies and advanced software engineering frameworks.

Then, in February 2001, a pivotal moment arrived: the Agile Manifesto was unveiled. This event sparked a slow but revolutionary shift in project approaches. What began as a ripple in the realm of software development has evolved into a tidal wave of change, influencing disciplines far beyond, from marketing to service improvement.

This chapter won't explain the Agile Paradigm in detail—that's a story for another book. Though understanding the essence of Agile is crucial: It lies in its systematic process to address the uncertainties that plague project deliverables. This ambiguity presents itself in two primary dimensions: the 'What'—the exact nature of the deliverable, and the 'How'—the methods and processes for constructing the deliverable.

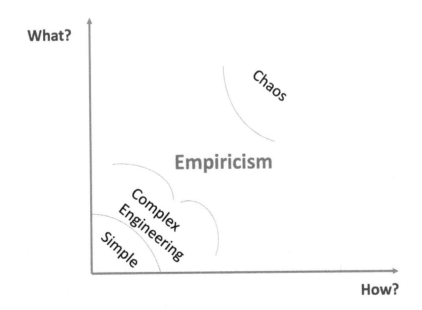

Figure 345: Empiricism at the center of the Agile Paradigm.

Traditional methods often assume a clarity that may not exist, leading to misalignments between expectations and outcomes. Agile, by contrast, adopts an empirical methodology, advocating for a process where knowledge and understanding evolve through experience and continuous observation.

It's crucial to recognize the contexts where Agile is most applicable. In scenarios with clearly defined outcomes and established methodologies, such as the onboarding process, Agile may not offer additional value—a standard workflow suffices. Even projects like bridge construction, despite their inherent complexities and initial uncertainties, still conform to established engineering protocols, making them suitable for a more structured, waterfall approach.

Conversely, there's the realm of total unpredictability—akin to major incident management scenarios— where the starting conditions are chaotic, and rapid, ad-hoc responses are necessary. Here, the focus is less on meticulous planning and more on assembling a versatile team ready to tackle immediate challenges through clear and concise communication.

It's within the spectrum between these polarities—the well-defined and the utterly unknown—that Agile methodology truly shines. This is the domain of innovation and creativity, where the outcomes are not just uncertain but are waiting to be discovered. Whether it's developing a groundbreaking product, designing a disruptive marketing campaign, or supporting continual service improvements, Agile offers a framework that embraces change, fosters iterative learning, and encourages collaboration and feedback. The 4me platform doesn't just 'support' Agile; it's designed to integrate Agile methodologies into the very fabric of enterprise service management. This integration ensures that Agile projects are not isolated endeavors but are harmoniously aligned with the organization's overall service management strategy. By doing so, 4me helps prevent the formation of 'Agile islands'—isolated teams operating independently of the broader organizational processes and objectives.

4me Agile Features

In a new 4me account, Agile functionalities are not automatically turned on. They require activation which can be easily accomplished by the *account owner*. This is done through a straightforward toggle within the Account Settings labeled 'Agile'. With this single adjustment, a range of Agile tools becomes available, opening up new possibilities for all specialists within the platform. These tools include Product Backlogs, Agile Boards, and Scrum Workspaces.

Product Backlogs

In the project management chapter, we discussed the importance of establishing a demand management process, treating business requests as potential 'demands'. These could signal new project opportunities or suggestions for enhancements. In an agile framework, organizations continuously harvest new ideas, ranging from proposals for brand-new projects to improvements on existing services or products. These suggestions might also stem from ongoing Agile projects, reflecting the Agile philosophy that enhancements emerge through ongoing observation and experience.

In 4me, all these ideas, whether for new projects or for enhancements to existing ones, can be added to a Product Backlog. Requests, and even Problems for which the root cause has been identified, can funnel into a Product Backlog. Concerning a Problem, once the underlying cause of an issue is pinpointed, it could reveal that the solution lies in a new feature or improvement.

A Product Backlog in 4me is streamlined, containing only essential fields: a Name, an optional avatar or image, a Product Owner, and a rich-text Description. The Description is particularly crucial in a Scrum framework; it should outline the product goals and the criteria for completion of the items ('Definition of Done'). Adding requests or problems to the backlog is straightforward: simply select 'Add to Product Backlog...' from the Actions menu. Once added, an item adopts an "On Backlog" status and exits the inbox of the assigned user or team. At this juncture, the support team, alongside the Product Owner, decides when to resume work on the item.

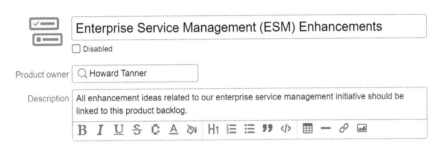

Figure 346: The 4me Product Backlog record.

The accessibility of a product backlog extends to all specialists within the account, aligning with Agile's call for complete transparency and confidence in teams and individuals. Specialists can contribute new ideas directly to the backlog via the Add New Request button, initiating a request that automatically assumes an "On Backlog" status.

Prioritization within the backlog is a vital function normally performed by the Product Owner, who adjusts the queue based on customer and stakeholder importance. This is achieved through a simple yet effective mechanism in 4me: items are dragged and dropped within the list to reorder them, with the highest priority items positioned at the top. This can be done by any specialist: while the Product Owner has significant influence in this process, prioritization should ideally be collaborative, involving discussions with all relevant stakeholders.

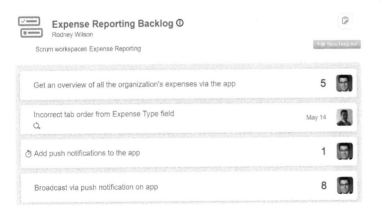

Hovering over an item in the backlog enables editing, revealing the standard ticket form plus an additional field for '**Estimate**', where story points can be allocated to each item. Further insights into estimates and story points will be explored as we dive into the Scrum workspaces within 4me.

Figure 347: The items on a Product Backlog are ordered by priority. Story points can be added in the Estimate field of each item.

Agile Boards

Agile Boards, often referred to as 'Information Radiators' within the Agile framework, are designed to transparently showcase the flow and progress of a project or of product development. This term underscores the concept of making project information as accessible and easily understandable as the warmth spreading from a radiator. An Agile Board is structured to provide a clear, at-a-glance view of the team's activities, with columns that sequentially represent the stages each item passes through until completion. These stages, labeled with straightforward terms such as 'Analysis,' 'Build,' 'Test,' and 'In Production,' are arranged from left to right, ensuring that anyone who views the board can instantly grasp the current project or product development status. Items on an Agile Board can be effortlessly dragged from one stage to the next, mirroring real-time progress.

In 4me, creating a new Agile Board is a straightforward process, accessible to any *specialist*. Like setting up a Product Backlog, establishing an Agile Board requires minimal inputs: a distinctive Name, an assigned Manager, and a comprehensive rich-text Description. The Manager of the board, who essentially 'owns' it, is responsible for curating and updating the board's columns—adding, deleting, moving, and adjusting their attributes to best reflect the project's or product development's workflow. The true value and functionality of an Agile Board lie in its columns, specifically in their logical, left-to-right sequence, which guides the team's work from inception to deployment.

In many scenarios, an Agile Board reflects the workload of a specific team, encompassing requests, tasks, problems, and even project tasks assigned to the team or individual team members. This brings up an important consideration: should a team primarily monitor their Inbox or the Agile Board for updates? When a team considers the Agile Board as the main stage, the team can opt for an approach where all items assigned to them are automatically placed in the first column of their designated Agile Board. This can be achieved by linking the Agile Board directly to the team through the team record settings.

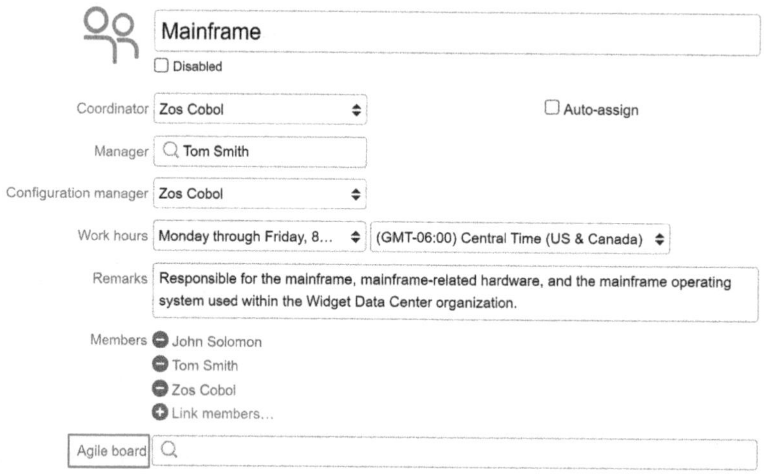

Figure 348: Linking a team to an Agile Board.

By integrating the team's coordination activities with the Agile Board, the reliance on checking the Inbox is reduced, except for approval or project tasks without a specific team assignment. Team members will still find tickets in their Inbox assigned specifically to them, but these will be clearly associated with the Agile Board. The Board's details are displayed at the bottom of the Inbox view, allowing specialists to quickly identify the relevant Board and even move the ticket to another column directly from the Inbox.

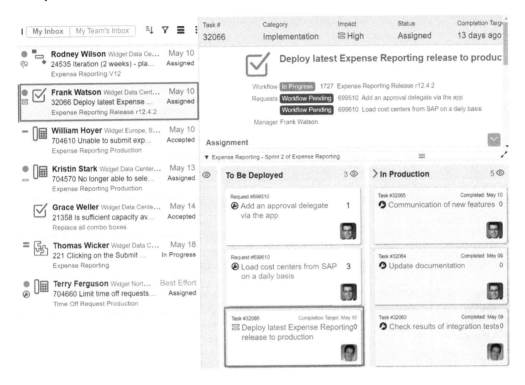

Figure 349: Integration of the Agile Board within the Inbox View. A specialist has the capability to transition a ticket to a different column of the Agile Board directly from the Inbox.

Agile Board Columns: Understanding the Settings

The functionality of an Agile Board largely hinges on the configuration of its columns. Let's examine the diverse settings available for an Agile Board column:

- **Remove After**: Once a ticket has moved to the final column, indicating that the task is completed, it could over time lead to clutter due to the accumulation of finished items. To maintain clarity, it's possible to set an automatic removal of items from a column after a set number of days, typically ranging between 14 and 28 days.
- **Action**: It's often practical to automatically update the status of a ticket as it progresses to a new column. Options include 'Assign,' 'Accept,' 'Start,' and 'Complete.' The 'Complete' action is typically used for the final column. 'Accept' and 'Start' (which changes the status to 'In Progress') are useful when the ticket needs to be actively picked up by the specialist moving the item. The 'Assign' action indicates that when the item moves to a new column, it should be re-assigned back to the team.
- **Dialog Type**: When a ticket is transitioned into a new column, additional information may be necessary. Choosing the 'Minimal' dialog type prompts a simple form for entering a public or internal note attached to the request. If more interaction is needed, selecting the 'Full' dialog type is advisable.

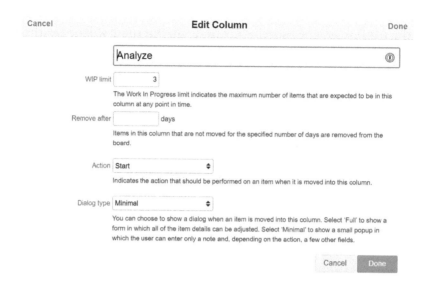

Figure 350: Agile Board column fields.

> **Tip**
>
> For Agile Boards that involve multiple teams, the necessary actions may need finer adjustments beyond the standard options provided. This complexity can be addressed through automation rules. By using the `'On update of Agile board column'` trigger along with attributes like `'agile_board'`, `'agile_board_was'`, `'agile_board_column'`, and `'agile_board_column_was'`, various scenarios can be efficiently automated.

Defining the WIP Limit: Embrace 'Start Finishing, Stop Starting'

A critical principle in both Agile and Lean methodologies, particularly embodied in the Kanban framework, is **'Start Finishing, Stop Starting.'** This principle advocates for the completion of ongoing tasks or work items before initiating new ones. This strategy aims to minimize work in progress (WIP), streamline workflow, and enhance overall productivity. In 4me, WIP limits can be assigned to each column on an agile board, and a clear alert is issued when these limits are exceeded. By implementing WIP limits, a 4me Agile Board can effectively function as a **Kanban Board**.

Transparency Through Shared Agile Boards

For service providers aiming to enhance transparency with their clients, 4me allows the sharing of Agile Boards directly with customer representatives through 4me Self Service. This functionality enables customers to monitor the progress of their requests, including the specific stage each request is in and the volume of active requests on the board. To facilitate this, an *account administrator* or *service level manager* can modify Agile Board settings to associate it with one or several Service-Level Agreements

(SLAs). Consequently, the Agile Board becomes accessible in the 4me Self-Service portal for users designated as '*customer representatives*' for the linked SLAs. This feature not only fosters transparency but also strengthens the trust between service providers and their clients by providing real-time insights into task progression and team workload.

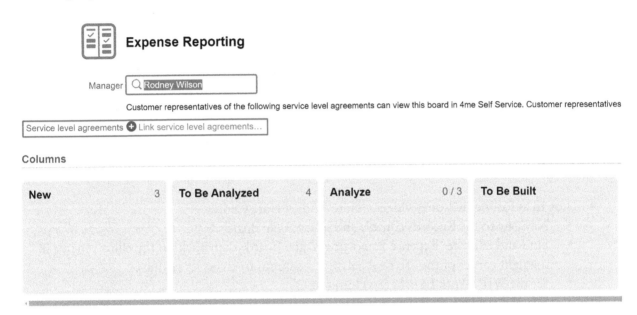

Figure 351: An Account Administrator or Service-Level Manager can link an Agile Board to Service-Level Agreements. This will allow the customer representatives to see the Agile Board in the Self-Service Portal.

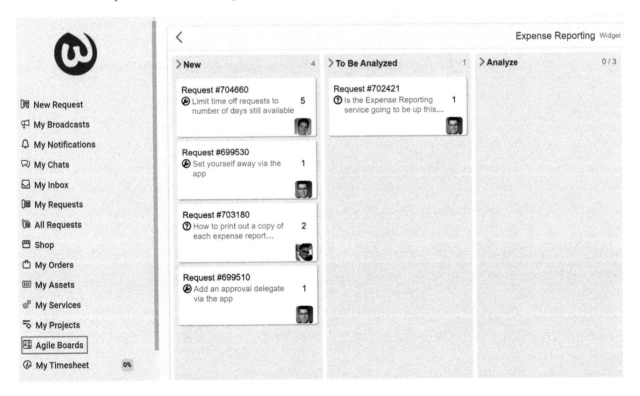

Figure 352: An Agile Board visible on the Self-Service Portal by a customer representative. The customer representative can only see the item details for requests linked to 'their' SLA.

Agile and Scrum
Defining a WIP Limit on an Agile Board

In Widget Data Center, the development of the Expense Reporting product is conducted following Agile principles, utilizing a product backlog and an Agile Board. However, the application development team realizes they are taking on too many analysis items, detracting from their capacity to develop new features. To address this, they decide to restrict the number of analysis tasks to two at any given time. Rodney Wilson, the owner of the Agile Board, will adjust the column settings to enforce this limit. Here's how Rodney proceeds:

- Log in as Rodney.wilson@widget.com to Widget Data Center.
  - Navigate to the Records console and select 'Agile Boards.'
  - Find and edit the 'Expense Reporting' Agile Board, then click on the ellipsis menu in the right corner of the 'To be Analyzed...' column to access its settings.
  - Set the WIP (Work In Progress) Limit to '2'.
  - Save the changes.
  - Observe how the column's color alters and note the WIP limit now displayed in the column's right corner.

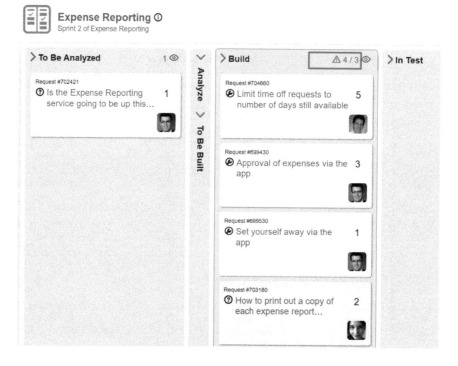

Figure 353: Defining a WIP Limit to an Agile Board column turns a 4me Agile Board into a 'Kanban Board'.

Implementing Scrum with 4me: Scrum Workspaces

In 4me, the use of Product Backlogs and Agile Boards enables an agile implementation across various organizational domains. For instance, Sales & Marketing departments can manage a broad spectrum of initiatives using these tools. Similarly, they are effective for driving continuous improvement initiatives within enterprise service management frameworks.

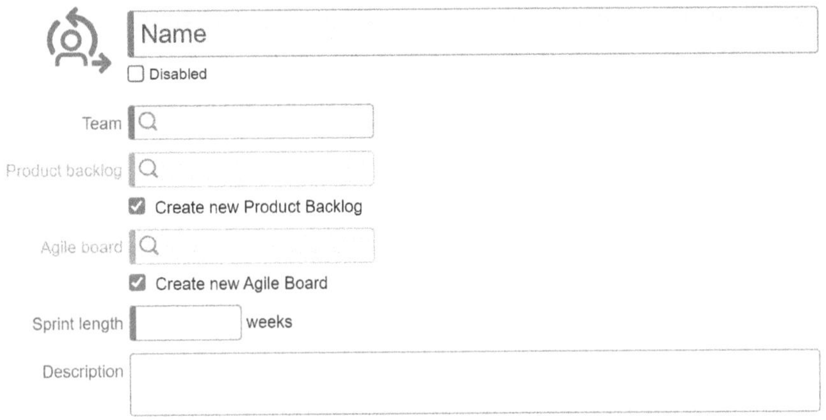

Figure 354: Defining a new Scrum Workspace.

For teams engaged in application development and adhering to the Scrum framework, particularly those working in sprint cycles, 4me offers the specialized feature of Scrum Workspaces. A Scrum Workspace bridges a team with a Product Backlog and an Agile Board via Sprints.

In setting up a Scrum Workspace, beyond just linking a team to these essential elements, one must define the Sprint Duration, typically ranging from one to two weeks.

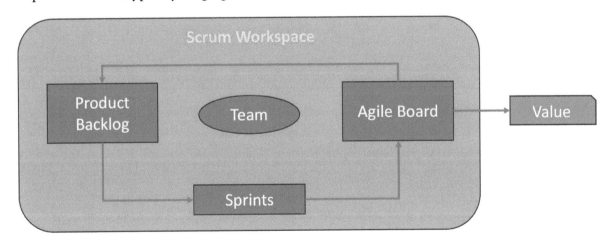

Figure 355: A Scrum Workspace: Linking a Team to a Product Backlog and an Agile Board through Sprints.

Overview of Scrum Workspaces

In 4me, accessing a Scrum Workspace immediately presents the active sprint's Burn-Down Chart. This graph illustrates the consumption of story points over the course of the sprint. It contrasts the '**Ideal Trend**'—how story points should ideally be completed over time—with the actual line ('**Remaining Line**') indicating the remaining story points. Optionally, a '**Scope Change**' line is featured, tracking any items added to the sprint post commencement. Once begun, the scope of a sprint in Scrum should ideally remain fixed. However, in the dynamic operational settings where 4me Scrum Workspaces operate, unforeseen necessities such as critical bugs or regression errors from a prior release may necessitate scope adjustments. Thus, despite traditional Scrum principles, these urgent issues can and should be incorporated into the ongoing sprint.

The Scrum Workspace also provides an overview of the sprints: the already-completed sprints, the active sprint, and the next sprint (with status 'Registered'). This allows team members and stakeholders to quickly assess past performance, current progress, and future planning.

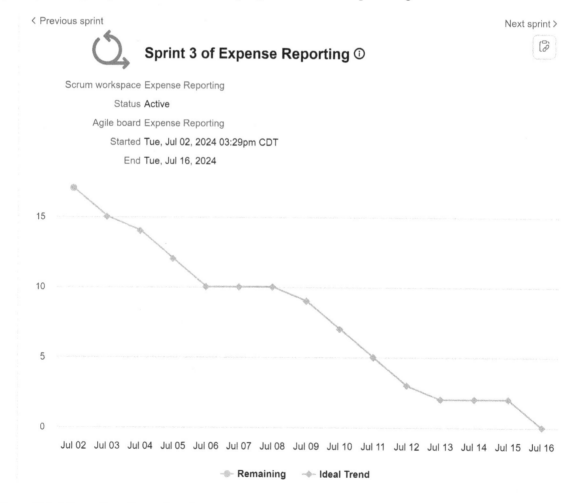

Figure 356: A Sprint Burn-Down chart for a new sprint.

Scrum Events in 4me

Scrum involves five principal events: Sprint Planning, Daily Scrum, Sprint Review, Sprint Retrospective, and the Sprint itself. Let's explore how 4me's Scrum Workspace aids in conducting the first three of these events effectively.

Scrum Planning

The Sprint Planning event is where the team, often with input from the product owner, decides on the workload they can realistically undertake for the upcoming sprint. 4me supports this crucial activity with its 'Plan a Sprint' feature, found at the top of the Scrum Workspace. This feature becomes particularly

handy after completing the actual sprint, smoothly transitioning into the new sprint's planning. Unfinished items from the current sprint are automatically carried over, giving the team a clear indication of where to start.

The Scrum Workspace layout in 4me presents the product backlog on the left and the upcoming sprint on the right, allowing for easy transfer of items between the two. Team members can drag backlog items into the new sprint, relying on previously-assigned 'Estimates' or story points on the product backlog to guide their decisions.

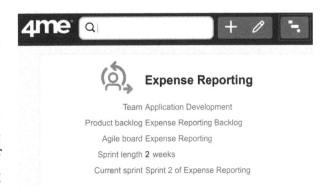

Figure 357: The Sprint Planning icon in the top header bar of the Scrum Workspace.

The aggregate story points for the sprint are visible in the top-right corner and adjust in real-time as items are moved. Crucially, team members can modify the '**Sprint Estimate**' for any item in the new sprint by hovering over it to access the edit icon. This feature is invaluable, as it allows the team to adjust estimates based on the actual progress of unfinished items or to account for any additional complexities encountered during the previous sprint. This adjustment capability ensures that the team's planning reflects their most current understanding and circumstances.

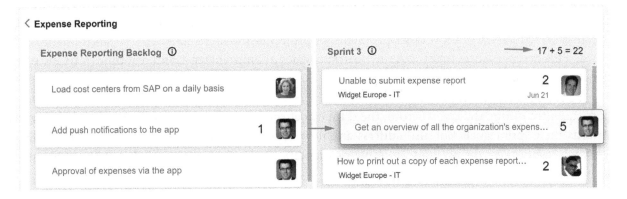

Figure 358: When moving an item from the product backlog to a sprint, the story points are dynamically added to the total number of story points of the sprint.

After finalizing the scope of the new sprint, team members can officially commence the sprint by pressing the 'Play' button, thereby starting a new focused cycle of work.

Tip   **Understanding and Applying Story Points**

The concept of story points is central to evaluating team velocity in Scrum—that is, the average amount of work a team can complete in one sprint. Story points represent 'relative effort' rather than exact hours, reflecting the combined aspects of task complexity, uncertainty, and effort required. This approach discourages equating story points directly to hours for several reasons:

- **Uncertainty in Agile Projects**: Agile and Scrum methodologies operate under conditions of uncertainty where the exact effort needed cannot be precisely known upfront. By using abstract units like story points, teams encourage discussion on an item's complexity and unknowns, fostering a deeper understanding of the work involved.
- **Focus on Team Velocity**: Story points are designed to measure the collective performance of a team, not individual productivity. In a diverse team, different members might take more or less time to complete the same task due to varying experience levels. By avoiding direct hour estimates, story points maintain the focus on what the team, as a whole, can accomplish, promoting a team-centric approach to project estimation and planning.

Remember, the goal with story points is to guide the team in understanding their own work pace and capacity, enabling more accurate sprint planning and performance assessment based on collective experience and past performance.

Daily Scrum and Sprint Review

The Agile Board stands as the focal point for a Scrum team's daily operations and is integral to conducting the **Daily Scrum**. As it is directly linked to the team, any ticket assigned to them—be it incidents, information requests, workflow tasks, problems, or project tasks—automatically appears on their Agile Board. This design ensures that the Agile Board provides a comprehensive and real-time overview of all activities impacting the Scrum team.

Consequently, during the Daily Scrum, the team can effectively review and assess not only the progress towards their sprint goals but also address any new issues or tasks that have emerged. This holistic approach ensures that the Scrum team remains adaptable and responsive to the dynamic environment of their workspace.

The Agile Board takes center stage not only during the Daily Scrum but also in the sprint review at the end of each sprint. It visually represents the achievements of the past sprint and highlights the items that remain unfinished. Within the context of the Scrum Workspace, navigating from the Agile Board to the current sprint is easy. Concluding the current sprint activates a seamless transition where all unfinished items are automatically moved to the sprint planning view for the upcoming sprint.

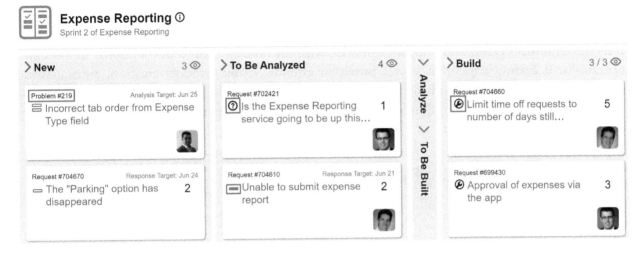

Figure 359: The Agile Board in the Scrum Workspace providing the complete picture including new incidents, problems, information requests, and workflow tasks.

Integrating Scrum with Organizational Processes

A significant strength of the 4me platform is its capacity to break down organizational silos. This capability extends to configuring Scrum Workspaces within the platform. The Scrum Framework, renowned for emphasizing team empowerment, fosters a bottom-up approach that grants teams

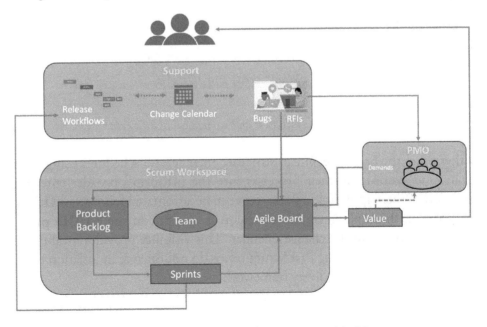

Figure 360: On the 4me platform the Scrum Workspace is fully embedded in the operating model of the organization.

substantial autonomy and responsibility. This departure from traditional top-down methodologies empowers teams to determine sprint contents, with the product owner ensuring alignment with business priorities. This approach has undoubtedly contributed to efficient and quality-driven product development, with 4me serving as a testament to its success.

However, integrating Scrum within 4me does more than just facilitate agile development; it aligns these activities with the organization's operating model, with the broader context of traditional support and operations. It acknowledges that service provision extends beyond product creation, encompassing ongoing support delivered to both internal and external users. In this integrated environment, requests—whether they are incidents (bugs), information inquiries, or enhancement requests—can be smoothly transitioned to the Scrum team.

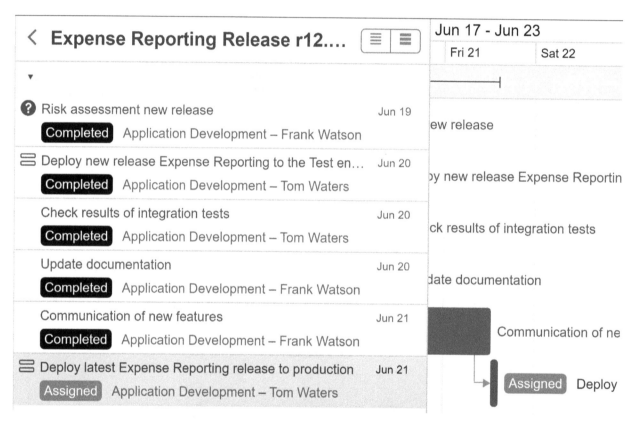

Figure 361: Using workflow templates to support and automate the CI/CD practice.

Furthermore, the Scrum team can structure their release schedules using release workflow templates within 4me, embedding their processes into the platform's broader enterprise service management framework. Where applicable, release steps can be automated following a **DevOps** approach, seamlessly incorporating the deployments of the items in a sprint in the **CI/CD practices** and making these deployments visible in the change calendar. This visibility provides invaluable context to service desk and support teams, ensuring that Scrum teams do not operate in isolation but are fully integrated into the organization's service delivery framework.

Demo

Agile and Scrum
Agile and Scrum Adventures at
Widget Data Center: Sprint Planning Unveiled

Dive into the dynamic world of Widget Data Center where the evolution of the Expense Reporting product unfolds. Join the application development team, anchored in the Scrum framework, as they navigate the conclusive phase of Sprint 12.4.2. Amid the hustle of wrapping up, they set the stage for the deployment of groundbreaking features. Join Frank Watson, a pivotal figure in the DevOps landscape, as he orchestrates the transition of new updates into the live environment. Here's how:

Launching the Process:

- Sign in as Frank Watson at widget.datacenter.com.
  - Head to the 'Scrum Workspaces' under the Records console.
  - Dive into the 'Expense Reporting' Scrum workspace and pinpoint the active Sprint 2.

Agile Board Updates:

- Hit the Agile Board icon to see the items awaiting migration.
- Frank takes the helm, shifting "Add an approval delegate via the app" and "Load cost centers from SAP daily" to the 'In Production' column, marking them with the Completion Reason 'Solved' and a note 'In production now', dedicating a minute for each request's closure.
- Seamlessly move the 'Deploy latest Expense Reporting release to production' task, spending 30 minutes to ensure flawless execution.

Concluding the Sprint:

- Tap the 'Show sprint' and then 'Finish selected sprint' icons. Encounter the alert: '8 items remain unfinished'. Bravely press 'End'.

The Art of Sprint Planning:

- Witness the new Sprint Planning view. Patiently allow 4me to reallocate unfinished tasks. The sprint's story points stand at 19, but due to diligent prior efforts, "Limit time off requests to number of days still available" needs just one more point. Refine by editing the item to a single Sprint estimate, revising the sprint's total to a compact 15.
- Decide the fate of 'Approval of expenses via the app', reallocating it back to the product backlog, slimming the sprint to 12 points.
- With a team velocity of 15, there's room for more: slide 'Broadcast via push notification on app' into the sprint's embrace.

Embark on the journey:

- Initiate the new sprint by hitting Play.

Crafting the Next Release:

- Transition to crafting the upcoming release. Navigate to 'Workflows' within the Records console and add a new workflow.
- Opt for "*Expense Reporting Release r<r.v.b>*" workflow template, tailor the release info to *r12.4.3*, and start the workflow.
- Return to 'Agile Boards', select the '*Expense Reporting*' board, and ensure the 'Risk assessment' task from the release workflow is added to the agile board.

Chapter 23 - The 4me Shop

Introducing the 4me Shop:
Empowering Enterprise Service Management

In a world where services frequently accompany products, the 4me Shop serves as a pivotal element in delivering a comprehensive solution. Whether it's Fleet Management Services or Employee Mobility Services provided by HR, involving vehicles, or the Personal Computing services by IT with desktops and laptops at their core, the demand for a seamless integration of products into services is undeniable. The 4me Shop brings this integration to life, offering a webshop functionality that users not only appreciate but also expect in today's digital era.

The 4me Shop enables service delivery organizations to extend their offerings to users through what we term 'Shop Articles.' These can range from tangible items like laptops and cars to intangible services such as consultancy and training programs. The beauty of the 4me Shop lies in its ability to morph a simple digital storefront into a dynamic service delivery platform. Beyond browsing and purchasing, the 4me Shop supports the intricate backend processes essential for delivering a premium webshop experience. Leveraging the familiar functionalities of requests, workflows, approval tasks, and automation rules, the 4me Shop showcases the full capability of these core platform features in creating a seamless service delivery experience.

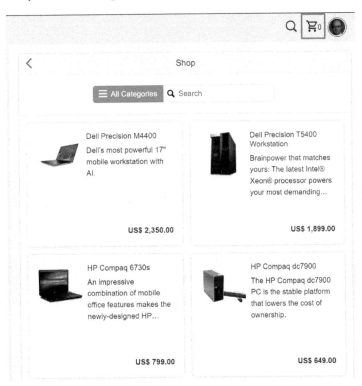

Figure 362: The 4me Shop providing webshop functionality to the Self-Service Portal.

Service Centered, as Always...

At its core, 4me remains service-centered, and the 4me Shop is no exception. It operates atop the service hierarchy, utilizing Service-Level Agreements (SLAs) and related service offerings to tailor shop article availability to end-users. The platform's versatility allows organizations to determine the accessibility of shop articles based on employee location, department, or specific groups defined within the SLA Coverage.

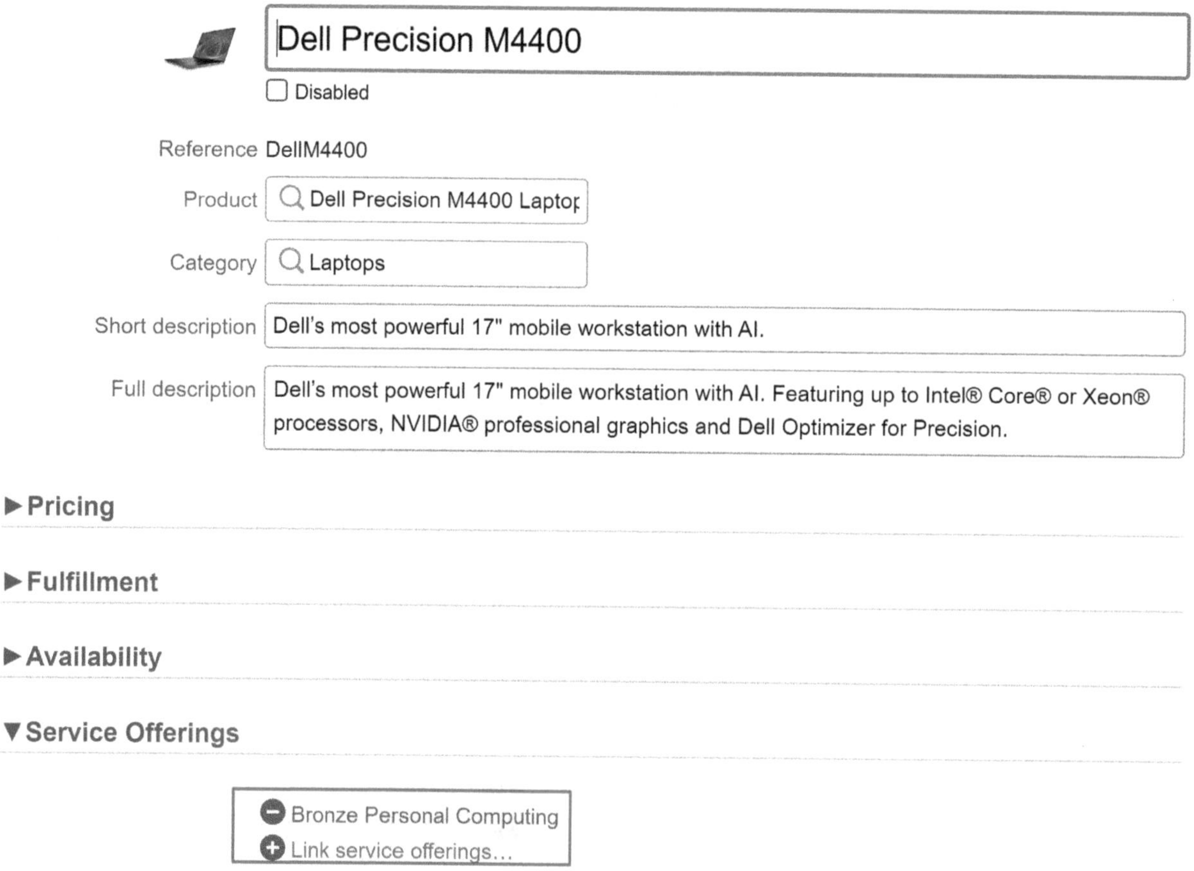

	Dell Precision M4400
	☐ Disabled
Reference	DellM4400
Product	🔍 Dell Precision M4400 Laptop
Category	🔍 Laptops
Short description	Dell's most powerful 17" mobile workstation with AI.
Full description	Dell's most powerful 17" mobile workstation with AI. Featuring up to Intel® Core® or Xeon® processors, NVIDIA® professional graphics and Dell Optimizer for Precision.

▶ **Pricing**

▶ **Fulfillment**

▶ **Availability**

▼ **Service Offerings**

> ➖ Bronze Personal Computing
> ➕ Link service offerings…

Figure 363: Publishing shop articles by linking them to a service offering.

Configuration simplicity is key: to publish a shop article, you only need to link it to one or more service offerings. For instance, when the HR department decides to offer health-focused training, they just need to create shop articles for each of the trainings and link these shop articles to the 'Learning and Development' service offering.

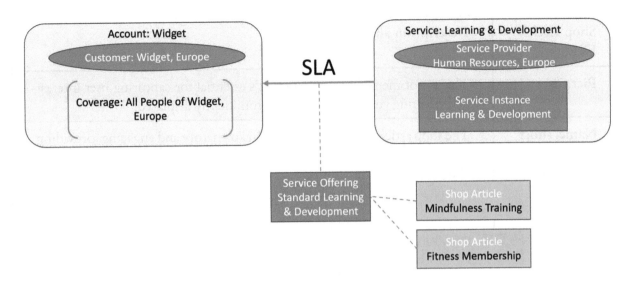

Figure 364: Shop articles are embedded in the Service Hierarchy via the service offerings.

Diving Deeper into Shop Articles

The essence of the 4me Shop is its shop articles, each equipped with fields designed to maximize flexibility and user engagement. From compelling imagery to detailed descriptions and customization options, every aspect of a shop article is crafted to engage and inform.

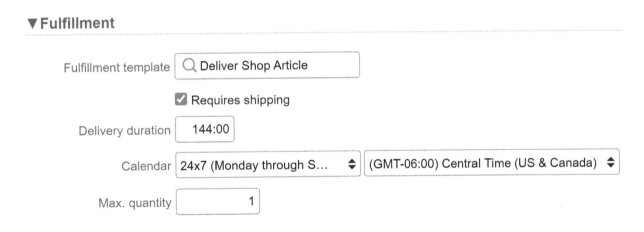

Figure 365: A shop article includes a Delivery section with a link to a request template for the fulfillment.

Shop Article Field	Description and Comments
Picture	This is not merely 'nice to have.' It's essential for capturing user interest and ensuring your shop items are prominently displayed.
Name, short and long description	The shop article name should be self-explanatory and engaging, providing a clear and immediate understanding of what the item is, with a touch of allure to draw in the shopper. Short Description: Offers a concise overview that highlights the key features and benefits of the shop article, making it compelling for the reader. Long Description: Here, you can expand on the details, include additional photos, and even embed videos. This section allows for a comprehensive explanation and visual showcase of the product, enhancing the user's understanding and interest.
Disabled	This setting allows you to control the availability of items in your webshop. It's important to refer to the section on cross-account 4me shop functionality, as this field plays a crucial role in managing what is accessible to customers in their 4me shop.
Reference	The reference field is automatically generated based on the item's name. It is utilized in automation rules and integrations to identify items uniquely. Please note that this field is immutable; once it is created, it cannot be modified.
Product	Refer to the section titled 'Shop Articles, Asset Management, and the CMDB' for an in-depth understanding of the benefits of linking a shop article to a 4me product. This connection can significantly enhance utility and efficiency.
Category	Consult the section 'The User Perspective' to gain insights into how categorization is implemented. This will help you understand the categorization process from the user's point of view.
Pricing	
	Prices can be established either as a fixed amount or as a recurring charge, with options for monthly or yearly billing. This flexibility makes the shop an ideal platform for implementing various charging and billing strategies.
Fulfillment	

Shop Article Field	Description and Comments
Fulfillment template	After an order is placed, the shop article must be delivered to the requester. This is the purpose of the fulfillment request template. Please refer to the section titled 'The Order and Fulfillment Processes' to understand the specifics of these procedures.
Requires shipping	The "Requires Shipping" checkbox should be selected for items that need to be shipped to either the user's organizational address or the address specified in the user's personal record. If both addresses are provided, the user will be prompted to choose one during the checkout process.
Delivery duration, Calendar	Managing user expectations is crucial. By specifying a delivery duration and selecting a calendar, the webshop will provide users with an estimated delivery date for their purchased items. For instance, if the calendar is configured for 'Monday to Friday from 09:00 AM to 5:00 PM' and the delivery duration is 24 hours, the system will calculate the estimated delivery time as 3 business days. This feature helps set realistic expectations for when users can anticipate receiving their orders.
UI extension	If the shop article comes with various options, a UI Extension is necessary. For instance, when employees are allowed to order a company car, the color option for each car model can be specified using a custom field on the shop article's form. Simply create a UI Extension of the type 'Shop Article,' and link it to the shop article to make the selection of options for that shop article available to users.
Max. quantity	The "Maximum Quantity" field specifies the maximum number of units of the shop article that a customer can purchase in a single order.
Availability	
Start date and end date	Two optional fields to define when the shop article is made available and/or when it should be retired.
Service Offerings	
Service offerings	Linking the shop article to specific service offerings allows you to precisely determine which users will see the shop article in their 4me shop. This targeted approach ensures that only relevant users have access to specific products or services, enhancing the shopping experience.

Crossing the Boundaries of 4me Accounts - Facilitating B2B Processes

The distinctive feature of the 4me Shop lies in its unparalleled capability to transcend the confines of individual organizations and companies, a crucial aspect for supporting B2B (Business-to-Business) transactions. This functionality is enabled through the integration with Service-Level Agreements (SLAs). Specifically, an SLA established by a Managed Service Provider (MSP) to deliver services to their clients can be leveraged to showcase shop articles within the 4me shop accessible by all (or selected) clients.

For instance, consider the scenario where the MSP GlobalNet offers WAN connectivity services to Widget Data Center. By associating shop articles with the service offerings of the SLAs with Widget Data Center, these articles become accessible to users within Widget, Inc. who are beneficiaries of these SLAs.

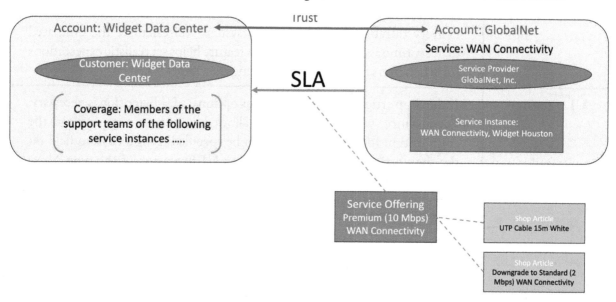

Figure 366: By linking shop articles to service offerings of SLAs to a trusted account, an MSP can share shop articles with their customers. These customers can publish these shop articles in their own 4me shop.

The customer retains comprehensive control over the availability of shop articles to their users, including the timing of availability and the specifics of the information and pricing shared. A key point of control originates from the coverage section of the Service Level Agreement (SLA), established by the Managed Service Provider (MSP) but defined at the customer's site. For instance, in the aforementioned example, it is the service level manager at Widget Data Center who determines the SLA coverage for WAN Connectivity.

The 4me shop introduces an additional layer of control at the customer's end. Shop articles created and activated by the MSP appear in the customer's account but are initially marked as disabled. This default setting allows the customer account administrator to tailor the visibility and details of these articles, including:

- **Name, Short and Long Description**: Customers have the flexibility to modify these fields with their own information. If no changes are made, the MSP's provided details are used by default.
- **Disabled**: By default, shop articles sourced from the MSP are disabled. This gives customers the autonomy to enable articles they wish to offer to their users.
- **Category**: As detailed in the section 'The User Perspective – One Shop and Multiple Categories,' customers can categorize shop articles independently of the MSP's categorization, tailoring the shop experience to their users' needs.
- **Pricing**: Customers can set their pricing for users, which may differ from the price charged by the MSP. Thus, a shop article could have two distinct prices: one for the customer organization called the *provider price* and another for the end-users within that organization.
- **Maximum Quantity**: Customers can specify the maximum quantity of each shop article that can be ordered, with the stipulation that this number cannot exceed the maximum set by the MSP.

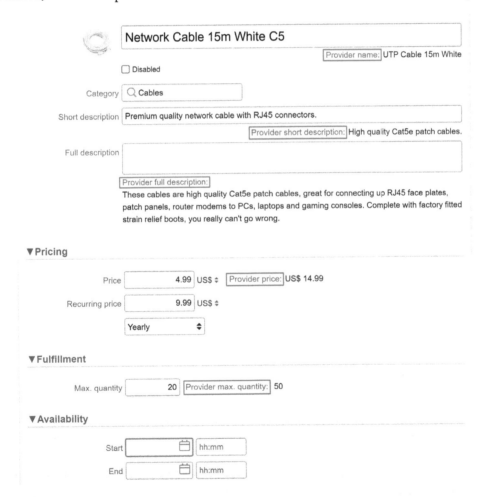

Figure 367: The account administrator in the trusted account can overwrite certain fields of a shop article provided by an external service provider, including the pricing visible to the users.

The End User Perspective -
A Unified Shop Across Multiple Categories

A user in 4me might be covered by SLAs from various internal and external accounts. For example, a user from the Widget Data Center organization could have access to services provided by Widget North America - Human Resources, Widget Data Center - Internal IT, and even GlobalNet, an external service provider. This diversity means that such a user can access shop articles from three distinct service delivery organizations.

4me simplifies this complexity: instead of navigating through separate shops for these services, there is only one integrated shop. Within a directory account structure, the Widget Data Center employee can seamlessly find, add to basket, and order items from all these sources in a single transaction.

However, this 'one directory account, one shop' approach presents its own set of challenges. Given that each service delivery organization may offer thousands of shop articles, it could be overwhelming for users to locate specific items, such as HR-related articles amidst a vast selection of IT products. This issue becomes even more pronounced when a single organization offers thousands of items.

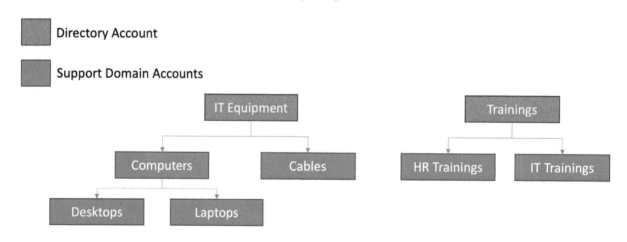

Figure 368: The shop categories can be defined and managed in the directory account and in the support domain accounts.

To address this, **shop article categories** are introduced. Like most web shops that use categories to organize their offerings, the 4me shop allows for the categorization of shop articles. These categories can be delineated between the directory account and the support domain accounts. It's important to note that a shop article can be linked to only one category, and each category can have only one parent. When multiple service delivery organizations utilize the 4me shop, they must collaborate to establish a unified category definition for shop articles.

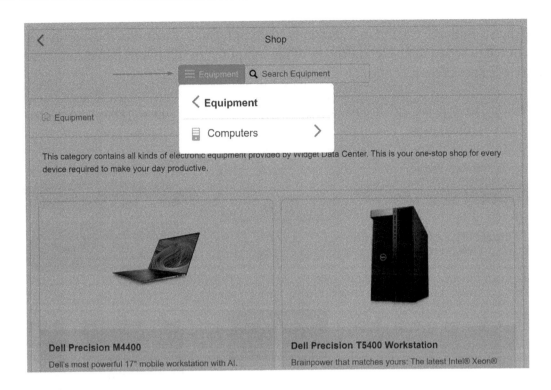

Figure 369: Navigating through the 4me Shop with shop article categories.

Shop Articles, Asset Management, and the CMDB

There can be a direct link between the shop articles provided by a service delivery organization through the 4me shop and the assets or configuration items (CIs) that the organization must manage.

Take, for example, Desktop Services. An IT organization might offer a selection of standardized desktop and laptop configurations through the 4me shop. After these computers are delivered, IT is responsible for supporting these devices. Effective support for desktops necessitates robust asset management, including tracking warranties and hardware support contracts. Consequently, these shop articles, once deployed, should be recorded as configuration items within the CMDB.

By linking a shop article to a product, the configuration management process that should be started when the shop article is delivered becomes more straightforward. This association between the shop article and the product clarifies for the service delivery organization exactly which product was ordered.

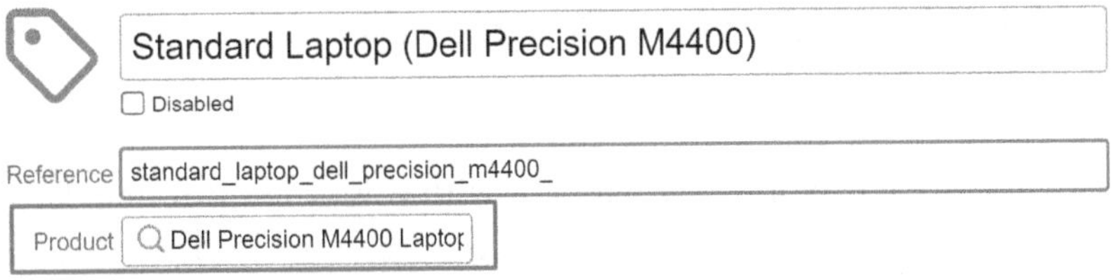

Figure 370: Linking a shop article to a 4me product.

They will then consult the CMDB to determine which configuration items for the specified product are in stock or need to be acquired. Upon delivery of the computer, the CI is linked to the user and its status is updated to 'In production'.

In the following section, we will discuss how the fulfillment request and workflow can be structured to effectively execute these steps.

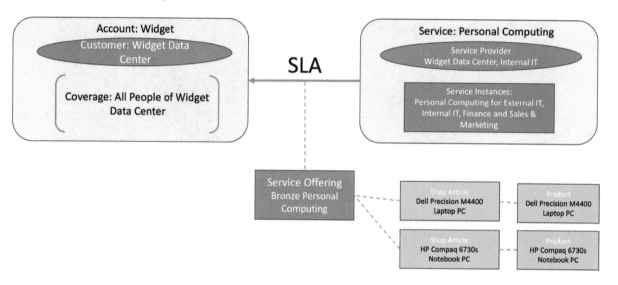

Figure 371: Shop articles with a link to a service offering and to a product supporting the configuration management process.

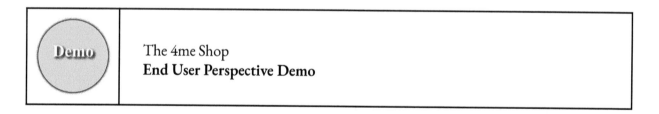

The 4me Shop
End User Perspective Demo

Let's take a look at how it all appears from an end user's perspective.

- Log in as beatrice.baldwin@widget.com to Widget International.
  - Click on the basket icon.
  - In the shop, Beatrice will find an overview of all computer models offered by the internal IT department of Widget Data Center for employees of the Widget Data Center organization.
  - Click on 'All Categories' and select a shop article category to narrow down the list of available computer models.
  - Add one of these PCs to the basket, proceed to checkout, and place your order. You are familiar with how this process works.

In the following paragraph, we'll explore what happens with this order. But first, let's switch to another user—Ellen Brown, a specialist and part of the Operations team in the Widget Data Center account who is entitled to certain technical services. Let's see what this means in the 4me shop.

- Log in as ellen.brown@widget.com to Widget International.
  - Click on the basket icon.

Some of the shop articles available to Ellen are from GlobalNet. For instance, there is the network cable and downgrade/upgrade packages to the WAN connectivity plan. In reality, these shop articles are not part of Widget Data Center's offerings; they are published by GlobalNet, Widget Data Center's external network supplier. You can find out how this is done:

- Log in as Frederic.anderson@globalnet.com to GlobalNet.
  - Go to the records console and select 'Shop Articles.'
  - Examine the service offerings and the related SLAs for these shop articles.
- Log in as ellen.brown@widget.com to Widget Data Center.
  - Go to the people record of Ellen Brown.
  - Go to the Coverage section and filter on WAN.
  - Check that Ellen is covered for the Premium and Standard WAN Connectivity SLAs.

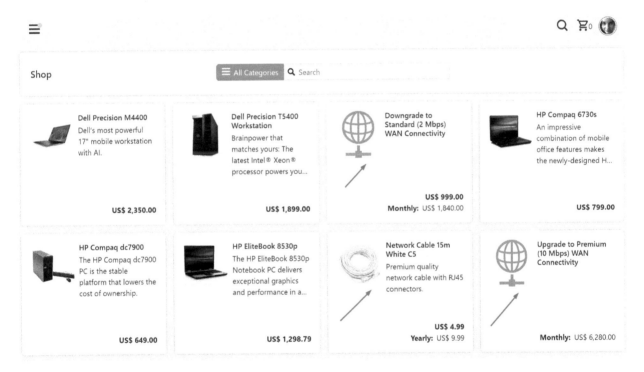

Figure 372: Shop articles from GlobalNet are published in the 4me shop of Ellen Brown on the Widget International Self-Service Portal.

The Order and Fulfilment Processes

The effectiveness of the 4me shop largely hinges on the backend processes activated by the ordering of shop articles. These processes are divided into two main parts: one governed by the customer and the other by the service delivery organizations providing the shop articles.

The Order Process

In a B2C (Business-to-Consumer) scenario, an order is considered accepted once the customer's payment has been approved. However, in a B2B (Business-to-Business) setting, the approach is slightly different: the customer organization should establish internal policies and rules regarding who is authorized to order items and define the spending limit. This is the order process. It should be auditable and the customer organization should have complete control and ownership over these procedures.

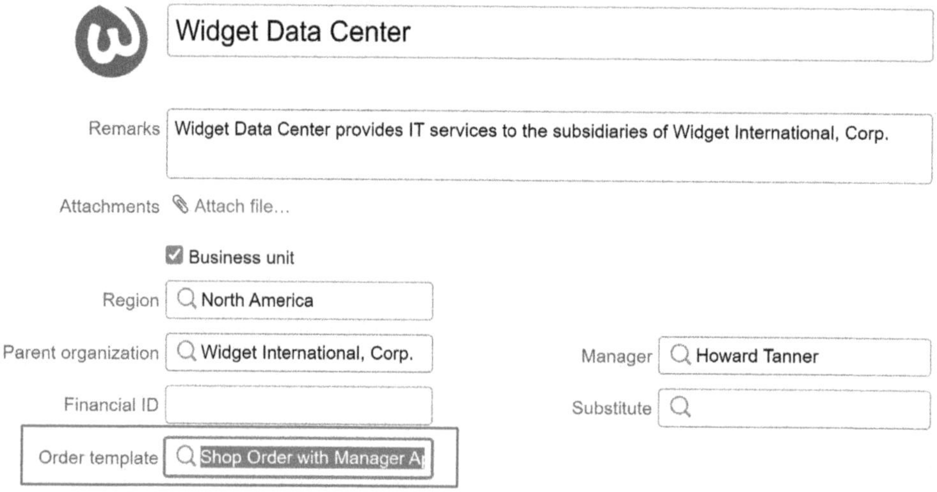

Figure 373: Linking a request template of category 'Order' to an organization will enable the 4me shop to all the users of the organization and their descendants.

Figure 374: The request template of category 'Order' requires a workflow template. The request template can be linked to multiple organizations.

To operationalize this framework in 4me, it's necessary to establish a workflow template and a request template with category '**Order**'. A request template of this category can be associated with one or more organizations. Once such a request template is linked to an organization the 4me shop will become visible in the Self-Service Portal of all the users of this organization and descendants. This setup enables each organization within a directory account structure to develop its own policies and procedures for ordering goods through the 4me shop. Customizations, such as UI Extensions, can be added to order request templates—for instance, allowing users to select a cost center when placing an order.

Be aware that making the shop visible to the users doesn't mean that the shop contains shop articles. Which shop articles are displayed in a user's 4me shop is determined by the specific Service-Level Agreements (SLAs) covering that user.

The workflow template categorized as 'Order' requires association with a service, while the request template for 'Order' does not. There's a deliberate rationale behind not linking order request templates to any service: these templates are not meant to be visible or selectable in the service catalog.

The Fulfillment Process

The responsibility for fulfillment or delivery of orders lies entirely with the service delivery organization once an order is placed. The specifics of preparing, packaging, delivering, and invoicing a shop article will vary depending on the product. For example, the process for fulfilling an order for a laptop will differ significantly from that for a training session. That's why a request template of category fulfillment must be linked to each shop article. Eventually a fulfillment request template can be linked to a workflow template. When a user orders more than one shop article, the 4me shop will generate a fulfillment request, and eventually a fulfillment workflow, for each shop article.

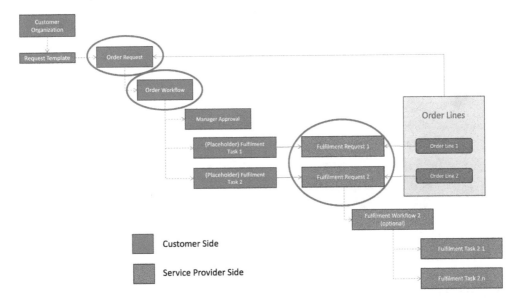

Figure 375: The order process and the fulfillment process are two independent processes in the 4me shop. Each article will generate a fulfilment request, and eventually a fulfillment workflow.

Shop Order Lines and Making the Workflows Dynamic

When a shop article is ordered, a corresponding **shop order line** is generated within the customer's account. The combination of the order request and the associated shop order articles constitutes the complete **order**. It's important to note that the order record itself is not separately visible within the 4me records console of the specialist interface. There's no need to search for it independently; to locate all 'orders,' simply navigate to the 'requests' section and filter by the 'order' category. A request categorized as 'order' will display the request with all related shop order lines, effectively serving as the order record.

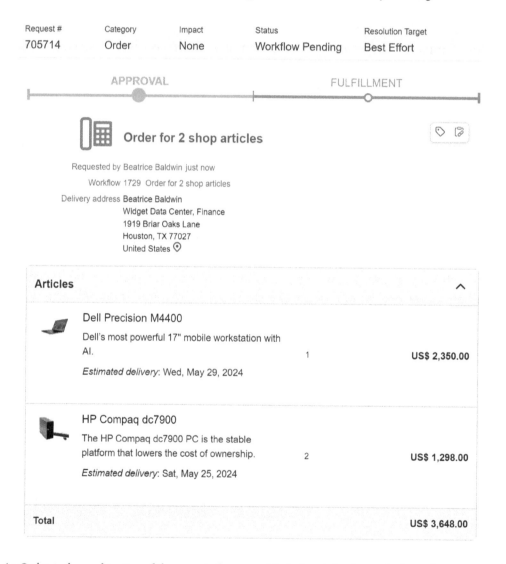

Figure 376: An Order is the combination of the request of category 'Order' and the shop order lines that are created for each ordered shop article.

In the Self-Service Portal, end users are provided with a '**My Orders**' option. Selecting this option opens again a list of requests of category order triggered by the user when ordering shop articles through the 4me shop.

Shop order lines appear as a distinct record type in the specialist record console. While shop order lines are created in the customer's account, they are also accessible in the service provider's account for obvious reasons: the service provider needs to deliver what is specified in a shop order line. In the service provider's account, each shop order line is linked to a separate fulfillment request. In the customer's account, both the price presented to the user when ordering and the provider's price are visible. However, in the service provider's account, only the provider's price is displayed. This setup ensures that the supplier does not have access to the pricing information at which the customer is offering the shop articles to their end users.

Both the order workflows and fulfillment workflows can be customized to accommodate specific requirements. For example, a customer organization may decide that certain shop articles do not require management approval. Additionally, the service provider can configure automatic actions, such as adding additional tasks for certain shop order lines. This flexibility is made possible by exposing the fields `order_lines` of order requests and `order_line` of fulfillment requests to the automation rules.

Consider the automation rule below as an example. It cancels the manager approval when only one shop article has been ordered, and the total price of the order is less than $100 USD. This level of customization ensures that the workflow aligns with the organization's specific processes and requirements.

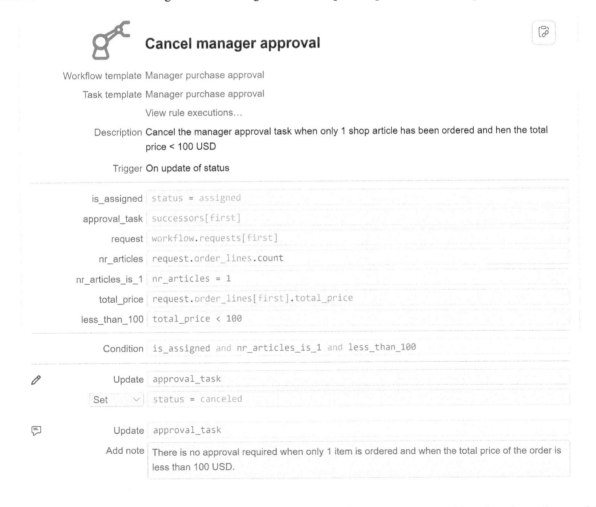

Figure 377: Example automation rule in an order workflow to cancel a manager approval based on the total price of the first order line.

The 4me Shop
The Backend Processes

Let's continue with the demo for the end users and take a look at the backend process. In the previous demo, Beatrice Baldwin ordered a PC. This order needs an approval from the workflow manager of the order workflow, Howard Tanner. He will find the approval task in his inbox.

- Log in as howard.tanner@widget.com to Widget Data Center.
- Check the inbox and open the approval workflow for the order made by Beatrice.
- Check the request related to the workflow: the request together with the related shop order lines represents the order.
- Approve the approval task.

Once the order is approved, the fulfilment request will be created. The assignment team of the fulfilment request template 'Deliver Shop Article' is set to the service desk team of the Widget Data Center (which is outsourced to VirtualSupport) and to Khunal Shrestra.

- Login as khunal.shrestra@virtualsupport.com to VirtualSupport.
- Check the inbox: you will find the order request(s) for the shop article(s) that Beatrice Baldwin has ordered.

Quick Start Guide: Setting Up the 4me Shop in 15 Minutes

Though initially appearing complex, the configuration of the 4me shop is quite straightforward once you grasp the underlying principles. In fact, with a clear understanding, setting up and launching a basic version of your 4me shop can be accomplished in just about 15 minutes. Here's a brisk walkthrough to prove just how manageable the process is:

Fulfillment Template Creation:

- Start by creating a request template of the category 'Fulfillment.' This template will streamline the shop article delivery process within your shop.

Shop Article Initiation:

- Proceed to create a shop article, a cornerstone of your 4me shop. Ensure this article:
  - Is linked to your freshly minted Fulfillment request template.
  - Is associated with an appropriate service offering to tie SLAs to your shop items.

Workflow Template for Orders:

- Add a workflow template of the category 'Order.' Just add one approval task template to it that is assigned to the manager of the requester.

Order Request Template:

- Establish a Request template of the category 'Order.'
  - Bind this template to your Order workflow template for the order approval.
  - Link the request template to the organizations (and their descendants) of the users that need access to the 4me shop.

The 4me Shop
Implementation Best Practices

1. Decide on the **shop article categories** at the company level. Establish shared top categories in the directory account, while also accommodating domain-specific subcategories in the support domain accounts.
2. Formulate company policies and procedures concerning the **shop order process.** If business units or organizations wish to establish their own policies, create specific order request templates for these entities. Manage these templates within a single support domain account, ideally the one responsible for providing 4me support to the company. Consider defining a dedicated Shop Ordering service with one or more order workflow templates and request templates (for each organization) in this support domain account.
3. The service delivery organization (the organizations responsible for providing shop articles) needs to define the types of shop articles they will distribute and how this will impact the delivery procedure. If the **delivery procedure** varies significantly based on the nature of the shop articles, it may be better to define multiple fulfillment request templates (and related workflows). If the delivery procedures are only slightly different, it is better to define a single fulfillment request template (and related workflow template) and use instructions or automation rules for differentiation.
4. Follow these steps to set up a 4me shop within a directory account structure:
   a. Define shop article categories in both the directory account and the support domain accounts.
   b. In the support domain accounts of the service delivery organizations:
      i. Define additional services, service instances, service offerings, and service-level agreements when the shop articles belong to a new service.
      ii. Define the fulfillment request templates (and related UI extensions, task templates, workflow templates, and automation rules).
      iii. Define the products to which the shop articles belong (if the deployed shop articles must be managed as configuration items).
      iv. Define shop article UI Extensions for shop articles that need to be made available to users or when extra information is required from users when ordering.
      v. Define the shop articles and link them to the shop article UI Extensions, fulfillment request templates, and service offerings.

c. In the support domain account responsible for managing the shop ordering process:
    i. Define a shop ordering service, service instance, service offering, and an SLA covering the company's organizations.
    ii. For each organization requiring a distinct shop ordering policy, define a fulfillment workflow template and fulfillment request template. Link these fulfillment request templates to the organizations.
d. When an external supplier (trusted account) publishes shop articles via one or more SLAs:
    i. Define in the coverage section of these SLAs the users authorized to order these shop articles.
    ii. Edit the supplier's shop articles, enable them, and link them to the correct shop article category. Optionally, define your own name, short description, long description, maximum quantity, and price.

PART V

Launching 4me

Guidelines for Effective
Implementation and Maintenance

Chapter 24 -
Implementing and Supporting 4me

Introduction

Gone are the days when implementing a service management platform began with laborious process design workshops, followed by building and testing these processes. Such approaches, focusing heavily on the 'how' of operations, often overlooked the 'what' — the very essence of service delivery.

Enter 4me: a next-generation enterprise service management platform that revolutionizes this paradigm. With core functionalities providing ready-to-use service management processes, 4me shifts the emphasis from the 'how' to the 'what'. Implementing 4me revolves around understanding and deploying the service delivery organization's operating model, gathering essential data, and integrating it seamlessly into the platform. This approach not only speeds up the process but also turns implementation into an exciting journey for all stakeholders. It's about making explicit what is already known, transforming every implementation into a unique opportunity for enhancement and fun.

Implementation Strategy: Agile and Empowering

At the core of the 4me implementation strategy are two pivotal elements: the agile approach and empowering the customer organization.

Agile Approach

Often, the operating model of a service delivery organization exists conceptually in the minds of its personnel, and interpretations of this model can vary significantly among specialists. This discrepancy can lead to chaos in incident management and request fulfillment, as tickets are handled inconsistently, leading to misassignments, overhead, and delays.

During the 4me implementation, this operating model is meticulously captured and explicitly defined in the account structure design and within the 4me service catalog. The service catalog acts as the platform's driving force, ensuring assignments align with the operating model and providing management with clear insights into service performance, quality, and cost.

Capturing the operating model requires active participation from key stakeholders within the service delivery organization. Their commitment to attend workshops and provide essential input is crucial to the project's success. To accommodate their schedules and ensure efficient use of their time, implementations in large enterprise environments are structured into multiple short iterations, each scoped to service delivery entities of no more than 300 specialists. This approach not only respects stakeholder availability but also enhances focus and effectiveness. Each iteration varies in duration, typically lasting from two to three months, though they can be as short as one week and should not exceed six months.

This iterative strategy ensures:

- **Focused Participation**: Reduces the duration stakeholders are needed for each iteration, preventing burnout and scheduling conflicts.
- **Limited Time Commitment**: Key stakeholders, often engaged in various activities, are only needed for short periods, preventing extended distractions from their primary roles.
- **Adaptability**: Allows the implementation to adapt to organizational changes and feedback in real-time.
- **Efficient Information Handling**: The project team can quickly capture, input, and validate operational data within 4me, enhancing both efficiency and accuracy.

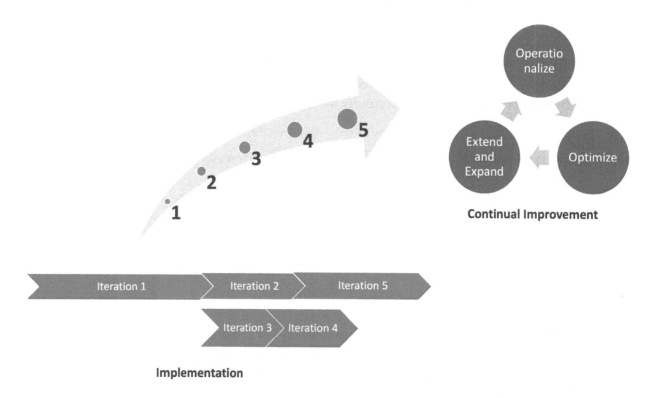

Figure 378: The agile approach of a 4me implementation. The scope of each iteration should be limited to a maximum of 300 specialists.

The agile method brings several additional benefits to the 4me implementation process, including:

- **Reduced Risk**: Agile methodologies decrease the likelihood of project failures.
- **Improved Quality**: Frequent iterations and ongoing testing enhance the overall quality of the implementation.
- **Faster ROI**: Agile allows for quicker reviews and adjustments, leading to a faster return on investment.

Empowering the Customer Organization

The successful implementation of 4me relies heavily on the guidance of experienced service management consultants. These experts may come from a 4me partner, directly from 4me, or from an independent consulting background. Regardless of their origin, it's essential that these consultants have a profound understanding of the 4me platform and the ability to effectively capture and translate the organization's operating model into the 4me configuration. Initially, the target organization likely lacks familiarity with these critical concepts, but by the project's conclusion, they should be well-versed and capable.

A key goal of any 4me implementation is to ensure that the insights gained from the platform—regarding the performance, quality, and cost of service delivery—are actively used to drive continual improvement. For this to be effective, it's crucial that the customer organization is equipped with the necessary skills, processes, and organizational structure to support ongoing enhancement efforts. This capability building is a fundamental part of the 4me implementation plan.

The implementation process is designed to empower the customer organization:

- **Consultant Shadowing**: In the initial phases, service management consultants from the customer's organization are expected to shadow the experienced service management consultants. This hands-on learning approach helps the customer's team develop a deep understanding and practical experience early in the project.
- **Support Structure Development**: Concurrently, a support structure for the internal customer support team is established. This framework is vital for enabling the customer to independently manage initial troubleshooting and minor configurations post-launch.
- **Gradual Handover**: As the implementation progresses, the customer's service management consultants gradually take on more configuration responsibilities, transitioning from a supervised to a more autonomous role. This phased transfer not only builds the team's confidence and expertise but also ensures they are fully prepared to manage and customize the platform.
- **Ongoing Quality Assurance**: Throughout the implementation, the experienced service management architects maintain a pivotal role in overseeing the quality of the implementation. Their involvement ensures that the configuration adheres to best practices and aligns with the strategic objectives of the project.

The Implementation Plan

Each iteration consists of five distinct phases

- Initiation
- Analysis and Design
- Account Population and Configuration
- Integrations
- Acceptance Testing, Training and Go-live

Two specific tracks extend through the complete lifecycle of the project: the organizational change management and project management activities.

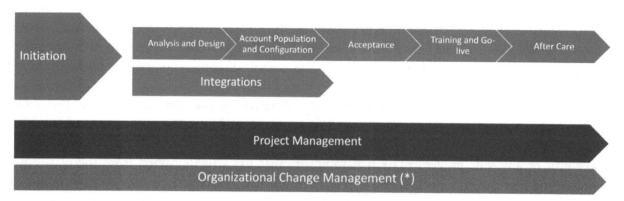

Figure 379: The phases in an iteration when implementing 4me. (*) Organizational Change Management is the responsibility of the customer.

The Initiation Phase

Objective: The primary goal of the initiation phase is to establish the project framework and raise awareness among all stakeholders. This phase involves identifying key stakeholders and formally introducing the project during a kickoff meeting.

Stakeholder Engagement and Expectations: Clear expectations are set for each key stakeholder during the kickoff meeting. It is crucial that stakeholders understand their roles within the implementation process and the extent of their involvement. They are expected to participate in an online 4me specialist training, which lasts approximately four hours, to gain a fundamental understanding of 4me's functionalities, including accounts, the self-service portal, and the service catalog. A brief demonstration is also typically conducted during the kickoff meeting to familiarize everyone with basic concepts.

Stakeholders must acknowledge the importance of their continuous involvement and commit to reserving sufficient time for the project. The availability of each stakeholder is a critical success factor, as their timely and effective participation is essential for addressing various project phases and ensuring smooth progress.

Account Structure Design: Designing the account structure is a crucial activity in this phase. This step may only be necessary during the first iteration and can sometimes precede the project kickoff. The account structure often dictates how to segment the project into multiple iterations. It is a good practice to discuss and confirm the proposed account structure with all stakeholders during the initiation phase to ensure a common understanding of the overall project scope and how the current iteration fits into the broader account framework. Basic settings for the accounts involved in the current iteration are also established during this phase.

Analysis and Design

Objectives

The primary objective of the Analysis and Design phase is to collect all necessary data to configure and customize the 4me setup effectively. This phase ensures that all foundational and operational elements align perfectly with the organizational needs and service delivery objectives.

Foundational Records Collection

The first iteration focuses on gathering foundational records essential for the 4me framework: organizations, sites, and personnel. This data is primarily loaded into the directory account. The sources of this data are identified, and decisions are made about whether and how this data will be automatically provisioned. If manual collection is necessary, tasks are assigned to designated customer stakeholders who are instructed on the data format required for importation into the 4me platform. This phase is typically unique to the first iteration; subsequent iterations build upon the foundational records established in the directory account.

Service Catalog Definition

The service catalog's definition is central to the implementation, conducted through several workshops with key stakeholders. Starting with a best practices catalog relevant to the business function, the process progresses through a staged approach—beginning with end-user-facing services and identifying supporting and supplier services. Once complete, the service catalog lays the foundational layer for the 4me configuration. Additional activities depend on the scope, but defining standard requests and related workflows is common to all iterations.

Request Fulfillment and Workflow Design Workshops

These workshops focus on identifying standard requests for each service and determining any associated workflows. They involve specifying the information to be captured during request registration to facilitate UI Extensions development. Workflows are identified, their schedule defined, and assessed for automation needs. Workflows are categorized by complexity and priority, influencing the project's scope; less critical workflows may be deferred to the continual improvement phase if initial estimates are exceeded.

Process Validation

Process validation workshops are optional. Whether these workshops are required depends on the scope and objectives.

Incident Management: for organizations needing compliance with specific frameworks. 4me's default process documents serve as a base, with major incident management procedures customized to organizational needs.

Problem Management: Activated as needed, starting with 4me's default documents and focusing on identifying problem managers for each service. Recurring workflows may be established to track problem management activities.

IT Change Management: Involves tailoring the organization's change policy through workflow templates, essential for IT management inclusion.

Service Configuration and Asset Management (CMDB): Determines which configuration items and assets are to be included in 4me, identifying source systems and provisioning methods (manual or via integration). Responsibilities for data collection and compliance with the 4me import API are clarified.

Knowledge Management (KCS): If in scope, the principles of Knowledge-Centered Service are explained, and 4me's default process documents are reviewed. Policies for knowledge article review cycles are set, and knowledge managers for each service are appointed. Knowledge article templates may also be designed.

Self-Service Design

A compelling self-service portal is crucial for implementation success. Decisions are made regarding the content available on the homepage and whether to base the design on an existing template or start from scratch.

Account Population and Configuration

This phase involves setting up and configuring the 4me accounts within the QA environment, focusing on establishing a solid foundation and ensuring all necessary elements are in place for the service operation.

Account Creation and Settings: The accounts and trusts are created and the Account Settings are validated. The following sections in the settings console are covered: Access & Security, Email & Notification, Account Design and Self-Service Settings, and Time & Calendars.

Initial Setup in the Directory Account: In the first iteration, foundational elements such as organizations, sites, and personnel records are established within the directory account. To streamline the management of user data, it is recommended to set up automated provisioning with the Identity Provider (IdP).

Team and Role Configuration: Once the foundational data is in place, teams are formed by assigning roles to specialists and adding them to the appropriate teams.

Service Catalog Development: The service catalog is meticulously crafted, detailing the services, service instances, service offerings and SLAs offered by the organization.

Request Templates and Workflow Templates: Next the request templates and workflow templates tailored to the organization's processes are added. If customizations are necessary, this phase also involves defining custom collections, elements, views, UI Extensions, and automation rules.

Configuration Management: If configuration management is included in the scope and manual data importation is necessary, this phase also involves collecting and importing relevant data into the 4me accounts.

Integrations

Integrating 4me with adjacent systems is a critical component of the implementation plan, especially in complex environments. For instance, Managed Service Providers (MSPs) may need to link 4me to their billing systems, or an integration might be required with a people management system like SAP SuccessFactors to maintain certain employee attributes.

Importance of Timely Integration: Integrations can be time-consuming and often sit on the critical path of the project. To ensure the project timeline is realistic, it is highly recommended to scope the integration requirements thoroughly before the project commences. 4me and its technology partners offer a range of standard integrations that can significantly reduce implementation time. However, it's crucial to assess whether these solutions meet the specific needs of your implementation.

Integration Design and Planning: The integration phase begins with a detailed design for each system connection. Completing the design phase is essential before technical architects can provide an accurate estimate of the time required to implement each integration. Given the potential complexity and impact on the project timeline, initiating the integration phase early in the project is a strategic move that can facilitate smoother progress and better alignment with project goals.

Acceptance Testing, Training and Go-live

Acceptance Testing

With 4me's robust architecture, the core functionalities, including built-in processes, do not require functional testing. Instead, acceptance testing should focus on validating the specifics of the operating model:

- **Service Catalog Accuracy**: Ensure the service catalog accurately reflects the organization's operational model, check for completeness, and assess user comprehension of service descriptions.
- **Service Hierarchy Validation**: Validate that the integration of supporting services offered by internal teams or external suppliers within the service catalog meets the support model.
- **Custom Workflows**: Test workflows, particularly those with extensive automation rules and custom fields, to ensure they implement the designated procedures effectively.

Training

Although 4me offers comprehensive online training for key roles—such as specialists, service desk analysts, problem managers, and workflow managers—it is advantageous to conduct hands-on classroom training. These sessions should cover:

- **4me Functionality**: Reinforce the online training with detailed explanations of the 4me specialist interface.
- **Implementation Specifics**: Focus on the unique aspects of the customer's implementation, such as the service catalog and tailored workflows.

For large environments, adopting a train-the-trainer approach can be effective, where team leads who participate in initial training sessions subsequently train their team members.

Go-Live Preparation

- **Configuration Transfer**: After testing and training, the configuration from the QA environment can be transferred to production using 4me's Sync functionality.
- **Dashboard Development**: Collaborate with team leads and service owners to develop dashboards that provide insights into activities within the 4me environment from day one.
- **Post Go-Live Support**: Schedule 1 to 3 weeks of support post-go-live, depending on the complexity of the environment, to address any emergent issues.

Project Management

Project management responsibilities are often shared between the implementation partner and the customer. While the implementation partner may oversee the general management of the project, the involvement of a customer-side project manager is crucial. This individual plays a key role in coordinating the involvement of necessary stakeholders, ensuring their participation in workshops, technical activities, and testing phases.

Responsibilities of the Customer's Project Manager:

- **Stakeholder Coordination**: The customer project manager is responsible for assembling the appropriate stakeholders at the right times throughout the project to ensure all necessary contributions are made.
- **Project Prioritization**: The customer project manager must ensure that the project receives the necessary priority within the organization, aligning project goals with organizational objectives and securing the resources needed to achieve success.
- **Inter-project Alignment**: The customer project manager coordinates with other ongoing projects within the organization. This includes managing relationships with other project managers to avoid conflicts and ensure that the 4me implementation is not adversely affected by external factors.

Organizational Change Management

Organizational change management addresses the human aspects of change within an organization. Transitioning from a traditional ticketing system to a service-driven enterprise management platform like 4me represents a significant shift in culture and operations. Effectively managing this change is crucial for the successful adoption of the new system.

Key Elements of Effective Change Management:

- **Responsibility and Ownership**: The primary responsibility for organizational change management activities rests with the customer. It is essential that they take ownership of this process to ensure alignment with their organizational culture and goals.
- **Involvement of Communication Teams**: Effective communication is foundational to successful change management. The customer's internal communications team must be involved throughout the process to craft clear, persuasive messages and engagement strategies that facilitate a smooth transition.
- **Cultural Integration**: The change management process must not only introduce the new system but also integrate it into the existing organizational culture. This requires careful planning and consideration of how changes in processes and tools align with the organization's values and practices.

Project Roles

The successful implementation of 4me involves a diverse team of specialists beyond just the project managers and key customer stakeholders. Here are the crucial roles:

- **Service Management Architect**: Leads the workshops and holds a deep understanding of 4me coupled with experience in service management implementations. This role guides the customer in aligning their operational model with 4me's account structure, service catalog, and workflows.
- **Service Management Consultant(s)**: Executes most of the platform configuration and customization tasks, including uploading foundational records, defining the service catalog, and building UI Extensions, request templates, workflow templates, and automation rules. It is advisable for at least one consultant from the customer's side to join the project team to shadow and learn from the 4me experts during the initial iterations.
- **4me Integration Engineer**: Takes charge of designing and building integrations. This role requires close collaboration with engineers from adjacent systems to ensure seamless connectivity.
- **Front-end Web Developer (optional)**: Needed if significant modifications are required for the self-service design, or if a completely new design is to be created from scratch. If only minor adjustments are needed to an existing out-of-the-box design, a service management consultant might suffice for these tasks.

4me Implementation Task and Role Assignment Table

In the table below, an overview of tasks along with the roles of the key profiles involved in a 4me implementation is presented. The involvement is defined as follows:

R: Responsible – takes ownership and accountability for the task.
P: Participant – contributes to the task but is not primarily accountable.
S: Shadowing – observes and learns from those performing the task.

Roles:
SMA: Service Management Architect
SMC: Service Management Consultant
IE: Integrations Engineer
CU: Customer. Could be different profiles depending on the activity.

Task Description	SMA	SMC	IE	CU
1. Initiation				
Kickoff and Awareness sessions	R	P	P	P
Account structure design workshops	R	P		P
Account settings definitions	R	P		P
2. Analysis and Design				
People, organization and sites - workshop	R	P		P
Service catalogue definition workshops (internal services)	R	P		P
Service catalogue definition workshops (3rd party services)	R	P		P
Standard Requests workshops	R	P		P
Workflow design workshops	R	P		P
Incident Management Process validation	R			P
Problem Management process validation	R			P
IT Change Management process validation	R			P
Knowledge Management (KCS)	R			P
Service Configuration and Asset Management (CMDB)	R	P		P
Self Service Design Workshop	R	P		P
Account Population and Configuration				
Account settings		R		
People, Organizations and sites - data collection		R		R
People, Organizations and sites - import		R		S
Service Catalog - configuration		R		S
Request templates and UI Extensions - simple		R		S
Request templates and UI Extensions - complex		R		S
Workflows incl automation rules - low complexity		R		S
Workflows incl automation rules - medium complexity		R		S
Workflows incl automation rules - high complexity		R		S
Configuration Items - data collection		P		R
Configuration Items - import		R		
Integrations				
SSO Configuration (Via SAML V2.0 or OpenID connect with IdP)		R		R

Task Description	SMA	SMC	IE	CU
User provisioning integration (Via SCIM integration with IdP)		R		R
<Other Integration Designs>			R	P
<Other Integration Build>			R	R
Acceptance Testing				
Prepare testers		R		
Test scenario preparation				R
Testing (max 3 iterations)				R
Corrections		R		
Training				
Online specialist training				R
Specialist training - train the trainer		R		
Specialist training sessions (4hrs)				R
Service Desk analyst training - train the trainer		R		
Service Desk analyst training				R
Workflow and change manager training - train the trainer		R		
Workflow and change manager training				R
Problem manager training		R		
Configuration Manager Training		R		
Administrator Training		R		
Go Live				
Dashboards and reporting	R	P		S
Migrate configuration to PROD		R		S
Post go-live support	P	R		
Organizational change Management				R

Managing 4me Configurations

Export and Import

From a technical standpoint, implementing 4me involves loading data into the platform. This is usually done via the specialist interface. However, creating nearly identical records repeatedly can be tedious. To streamline this process, you can utilize 4me's export and import functionalities.

The import functionality allows for the creation or update of records in batches. This feature is accessible to account administrators through the Actions menu. The data for import must be in UTF-8 encoded comma-separated values (CSV) or tab-separated values (TSV) files, adhering to the RFC4180 standard:

Basic Format:

- Each line in the file represents a single data record.
- Records are separated by newline characters.

Fields (Data Columns):

- Fields within each record are separated by commas or tabs.

Encapsulation:

- Fields containing line breaks, double quotes, or commas must be enclosed in double quotes.
- To include double quotes within a field, they should be escaped by using two consecutive double quotes.

Header Row:

- The first line of the file serves as the header row, naming each field.

There is no need to create your own CSV template. Simply perform an export for the record type you need, and use the resulting file as your template. The export will include a header row with the correct field names.

Important Considerations

- Omitting a column for a field in the import file is possible: 4me sets that field to its default value, which usually means it remains empty. However, ensure you include all mandatory fields when creating new records.
- Each line in an import file corresponds to one record in 4me. If the record exists, it will be updated; if not, a new record will be created.

- A record may include references to records that are defined in another account. For instance, a service record includes a "Service Owner" field where you must specify the primary email address of a person. Often, the person associated with this email will not be defined within the support domain account of the service but in a related directory account. In such cases, you should append an account identifier using the "@" symbol to indicate the specific account. For example, you would enter

`'john.doe@widget.com @widget'.`

Create or Update Logic

Each record in 4me is assigned a unique ID. If the ID column in the import file is filled for a row, 4me will attempt to locate the existing record using this ID and update it. If the record with the ID cannot be found an error is raised. If the ID column is empty, but both the Source and Source ID columns are filled, 4me uses these to locate or create records. If a match is found, the record is updated; otherwise, a new record is created with the Source and Source ID from the import file.

When importing new records into 4me, utilize the Source and Source ID fields effectively. You can enter your name in the Source field and append a sequence number to the actual data as the Source ID. For example, if you are importing several hundred records and encounter some errors, you can easily make the necessary corrections and re-import the file. By specifying a Source and Source ID, 4me will recognize any records that were already created during the initial import and will not alter them on subsequent imports.

Special Identifiers for Import Types:

- Organization Contact Details: Use the organization's name.
- People: Use the primary email address.
- People Contact Details: Use the person's email address.

Editing CSV Files

To edit CSV files, such as duplicating records, use spreadsheet applications like Microsoft Excel, Google Sheets, or LibreOffice Calc. Although widely used, Excel does not fully comply with the RFC 4180 standard, particularly with encapsulation rules and special character handling. Google Sheets or LibreOffice Calc might be preferable for strict compliance.

The 4me Sync Feature

Exporting a full configuration from a QA account to a Production account manually is time-consuming, typically requiring 4 to 8 hours. It also demands a thorough understanding of the relationships between different record types to ensure correct import order. To streamline this process, the 4me Sync feature is highly recommended.

How 4me Sync Works

4me Sync utilizes the 4me OAuth security framework to connect two accounts: the source (normally QA) and the target (Production). The initial step involves creating a **Sync OAuth application** in the source account. This application is configured to grant read-only access to **Sync Sets**. The credentials generated—client ID and client secret—are then used to establish a **Sync Link** in the target account. Within this Sync Link record, you specify the source environment, the account ID of the source account, and the credentials. This setup enables the Sync Link in the target account to access Sync Sets in the source account.

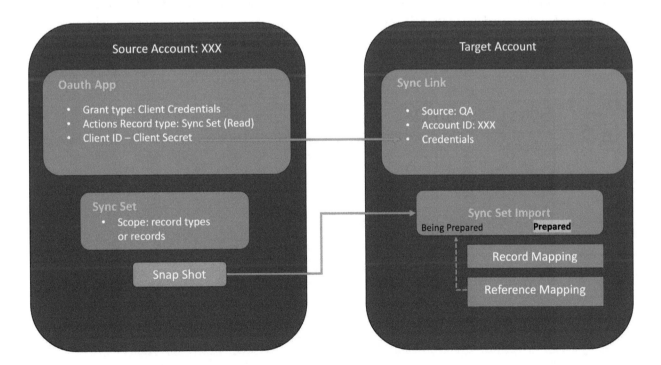

Figure 381: The components of the powerful 4me Sync Set functionality.

Next, define the data to be provisioned using **Sync Sets** and **Sync Set snapshots**. A Sync Set outlines the scope of records for inclusion in a snapshot. You can either select record types or choose individual records such as a request or workflow template for ongoing maintenance. To prepare a go-live you will select all record types.

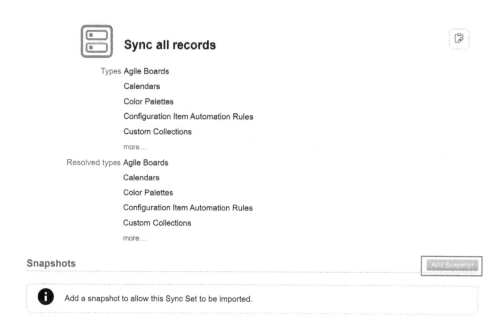

Figure 382: Creating a Sync Set in the source account. Once the scope is defined, in this example by specifying all the record types, a snapshot can be added.

After defining the Sync Set's scope, a snapshot is taken in the source environment. The sync feature then aggregates all related items. For example, if a request template is added, related items like workflow templates, UI extensions, task templates, custom views, collection elements, and automation rules are also included in the snapshot.

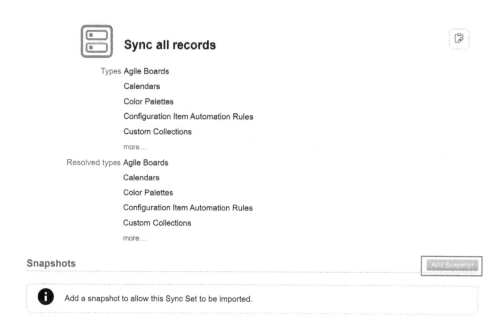

Figure 383: Defining a Sync Link in the target account. Specify the 4me environment and account ID of the source account.

These snapshots appear in the Sync Link in the target environment, where you can initiate a **Sync Set Import** based on the snapshot. The Sync Set Import acts as a mapping table, linking records from the source to the target account. New records are created when no corresponding record is found, existing records will be updated. Disabled records in the source account will disable the linked record in the target account. However, if a disabled source record is absent in the target, it will not be provisioned.

3ba61c74-f428-4c54-a078-06ce99171b29

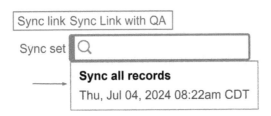

Figure 384: Adding a Sync Set Import to a Sync Link in the target account. Select one of the available Sync Set Snapshots from the source account.

An additional aspect of the Sync Set Import involves reference mapping for foundational records like Organizations, Sites, and People, which are not covered by the sync set functionality. Reference mappings are necessary when references to these records exist. This part of the process can be somewhat time-consuming but is simplified if the same organizations, sites, and people are present in both QA and PROD environments.

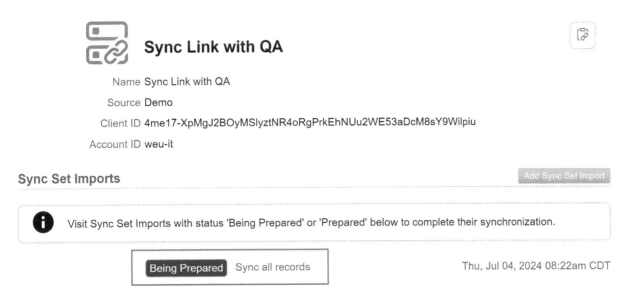

Figure 385: When a Sync Set Import gets the status Being Prepared some reference mappings need to be added.

The Sync Set Import remains in the "**Being Prepared**" status until all reference mappings are completed. Once done, the status changes to "**Prepared**," allowing you to execute the provisioning by clicking the play button.

References   Reference mapping

Organizations 7

People 12

Figure 386: Click on the Reference mapping button in the Sync Set Import to map organizations and people from the source account to organizations and people in the target account.

- Ensure that the QA and PROD environments have consistent account trusts and trust settings. A 4me account interacts with other accounts, affecting certain records in a sync. For example, a task template assigned to a team in a trusted account requires that trust settings in the trusted account are configured identically in both QA and PROD.
- Settings specific to accounts, like those allowing agile methodologies (e.g., agile boards, product backlogs, scrum workspaces), must also be aligned between environments.

Moving the Configuration from QA to Production

The 4me Sync feature focuses on transferring account configurations but does not include data such as organizations, sites, people, product categories, products, and configuration items. Therefore, transitioning a complete account configuration from a QA account to a production account involves a combination of manual export/import alongside the Sync feature. Since the directory account primarily comprises organizations, sites, and people, the Sync feature does not support directory accounts. To prepare for a go-live of a directory account structure, execute the following steps:

Directory Account Migration from QA to PROD:

- Export/Import custom collections and custom collection elements.
- Export/Import custom views.
- Export/Import UI Extensions.
- Export/Import organizations, excluding the Managers and Substitute columns.
- Export/Import sites.
- Export/Import people and their roles.
- Export/Import people contact details.
- Export/Import people roles.
- Export/Import organizations, including the Managers and Substitute columns.

Support Domain Account Migration:

It is also possible to define organizations, sites, and people within a support domain account. These records can be linked to UI Extensions that reference custom views and collections. That's why migrating a support domain account from QA to PROD follows a four-step process:

1. Create Two Sync Sets in the QA Account:
   - *Sync Set Customization*: Includes record types for UI Extensions, custom views, and custom collections.
   - *Sync Set All Records*: Selects all record types.
2. Transfer Customizations to Production:
   - Use the 4me Sync feature to move the *Sync Set Customization* to production.

3. Manual Export/Import of Data from QA to Production:
   - Export and import organizations defined within the support domain account(s).
   - Export and import sites, people, people roles defined within the support domain account(s).
   - Export and import teams. This can be important. The teams export/import should include the team members. When task templates are defined with the assignment set to a team and a team member, the Sync will fail when the team members are missing.
   - Export and import product categories, products, and configuration items defined within the support domain account(s).
4. Finalize with 4me Sync:
   - Use 4me Sync to import all records into production.

Ongoing Maintenance

4me Support

A critical outcome of each 4me implementation project is the establishment of an internal 4me support structure. This structure should define a service that covers all end users, enabling them to register issues, ask questions, and access knowledge articles related to 4me. The unique account structure of the 4me platform allows for defining trusts with other 4me accounts for escalating any issues or questions to a 4me partner, or directly to the 4me support organization if the customer has a direct contract with 4me.

Continual Improvement

The internal 4me support structure should also spearhead improvement initiatives. Continual improvement is vital in service management, especially following the agile implementation approach of 4me. The platform allows for short implementation cycles that deliver a Minimal Viable Product (MVP). Generally, a 4me MVP provides a high level of maturity due to its service-driven architecture. It is also designed to be easily enhanced by adding extra workflows, automating steps in existing workflows, fine-tuning the support model, etc. The go-live of a 4me implementation should mark the beginning of continual improvement for several reasons:

- **Enhanced Customer Satisfaction**: Continual improvement enables organizations to better meet customer needs and expectations by continuously refining services and delivering higher quality outcomes.
- **Cost Reduction**: Identifying and eliminating waste, duplication, and unnecessary steps in processes can lead to significant cost savings.
- **Adaptation to Change**: The business environment is constantly evolving with new technologies, shifting customer expectations, and changing market dynamics. Continual improvement ensures that service management practices remain relevant and effective.
- **Optimization of Processes**: Regularly reviewing and refining processes helps identify inefficiencies and bottlenecks, leading to smoother operations and better resource utilization.

- **Competitive Advantage**: Organizations that embrace a culture of continual improvement are better positioned to outperform competitors by continuously innovating and delivering superior services.

A practical approach involves collecting enhancement requests and using 4me product backlogs and agile boards to prioritize and implement changes in a lean and transparent manner.

Syncing QA and Production Accounts

It is a best practice to implement all enhancements in the QA accounts, conduct thorough testing, and then provision these modifications to the PROD accounts using 4me Sync.

Start by defining a 4me Sync Set in the QA accounts that is not linked to any specific record type. Then, add the modified records to this Sync Set using the 'Add to sync set...' option found in the Actions menu.

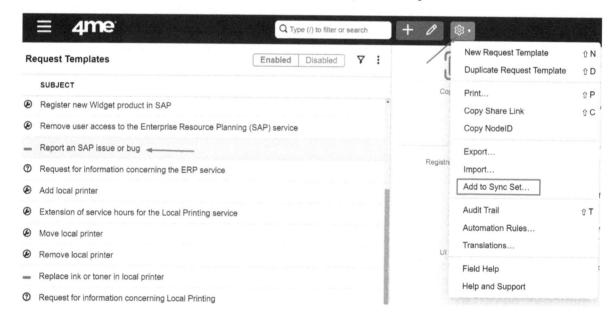

Figure 387: Adding a request template to a sync set via the 'Add to Sync Set...' option in the Actions menu.

Prerequisites

Using 4me Sync as a strategy to create and test all modifications in QA before provisioning these modifications to PROD will be successful only if the QA environment is completely aligned with the PROD environment. Misalignment can lead to unexpected errors and may result in provisioning outdated or invalid configurations to production. Here are some best practices to ensure this alignment:

- **Strict Change Management**: Adhere to rigorous change management procedures. Avoid making direct modifications to the configuration in PROD. Limit the number of people who have roles such as administrator, account designer, and service desk manager in the production environment to minimize risks.
- **Handling Disabling Records**: Always disable records in the QA environment first. Inactive records can be included in a sync set and then provisioned to PROD, ensuring that changes are tested before being made live.
- **Consistent Data Across Environments**: Data such as organizations, sites, people, people roles, team members, product categories, products, and configuration items are not included in the 4me snapshots. It is crucial to maintain consistent configurations for these records between QA and PROD. This can be achieved by provisioning these records from the same master database in both environments, or by including manual updates for specific record types as part of the procedures or workflow templates in both the QA and PROD environments.

Data Integrity Reports

When offboarding personnel, inconsistencies in the configuration may emerge, for instance if the individual acted as a change manager for a service or as a manager of an organization. Such scenarios can lead to disabled person records disrupting workflows. Additionally, these inconsistencies can cause errors during syncing processes, such as when a service owner's record should be active but is not.

Utilizing data integrity reports is crucial for detecting these anomalies. It is a good practice to incorporate checking these reports into the offboarding procedures. To maintain consistent data integrity, it is advised to perform these checks at least once a month. This can be facilitated through a recurring workflow.

- People With Disabled Manager
- Risks With Disabled Manager

Product Integrity Reports

- Configuration Items With Disabled Product

Organization Integrity Reports

- Service Level Agreements With Disabled Customer Organization
- Service Level Agreements With Disabled Covered Organization
- Products With Disabled Organization

Site Integrity Reports

Figure 388: Explore an extensive collection of Data Integrity Reports in the Settings console. It is best practice to review these reports monthly.

Annex A: References

Axelos (February 4, 2020). *ITIL Foundation, ITIL (ITIL 4 Foundation)*. ISBN-13 : 978-0113316076

Alexander Osterwalder , Yves Pigneur , Gregory Bernarda et al. *Value Proposition Design: How to Create Products and Services Customers Want*. ISBN-13 : 978-1118968055

Andrew Cambell, Mikel Gutierrez and Mark Lancelott. *Operating Model Canvas*. ISBN-13 : 978-9401800716

Jeanne W. Ross , Peter Weill, David C. Robertson. *Enterprise Architecture As Strategy*. ISBN-13 : 978-1-59139-839-4

Donald Sull, Stefano Turconi, Charles Sull, James Yoder. *No One Knows Your Strategy — Not Even Your Top Leaders*. MIT Sloan Management Review. Reprint # 59329

Michael Porter. *The Competitive Advantage: Creating and Sustaining Superior Performance*. Free Press, 1985.

Annex B: 4me Demo Accounts

Below is an overview of the 4me accounts available in the demo environment. Each account listing includes the designated account owner. Additionally, for certain accounts, we suggest principal users to help you further explore and understand the specific configurations within each account.

Widget International: This directory account represents the core enterprise structure of Widget International. Log in using various user accounts to explore how content dynamically adapts to different regions. Customize the self-service portal to align with your company's branding and style preferences.	
Account Owner account.owner@widget.com	This is a virtual user profile designated as the **owner** of the account, a best practice for system administration. The account owner possesses comprehensive administrative privileges, including access to security-related settings.
Howard Tanner howard.tanner@widget.com	Howard operates as a **directory account administrator**. He does not have permissions to modify security-related settings within the directory account. Use his profile to see how a specialist can access the team inbox within the self-service portal.
Arizona Bachus arizona.bachus@widget.com	Arizona is part of the European finance department, working as a Financial Controller with her language preference set to Dutch. She has the **end user** role. To test in English, you can modify her profile language settings. She has access to the ERP (SAP) service—examine the well-designed workflow for registering a new Widget product, which requires approval from her manager, David Whitney.
Beatrice Baldwin beatrice.baldwin@widget.com	Beatrice serves as a Financial Controller in the finance department at Widget Data Center. She has the **end user** role. For processes that necessitate managerial approval, her direct supervisor is Matt Leach. Utilize her account to explore and test functionalities like the W.
Adam Blackburn adam.blackburn@widget.com	Adam operates machinery at the Widget Manufacturing Center in Chicago, part of Widget North America. He has the **end user** role. Use his account to test the reservation system; simply navigate to Facilities Management and select the 'Company Cars' service to reserve a vehicle.
David Whitney david.whitney@widget.com	David holds the **key contact** role for both IT and Facilities Management at Widget Europe. He is also listed as the manager for Arizona Bachus, overseeing certain approval workflows.
Matt Leach matt.leach@widget.com	Matt manages the Finance department at the Widget Data Center and is the designated manager for Beatrice Baldwin. In addition to his managerial duties, he fulfills the role of an **auditor** in both the directory and the Widget Data Center accounts.

Widget Data Center: This support domain account provides shared services to regional IT support domains. Observe how user requests for email assistance, originating from any region, are instantly allocated to Widget Data Center. The center also maintains support contracts with external service providers within 4me, such as GigaTera Managed Services and GlobalNet. Explore the process by which an ERP-related incident, reported through a regional IT account, can be escalated to Widget Data Center and then directed to GigaTera Managed Services. The service desk of Widget Data Center is outsourced to VirtualSupport. Additionally, this account has project management and agile capabilities enabled, featuring multiple projects, a product backlog, an agile board, and a Scrum workspace.

Howard Tanner howard.tanner@widget.com	As the **account owner** of this account, Howard has full administrative rights and is integral to the Operations team's activities.
Billie Stylish billie.stylish@widget.com	Billie, with her **account designer** role, specializes in tailoring the configuration and customization of workflows. She is adept at creating request and workflow templates, UI Extensions, and automation rules, though she does not handle ticket resolutions nor can she see any tickets .
Ellen Brown ellen.brown@widget.com	Ellen has several roles. She has the **account administrator** role and also serves as a **project manager** overseeing various projects. She is also assigned as the **coordinator** for the Operations team.
Frank Watson frank.watson@widget.com	Frank serves as the **coordinator** of the Application Development team, fulfilling multiple roles including **knowledge manager**, **problem manager**, **workflow manager**, **release manager**, and **configuration manager**. His profile is ideal for demonstrating the agile methodology, particularly in managing the transition between concluding a sprint and initiating a new one.
Abbie Lindt abbie.lindt@microsoft.com	Abbie is an external consultant from Microsoft. Within the Widget Data Center account, she has an **end-user** role, allowing her access to the self-service portal of Widget Data Center. Abbie can be assigned approval tasks and project tasks as required.
Ron Bartlett ron.bartlett@widget.com	Ron is an accountant who belongs to the Widget Data Center, Finance department. He has the **financial manager** role.

Widget Data Protection: This support domain account specializes in providing Security and Data Protection services to the Widget company. It features risk management dashboards and recurring workflow templates designed to enhance the Governance, Risk, and Compliance (GRC) functions. This is a **strong privacy** account.

Howard Tanner howard.tanner@widget.com	Howard is the **account owner**.

Michael Burgess michael.burgess@widget.com	Michael is a key member of the Information Security team at Widget Data Protection, holding both service desk analyst and workflow manager roles within this account. Additionally, he is involved in similar roles in the Widget Data Center account. As part of an agreement between Widget Data Center and its suppliers, Michael even acts as a service desk analyst in the GlobalNet and GigaTera Managed Services accounts.
Melissa Swanson melissa.swanson@deloitte.com	As part of Widget's outsourced data protection initiative with Deloitte, Melissa plays a crucial role on the Data Protection team. She holds the positions of service desk analyst and workflow manager, bringing external expertise to bolster Widget's data protection strategies.

Widget Europe, FM: This support domain account serves as the Facilities Management hub for the European region.

Martin Koning martin.koning@widget.com	Martin is the **account owner** of Widget Europe, FM, responsible for managing and overseeing all facilities management activities within the European region.

Widget Europe, HR: This support domain account functions as the Human Resources center for the European region, managing all HR-related activities. This is a **strong privacy** account with **case management** enabled.

Stacy Winter stacy.winter@widget.com	Stacy serves as the **account owner** for the Widget Europe, HR account. She is fluent in Dutch

Widget Europe, IT: This support domain account operates as the IT Support center for the European region, handling all regional IT-related activities and support.

Ander Alkin ander.alkin@widget.com	Ander is the **account owner** of this support domain account. He is the IT manager and also fulfills the role of **service desk manager**, overseeing IT support operations.
Joseph Baker joseph.baker@widget.com	Joseph serves as the **coordinator** of the service desk with a **service desk analyst** role. Use his profile to test the scenario of replacing a user's broken laptop.
Chris McNulty chris.mcnulty@widget.com	Chris is the **configuration manager** for the End-User Support team based in Amsterdam. He plays a key role in the workflow for replacing broken laptops.
Bert Jansen bert.jansen@widget.com	Bert is a German-speaking SAP specialist and **coordinator** of the SAP Development team. His profile is ideal for testing the 4me auto-translate feature. Bert handles the escalation of SAP requests to the SAP Basis managed by the Widget Data Center.

Widget N. America - FM: This support domain account delivers facility management services across the North American region, spanning multiple sites. It showcases excellent examples of integrating configuration items with the service catalog. Be sure to explore the reservations module for company cars available in this account.

Hank Williams hank.williams@widget.com	Hank is the account owner for the Widget North America - FM, overseeing the provision of comprehensive facility management services throughout the region.

Widget N. America - HR: This Human Resources support domain account serves the North American region and emphasizes stringent privacy measures being defined as a **strong privacy** account. With specialists that can belong to two different teams, check the effective data segregation between teams. You also might want to explore the offboarding workflow template to see how automation rules efficiently schedule various tasks, aligning precisely with the necessary timing for offboarding processes. Note also that **case management** is enabled.

James Balance james.ballance@widget.com	James is the **account owner** of Widget North America - HR and participates in both the Human Resources and Payroll Administration teams.
Ann Review ann.review@widget.com	Ann serves as an HR support specialist within the Human Resources team. She holds the roles of **knowledge manager** and **problem manager**, contributing to the management and resolution of HR issues.
Herman Ramirez herman.ramirez@widget.com	Herman is a payroll specialist and a key member of the Payroll Administration team, focusing on managing and executing payroll functions.

Widget N. America - IT: This support domain account functions as the IT Support center for the North American region, managing all regional IT-related activities and support. Chess Cole (*chess.cole@widget.com*) serves as the account owner.

Best IT: A small supplier for the Widget Data Center, Best IT provides technical support for printer hardware and UPS devices. The account is managed by Howard Tanner, whose contact is *howard.tanner+bestit@widget.com*.

GlobalNet: A key supplier for the Widget Data Center, GlobalNet provides network services. In this **standard account** the account owner is Frederic Anderson (*frederic.anderson@globalnet.com*).

VirtualSupport: Widget Data Center and Widget North America have outsourced their service desk operations to VirtualSupport, which also maintains a First Line Support Agreement with UltraMax Super Stores. Log into this account to explore the service desk functionality and access First Line Support Agreement (FLSA) reports.

Khunal Shrestra khunal.shrestra@virtualsupport.com	Khunal is the account owner and **service desk manager** at VirtualSupport. He oversees the service desk functions for both Widget North America, IT and Widget Data Center, holding both analyst and manager roles.
Susan Spoc susan.spoc@virtualsupport.com	Susan serves as a **service desk analyst** for VirtualSupport's three key clients: Widget North America, IT, Widget Data Center, and UltraMax Super Stores, providing first-line support across these accounts.

GigaTera: The directory account for GigaTera, Inc., a Managed Service Provider specializing in storage and data center services. Sandra Store (*sandra.store@globalnet.com*) is the account owner.

GigaTera Managed Services: This support domain account delivers managed services, featuring enabled time tracking and billing options. The account is noted for its efficient and streamlined change management workflow.	
Sandra Store sandra.store@gigatera.com	Sandra is the **account owner** and coordinates the Storage team at GigaTera. She holds multiple roles within the account, including **financial manager**, **workflow manager**, and **service level manager**.
Sarah Hendrix Sarah.hendrix@gigatera.com	Sarah is the coordinator of the service desk team. She fulfills both the **service desk analyst** and **service desk manager** roles in the GigaTera Customer Portal account.
GigaTera Whistleblower: This account showcases the whistleblower feature, enabling guests to register requests anonymously. Sandra Store (sandra.store@globalnet.com) manages this account, ensuring the confidentiality and integrity of the process.	
GigaTera Customer Portal: This standard account lists GigaTera's customers who have not implemented their service management on the 4me platform. This account has user self-registration enabled. Sandra Store (*sandra.store+customerportal@gigatera.com*) is the account owner.	
Sandy Stew sandy.stew@imbitto.com	Sandy serves as a **key contact** and customer representative for Imbitto, a customer of GigaTera. She is defined as the **customer representative** for the Premium AWS Fsx and Premium AWS S3 services, acting as the main point of contact for these offerings.
Amazon: A principal supplier for GigaTera Managed Services. Marty Stone (marty.stone@amazon.com) is the account owner.	
Ultra Max Super Stores: This account provides dedicated support to a chain of retail shops, exemplifying efficient management of retail operations. The account is owned by Will Selsom (will.selsom@ultramax.com).	
4me: Similar to production environments, this account is designed for customers and partners to direct their issues, questions or enhancement ideas related to the 4me platform. The account owner is named to one of the founders of 4me, Mathijs Sterk (*mathijs.sterk@4me.com*).	

Annex C:
Examples of Best Practices Service Catalogs

IT Service Catalog

Service	Short Description
End-user Services	
Email and Calendar	Offers email services for sending and receiving messages, scheduling appointments, maintaining personal and enterprise contacts, and accessing functional mailboxes.
Fixed Telephony	Manages traditional landline services, including private branch exchange (PABX) systems, voicemail, and DECT devices.
Meeting Rooms	Support for IT equipment in meeting rooms, such as projectors, monitors, and ClickShare systems, along with assistance in reserving meeting rooms.
Mobile Devices	Support and maintenance for company-owned mobile phones, handhelds, and tablets, including assistance with SIM cards and data roaming.
Network Connectivity	Provides access to the organization's local network through both wired and wireless (Wi-Fi) connections.
Personal Computing	Desktop or laptop computers provided to users, complete with all necessary hardware (monitor, keyboard, mouse, external drive) and software, including the operating system.
Print, Scan and Copy	Provides access to printers and multifunction devices for printing, scanning, and copying.
Remote Access (VPN)	Provides users with secure, remote access to the organization's network via a Virtual Private Network (VPN), simulating direct LAN connectivity.
Shared Folders - Network drives	Enables storing and retrieving files on network drives.
User Management	Handles IT-related tasks for user onboarding and offboarding, managing profiles in the Identity Provider, single sign-on, password resets, and multi-factor authentication.
Application Services	
Enterprise Resource Planning (ERP)	Utilizes platforms like SAP or Microsoft Dynamics to centralize and streamline core business processes, enhancing resource efficiency and decision-making across the organization.

Service	Short Description
Microsoft Teams	A unified communication and collaboration platform that combines persistent workplace chat, video meetings, file storage, and application integration.
Office 365	A comprehensive suite of productivity tools including Word, Excel, Outlook, and more.
List all cloud and on-site application services here	

Infrastructure Services

Service	Short Description
Antvirus and Malware Services	Provides continuous defense against viruses and malware through detection, prevention, and removal to ensure system security.
Backup and Restore Services	Protects data by regularly creating backups and providing swift recovery solutions.
Cloud Services	Delivers scalable computing resources over the internet, facilitating remote access and collaboration.
Database Services	Provides robust database management and support for critical data storage and retrieval to business applications.
Directory Services	Technical management of the Identity Provider solution. Manages user access and authentication across company networks and systems.
Firewall Services	Protects network integrity by managing and maintaining firewall infrastructure to prevent unauthorized access and cyber threats.
HVAC	Controls the heating, ventilation, and air conditioning of the computer rooms to keep server environments, network components and storage devices at optimal conditions.
Monitoring Services	Continuously observes system performance to ensure operational integrity and uptime.
Network Services	The organization's network backbone. Ensures reliable connectivity and network performance across the organization.
Rackspace	Allocates physical and virtual server space for efficient data center management.
Server Services	Maintains the server infrastructure essential for hosting business applications.
Storage Services	Offers secure data storage solutions to accommodate various organizational needs.

IT Security Services

Service	Short Description
Access Management (IAM and PAM)	Ensures secure control and monitoring of user and device access through Identity and Access Management (IAM), and manages privileged accounts with Privileged Access Management (PAM).
Business Continuity and Disaster Recovery (BCDR)	Plans and implements strategies to continue operations in the event of a significant disruption, with methods for data backup and system recovery.
Compliance Management	Ensures that IT systems and processes meet industry standards and regulatory requirements to protect data and privacy.
Cybersecurity Training and Awareness	Provides education and resources to employees about cybersecurity best practices, phishing, and proactive defense measures.
Data Breaches and Security Incidents (SIR)	Offers structured procedures to respond to cyberattacks (Cyber Incident Response or CIR) and data losses, ensuring compliance with the EU GDPR and the NIS Regulations.
Data Subject Rights	Manages and fulfills the rights of individuals under privacy regulations, such as access requests, rectification, and erasure of personal data.
Encryption Services	Protects sensitive data through encryption both at rest and in transit, across the organization's networks and devices.
Information Security Policy Development	Creates and maintains comprehensive security policies to govern the organization's approach to protecting its information assets.
Intrusion Detection and Prevention Services (IDPS)	Monitors network and system activities for malicious activities or policy violations and takes action to prevent breaches.
Vendor Risk Assessment (VRA)	Evaluates and mitigates risks associated with third-party vendors, ensuring their compliance and the security of their products and services.
Vulnerability Management	Implements ongoing identification, classification, and remediation of security vulnerabilities, includes penetration testing and ensuring timely system updates.

HR Services

Service	Short Description
Company Handbook	The Company Handbook outlines the company policies, procedures and expectations for and of an employee.
Conflict Resolution	Offers mediation and conflict resolution services to address disputes among employees and prevent escalation.
Diversity and Inclusion Programs	Develops and implements initiatives to promote diversity and inclusivity within the workplace.
Employee Benefits	Manages comprehensive employee benefits including health insurance, retirement plans, paid time off, and salary structures.
Employee Communications	Facilitates effective communication between employees and management through newsletters, social media, and company meetings.
Employee Recognition Programs	Manages and coordinates recognition programs to reward and acknowledge employee contributions.
Expenses	Processes reimbursement requests for business-related expenses incurred on personal payment methods.
HR Compliance & Legal Issues	Ensures adherence to employment laws and regulations, managing legal aspects of HR and safeguarding workplace rights.
Immigration and Mobility Services	Assists with the legal and logistical aspects of employee international relocations and work authorization.
Joiners, Movers and Leavers	Manages transitions for employees joining, moving within, or leaving the organization, including all associated administrative processes.
Learning & Development	Provides training and development opportunities such as workshops, seminars, and online courses to enhance employee skills and knowledge.
OT (Overtime) / TOIL (Time Off In Lieu)	Oversees arrangements for overtime and compensatory leave, providing guidance on relevant company policies.
Paid Time Off / Annual Leave	Administers policies and supports for managing paid time off and annual leave.
Payroll	Manages payroll processing to ensure accurate and timely payment to employees.
Performance Management	Handles the performance review process, offers feedback, and assists managers in setting performance goals for their teams.

Service	Short Description
Personal Data	Ensures secure and compliant management of employee personal and professional information.
Sickness & Absence	Provides support for managing employee absences, including sickness and other leave types, aligning with organizational policies.
Wellbeing Options	This service supports employee physical and mental health by offering access to wellness programs, health coaching, counseling, and additional wellbeing resources. It aims to enhance employees' overall health and productivity, fostering a positive work-life balance.
Workplace Health & Safety	Ensures a safe and healthy work environment by identifying hazards, providing safety training, and ensuring compliance with health and safety regulations.

Facilities Management

Service	Short Description
Building Access & Security	Oversees the security measures in place to safeguard the premises and ensure restricted access.
Building Maintenance	Maintains the integrity and safety of the workplace through regular upkeep and repairs.
Catering & Event Setup	Coordinates the provision of food services and the arrangement of spaces for events and meetings.
Cleaning & Hygiene	Ensures a hygienic work environment with the cleaning of common areas and maintenance of hygiene products in facilities.
Company Cars	Manages the allocation and reservation of company cars for business use.
Electricity and Lighting	Ensures the provision and maintenance of electrical services, lighting, and electronic appliances like fridges and microwaves.
Environmental Sustainability Initiatives	Implements green practices in facilities management, focusing on energy efficiency, waste reduction, and sustainable resource use.
Landscaping & Grounds	Maintains outdoor spaces, including lawns, gardens, and walkways to enhance the aesthetic appeal of the facility.
Heating, Ventilation & Air-Conditioning (HVAC)	Maintains a comfortable indoor climate and air quality by managing the heating, cooling, and ventilation systems throughout the facility.
Mailroom Services	Handles the distribution and dispatch of mail and packages within and outside the organization.
Office Furniture	Offers a selection of functional office furniture to create an effective workspace for optimal performance.
Parking	Manages on-site parking facilities, including assignments, permits, and enforcement.
Safety	Provides personal protective equipment like safety glasses and hearing protection, prioritizing the well-being of all personnel.
Sanitary and Water	Maintains the shop's sanitation facilities, plumbing, and addresses any leakages.
Space Management	Optimizes the use of workspaces and manages office layouts to support organizational needs and employee comfort.
Trash & Recyclables	Manages the prompt collection and proper disposal of trash and recyclables to maintain a tidy work environment.
Vending Machines	Provides employees with easy access to a variety of snacks and both hot and cold beverages.

Retail Shop

Service	Short Description
IT Services	
Backoffice PC	Provides a dedicated computer system in the back office for inventory management and administrative tasks.
Email & Calendar	Facilitates internal and external communication via email, supports attachment sharing, scheduling meetings, and provides an integrated address book for organizational contacts.
Point of Sale (POS) System	Includes cash registers, handheld terminals, and POS printers for transaction processing.
Printing	Offers multifunctional printing capabilities for back-office use, separate from the POS system.
Wi-fi	Delivers wireless internet access for both customers (public) and staff (private) within the shop.
Wiring Cabinet	Houses and organizes the shop's network and telephony infrastructure.
Facilities Management	
Advertising	Manages illuminated displays for advertising both inside and outside the shop.
Cleaning and Waste Treatment	Covers cleaning services, pest control, and responsible waste management for the shop.
Electricity and Lighting	Ensures the provision and maintenance of electrical services, lighting, and electronic appliances like fridges and microwaves.
Entrance Gates and Deactivation Plates	Manages security gates and deactivation plates to secure the shop entrance and exit points.
Heating and Airco	Controls the shop's heating and cooling systems, ensuring a comfortable shopping environment.
Information Display	Operates and maintains digital screens for displaying information to customers.
Interior Design	Encompasses floor design, entrance mats, furniture, and play areas for children.
Safes	Provides secure storage for cash and valuable items within depository safes and vaults.
Sanitary and Water	Maintains the shop's sanitation facilities, plumbing, and addresses any leakages.

Service	Short Description
Security Systems	Includes alarm systems, surveillance cameras, disinfection units, and fire safety measures.
Shop Access	Manages access points including automatic doors, key-based locks, and entry alert systems.
Back-office Services	
Product Management	Addresses inquiries and manages feedback related to the shop's products, including damage or complaints.

Financial Services

Service	Short Description
General ledger	Offers assistance with the central system for tracking financial transactions, ensuring accurate, organized financial data and aiding in the generation of financial statements for strategic decision-making.
Payroll	Provides support for payroll processes, ensuring employees are paid accurately and punctually.
Aging reports	Supplies reports detailing the age of receivables and payables, helping to quickly identify and address potential financial issues.
Anti-Money Laundering (AML)	Offers guidance to prevent money laundering, ensuring compliance with AML regulatory standards and practices.
Foreign Corrupt Practices Compliance	Assists with maintaining ethical business practices, ensuring adherence to domestic and international anti-corruption regulations.
Global Compliance and Reporting	Supports adherence to diverse international legal and regulatory requirements, ensuring global compliance across all jurisdictions of operation.
Sanctions Compliance	Helps ensure the organization avoids transactions with sanctioned parties, maintaining compliance with international sanctions laws.
Accounting Software Support	Provides assistance with accounting software like QuickBooks, Sage 50, and Microsoft Dynamics GP for tracking transactions and generating financial statements.
Payroll Software Support	Offers guidance on payroll software systems such as ADP, Paychex, and Gusto for managing employee compensation and benefits.
Reporting Software Support	Offers assistance with financial reporting software such as Microsoft Power BI, Qlik Sense, and Tableau, enabling the generation of detailed financial performance reports.
Budgeting Assistance	Provides guidance and support for creating and managing budgets to ensure financial objectives are met.
Financial Analysis Consultation	Offers expert advice to gain insights into the organization's financial health, aiding in strategic decision-making.
Financial Modeling Support	Assists in building and testing financial models to project and understand the organization's financial outcomes.
Financial Statement Analysis	Supports the in-depth review of financial statements to gain a clearer understanding of the organization's fiscal status.

Service	Short Description
Financial Risk Management Advice	Provides strategies for identifying and mitigating potential financial risks to safeguard the organization's fiscal performance.
Financial Strategy Development	Helps in crafting a comprehensive financial plan to reach long-term organizational financial objectives.
Forecasting Guidance	Offers support in forecasting to predict future financial trends and inform proactive business decisions.
Mergers and Acquisitions Support	Offers financial expertise for navigating mergers or acquisitions, facilitating business expansion and strategic development.
Financial Reporting	Provides comprehensive reports on the organization's financial performance, aiding in monitoring progress and pinpointing improvement opportunities.
Auditing Services	Assists with the independent evaluation of financial information, ensuring accuracy and building trust in financial reporting.
Risk Management Services	Delivers strategies and support to identify and mitigate financial risks, protecting the organization from potential losses.
Investor Relations Guidance	Supplies advice and support for managing investor relations and investments, essential for capital growth and maintaining investor trust.
Portfolio Management	Advises on the strategic allocation and oversight of the organization's investment portfolio to optimize financial performance.
Indirect Tax Compliance	Ensures adherence to indirect tax laws, including sales tax, VAT, and excise tax, affecting pricing and company compliance.
Tax Accounting	Manages the accurate reporting and recording of the company's tax obligations, aligning with all tax laws and regulations.
Banking Services	Oversees bank account management, optimizing interest rates on deposits and loans for the organization's benefit.
Cash management	Forecasts cash flows to maintain sufficient liquidity for operational needs and financial commitments.
Investment management	Manages short-term investments to generate returns on idle cash reserves.
Foreign Exchange Services	Provides strategies to manage foreign currency exposure, safeguarding against losses from exchange rate fluctuations.

Legal Services

Service	Short Description
Compliance Services	Ensures the organization adheres to all relevant laws, regulations, and guidelines, minimizing risk and maintaining the company's integrity.
Contract Support	Provides expert review, negotiation, and drafting of legal contracts to protect the organization's interests and facilitate smooth business operations.
Corporate Governance	Advises on best practices for corporate governance, supporting the board of directors and ensuring ethical conduct and compliance with fiduciary duties.
Corporate Law	Offers counsel on a range of corporate legal matters from company formation to governance, ensuring legal compliance in all business activities.
Data Privacy & Security legal support	Advises on data protection laws, helping to establish policies and practices that safeguard personal data.
Employment & Immigration Support	Advises on employment law, workforce regulations, and immigration matters to ensure compliant hiring and employment practices.
Environmental Law	Provides guidance on environmental regulations and compliance, ensuring the company meets its sustainability commitments and regulatory obligations.
Insurance	Manages risk by overseeing the company's insurance policies, including coverage evaluation and claims management.
Intellectual Property Support	Protects the organization's intellectual assets by securing patents, trademarks, and copyrights, and addressing infringement issues.
Legal Advice & Counsel	Provides legal guidance across various facets of the business, from strategic decision-making to dispute resolution.
Litigation Management	Manages legal disputes and litigation processes, representing the company's interests in court or through alternative dispute resolution.
Mergers & Acquisitions (M&A)	Supports the legal aspects of mergers, acquisitions, and divestitures, from due diligence to integration.
Regulatory Affairs	Keeps abreast of regulatory changes, advising on their implications and ensuring the company responds appropriately to policy shifts.

Annex D: The 4me Infrastructure

The 4me platform is engineered for unmatched stability, exceptional performance, robust security, and a reliable weekly release cycle. It boasts a remarkable track record, maintaining nearly 100% availability in recent years. Below is a high-level overview of the platform's architecture:

Figure 389: The 4me architecture, a high availability platform designed for zero down-time.

Key Highlights:

- **Hosting and Regional Independence**: 4me is hosted on Amazon Web Services (AWS) across five independent regions, with no data exchange between them, ensuring localized data handling and resilience.
- **Security Testing**: Penetration tests and vulnerability assessments are conducted biannually by external parties, complemented by automated testing with each software release to uphold stringent security standards.
- **Data Backup**: Multiple daily and weekly backups are performed, stored within the primary operational region, and replicated in a secondary region located at least 800 kilometers away (where available) to ensure data durability.
- Availability and Redundancy: All components are configured for high availability, with critical systems deployed across three availability zones to minimize risks of downtime.
- **Data Encryption**: All customer data is encrypted both in transit and at rest, safeguarding sensitive information against unauthorized access.
- **Continuous Deployment**: New releases are deployed every weekend without any downtime, thanks to an architecture that supports seamless updates of service components and code.
- **Certifications**: The 4me SaaS solution is certified under ISO 27001:2013 and ISO 27018:2019, and holds a SOC 2 Type 2 attestation.

Index

Starting with a number

A

D

E

F

N

O

P

Q

R